SEXUALITY IN THE LAND OF OZ

Searching for Safer Sex at the Movies

Wayne Wilson
Department of Psychology
Stephen F. Austin State University

UNIVERSITY
PRESS OF
AMERICA

Lanham • New York • London

Copyright © 1994 by
University Press of America,® Inc.
4720 Boston Way
Lanham, Maryland 20706

3 Henrietta Street
London WC2E 8LU England

Library of Congress Cataloging-in-Publication Data

Wilson, Wayne.
Sexuality in the Land of Oz : searching for safer sex
at the movies / Wayne Wilson.
p.   cm.
Includes bibliographical references and indexes.
1. Sex in motion pictures.   I. Title.
PN1995.9.S45W53   1994
791.43'6538—dc20   94–21615 CIP

ISBN 0–8191–9622–3 (cloth : alk. paper)
ISBN 0–8191–9623–1 (pbk. : alk. paper)

In Memory Of My Mother...

The Last Of The Luckey Sisters

Table Of Contents

Preface

Going to the movies? Chances are you'll see a little sex, maybe a lot of sex. Chances are, too, that you may not think much about it later (or so you believe). After all, you've been watching movies for years and years. Why should one more portrayal of seduction change your attitude regarding the use of sex as entertainment?

Filmmakers show a penchant for avoiding tepid moods where sexual matters are concerned. Moderation, of course, seems unlikely to earn much revenue for the industry. Still, where do these peak-and-valley experiences leave the viewers' conception of sex? How do scenarios of Good Sex and Bad Sex affect viewers like ourselves who search out movies for pleasure and escapism? I wonder how many people find the illusions of Good Sex and even Bad Sex so inviting that they encourage cinematic realities to drift into assumed realities.

I wonder especially about the movies' strongest suit--telling stories--and how such vivid tales influence the youthful viewers' psychology of what they see. I present the *Land of Oz* as a process in this relationship. Oz does not refer to the movie's fantasy world, but to the moviegoer's response *to* that world. We become enamored of what we see, especially when the images portray seductive actors in exotic settings. The moviegoer's role is not a passive role. We participate in these illusions, bringing forth our personal Oz to fantasize alongside those seductive actors and their adventurous rendezvous.

So, hang on. I can't guarantee you a journey that will prove calm and routine. Movies don't work that way. Quite the contrary, films go for the Heaven-or-Hell approach, with a disdain toward staid, middle-of-the-road excursions. Sex becomes SEX with a dash of humor here, a cry of pathos there, and enough passion in between to drive a flotilla of warships. As one famous actress remarked, posturing herself on a stairway to claim center stage: "Fasten you seat belts, it's going to be a bumpy ride."

Acknowledgements

Most of the movies in this book are mainstream American movies. Analyzing movies can, like analyzing humor, remove the magic of spontaneity from the creation. But I am a movie lover, and I hope that my enthusiasm for this world of illusions shines through on occasion. Movies, after all, have stood the test of turbulent times for a century now. The filmmakers must be doing something right to give their product a history that continues to capture millions of fans.

On a more personal note, I wish to thank Michelle Jamnik and Sheree Helge for their diligence in proofreading the manuscript. Finding an "i" to dot and a "t" to cross can prove tedious, and I appreciate their devotion to giving my prose a healthy dose of professionalism.

Finally, a special thanks to Robert and Cheryl Verner for many pleasant evenings of viewing companionship. Over the years, we have critiqued almost every conceivable kind of film: some of them delicious, some spare, and some vehicles best left to the netherworld of anonymity. The critiquing, however, has always been offered in the spirit of entertainment. Indeed, I hope that this same spirit will have invested its presence in the pages to follow.

Lesson 1

A Sex Education In The Dark

Millions of moviegoers receive mixed signals from the movies' visceral portrayals of sex. Sex appears rosy one moment, barbarous the next. Richard Gere and Debra Winger make leisurely, sensuous love in *An Officer And A Gentleman* (1982), a romantic interlude of luxurious, physical pleasure. Janet Leigh, by contrast, gets punctured to death in *Psycho* (1960) because she awakens Norman's erotic feelings, and thereby distresses his alter ego, Mad Mama Bates. Sexual expressions soar from cinematic peak to cinematic valley, with few stops to catch a breath, think sensibly, or consider the virtues of moderation.

This **double standard** places a high price on sexual illusions. Sex isn't just good, it's terrific, as in the fireworks that accompany the tryst between Cary Grant and Grace Kelly in Alfred Hitchcock's 1955 film, *To Catch A Thief*. And sex isn't merely bad, it's ruthless, as in Marlon Brando's rape of the delicate Vivian Leigh in *A Streetcar Named Desire* (1951). Good sex and bad sex may fare well or fare poorly, depending on the movie's capacity to provide quality entertainment. Broadly stated, this range of entertainment can carry us to a visionary experience of grand emotions--but also displays the proficiency to sell us the dumbest, most tasteless trash imaginable. A sex education of sorts, often glamorous, though frequently misleading. Critics seldom accuse the movies of fostering the kind of high intellect that ennobles human nature. What movies do best, actually, concerns their potential to rouse feelings of gut-level intensity. This accomplishment hardly appears laudable, except to say that intense feelings may only look chaotic. Feelings have a strategy to them, and this strategy--in good movies--reflects the presence of a lurking intelligence.

Still, where do these split portrayals of good and bad sex leave the moviegoer's conception of real sex? Where do these peak-and-valley experiences leave you, and me, and those millions of viewers who adore the big screen? A sex education in the dark, but an education engineered, first and foremost, for entertainment...and for profit.

Praise Be

Sex represents the movies' **fuel**; a fuel that has propelled filmmaking through some hard times. Imagine two actors gracing the big screen: Give them the professional's touch on makeup, the right lighting, the best camera angles, the perfect music, and these lovers will transform sex into a bewitching production. Shangri-La. A more exotic paradise than the average girl and guy can re-create in their little bedroom.

Real sex never measures up to luscious, cinematic sex, but why should viewers pay money to see real sex? They can manage that feat themselves, some with creative abandon, some less so. What fans wish to see is sex that drifts into **captivating illusion**: bigger than life, better than life, sex with trappings of gold. And if the movie's fantasies prove especially fetching, who knows? Viewers may dupe themselves into giving the desired illusions more credence than these illusions deserve.

Sex, along with violence, constitutes the industry's staple entertainment. But sex, as a fuel, must undergo adornment and diversity to remain consistently attractive. The one-two-three mechanics of sex aren't entrancing. Filmmakers toy with the mechanics to make the process more inviting, more outrageous, more humorous. They find a way--and there are many ways--to fuel the viewer's imagination and generate entertainment. In *No Way Out* (1987), Kevin Costner and Sean Young, who have met only an hour before, make love in a limousine. The driver, understanding as only limousine drivers can be, tours Washington's national monuments, allowing the couple to indulge their passions. Once the lust dwindles to a sigh, the lovers decide to introduce themselves. First things first.

Probably you will never realize love's ecstasy in the back seat of a limousine. Indeed, you may not wish to experience ecstasy with a near-stranger in the back seat of anything. But you hold no reservations in watching actors do it skillfully and seductively. Viewing the scene becomes exciting unto itself because you are a voyeur who pays for the right to watch.[1] What you find exciting dwells in the camera's eye. And what you fail to find in the camera's purview continues through your fantasies. The movies dress up sex and give it somewhere to go.

Sex in mainstream movies, nonetheless, subscribes to certain taboos. You can show the two lovers in their limousine, passionate and throbbing, but you dare not show it all. Truly, you need not show it all. You need not show his penis or her vagina. You need not even show them completely disrobed. Illusion and the viewer's imagination should count for something. That's sophistication; that's class; that's artistic integrity, or at least a smattering of it.

Clearly, not all films convey these qualities. The attitude-- the sophistication--that a filmmaker brings to sexual expressions deserves analysis. One reason for this query concerns the assumption that sex, the same old sex, harbors quite a cinematic wardrobe. Some styles appear debonair, others gaudy, still others drab. Each style, however, evokes a message about sexual attitudes.

Has this message gotten out of hand? Do today's fledgling lovers profess a sophistication about real sex that mimics the cavalier treatment exhibited in *No Way Out*? If so, the intimates, novices that they are, have made the risky move from **illusions** to **delusions**. They have lost sight of cinematic love as pretense, and have eased into the domain of false beliefs (Boorstin, 1987, p. 3).

Hmmm. Not so good for lovers just starting out. And what about the rest of us? Frankly, given the daily tally produced by soap operas, prime-time programs, cable fare, theatrical films, and videotapes, our thinking cap about sex probably sits askew as well. We may have developed a nonchalant acceptance regarding the glitz and appropriateness of cinematic sex. If so, a sensible recognition of real sex must suffer by comparison. A sensible recognition includes properly acknowledging the risks of sexual intimacy, such as the HIV virus. But even "informed" lovers may decide that the HIV virus and other sexual pitfalls do not pose a true risk for them (Pinkerton & Abramson, 1992).

The movies frequently portray physical love as unerringly rapturous with no timeouts for caution. John and Marsha, say, thirst to bring their loins together. They desire to attain--not exactly what they see on the screen (they're not that foolish)-- but at least something memorable. John and Marsha want **good sex**: They want it now; they want it effusively; they want it with nary a hitch; they want it in the same spirit that big-time lovers demonstrate on the giant screen.

Good sex, according to the movies, plays out as terrific sex. But conventional sex, the sense of straightforward physical love, does not cater to entertainment. No exquisite lighting, no mood music, no rippling acrobatics grace the love scene. Rather, the lovers find themselves immersed in grunt-and-groan motions that suggest a pale imitation of cinematic paradise.

If a movie shows conventional lovemaking, it does so to highlight a sexual problem, or to illustrate a mundane existence. Robert Mitchum, playing a sexually reticent schoolteacher, climbs haltingly into bed with his hot-blooded bride, Sarah Miles, to perform a husbandly duty in *Ryan's*

Daughter (1970). He performs that duty, and he's not happy about it. The "lovemaking" becomes nothing more than a painful interlude of wooden movements, absent of gusto, absent of desire, absent of any of the expected passions.

Contrast this wedding-night misery with the more familiar gangbusters consummation that occurs in John Ford's *The Quiet Man* (1952). John Wayne and Maureen O'Hara, fire-snorting lovers, create a combustible wedding night out of conflicts, stubbornness, and explosive tempers--all of which lead Wayne to eventually storm into their bedroom and refuse to be refused by O'Hara's tempestuous denial of his groomly rights. No need to show the bride and groom in action (the censors wouldn't have permitted it, anyway). Instead, Barry Fitzgerald, the village cabman, visits the next morning to find their bed collapsed and the lovers' cottage in disarray. Fitzgerald then waxes poetic and expresses his admiration for the lovers' ferocity at what must have been an evening fit for the gods.

The gods and cinematic sex comprise a succulent relationship. Wayne and O'Hara deliver entertainment because they register as god and goddess of the screen, more handsome and commanding than any couple has a right to be. The two lovers spell the stuff that dreams are made of. But emulating the gods also amounts to a daunting challenge--a tall order for a pair of novice lovers to fill.

Damnations

Movie entertainment thrives on exaggeration. It's geared to offer moviegoers a sweeping euphoria that, presumably, they have no way of capturing themselves. There's profit in creating alluring fantasies, and the movies have mined this profit since the days of silent pictures. The exaggeration, moreover, comes in two flavors. One assortment pertains to physical love in its most enveloping, endearing light. This beguiling flavor, as Thumper in *Bambi* (1942) would say, "twitterpates" young lovers like John and Marsha. These portrayals represent good sex. The harm that derives from good sex pertains to hyperbole, but not to coercion and destructiveness.

The other flavor, unfortunately, gives viewers a grotesque look at sex in the fast lane. A hollow vision that speaks more of physical dominance and violence than any semblance of physical love. Predation, lust, possessiveness, control--call it what you will--it's **bad sex**. Bad sex hits the screen as victimization, whether the victimizing occurs in the shower, the dark alley, or the parked car. These locales mark the plight of not just any victim, but the female victim: a young female, usually helpless and nearly always at the mercy of a deranged male. The happening of import here is not sex, but sex subordinated to the more forbidding urge of violence.

If sex symbolizes the fuel for films, violence engenders the **fire**. This fire roars with a multitude of expressions, so much so that physical violence overshadows physical sex in its diversity and box-office power (Fraser, 1974, p. 9). Violence constitutes the dominant entertainment of our society. Some male-only films like *Twelve Angry Men* (1957), *Birdman Of Alcatraz* (1962), *Sleuth* (1972), and *The Hunt For The Red October* (1990) entertain violence, or the suggestion of violence, to the exclusion of physical sex. Sex conjures up its own fascination, but violence endures as the backbone of the film industry.

What violence has wrought on sex is more than deplorable. Violence resolves itself into different orientations that are by varying degrees sanitized, humorous, absurd, and graphic. These perspectives do not always remain apart--sometimes they blend--but they all cast sexual expression in a supporting role. To choose one of the more mystic perspectives, consider the **absurd orientation** to violence. Consider, in particular, its distinctive application to one of entertainment's more visible pastimes: the sexual humiliation of women.

One scenario of absurd violence takes the unwitting woman and fancifully renders her dead meat. Apparently unkillable villains like Michael from *Halloween* (1978), Jason from *Friday The 13th* (1980), and Freddy from *A Nightmare On Elm Street* (1984) prey on the female, who, oblivious to her last few breaths, shows us a tantalizing moment of terminal passion. The artistry centers on the style of execution--a different girl, a different way to die. This formula demands that the females (and a sampling of males thrown in for variety) exercise sufficient denseness to deserve their death. Filmmakers often apply the formula by exhibiting nubile teenagers without a sound thought to their name, roaming about in places they shouldn't be. Not too surprising, they leave themselves open for a sexual atrocity or two.

Sex, in this context, becomes the filmmaker's instrument of rapture. Arouse your audience sensuously, then bring out the blade, the ax, the sledgehammer, the chain saw, or the vampire fangs. Edward Donnerstein, Daniel Linz, and Steven Penrod (1987, p. 114) note that in one variety of horror films, known as slasher movies, filmmakers frequently preface the absurd violence by including a previous scene of eroticism. A teenage girl undresses for bed and projects a titillating image, vulnerable and poised like a promising victim. The authors point out that the effect of pleasant arousal followed by aggression lulls viewers into a **desensitization to violence.** The positive arousal that arises just before a horrific scene not only makes the violence more exciting, but more acceptable to moviegoers.

And what if we add one final ingredient? Suppose we deem the girl expendable (say, she's a bitch). Having her appear cruelly seductive just before her grand demise suggests the makings of a **good murder** (Wilson, 1991, p. 121). A subtle, cinematic rule is worked to perfection: The girl dies horribly because her unseemly behavior indicates that she deserves to die. Moviegoers find her death especially enticing since the girl also loses her ability to seduce--perhaps a talent that she used selfishly before her murder. Directors of exploitation movies know how to score a cinematic knockout: use sex, then violence; the one-two punch of horror films.

Movie viewers need not embark on a stirring leap of imagination to realize that bad sex penalizes the female. If a temptress fails to appreciate her susceptibility to harm and chooses to flaunt her womanly wiles, then, yes, commercial entertainment dictates that maybe she should suffer according-ingly. A good murder sounds contradictory, but in cinematic jargon this phenomenon serves a valued purpose: A good murder primes the audience to wait expectantly for the victim's likely termination.[2]

True, critics can argue that youthful viewers who recognize the dangers of placing themselves in a car on Lovers Lane will act on this lesson and engage in more prudent lovemaking. Perhaps yea, perhaps nay. I know of no body of research that bears on what fans find educational about absurd violence. I suspect, however, that any such lesson becomes displaced or lost in the overwhelming tandem of sex, then violence. Bad sex denotes bad sex only as we choose to contrast it with good sex in the movies. From a different perspective, millions of action fans interpret the "slice-and dice" scenarios of bad sex as quite captivating. Bad sex, for them, translates to good entertainment.

The bad sex that these viewers enjoy concerns exploitative sex--sex portrayed for shock value. But the violence of sex can take a constructive turn, despite the movies' generic reputation for pulling out all the stops to flaunt physical perversity. Filmmakers can treat bad sex deftly, usually by minimizing the act's explicitness and emphasizing the act's capacity to change characters and storylines.

To wit: First, the sexual assault of a young, deaf mute in *Johnny Belinda* (1948), suggested rather than shown graphically, leads to positive consequences for the girl. Second, the incest of a father and daughter, when revealed, figures prominently to explain the tragic conduct of both parties in *Chinatown* (1974). And third, a false charge of rape against a young, black male proves integral to the conclusion of *To Kill A Mockingbird* (1960).

These examples reflect a productive use of sexual violence to show, not the bare bones of sexual assault for its own sake, but the far-reaching aftermath of such volatile behavior. Compare this aftermath, then, to the shallow depictions of rape-and-revenge killings in films like *Lipstick* (1976), *I Spit On Your Grave* (1980), and *Sudden Impact* (1983). Make these comparisons and the distinction between a constructive versus an exploitative use of bad sex becomes clearer. Moviegoers need not puzzle over the difference: Bad sex in a sexually exploitative film serves to place thrill-seeking viewers on a starvation diet for substance. They gain little insight from such movies except to conclude that violence appears to solve problems quickly, whatever the consequences.

The carnal nature of what we see still leaves us unfulfilled, however. Something's missing. Something as yet undefined from the lovers' portrait. John and Marsha, for instance, are well aware of their physical relationship, whether bolstered by the enticements of good sex or complicated via the perversities of bad sex. But they admit puzzlement over the intangibles of their intimacy. Beyond the passionate huffing and puffing of physical ardor, "something" must surface to hold this relationship together. Marsha. John. Hang on.

Sexuality As A Cohesive Force

Good sex can be cavalier, capricious, and chaotic. But good sex also proves mutually consenting--virginal for some lovers, a more seasoned pleasure for others. Bad sex, by fiat, abhors a democratic relationship and prefers to rely on domination and stupidity. Bad sex, the appetizer, dwells on a victim's helpless desire to escape before the main meal of violence lurches into view.

Good heavens, if all our marbles rested on one of these primal urges--good sex, bad sex, let me see it baby, oh, yeah, here it is, what do you think, darlin'?--we might as well trudge soullessly away. Our days and nights would become labored since the only tune played comes from a physical arsenal of penises and vaginas in juxtaposition. Fortunately, the sexual relationship carries experiential baggage that goes beyond the mere rhythm of thrusting bodies.

The baggage in question? **Sexuality**. Sexuality as a psychological tie that communicates the affections shared by a couple like John and Marsha. Because sexuality covers a vast conceptual territory, it becomes subjective and open to numerous, inventive descriptions. Lesser abstractions like gender, femininity, and masculinity are used to explain the greater abstraction, sexuality. For instance, one group of sex educators settled on this definition:

> **Definition:** The concept of **sexuality** refers to the totality of being a person. It includes all of those aspects of the human being that relate specifically to being boy or girl, woman or man, and is an entity subject to life-long dynamic change. Sexuality reflects our human character, not solely our genital nature. As a function of the total personality it is concerned with the biological, psychological, sociological, spiritual, and cultural variables of life which, by their effects on personality development and interpersonal relations, can in turn affect social structure (Hawkins, 1980, p. 1).

Whew. This definition overlooks the cosmic connection but that's about it. The educators, in fairness to their efforts, understood that this omnibus declaration required analysis and more precise elaboration. The overall definition, nonetheless, holds two clues for us. First, it says that sexuality includes sex (our genital conduct), but is more than sex. This surplus meaning can embrace many influences, although we will concentrate on one such influence: the psychological domain. And second, the definition notes that sexuality is subject to change. The change makes sense because as we continue to develop, however imperceptibly, our sexuality changes with us.

Sexuality can make its presence felt through a gesture, a touch, a kiss, or an all-out affectionate assault. The presence is not defined so much by what you see on screen as what you experience between the lovers. Alfred Hitchcock, to circumvent the Production Code's constraints on kissing, devised a kissing sequence between Cary Grant and Ingrid Bergman that extended to longer than three minutes. Grant nibbles on Bergman's ear, and the two kiss and caress each other as both talk about the chicken dinner they are to eat (Wood, 1989, p. 322; Nash & Ross, 1986, p. 2203).

The talk of food, of course, only makes the nibbling and caressing more symbolic. Following this sequence, Bergman clings to Grant, caressing him even when he moves into another room to use the phone. Hitchcock, while traveling by train through Europe, gazed out the window and observed a young girl holding a young boy's arm as he urinated against a wall. She stood there, looking elsewhere, patiently waiting for him to finish but refusing to relinquish her grasp. Hitchcock borrowed that moment of intimacy and introduced it in *Notorious* (1946) as a gesture of attachment, with Bergman refusing to pull herself away from Grant.

For movies, sexuality springs from the **image** that actors portray. This image dictates the kinds of physical presence that moviegoers expect from well-known performers. Thus, Cary Grant's suaveness and Ingrid Bergman's earthiness complement their nibbling, caressing, and Bergman's clinging to Grant's arm. The lovers' relationship is, momentarily, open and free of suspicion, allowing them to declare an unrestrained closeness.

An image may prove so overwhelming that the performer need exhibit only subtle physical overtures to reflect the sexuality in force. James Dean, who starred in just three movies before his death, captured the charisma of a brooding, smoldering rebel--so brooding and so smoldering that fans easily imagined his sexual skills. Dean's outward responses of affection remained terse and detached, but moviegoers never doubted Dean's potential as a potent lover.

Image, nonetheless, has its delicate nature. Julia Roberts in *Pretty Woman* (1990) plays a young prostitute, although a prostitute not possessed of greed, guile, or bitterness. She's an open person, one familiar with the attractiveness of her body, yet one who surpasses her physical presence through a winsome personality. She's a nice person, still capable of showing genuine delight. Richard Gere, softly underplaying his customary amoral character, appears less comfortable with intimacy than Julia, despite all his wealth. Gere's controlled, distant sexuality makes her character all the more animated and delicious.

So, what's the point? The point has to do with age and the cumulative history of an image. Julia Roberts is young and a relative newcomer to her role. How effectively might an older actress, such as Elizabeth Taylor or Jane Fonda (each of whom won an academy award for playing a prostitute), have substituted for Roberts in this movie? The answer is, they couldn't and they wouldn't. Writers would have to redo the part to fit a possibly darker theme and a different image for the female. An older, likely jaded prostitute could not enliven the fairy-tale spirit as positively as did Julia Roberts's character in *Pretty Woman*.

Sexuality functions as the heartbeat of a relationship. This palpable force relies on sex, but also on image in conjunction with attractive actors, apt settings, and good writing to establish its demeanor in movies. The physical paraphernalia of a come-hither look or a shuddering sigh helps to remind us of sexuality's intrigue. Still, we are reminded only if the filmmaker permits sexuality to breathe and become more than the sum of its viewable parts. This likelihood seems plausible when the movie depicts good sex rather than bad sex, because filmmakers use bad sex more frequently to exploit sexuality than to enhance it.

Enhancing Sexuality's Image

Sexuality suffers artistically, along with everything else, in a poorly crafted film. A film misfires if the actors falter in their performance, the director directs haphazardly, or the screenwriter substitutes well-worn dialogue for inspiration. Actors, most visible and most vulnerable, typically are not the problem. They may give less than they should, or they may find themselves miscast, but, normally, actors will strive to make the best of a good or bad project. Directors exercise greater influence, sometimes a singular influence, and may even bring a mediocre screenplay to dazzling life on screen. More likely, though, directors find mediocrity a tough nut to crack.

Experts will argue the point of course, but the ruling passion for predicting a good film rests with the **screenwriter** (or writers). Actors and directors, especially directors, can compromise a good script. But as professionals, the odds are that they and their collaborators will rise to the creative word and transform that word into a compelling film. When this wonderful transformation happens, sexuality assumes the acquisition of an extraordinary presence. This presence conveys more than the mechanics of lovemaking--it offers a little mystery, a little novelty, and more than a little integrity. Something magical transpires, not witnessed before; something magical that adorns sexuality, gracing womanhood and manhood with a special screen image.

Therefore, what you see and how you remember begin with the screenplay. Aptly posturing and vocalizing a fine line of dialogue distinguishes the world of image from the world of print. *All About Eve* (1950) provides one of the few films that uses inspired dialogue to capture a sparkling look at theatre people. This creative chain of events began as a short story, "The Wisdom Of Eve," by Mary Orr (who never received screen credit for her original story); then became a film garnering 14 Academy Award nominations, winning six awards; and, finally, it marched forth as a stage musical, entitled *Applause*.

Margo Channing (Bette Davis) feels that age has placed her career at a turning point, although she still reigns as a star of the theatre. Margo graciously takes in Eve (Anne Baxter), a self-deprecating individual on the surface, who, secretly, conducts herself as a scheming, young actress fervently determined to succeed. Margo eventually realizes Eve's true personality, and this disarming insight, along with Margo's concern about aging and the fear of losing her lover, put the star in a foul mood. Margo's dark temper comes through at a party with one of those rare lines that moviegoers remember over the years. Margo, positioned on a stairway like the stage actress she is, says to her guests: "Fasten your seat belts, it's going to be a bumpy ride."

The line says it all. Margo issues fair warning that she's ready to bitch and that trouble's afoot. Shortly thereafter, true to her word, she institutes her own brand of Margo friction. Notice that if Margo speaks the line sweetly, or mischievously, or jokingly, she will cause viewers to dismiss the dialogue's true intent. No, Margo gives her warning as a challenge, saying in effect, "Watch out, I'm going to throw a temper tantrum." Notice, too, that if she speaks the line using those exact words, the style of delivery remains a challenge, but the line's substance will diminish. There's no mystery when you tell the audience what you plan to do. "Fasten your seat belts, it's going to be a bumpy ride" grabs your attention and makes you wonder what Margo has in mind.

The script of *All About Eve* leaves little room to take a breath. The rapid exchange of witticisms, pointed remarks, and wicked humor generates a campy atmosphere. By contrast, everyday conversations have no place in novels, the theatre, or film. Such talk consists of redundant expressions and incomplete sentences: "Um, you know, I tried to kiss her, but, well, you know, maybe next time." Movie dialogue demands an edginess, an unpredictability that provokes interest and advances the story. The dialogue of *All About Eve* **sounds realistic**. It reflects dramatic realism in the sense of according theatre people a style and substance of speech that entertains.

Such plausibility, however, does not rest wholly with the movie's dialogue or the movie's characters. How we use our imagination to heighten the moviegoing experience--and the sexuality--concerns you and me.

We, The Moviegoers

You have, no doubt, seen your fair share of movies. If your viewing habits do not include the theatre or the renting of videos, then you may find yourself watching television at some percentage of that statistical viewing average of seven hours per day. You have a voice concerning what movies you prefer, although it's a voice for which little incisive data exist. Filmmakers, if they could really anticipate what moviegoers desired to see at a given time, would enjoy a better history of success than their accomplishments reveal.

Failing to discover the holy formula for cinematic success, filmmakers accept the challenge to pursue Plan B. Plan B reflects an artistic attempt to manipulate our sentiments. **Entertainment** denotes the business of involving us to root for the protagonist and boo the antagonist (Zillmann & Bryant, 1986, p. 312). To achieve this goal, the makers of movies must take care to imagine what viewers will pay to see, and, if blessed with a popular movie and exquisite timing, what viewers will pay to see more than once.

One condition to understanding moviegoers involves anticipation. We entertain **expectations** about what should happen in a movie. Probably, we will not go to a movie without a bit of forethought. We need a tad of rehearsal or mental preparation before surrendering ourselves to the emotional ride of a potentially engrossing experience. We may not know much regarding a particular movie, but guidelines are usually there. The star's familiarity, for example, may prove adequate to accommodate our entertainment needs. Too, our interest varies in wanting to watch a specific movie. We are beset by **moods**, by a desire to match our feelings with the right film. Perhaps a comedy to counter depression, or a melodrama to celebrate good news. As movie fans, we constitute an elusive lot.

So, how do you classify moviegoers? Mostly, we are not easy to judge because we are not automatons in our artistic tastes. Occasionally we surprise friends by our willingness to view a film that they predict we shall not wish to see. Why the change? Possibly our expectations remain low, but our mood wins out. We feel the need for a little mystery, a little love, a little sex, thus we allow our mood to carry us to a vehicle that otherwise holds limited appeal. Reason (expectation) wavers, and feelings (mood) persevere. Other variations arise--such as a friend's persuasion, or just sheer boredom--resulting in numerous reasons why you might watch a movie that, typically, you would dismiss.

Seeing a number of movies makes us more than plebeian observers. We fashion our own ideas about good movies and bad movies. We know when a character steps out of character, and we grow restless when too many implausibilities mar a film's artistic integrity. We aren't dumbbells about what we find entertaining. We even recognize cinematic junk as cinematic junk, but if the fancy strikes us we will go slumming and watch movies that we feel are "beneath us." What we fail to comprehend so readily, nonetheless, is the movies' devious presentation of sexual issues.

The more diverse our independent sources of sexual information, the more likely we are to have a critical frame of reference in assessing sexuality on the big screen. This proposition holds true if the independent sources prove valid and reliable. But if such information comprises an unknown mix of truth and falsehood, or if there is precious little information to draw upon, then sexual entertainment in the dark becomes less illusion and more delusion; less pretense and more the possibility of assuming false beliefs about what you see. We subject ourselves to a sex education by actors following a script, actors who are given the luxury of rehearsals and the technology to make their sexual moments appear spellbinding.

Contrary to popular ballyhoo, all roads linking unbridled sex and the movies do not lead inevitably to pornography. Other, equally important sexual conflicts are at stake in the world of entertainment. What do we know, for instance, about the cinematic treatments of AIDS and abortion? Given the focus and intensity of such dramatizations, how do presentations covering these two controversies affect our expectations and moods? The less we discern of arguments about AIDS and abortion in reality, the more we tempt ourselves to accept their cinematic excursions at face value.

Even less controversial themes prove deceptive in the hands of filmmakers. Consider the seemingly benign subject of romantic love. We feel intuitively that we understand romance, especially our personal reality of experiencing the rise and fall of several promising relationships. But I doubt if we can prepare ourselves for Hollywood's version of such escapades. Love romanticized through absurd humor differs, for example, from love romanticized via the supernatural. And neither love--humorous or supernatural--tells us much about the "cinematic realities" of romance. These pretend realities come into dramatic play when we view young love; when we watch attractive males and females struggle to find the "right" love; and when we see failed lovers trying to recapture their romantic past. Love is not a simple matter, on screen or off.

Thus, our one and only axiom presents itself: **We must never, ever, under any circumstance, accept what a movie tells us at face value.** Never. Ever. Under any circumstance. The good movie may provide us with a provocative message about AIDS, abortion, romance, adolescent temptations, machismo, beauty, homosexuality, adultery, lust, sexual assault, prostitution, or how to get a sex education in the dark. But a movie, good or bad, delivers its theme tempered with considerations of art and commerce. It is the rare movie that subordinates entertainment and commercialism to instruction. Instruction, frankly, is not the business of theatrical movies. The business of theatrical movies is to kick-start our emotions for a roller-coaster ride into the Land of Oz.

Oz

For us, the Land of Oz does not indicate another synonym called Hollywood. Nor does it designate the fanciful world of any given movie. **Oz** refers to a state of mind: your mind, my mind, the viewer's mind. Oz denotes that special connection between viewer and movie known as viewer imagination. We think of the connection as special because moviegoers supply their own desirous interpretations of the cinematic fantasies before them.

Recall that the Wizard (Frank Morgan) in *The Wizard Of Oz* (1939) isn't all that his title suggests.[3] Recall, too, that Dorothy (Judy Garland), although fascinated with the splendors and dangers of her fantasy world, wants most of all to return home. Home in the movie appears bleak and desolate, the flat, flat, flat land of heartland Kansas. Not much of a home, but at least it's real. When Dorothy exhorts at the film's end, "Oh, Auntie Em, there's *no* place like home!", she says it with such feeling that we suspect Dorothy may have thought herself trapped in Oz forever.

Oz is not reality but a **transitory process** by which a movie helps us to imagine a fanciful existence. For Dorothy, Oz proved a poignant dream, filled with joy and fright. Eventually, she finds Oz too fanciful and too confining, a lesson that endows the familiar turf of Home with an appealing radiance, heretofore unappreciated.

For us, Oz becomes an escape from reality, though the escape depends on experiencing a cinematic reality that threads the familiar with the absurd. Too much Oz and the fantasies lose their sparkle: too much incredulity, too many Munchkin characters, too bizarre the happenings, and Oz exceeds its welcome. Too little Oz, by contrast, and we find ourselves checking the time. Will this boring movie ever change its tune?

Oz thrives best on an imaginative balance of the rational and irrational, but the balance responds to our call. We decide, via our expectations and moods, what we hope to enjoy as entertainment. The viewing experience represents a three-stage process: First, as our discussion already shows, we anticipate; we prime ourselves for the kind of movie we hope to see (not, regrettably, that we always fulfill that hope). Second, we engage in mostly a physical reaction as we view the movie--more gut than high intellect--to acknowledge the authenticity of characters and story. We identify emotionally with one or more of the characters, and prepare ourselves for the kind of strong sensations that only a movie can safely provide (Boorstin, 1990, p. 135).

Third, we reflect, so that what happens after our viewing experience also includes Oz. Once the immediacy of watching a film has passed, we entertain the luxury to deliberate more leisurely on how the characters and story affected us. The relationship of what we view, and, later, what we evaluate of our viewing experience, need not constitute a straightforward connection. A movie like *Basic Instinct* (1992) can bombard our senses with the agony of mesmerizing sex and bigger-than-life characters, spiced by a lethal twist or two. Afterward, however, we may find our praise allayed with the sober realization that the true value of seeing this film resides in the viewing per se, and not in any substantial message that subsequently gives the movie much creative weight.

Consequently, Oz involves anticipation, affectivity, and aftermath: We anticipate, we experience, we reflect. The future (anticipation of what we will view), the present (emotionality of the viewing experience), and the past (contemplating what we have viewed) combine to give Oz its special meaning; or, upon viewing a disappointing movie, its not-so-special meaning. Oz becomes our package of fantasies, tinkered, polished, and sometimes bludgeoned by the cinematic worlds that filmmakers concoct to entertain us.

A Lurking Intelligence

Therefore, acknowledging that Oz depicts your interpretation of the movie experience, what should you, the viewer, look for? As a patron of Oz, you assume an intelligence to imagine more complex fantasies of what you see, presumably during the movie, certainly afterward. How can you learn to appraise these fantasies in sorting out a good movie from a lackluster effort? And, more difficult, how can you learn to judge, through characters and story, a creative rendition of sexuality?

A film's theme becomes the place to start because it presumes a basic or native intelligence. Movie messages convey fundamental ideals about sexuality: the conflict between loyalty and adultery (*Eye Of The Needle*, 1981); the pain of losing a lover (*Love Story*, 1970); the dangers of sexual rejection (*Fatal Attraction*, 1987); the nostalgia of adolescent desires (*The Man In The Moon*, 1991); the political manipulations of homosexuality (*Advise And Consent*, 1962); the retribution for a sexual assault (*The Accused*, 1988); the virtues of an enduring love in preparation for death (*On Golden Pond*, 1981). Film can visualize these cardinal ideas, can even present them delicately, although not with the depth of exposition that a novel commands.

Good films, nonetheless, possess a **lurking intelligence.** This delayed awareness surfaces only when the cumulative effects of a well-played emotional scene shock or nudge the viewer into realizing the filmmaker's heretofore hidden theme. The emotion reminds the viewer--indeed, **primes** the viewer-- to consider ideas that will explain the characters' actions. A movie that addresses its theme well emotionally can serve as a

conduit of intellectual ideas--if the viewer is thinking to
permit such ideas to arise (Schank & Childers, 1988, p. 91).

So, what "lurks" exactly?   The filmmaker's scheme,
actually.   A scheme designed to entertain by creating
anticipation, humor, tragedy, passion, but most of all, by
cultivating deception.   The filmmaker does not want you
bored, mouthing the character's next lines before the character
reacts.   The story--a good story--delivers its native intelligence gently yet invincibly, articulating the characters and
plot with sufficient mystique to entertain and to enlighten.

Characters and plots, in fact, prove less flexible as they
progress.   Surprises are easier to introduce early in a story
when the performers and their purpose remain ambiguous.
Later, surprises with established characters require more
careful thought.   Entertainment relies on deception to
maintain at least a hint of unpredictability, but entertainment
also relies on the film's cohesiveness to clarify and consolidate
storylines. A sexually repressed wimp does not blossom forth
miraculously as a suave lover--not in any plausible sense--
unless the filmmaker legitimately prepares you for this
"revelation."

A film's intelligence slowly manifests itself through the
viewer's **cumulative experience** with characters and story.
Actors who must exhibit deep feelings can do so effectively if
the audience identifies with them and their hardships (a
vicarious identification; see Boorstin, 1990, p. 65).
Moviegoers will not likely grant actors instant identification,
unless you speak of stereotyped personalities comparable to
James Bond or Dirty Harry. Very probably, an actor must
earn his or her rapport with the audience. Thus, the greater
the familiarity with a character, the more viewers will become
involved, and the more they shall anticipate **why** the character
behaves as he or she does.

The 1960 melodrama *Home From The Hill* illustrates the
value of this cumulative experience in the film's climatic scene
(Harvey, 1989, pp. 262-263).   Rafe (George Peppard) is the
illegitimate son of Captain Wade Hunnicutt (Robert Mitchum).
Hunnicutt respects Rafe, but refuses to publicly acknowledge
him as his son.   Rafe, a self-made man, does not allow this

longing to ruin his life. He feels no resentment, for example, that his half-brother, Theron (George Hamilton), receives the Captain's blessings as his true son. Rafe, in fact, remains protective of Theron, who has yet to work his way into manhood--at least into the style of manhood that the Captain favors.

Wade Hunnicutt, however, bears a name that gains more respect than the man himself. He denotes a darker character by sporting the deserved reputation of a womanizer, and he has enemies because of this indulgence. One father, learning of his unmarried daughter's pregnancy, grabs a rifle, and, enraged, shoots the Captain. Ironically, Hunnicutt has no part in the daughter's misfortune--that responsibility belongs to Theron, still learning about manhood--although the Captain can hardly savor this thought as he lay dying. Rafe rushes to Hunnicutt's side, but Wade dies before he can acknowledge Rafe as his son.

Rafe gradually comes to dominate the story, yet only after a series of happenings painful to him and to the Hunnicutt family. Viewers realize over time that the denial of Rafe's birthright proves an inner loss sufficient to diminish his self-respect. Family names are important in rural America, and Rafe wants his. Not the family wealth, not the bragging rights, just the name. Viewers grasp this truth when they discover, through Rafe's emotionality, how earnestly he relates his birthright to his manhood. Feelings of this nature give rise to a gem of wisdom, a lurking intelligence that requires time and tribulation to find recognition.

These tumultuous experiences culminate in the graveyard scene. The Captain's estranged wife, Hannah (Eleanor Parker), stands beside Wade Hunnicutt's headstone, waiting for Rafe to join her. He arrives and reads the headstone's inscription. The inscription, at Hannah's request, includes him as the Captain's son. Rafe's face offers the audience a "roll" of emotions--initial surprise, then bitterness, then anguish. He asks Hannah if she wants the inscription there for everyone to see. Hannah assures him that she does.

Viewers know why Rafe must grapple with these feelings. Viewers know because they have tied themselves emotionally to him during his trials with the Captain. Rafe, still unfulfilled, stands too generous of nature to pursue his bitterness. He desired the Captain's acknowledgment before death, not after. But, finally, Rafe retreats from his pain, understanding that he enjoys a good life. The audience, too, feels Rafe's longing. His hopes become the viewers' hopes, assimilated individually through an Oz experience that personalizes Rafe's story and gives each moviegoer a presence in that story.

It seems silly to say it, but, yes, we can feed upon a movie's illusions all we want--as long as we divine between illusions and delusions; as long as we manage a comfortable distance between pretense and false beliefs. Pursuing this distinction concerns the remaining lessons of *Sexuality In The Land Of Oz*: How creatively do movies embrace sexual issues as a practice or a theme?

To answer this query we must learn how movies present sexual matters constructively, though admittedly in exaggerated form. We must search for that manifestation of a film's lurking intelligence. And, as moviegoers, we must remind ourselves that movies appear real at times, yet, in essence, they are truly phony baloney. Illusions. Pretense. Make-believe. A sexual experience to enjoy, but a sex education in the dark that calls for caution.

Notes

1. Technically, **voyeurism** refers to individuals (usually male) who become sexually aroused upon observing nude or partially nude individuals (usually female) who do not know they are being observed (Haas & Haas, 1993, p. 544). But technical terms that assume more general usage, as voyeurism has, frequently find their meaning altered and commandeered to serve other interpretations.

Voyeurism, for our purposes, includes males and females who privately, yet dispassionately, appraise the legitimacy of the characters they see in various cinematic situations (Boorstin, 1990, p. 11). Voyeurism, in this context, focuses on the logic--the common sense--that a character makes in behaving sexually or nonsexually. Sexual arousal as an emotion becomes identified therefore, not with voyeurism, but with the moviegoer's ability to experience cinematic sex **vicariously**. A sexually vicarious experience indicates the viewer's success in feeling aroused at a character's erotic portrayal.

2. A **bad murder**, by default, indicates an innocent victim, a person who does not deserve to die. This kind of murder seems redundant since murder defines a deliberately negative act. But in movie lore a value judgment changes the equation: A bad murder helps to catapult the hero into action, if for no other reason than to avenge the dastardly deed. What our hero customarily arranges, of course, pertains to the enactment of a good murder. He or she kills the villain and conveniently serves as judge, jury, and executioner to redress the earlier, bad murder (Wilson, 1991, p. 2).

3. The public's loving reception of this film belies all the tales of woe that went into its production (Sennett, 1989, p. 127). Numerous writers, at least four directors, a cadre of drunken Munchkins, and other digressions made *The Wizard Of Oz* a remarkable achievement of mind over matter. The film derives from a series of Oz stories by Lyman Frank Baum, who, himself, made three silent films of his work (Sennett, p. 129).

The Wizard Of Oz addresses other fantasies too, such as the folklore that Oz actually refers to the abbreviation for an ounce of gold. The gold allegory finds expression through controversial symbols like the "yellow brick road" (as the gold standard) and its path to Emerald City (standing in for Washington, D.C.). A dispute over the gold standard parallels--and may have inspired--the arrival of Baum's *Oz* in 1900 (Chism, 1992). Still another interpretation comes from Geoff Ryman's 1992 novel, *Was*, in which the author tells his own story of Dorothy and Oz, and it's not a pleasant trip (see Crowley, 1992).

Lesson 2

Sexual Practices

"**I** loved *Sassafras Pass* when I read it," says Helen. "I knew what the characters were thinking. I could see the purple mountain majesties and amber waves of grain. I liked how the author tied the five tales of incest, adultery, rape, prostitution, and bestiality into one whopping finale. So, how come the movie didn't do all that?"

How come, indeed? Helen goes to the theatre or plops a tape in the VCR and spends two hours watching *Sassafras Pass*. Compared to Helen's brief time at the movies, she may cheat by peeking at the last chapter--a practice less likely to happen when watching a film. Readers usually consider books an extended investment. They prolong the leisure of reading because they possess the patience to delay closure.

The novel, although usually structured in plot and progressive in telling a story, requires the reader to do some inventive work (Corliss, 1991; Hailey, 1991). An author describes (more or less) the character's appearance and personality, and the reader builds on this description to suit his or her fancy. But unlike a novel, a movie must **move** to entertain. It moves in the sense of injecting breathtaking action or steamy love scenes, and by presenting lively dialogue that presses the story onward. Sometimes events occur so swiftly that a viewer can only watch, not think. Therefore, what Helen "does" when she reads a book is generally not what she "does" when she views a film (see Brown, 1988, p. 179).

Films depart from novels by adding or eliminating characters, changing the book's locale, the book's message, the book's tone, the book's ending. Normally, of course, a book and film will share at least a few experiences for someone who reads the novel and sees the movie. But even if the two events manage a close relationship, the moviegoer may wonder, as Helen wondered after seeing *Sassafras Pass*--why didn't "they" do the movie more like the book?

What Movies Do Poorly

A movie's strength lies more in its **image** than its word. But a film's imagery cannot handle certain story elements well. A running commentary, for instance, spells trouble on the big screen. How would a filmmaker, say, translate the narrative present in this bit of macho business?

> I took the call on a day when a light breeze would white-face your eyebrows and glaze your lips for posterity. But I must admit that my eyebrows and lips felt better than Calvin's. He lay coiled by the hearth next to a fire that only the dead could ignore. He had my card, so they called. The card baffled me. What I remember of Calvin would have encouraged me to kick him in the groin, not leave a card. Calvin the creep. Calvin the monster. Calvin the bully. He bullied me. Guys don't forget those primal tokens of terror. The bully may be gone, but the bullying stays with you. I could kick him in the groin now, but it's too late. Even if Calvin were alive, it would be too late.

The author's **first-person narrative** conveys a viewpoint that prevails exclusively with the novel's narrator. How did

Calvin obtain the narrator's card, and why did Calvin die? Something's brewing here, although presently we are simply left to wonder. The narrator wonders, too, about Calvin's possession of his card, a query that prompts him to hark back to an unpleasant memory. A memory that strikes at the narrator's masculinity; a vulnerability that the narrator has never resolved, and feels he cannot change by any immediate action.

Now, what about adapting this scene to film? Aside from the logistics of making the narrator appear wintry cold--perhaps shaking ice crystals from his nose as he enters Calvin's lodge--what difficulties arise for the filmmaker? The tangibles in our narrator's thoughts are no obstacle. The filmmaker can reproduce and even enhance these tangibles to imply a mood for the setting. The fireplace, a "busy" fire, and a dead Calvin offer no problems for visualization on film. Calvin's den, let us say, is rife with background items--tennis trophies and photos of attractive women--to indicate Calvin the sportsman and Calvin the ladies' man. The set decorator arranges the den's furnishings, placing objects in strategic spots to acquaint us with Calvin's style of living (when he lived). No, the barrier lies not with Calvin, nor his hearth. The barrier concerns the narrator. **He's** the problem.

Specifically, the trouble involves our narrator's stream of consciousness. The first-person narrator of a novel functions as the reader's conduit for everything that happens. If a sultry lady flirts and attempts to seduce the narrator (who is married), we learn of this perturbing moment through the narrator's first-person account. But the reader learns only what the narrator supplies, and, customarily, accepts his account at face value as the unvarnished truth (Seger, 1992, p. 19).

How can a film express this stream of consciousness? Answer: not very well. A first-person viewpoint in film, taken precisely, means that the individual shall appear in every scene. This demand makes the role rather rigorous for the lead actor. One of those rare attempts to include the viewer as a first-person hero occurs in *Lady In The Lake* (1947), a private-eye film. The camera's "eye" becomes the viewer's eye.   Other than showing the hero's hands and arms as appropriate extremities, and flashing an occasional mirror image, the viewer and the camera are one (Huss & Silverstein, 1971, p. 57).   Unfortunately, the experiment does not work well since empathizing with the hero doesn't help much if we can't see the hero's face (Boorstin, 1990, pp. 114-115). This radical approach shows the artistic differences between a novelist's first person and what a filmmaker must do to achieve the effect literally.

The narrator's brief reminiscence about Calvin the bully calls for another actor to hear the narrator divulge his memory. Or the narrator narrates; he performs a "voice over" that the audience hears--but need not accept as the naked truth--while the narrator walks silently about Calvin's den. The novelist accomplishes this feat by letting the narrator think and feel for the reader.   The filmmaker, however, cannot indulge a continuous recital. The actor must manifest his memory about Calvin, perhaps through an embittered glance at the body. Or possibly the actor shows perplexity, followed by a grimace of recognition to tell the audience that he knows Calvin; and that the knowing, though not pleasant, also is not recent.   Still, even if the actor manages these nonverbal signals, the business about Calvin the bully will not emerge as easily on film as in print (McKibben, 1992, pp. 211-212).[1]

Perhaps the trickiest feat of narration for filmmaking involves breaking down the **fourth wall**. This expression concerns the "wall" that exists between performers and audience.   Novelists, of course, can speak to the reader through the first-person "I" narrative. Stage plays occasionally permit a performer to speak directly to the audience as an "aside" from the ongoing action. But movies run a greater risk of disengaging viewers from the story by allowing an actor to turn and speak, facing the camera directly.

When the technique works, it enhances the story's magic. When it doesn't work (sigh), the technique deteriorates to a series of annoying interruptions. Michael Caine (1990, p. 96) comments, for example, that his role as the sexual wayfarer in *Alfie* (1966) required him to speak to the camera. Conversing with the audience allows the amoral Alfie to become more likable, because Caine learns to covet the camera and pretend to speak with one person rather than to a large, unseen audience. (Caine also developed a video on acting, and plays a scene from *Alfie* to demonstrate the fine points of using the camera to an actor's best advantage.)

He shares intimacies with the viewer, thinking of the viewer as an old friend. Alfie, confiding to you as the friend, puzzles over his inability to bring himself to marriage, given the fact that he has had numerous opportunities. Nor can he bring himself to worry much about another fact, namely, that he has left so many wenches in sexual disarray. Note, however, that without Alfie's shared confidences, his unflattering lifestyle would leave viewers with less reason to foster any affection for him.

On a more plaintive chord, Shirley (Pauline Collins) of *Shirley Valentine* (1989) speaks to the walls and various paraphernalia, including the camera. Shirley's in a mid-life crisis and convinces herself that a trip to Greece will rescue her from the doldrums of an overly-contented, exactingly predictable routine. Shirley's husband is bewildered but indifferent to his wife's desires, causing her to move haltingly, though inevitably, to a decision.

Shirley, like Alfie, "converses" intimately to make you feel a participant and also a confidant. If you sympathize with Shirley's dilemma (i.e., that she should go), you will quickly forgive the disconcerting nature of her early asides, and soon learn to anticipate the character's interludes of direct contact. Once your identification with Shirley's wishes and travails becomes second nature, she need give you only an occasional look to communicate her feelings. Such emotional closeness demands personable performers who can win your trust, as Michael Caine and Pauline Collins demonstrate. Both Alfie and Shirley, incidentally, were stage characters before they successfully made the precarious transition to film.

Clearly the novelist and filmmaker attempt to do many of the same things, but do them in different ways. A novelist creates a character for us by probing the character's innermost thoughts. The filmmaker relies on our discovering the character through show and tell. The "show and tell" can include the story's cumulative effects, narration, and other visual/audio techniques that provide the audience with a sense of identity. As one critic remarked, "In the novel, we see because we remember; in film, we remember because we see" (Linden, 1971, p. 158).

What Movies Do Well

So, how can film handle a novel's abstractions? The best way, as we have seen, does not mean a literal reconstruction of these abstractions. Sometimes the most effective treatment of complexity is to ignore it. Go with the medium's strength, and the strength of film involves its **immediacy of vision and sound**. This immediacy carries the potential to provoke an **intensity of experience** that books find difficult to rival.

Recall for a moment the **Oz** experience. We assumed in Lesson One that Oz refers to a viewer's interpretation of seeing a movie. The movie influences what a viewer contrives as entertainment, but the viewer is not a blank tablet. He or she conjures up a personal conception of what transpires on the screen. This conception involves the viewer's expectation and mood, both of which are susceptible to the physical effects of emotion during the movie, and to a more abstract emotionality that the person experiences afterward.

The **physical emotionality of Oz**, frankly, can prove overwhelming at times. A filmmaker counts on certain emotional experiences that will bind the viewer to the image. According to Jon Boorstin (1990, p. 9), author of *The Hollywood Eye*, a movie illuminates three pleasures that compete for attention, and that comprise the viewer's emotional investment in a film. The **voyeur's eye**, Boorstin argues, indicates a "prying observer," someone who dispassion-ately analyzes the film's unfolding events for their sense of logic and their plausibility (Boorstin, pp. 12-13). To wit, does a character's feelings and behavior make sense to the moviegoer? Does the actor's conduct ring true?

A second pleasure, the **vicarious eye**, relies not only on the viewer's ability to comprehend the characters' emotions, but the viewer's willingness to identify with those emotions--what Boorstin calls "our sense of emotional truth" (p. 75). If the moviegoer, becoming familiar with a character, does not believe a character would react a certain way, then the moviegoer will not find that emotion credible. Hence, the failure to achieve emotional "common sense" through voyeurism also impairs any emotional truth gained through the vicarious experience (this standard covers other creative efforts too, including the novel; see Vornholt, 1992).

Boorstin's third pleasure, the **visceral eye**, depends on the movie's capacity to shock the viewer into sensing raw emotions, such as lust, fear, anger, or surprise. An effectively choreographed roller-coaster ride will do it, and so will an explicit rape scene. The emotions felt here are not vicarious, but given in direct response to what the viewer sees. Boorstin contends that "Visceral thrills are filmmaking's dirty little secret. Though they can require considerable art to achieve, there is nothing artistic about the results--thrill of motion, joy of destruction, lust, blood lust, terror, disgust. Sensations, you might say, rather than emotions. More complex feelings require the empathic process [the vicarious eye], but these simple, powerful urges reach out and grab us by the throat without an intermediary" (Boorstin, p. 110).

Boorstin's scheme of the voyeur's eye, the vicarious eye, and the visceral eye provides us with a profile for examining the physical emotions of Oz. But the three "eyes" do not say much about the more **abstract conceptions of Oz**--notably the practice of reflecting on a film's worth to the viewer. Viewing often leaves little time for such reflections during a story's progress. The physical conception to make sense of what you see (voyeur's eye), identify with the characters emotionally (vicarious eye), and feel the onslaught of strong sensations (visceral eye), will dominate the Oz process as you watch a movie.

A case in point concerns *The Exorcist*, a best-selling novel by William Blatty that blended the familiar and unfamiliar into a horror tale. The familiar, a previously normal 12-year-old girl, finds herself possessed by the unfamiliar, a demon. The question is, How do you get her unpossessed? Therein lies the story, and thereby enters the 1973 film based on Blatty's novel.

The novel no doubt delivered shivers to readers who tried to picture the young girl in that ghostly bedroom. But the novel's terror pales compared to the film's special effects. The movie did with this story what a movie does best--"show" viewers the girl slowly becoming emaciated; "show" the demon's handiwork; "show" the demon's utterances in its sexually "dirty," god-awful voice. The movie, in short, exhibits a vivid presence of evil through sight and sound.

Viewers' reactions involved more than shivers: Moviegoers unleashed reactions to what Jon Boorstin would call the film's visceral effects. Some patrons could not stay seated to watch the more intense scenes, and many individuals found that the movie put them through an emotionally wrenching experience. To filmmakers, the viewers' reactions are pure gold. Such emotional responses constitute another way of saying that the movie mesmerized its audience.

These reactions are not the reactions you associate with reading a book. Nor can we assume that the filmmaker merely duplicates the novel's message. The movie's capacity to invoke greater intensity encourages a **carry-over effect**. The intensity of key scenes enlivens the entire film. *The Exorcist* unfolds an intriguing tale to complement its special effects. The novel and the movie explore a fascinating relationship between sexual taboos and religion.

The film does not rely on extended dialogue to make its point, however. Rather, the camera bares the demon's power by displaying a young girl's face and body to project her desperation as a girl, and her sexual ferocity as a demon. The novel, although a good read, cannot match the immediacy of the movie's visceral power to create a startling visual and auditory ordeal.

Sexual Practices: Thinking About Our Feelings

Speaking to the sexes, do you remember the first time you saw a vagina? A penis? The vagina requires close inspection, hidden as it is by anatomical design, and, in mature females, by a more-or-less dense pubic forest. But the penis hangs out in all its flaccid and, occasionally, upright glory, although this remarkable organ appears unlikely to win any beauty contests. For a female, therefore, her first observance of the male's secret joy probably inspires a surge of mixed emotions.

Imagine Eugenia (Laura Antonelli) in *Till Marriage Do Us Part* (1979), a virgin seeking her first encounter with...the THING. She marries, apprehensive, yet fully expecting to consummate the relationship on her wedding night. Then, she receives a staggering revelation that leaves her sexually unfulfilled and searching for release: A groom is not always a groom, it seems, especially if he happens to be your unknown brother. Dismayed though not deterred, Eugenia tries again with an admirer, engaging in a hilarious contra-diction of behaviors that pits womanly lust against ladylike diffidence (she wants to, yet knows she shouldn't). But her admirer, learning that Eugenia is a virgin, reluctantly withdraws and decides the whole business will become too complicated.

Finally, Eugenia strikes pay dirt with her swarthy chauffeur. Pretending that the car has broken down, he guides her into a hut, arranging clusters of hay for the big moment. Eugenia protests feebly as the chauffeur attempts to remove several layers of her clothing. The removal job almost exhausts him, and he stops to ponder if she's worth the experience. Eugenia protests more strongly as a signal for him to continue. Continue he does, ultimately making his way to her skimpy garments. He pauses, walks a few steps away, and begins to disrobe. Eugenia rises up in rapt curiosity as he lowers his pants and reveals...the THING! Her eyes widen, she flies back on the hay, covers her face, and emits a piercing scream.

Welcome to the world of cinematic reality. Whatever
Eugenia expects, given her dearth of preparation, what she
sees goes beyond comprehension. The scream somehow
embodies all her worst fears about the "first time." No doubt
real females in real time have reacted strongly to their initial
glimpse of the penis. Who knows? Some feminine observers
may have hiccupped, passed out, or barfed up their lunch.
More likely, though, they giggled (as opposed to laughing
uproariously), checked out its peculiar anatomy, or wondered,
ultimately, about all the fuss and secrecy.

If Eugenia had merely shrugged her shoulders, the hilarity
and the entertainment would have been for naught. Cinematic
reality, however, advances true reality by embellishing the
viewer's Oz process. This embellishment demands an
enhancement of real life. Enhancement means a twist, an
exaggeration, possibly an absurdity. All three happenings
indicate a distortion of reality; distortions that carry implica-
tions--good and bad--for moviegoers.

Cinematic sexual practices, aside from their choreographed
intent to entertain, constitute a special consideration. Movies
can and do present masturbation, intercourse, seduction,
lustful liaisons, and other activities in outlandish fashion. But
sheer sexual exaggeration wears thin as the sole explanation
for maintaining viewer interest. No, such practices retain
their longevity because of the viewers' fascination with **sexual
intimacy**. In essence, moviegoers delight upon seeing
attractive performers practice their sensuality--physical and
psychological--in a style and setting that makes Tuesday-night
sex in the back room humdrum by comparison.

The movies' illicit intimacies, in particular, violate society's
social regulation of sexual conduct (Davies, 1982). Movies,
however, can defy these boundaries, usually with impunity.
Want to walk in the prostitute's world and vicariously live her
life? Okay, walk along. Want to seduce a vulnerable someone
for all the wrong reasons? Very well, go for it. You may do
so because its pretense, and because Oz permits you the
fantasy.

If the filmmaker knows his or her craft competently, a
movie should engage you to respond physically to the

characters and story, as suggested by Boorstin's voyeuristic, vicarious, and visceral eyes. But a better filmmaker, by fiat, should do more. "More" involves a foray into **abstract emotionality**, mentioned earlier: A movie possessed of lurking intelligence, capable of making you think and reflect on the sexual intimacies viewed, especially after your physical pleasure in seeing the movie has diminished.

Interestingly, a film claims greater artistic integrity when it does challenge the viewer's imagination. An actress playing a sensuous character remains more beguiling when she stays partially robed than if she exhibits herself completely nude. Partially robed, she provokes the imagination of that unseen vision. Completely disrobed, she plays her ace and the tantalizing mystery of her physical allure becomes compromised.

Michelle Pfeiffer, who portrays a torch singer draped in a red gown and jeweled bracelets, provides the movie's memorable twinkle of eroticism when she warbles "Making Whoopee" and performs her psychological strip tease atop a piano in *The Fabulous Baker Boys* (1990). Male and female viewers, in their own way, find themselves free to interpret this scene beyond what they see, an opportunity that would prove more restrictive if Pfeiffer had undulated through a physical strip tease.

Oz thrives on **mystery**. A filmmaker who belabors the obvious is a filmmaker whose work harbors little artistry. Instead of scoring exquisite moments on film and trusting the audience to use its imagination, the pedestrian filmmaker talks down to viewers and leaves nothing of substance to fantasize. The sad outcome of this literal entertainment concerns those moviegoers who permit the movie to do all the imaginative inducement for them. They need not think about their emotions, just feel. For them, imagination extends only to the immediacy of what they see. And what they see, perhaps too often, is cinematic trash.

To examine this psychological dimension of Oz, imagine the delights and despairs of five sexual practices: gender reversal, masturbation, seduction, the vagaries of lust, and a first intercourse, knowing what we now know about the value of thinking through our emotions. Misinformation surrounds all five practices, so stay vigilant and note the differences between cinematic reality and the real thing.

The Gender Twist

Considering the five sexual practices cited--gender reversal, masturbation, seduction, lustful behavior, and intercourse-- **gender reversal** emerges as the most purely cinematic. Transform a male to a female, a female to a male, or either sex to "something else" and the movies can do it, and do it with panache. Viewers, if they wish, can witness just about every gender enchantment and vulgarity known to humankind. As Toddy (Robert Preston) of *Victor/Victoria* (1982) observes after completing his song and responding to the applause, "Thank you, you're most kind. In fact, you're every kind." Toddy knows whereof he speaks: He's gay, an aging Queen in fact, and he's just sung to "every kind" at a gay club, the Chez Lui.

True, in reality we know of **transvestites** who dress as the opposite sex for psychological gratification. We know of **transsexuals** as males and females who feel more oriented to the opposite sex and cross dress for gender security. We know of **gays in drag** who dress as the opposite sex for entertainment. And we know of males and females who impersonate the opposite sex for reasons not easily categorized, for example, to obtain and hold a job. But the movies' idea of gender reversal concerns less these possibilities, and more the use of gender twisting for humor. What filmmakers do with gender as a practice does not bear much correspondence to actual behavior.[2]

Defining gender scientifically can become a full-time obsession. The "dichotomous" camp prefers to keep a respectful distance between sex and gender, choosing to interpret sex biologically and gender culturally (Gentile, 1993; Doyle & Paludi, 1991, p. 4; Prince, 1985). The "relatedness" camp compromises this distinction and concludes that sex and gender act in concert (and sometimes out of concert) too splendidly to force a separation (Deaux, 1993; Unger & Crawford, 1993; Benderly, 1987, p. 11).

The two camps appear to agree, nonetheless, that the more exclusive the biological and cultural origins of a function, the more likely one can distinguish between sex and gender. Thus, the gestation period invokes a female biological function, whereas the strong preference in India for male infants over female infants indicates a cultural prejudice. Most of the time, however, sex and gender prove difficult to untangle. I acknowledge the positions of the dichotomous and relatedness camps, although in the present lesson, for convenience, I use the expressions "opposite sex" and "opposite gender" interchangeably.

This academic debate over sex and gender, however, does not really address the portrayal of gender in movies. Cinematically, **gender** denotes an **image**. The more charismatic the actor, the greater his or her potency to convey an entertaining masculine or feminine image. Sex, defined as a constellation of primary and secondary bodily functions, finds its domain overwhelmed here by the psychological presence that actors emanate to an audience. This "psychological presence" includes physical attractiveness, as well as other cultural evaluations of womanliness and manliness that come closer to what social scientists call gender.

Movies customarily follow the tradition of American culture and contrast masculine and feminine conduct. But when blending occurs, androgyny arises as a description. **Androgyny** seems easier to detail on paper than to recognize in practice: Males and females blur gender boundaries by accommodating both masculine and feminine qualities. The qualities may reflect appearance, but need not. More reliably, androgyny involves behaviors that do not readily fit the traditional feminine or masculine niche, such as competitiveness in women and crying in men.

Filmmakers show an inclination, when necessary, to enhance the female's masculinity, yet they refrain from softening the male's manhood by emphasizing his femininity (Bell-Metereau, 1985, p. 1). Consequently, viewers find greater acceptance in watching Sigourney Weaver play an

assertive Ripley in the *Alien* films, than in viewing Clint
Eastwood's effeminate nature, should he ever attempt such a
variation. The matter does not rest simply with addition or
subtraction, but occurs through a pleasing conglomeration of
traits: Ripley can behave ferociously and express her courage
with the best male fighters, but Ripley's also a woman and a
mother who does not sacrifice her femininity to the callousness
of a wholly masculine portrayal.

Gender, of course, represents a state of being and not a
practice. It becomes a practice when given movement and
direction--when it lends itself to purposive activity.
Filmmakers being filmmakers, their idea of purposive activity
is to stand gender on its head. Reverse it, shift it, switch it,
give the image of gender a twist for the sake of entertainment.

Toddy (Robert Preston) meets Victoria (Julie Andrews) in
Victor / Victoria (1982) when both are out of work and down
to their last doughnut. He's not feeling well, and she's been
fainting due to hunger, so each commiserates with the other as
they soak their cold, tired feet in a tub. Victoria wants to
know how long Toddy has been a homosexual, and he retorts
by asking her how long she's been a soprano. These lively
exchanges set the tone for a cavalier treatment of gender
throughout the story.

It is Toddy's brainstorm that kicks the plot forward.
Victoria, her clothes unwearable, dons a suit owned by
Toddy's rather heartless lover. Then the brainstorm: Victoria
can pretend to be a man pretending to be a woman. A tricky
charade since Victoria must sing like a Victor, yet not so
convincingly that patrons will miss the revelation of Victoria
dressed as Victor to play Victoria. (Movie and stage
productions proclaim a history of engaging in these convoluted
games and, occasionally, playing them well enough to get away
with the farce.) Victoria's finale is to doff her wig dramatically and leave the audience believing that she really is Victor.

One person who doesn't believe it is King Marchand
(James Garner), a Chicago nightclub owner visiting Paris and
quite enamored of Victoria. King confronts Victoria and tells
her bluntly that he's practically certain "He" is really a "She."
Victoria counters, "Ah, but to a man like you, someone who

believes he could never under any circumstances find another man attractive, the margin between 'practically' and 'for sure' must be as wide as the Grand Canyon."

King, undeterred, secretly invades Victoria's quarters, hides in the linen closet, and spies on Victoria as she disrobes for her bath. The smug smile on his face tells viewers all they need to know. Now, he's 100 percent certain. His certainty, however, is not shared by King's crusty girlfriend, Norma (Leslie Ann Warren), who, sensing Victoria as a threat, needs to believe that Victor is really Victor. Hence, to convince King that Victor/Victoria is really is a man, she declares pompously, "A woman can always tell."

King's discovery, nonetheless, does not prepare him for the challenge to his manhood. King and Victoria become lovers, first privately, then publicly. Scenes show them at a bloodthirsty prizefight, with King in his element and Victoria (as Victor) ready to barf; then they're at the opera, with Victor in tears at the performance, and King in agony at how to handle this crying "male" next to him; finally, we see them dancing in a gay club, a final gender twist that King cannot handle. Victoria compounds the problem when she admits that being a man is fascinating: "I mean there are things available to me as a man that I could never have as a woman. I'm emancipated." "Emancipated?" King asks. "Well," Victoria replies, "I'm my own man, so to speak. You should be able to relate to that..."

King can, but not at the expense of his masculinity. Victoria enjoys the perks that come with the male prerogative, whereas King longs for the more traditional male/female relationship. *Victor/Victoria* carries this dilemma to the only solution acceptable in the comedic game of erotic intrigue: Victor must go. The alternative, that King neutralize his manhood for the sake of romance, does not compute in the Oz experience. Victor, after all, merely pretends to be male, and, as such, has no claim on the male province. Easier for Victor, then, to relinquish "his" perks and prerogatives, and help the beleaguered King to restore his inherent masculinity.

Victor/Victoria depicts an unusual farce for Hollywood. Unusual in that a woman must pass, however frivolously, as a

man. A female typically does not possess the deeper voice,
angular features, accentuated muscles, and broad-shouldered
physique to convince moviegoers of a male impersonator.
Males, conversely, realize the easier deception in assuming
those feminine wiles that they must emulate. Certain rules
apply, of course: You don't embellish your impersonation by
swinging the hips to and fro like a battering ram; you don't
squeal the falsetto voice; and you don't wave the arms
flamboyantly to express giddiness. You don't, in other words,
exaggerate. Instead, you pull in, walk sedately, talk quietly,
and behave for all the world as a demure lass, a lady from
head to toe. This transformation does not mean that the male
now comports himself as a woman; but it does mean that if
he's careful, he may not fall prey to a caricature of female
behavior (Bell-Metereau, 1985, p. 9).

Crossing over, the male finds, serves up a daunting
experience. Joe and Jerry (Tony Curtis and Jack Lemmon) are
two desperate musicians who must give female impersonation
a shot in *Some Like It Hot* (1959). Literally, their lives and
their livelihood depend on it. The partners are witnesses to
the St. Valentine's Day massacre of 1929, so it's important that
they leave Chicago fast. Joe becomes Josephine and Jerry
changes to Daphne, two "girls" who must learn quickly about
dress and decorum--especially since they have signed
themselves on to play with an all-girls' band, bound for
Florida.

The entrancing feature of such gender twists concerns
those little feminine insights that males realize when, for
whatever reason, they portray the opposite gender. Daphne,
having trouble with her heels and the winter draftiness of her
dress, marvels at the fluid locomotion of one Sugar Kane
(Marilyn Monroe) as Sugar hurries past to join the band:
"Look at that! Look how she moves. Just like Jell-O on
springs. Must have some sort of built-in motor or something...I tell you it's a whole different sex!"

Different enough so that, in close quarters with a parade of
nighties, Daphne (Jerry) must keep reminding herself "I'm a
girl, I'm a girl, I'm a girl..." Furthermore, an interesting
switch in attitude occurs at this juncture between Joe and

Jerry. Joe, the ladies' man, gambler, and con artist, has heretofore driven Jerry, the worrywart, wild with his crazy schemes for a quick buck. But now, as Josephine, Joe behaves more like a chaperon. He feels obligated to monitor Daphne, lest Jerry as Daphne become too taken with the luscious pearls about him.

Daphne, however, encounters a novel problem: She must fend off the amorous overtures of Osgood Fielding III (Joe E. Brown), millionaire playboy who wants to play with Daphne. Daphne storms into her hotel room: "Dirty old man! I just got pinched in the elevator!" Josephine replies, "Now you know how the other half lives." But Daphne checks herself in a mirror and complains, "I'm not even pretty!" Josephine replies, "They don't care as long as you're wearing a skirt. It's like wearing a red flag in front of a bull." This outcome proves too much for Daphne: "Really? Well, I'm sick of being a flag. I want to be a boy again..."[3]

An unsung blessing of *Some Like It Hot* involves the disparate personalities of Joe and Jerry. Joe, as Josephine, never forgets his maleness. He's uncomfortable as a woman, partly because of his avocation to pursue the opposite sex, an erotic game that he plays well. Jerry, by contrast, looks upon his previously suppressed Daphne skills as an enchanting experience. He knows he's male but finds his paler masculine image less satisfying. Jerry, after an awkward initiation into the world of femininity, embraces Daphne as a delightful diversion. Indeed, Daphne informs Joe that "she" plans to marry Osgood. Joe is stunned: "What are you talking about? You can't marry Osgood." Daphne, more than a little gender-struck, replies: "You think he's too old for me?" Joe persists: "But you're not a girl, you're a guy. And why would a guy want to marry a guy?" Daphne's answer: "Security."

The closing scene finds Osgood steering a boat to his yacht, contentedly expecting to marry Daphne. Jerry, as Daphne, tries a few artful maneuvers to dissuade Osgood, but ultimately whisks off his wig and exclaims: "Oh, you don't understand, Osgood! Ahhh, I'm a man." Osgood, unfazed, replies calmly, "Well, nobody's perfect." This last line is a classic in movie history, and, if you analyze it, the conclusion follows that even gender becomes unimportant for a male (Osgood), who, after seven or eight failed marriages, now decides he's finally on to something.

The most fulfilling male-to-female impersonation occurs in *Tootsie* (1982) when Michael Dorsey becomes Dorothy Michaels (Dustin Hoffman) to find work as an actor. Note that the gender exchange in *Victor/Victoria*, *Some Like It Hot*, and *Tootsie* all happen because the characters need a job. This nonsexual beginning, regardless, gives way to a bit of gender magic that cross dressing inspires. The cross dressing helps the stated gender to tap into the opposite gender with a little insight, a little humility, and sometimes more than a little verve.

The case in *Tootsie* illustrates that Dorothy Michaels boasts a charitable nature to outshine her more selfish creator, Michael Dorsey. Dorothy seems nicer and more considerate as a woman than Michael does as a man. Critics have argued over what the Dorothy/Michael impersonation truly says, but the point to remember is that Dorothy and Michael are **one** (Garber, 1992, p. 5; Bell-Metereau, 1985, po. 200). Dorothy does not add a dimension to Michael's personality that he does not already possess. She does, however, give life to a more gracious Michael at the movie's end, without changing him radically in the process. Because of the Dorothy in him, Michael moves closer to an understanding of the opposite gender.

The fascination with gender reversal comes in two flavors--the physical and the psychological. Physically, as a male you can imagine the sensation of movement that a female experiences, although stretching yourself to imagine her menstrual cycle may prove too ambitious. Physically, as a female you can empathize with the male swagger and gait, but likely will find more trouble in imagining the wave of stimulation that accompanies a penile ejaculation. Physically, then, each gender can be in touch with the other...if they wish.

Psychologically, hobnobbing with the opposite gender becomes more problematic. Is it easier for the male to think and feel as a female, or for the female to show better rapport with being a male? The question may not prove fruitful to social scientists, but it poses a potential issue for self-appraisal. Dustin Hoffman's creation of Dorothy left him with emotional ties to her, in part because he used his mother as inspiration for the role: "...I'm still taken by that fantasy girl. When I tried to become this character, Dorothy Michaels, I couldn't become as pretty as I wanted to become, and we tested for over a year, because I felt that I should try to look as attractive as I could, just as I want to be in a man....It suddenly occurred to me after doing Dorothy for a while that if I'd met her at a party, I'd never so much as condescend to talk to her, because physically she was a write-off. It's a shallow attitude, certainly, to judge people by the way they look, and I think that is what started to make me sad" (Tuchman, 1983, p. 26).

Those Precious Bodily Fluids

Losing one drop of **precious bodily fluids** (semen), so proclaimed an 18th-century dilettante, produces more physical weakness than losing 40 drops of blood (McCary, 1971, p. 112). Important and influential people listened to such pronouncements, in part because the rhetoric could be traced to the King James Book of Genesis (Genesis 38: 1-11). God's commandment dictates that Onan must impregnate his brother's widow, but Onan decides that the seed will belong to his dead brother and not to him. He chooses, instead, to spill his fluids on the ground, defying Hebraic tradition. According to this anti-masturbatory version, God struck Onan dead for wasting seed. The idea that God may have sanctioned Onan (as God did Onan's brother, Er) for disobedience somehow gets lost in the interpretation.

One early health manual included the before-and-after picture of a man who succumbed to the dreaded practice, **masturbation**. Before, his face conveys the glow of health; after, we view a face haggard and emaciated, a deterioration triggered by too much hand-to-penis fraternization. The Boy Scouts of America got into the act during the 1940s with a segment in their handbook entitled "Conservation." Conservation referred, not to soil or water preservation, but to the retention of seminal fluids needed to maintain manhood (Miller, 1974). Carl Miller, knowing the score, wrote several letters to the scouts, expressing his concern that the hip baths, recommended in the manual, no longer proved effective to keep him above "temptation." Miller adds that the scouts finally replied, suggesting politely that he see a good psychiatrist.

Surely though, as our sexual culture moves brashly into the 21st century, the myth of precious bodily fluids should have met its Waterloo. But no, not when you compare masturbation against other, more desirable sexual practices. Understandably, adolescents don't care to discuss their masturbatory habits, since, for males in particular, to masturbate means to fail. Masturbation signifies the male teenager who finds himself unable to engage in intercourse or oral-genital contact with a desired partner. His indulgence in autoeroticism also denotes a youth who cannot maintain the necessary discipline to keep from succumbing to this awful practice. Masturbation reflects a sign of weakness, and, for some adolescents, envelops an insidious act that dooms them to foolish beliefs and a guilty conscience.[4]

Teenagers today acknowledge many of the fallacies concerning masturbation, yet their recognition does not always dispel feelings of shame over the practice. And certain adolescents, like one 14-year-old boy, still feel the need to conserve those precious fluids: "It makes you weak, that's what I heard. My mom's old boyfriend played on a professional soccer team and he said making love or having sex makes you weak--that's shooting sperm, so shooting a lot of sperm makes you weaker and weaker and weaker, and you don't want to walk around school sagging around 'cause you can't even hold yourself up" (Stokes in Coles & Stokes, 1985, p. 68).

True, masturbating seven or eight times an evening can produce a weary penis, although the owner of that penis will find himself no closer to perdition. And, unlike the more acceptable practice of intercourse, masturbation signals certain drawbacks. Among its liabilities is the belief that each male harbors only so many "shots" of semen. Placing a quota on the semen a teenager expels illustrates one way of frightening the naive adolescent into foregoing his "evil" habit.

No evidence exists, however, that the "quota" myth keeps males from masturbation, or even slows the practice. This misbelief simply provides another variation on the theme of retaining those precious bodily fluids. Interestingly, the myth has no application to female teenagers, who, although demonstrating less exhibitionism than males, find masturbation just as pleasurable. Indeed, females learn that through clitoral stimulation they can orchestrate more orgasms--and more intense orgasms--than those experienced when the penis thrusts away vigorously in the vagina (Bakos, 1990, p. 114).

Masturbation, nonetheless, can assume a **dark practice** in the movies. Despite the act's rich source of sensual gratification, its image remains tainted as an example of social ineptitude. When the inept male finds his first choice denied, such as sexual companionship through intercourse or oral-genital contact, masturbation emerges as a jaded second choice.

Movies, furthermore, can treat the act harshly merely by the **context and character** through which it occurs. One scene in *The Silence Of The Lambs* (1991) shows Clarice Starling (Jodie Foster) leaving serial murderer Hannibal Lecter (Anthony Hopkins), frustrated because Lecter chooses to give her little information. But as Clarice passes a neighboring cell, the inmate, who has not seen a woman in years, throws semen in Clarice's face. He times his masturbation, cups the semen in his hand, and delivers his fluids--an act that serves the dual purpose of insulting her and arousing him. The point is that masturbation benefits an ugly purpose in this scene. Lecter reinforces the ugliness when, later, he exacts revenge on his adjacent cell mate by somehow talking the man into swallowing his tongue. Lecter does so because, by his own perverse standards, he finds the semen-throwing incident "rude."

Therefore, cinematic magic, via context and character, alters the value that we attach to masturbation. Change the context and character, and you change the value judgments

associated with the practice. *Fast Times At Ridgemont High*
(1982) creates an adolescent's nightmare when Brad Hamilton
(Judge Reinhold) returns home, disgruntled and disenchanted.
He finds his sister, Stacy (Jennifer Jason Leigh), and her best
friend, Linda (Phoebe Cates), by the pool.

Brad fantasizes about Linda: How she dives into the pool,
how she emerges wet and sleek, how she glides towards him,
how she pulls away her halter top, how she tells him of her
desire...Brad, in a dither, conjures up the ultimate male
fantasy as he pumps away in the bathroom, not hearing Linda
walk to the door, not hearing her open the door, and not
realizing that she discovers him until it's too late. The risk of
discovery offers perhaps an added sense of excitement to the
adolescent; but the trepidation of having a beautiful girl open
the door and see a male lamely exercising his second choice
becomes the adolescent's devastation. Defensively, Brad snaps
at Linda about the lack of privacy, yet he vents his anger
because reality intrudes on fantasy--a reality that tells him
sharply of the chasm between what he desires and what
actually happens.[5]

The humor in eavesdropping on the sexual misfortunes and
misunderstandings of others denotes a longstanding cinematic
berth for comedy. Misfortune reigns in *Dr. Strangelove* (1964)
when a bonkers general, Jack D. Ripper (Sterling Hayden),
initiates a nuclear attack on Russia. Everyone scurries about,
desperate to recall Ripper's bomber wing of B-52s; bombers
that barrel relentlessly forward to the toe-tapping irony of
"When Johnny Comes Marching Home Again." Government
forces, directed by buffoons from the "War Room," frantically
attempt to penetrate Ripper's fortified air force base and to
squeeze the recall code from him. The general, however,
remains serene--a truly demented tranquility--convinced that
he must fight fire with fire.

His opposition are the Ruskies, and his reason for
launching Armageddon is fluoridation. To Ripper, fluoridation in water designates an impurity, and represents the
Ruskies' secret weapon for capturing the U. S. of A. But the
general arrives at his "theory" from an earlier experience, an

act of lovemaking that convinces him of the need to preserve his "precious bodily fluids."

Under siege from an attacking force that he believes to be Russian, but is actually a detachment of American troops, Ripper confides to a shaken Major Mandrake (Peter Sellers) that his belief began during the physical act of lovemaking. Lovemaking, he adds, that left him with a deep fatigue and a feeling of emptiness: "Luckily, I was able to interpret these feelings correctly....Loss of essence. I can assure you it has not recurred, Mandrake. Women sense my power and they seek the life essence. I don't avoid women, Mandrake. But I do deny them my essence."

Here we encounter the myth of losing one's "essence" again, only now it's a myth that compounds a monstrously humorous theory of Why an American male must conserve his bodily fluids from waste and contamination. The general's conviction that losing his fluids also means losing his essence sets the stage for an off-the-wall satire on human frailties--of men in authority who mawkishly try to forestall an overkill of technological power. This time, regrettably, human efficiency (getting to Ripper) lags behind electronic efficiency (getting the Bomb to Russia) to the peril of all involved.

The general's madness, his military capabilities, and even his surname heighten the ludicrous lengths to which the film's director, Stanley Kubrick, carry this mistaken belief. Kubrick plants a presumably innocuous fallacy in the wrong mind at the wrong time, allowing Ripper's concern over his precious natural fluids to culminate in a gigantic nuclear cloudburst for the world.

The movies tend to treat masturbation and its myths rather shabbily. We recognize that those precious bodily fluids can be used abusively for shock value (*The Silence Of The Lambs*); for embarrassment (*Fast Times At Ridgemont High*); and for absurd humor (*Dr. Strangelove*). All three examples, moreover, constitute negative outcomes associated with adolescent beliefs. Do filmmakers have the creative clout to show "the other side"? Can a movie include masturbation as a wholesome practice? A practice free of the usual tawdriness and ridicule that accompanies references to the act? The answer is yes, depending on your interpretation of "whole-some."

Misunderstanding prompts the humor of *Being There* (1980), but this humor proves more gracious in its treatment of masturbation.   Chance (Peter Sellers), a simpleminded gardener, finds himself thrust into the real world after his master dies. For Chance, who has lived the most gentle and sheltered of lives, the real world becomes comprehensible only through a passion that he has nurtured all his years--watching television.

Two developments bring humor to the audience and new-found friendships to Chance: (1) his ability to conduct himself according to television etiquette, and (2) the tendencies of sophisticated, cynical people to misinterpret Chance's elementary comments on gardening as profound insights into the nation's economy. Inadvertently, these developments become important when he wins the trust of a bedridden, billionaire industrialist, Ben Rand (Melvyn Douglas), and his wife, Eve (Shirley MacLaine).

Eve, like Chance, behaves as an innocent regarding sexual matters. Ben, knowing he will die soon, gives Eve his blessing to accept Chance as a companion. But Eve, shy and delicate, does not know Chance's preferences for sexual engagements. When she asks, Chance replies with the one line that he uses often, and that others reliably misconstrue: "I like to watch."

Chance means that he likes to watch television, and, unexpectedly, kisses Eve in an apparent lustful manner, but only because two lovers are kissing passionately on television. Once the lovers stop, Chance stops. Bewildered at this interruption, Eve takes Chance's response of "I like to watch" as a cue. Holding to his ankle, Eve lies on a bearskin rug and, hesitantly, begins to masturbate. Her hesitancy quickly gives way to uninhibited pleasure, then to laughter and orgasm as she observes Chance mimicking another television show by attempting to stand on his head.

Chance misunderstands because he views life dispassion-ately, including Eve's masturbation, as another television event. Eve misunderstands Chance's "I like to watch" because she believes that, as an observer, he becomes sexually aroused.

But moviegoers didn't misunderstand. The bedroom sequence conveyed a delightful comedy of errors, one of those rare experiences where a film presents masturbation as modest and pleasurable, rather than an act emphasizing ugliness, depression, or ridicule.

Seduction

"Nobody stays married for six," remarks a valet, as he ushers Mickey and Ray Davis (Barbara Williams and John Getz) into a restaurant to celebrate their sixth wedding anniversary. The Davis's seem secure and content, he a successful writer of children's books, and she a promising interior designer. But their success belies a passive marriage. Ray makes a fashion statement with his bow tie, nearsighted frown, and shopworn appearance. Mickey gazes at her husband with concern, wondering what it will take to spark him--and her--to a more loving relationship.

The spark arrives in the person of Scott Muller (Steven Bauer), a professional thief who burgles the Davis's home even as they celebrate. Scott absconds with the usual valuables, including a portrait of Mickey, and, most telling, a cache of her private journals. The thief, who needs a spark or two himself, finds Mickey's journals more than inviting--he reads of a woman who searches desperately for change: "There are two me's really--Mickey and Michelle. Mickey is this mousy little hausfrau who hasn't taken a real chance in her whole life. Michelle on the other hand is up for anything. The only trouble with Michelle is that she lives and breathes only on these pages."

Scott decides to emancipate Michelle by initiating an erotic game of deception in *Thief Of Hearts* (1984). He sees in Mickey a prospect worthy of pursuit, with good reason. Her diaries are a chronicle of sensual thoughts, thoughts that also express the unhappiness she feels in her marriage. Mickey, in turn, senses the unknown intruder's invasion of her private life, senses his fascination with her, feels him "turning each page." And...she's right.

The seduction begins. Scott "accidentally" bumps Mickey at a grocery market, retrieves her dropped parcels, and names her favorite ice cream flavor. Mickey, wary, wants to know how he knows, whereupon Scott selects the ice cream from her groceries and "admits" his ruse. Provocatively, Scott licks the melting ice cream from his fingers as he watches Mickey drive away, knowing that her transformation to Michelle represents a challenge far more exciting than the practice of mere thievery. Mickey later uses the ice cream to tempt Ray into an amorous encounter. She straddles his lap suggestively and forces him to taste the ice cream, but he puts her off and retreats to his self-absorbed world of the typewriter. Mickey, unsettled and unhappy, slips into a vulnerable state of mind.

Scott's manipulations escalate when he convinces Mickey to design the interior of his apartment. Complimenting her on her attractiveness and her talent, Scott adds, "Well, we'll find out soon, won't we?" Indeed, they will. Scott's first ploy is to take Mickey sailing, knowing from her journals that she thinks of water erotically. Scott recalls Mickey's description of an arousing childhood experience--watching her father cover himself with suntan oil. Naturally, Scott does the same, an effect that excites yet also puzzles Mickey. Something's happening here, something odd, but she's too captivated by this mysterious male to stop.

Mickey, frightened yet fascinated by guns, allows Scott to instruct her on the fine points of using a .45 caliber automatic. She murmurs "What a sense of power," as Scott seizes the moment to exercise his next tactic, the caressing and disrobing of Mickey as she fires at a target. Mickey, caught up in the excitement of a daring relationship, yields to Scott. He beds her, talks her into an orgasmic state, and preens at his mastery to bring Michelle alive.

Meanwhile, back home, Ray realizes his problem, although not the solution. Ironically, Mickey and Ray invest their most sensitive feelings into writing--his earnest thoughts find expression through children's stories, and her innermost desires become manifest in the pages of a private journal.

Neither party, however, communicates easily with the other. So their resolution, when it happens, does not derive from the resourcefulness of either partner, but from the flawed character of Scott Muller. Mickey, though entranced with Scott, also understands that she knows little about him. Knowing so little bothers her, a bother that Scott cannot allay. He likes the game of being in command, of knowing everything about her, of playing by his rules. She doesn't, disturbed over the one-sidedness of their relationship.

Scott's criminal past prompts him to consider leaving San Francisco for safer haunts. He wants his creation, Michelle, to join him. Mickey, reluctant to relinquish herself as Mickey, wants to learn more about him. Scott replies with his customary arrogance that she knows him as well as anyone can. Then, he commits a crucial mistake and reveals his startling secret: "And you know what? I know you--I know you like no one's ever known you, don't I, baby, hmmm? Don't I, Michelle?"

Stunned, Mickey finally fathoms the depth of Scott's seduction. And Scott, underestimating Mickey's reaction to the violations of her private world, overplays his hand: He compounds his mistake by telling Mickey that she no longer loves her husband. Mickey, in all sincerity, tells Scott that she still cares for Ray, despite her unfaithfulness. Scott refuses to accept Mickey's claim, unable to imagine any denial of him. Her declaration does not fit with Scott's journal portrait of Michelle. He envisions Michelle as his success, free of the repressed Mickey, and rid of the lackluster Ray.

Scott invades the Davis's home once again, but the journal he reads no longer harbors the old Michelle. Instead, he learns of a changed Mickey, and of a marriage renewed in spirit. Circumstances at the home lead to a final confrontation between Mickey and Scott: a parting of the ways, electrified by the attraction they still experience, yet sobered by the thought that each lover must follow a different life.

Thief Of Hearts offers the premise of erotic diaries that fall in the hands of a schemer. Armed with such intimate revelations, Scott Muller does what he does habitually anyway--he deceives, manipulates, and carries his sexual advantage to the wall. He plays the game for all its worth. The trick in being Scott Muller is not so much what he does, but who he is. He's a thief, he's arrogant, he's macho, but he's not insensitive. Scott's upset with himself for what he is--a thief--yet these concerns do not make him oblivious to the problems of others. A case in point: Earlier in the story, when Scott cannot reach a climax with a young hooker, he quietly assures her that the fault rests with him, not her.

The seduction becomes more sexually involving if the audience detects a glimmer or two of compassion in Scott Muller's character. Viewers, of course, also need to realize rapport with Mickey, the unfulfilled wife. Mickey's guided emotional attraction to Scott brings sympathy her way, with reservations. After all, she's engaged in an affair.

Viewers, if they're involved voyeuristically and vicari- ously, will grant Mickey this affair because of Scott's betrayal of her secret longings, and because of her husband's unresponsive behavior. But to keep the seduction flourishing, Scott and Mickey must project a certain likability. They need to emanate a sensual appeal to the audience, an appeal suitably positive to counter their illicit ways. If they do, they're in the catbird seat to entertain; if they don't, then she's a Jezebel and he's a mocking harlot.

The **cinematic formula of seduction** denotes an overarching enterprise that translates erotic tomfoolery into rash and improper games of secrecy, all in the name of entertainment. Indeed, the label of **sexual audacity** better reflects the movies' swashbuckling spirit of SEX than do more benign descriptions like sexual indiscretions or sexual improprieties. The movies prefer charging to walking, fighting to talking, and panting to sighing. Frequently, sexual audacity is what we pay to see and, perchance, the Oz we wish to experience through the film's characters and story (such as a sultry Mrs. Robinson seducing a naive Benjamin in *The Graduate*, 1967).

Seduction has its cinematic confines, however. To allow Scott and Mickey, say, to murder a benevolent Ray and then sail away free and unremorseful, does not seem a credible formula (although this ending surely qualifies as audacious). Nor does the possibility seem likely that Ray or Scott or

Mickey shall murder the other two principals, although you may find some takers willing to let Mickey extract her pound of flesh.

No, seduction, for all its boldness and daring, requires fine tuning to work well cinematically. Part of the tuning process concerns how much moral slack the players can exhibit and still adhere to the "Wages of Sin" doctrine. Scott, for example, loses Michelle, but he also slips into the night and, presumably, loses the law as well. Given his thievery, is this resolution just? Considering the traditional nature of morality in crime and punishment, probably not. But considering Scott's sexual gamesmanship of seeking to unravel a shaky marriage for selfish gain, viewers may decide that losing Mickey constitutes sufficient punishment.

Seduction warrants closer examination because of its packaging as entertainment, unwitting or not, to slight moral conduct. Endings weigh heavily in finalizing our thoughts about a character like Scott. We may find it easier to award him a changed personality and hope for his freedom. By contrast, we conveniently forget the emotional damage inflicted when Scott plays his deceitful game to possess Mickey. And it is his deceit--his secrecy--that makes the seduction a fascinating, if, in Scott's case, complex moral experience.

Moviemakers have many reasons to honor secrecy, and sexual secrecy in particular, as entertainment. David Bakan (1967, p. 104), relying on both the spontaneity and rigorous analysis that introspection can invite, generates a number of testable hypotheses about secrecy. **Secrecy**, he proposes, "...is maintained in order to maintain some given perception of one's self in others" (p. 105), a supposition that Scott fulfills when he presents himself deceptively to Mickey. And, another Bakanian thought, "To conceal a secret, one may tend to reveal a fabricated 'secret,' or a less-secret secret, in order to generate the impression that one is being open and frank" (p. 105)--which Scott does when he teases Mickey about her favorite ice cream flavor at the grocery market. He "admits" he knows her special flavor because he spots the ice cream among her parcels, but, in truth, Scott knows because of his knowledge of Mickey through her diaries.

Secrecy helps to make seduction not only suspenseful to moviegoers, but engaging, too. The duplicity in *Thief Of Hearts* gives Scott's Machiavellian boldness a measure of intrigue and verve. The tension, the uncertainty, the anticipation of Scott telling Mickey THE SECRET becomes not only paramount, it captures us as co-conspirators, an Oz process that enhances the moment of truth, when it comes. So, under these absorbing circumstances, who has time to think about morality?

Now, add to this stew a dash of comic philosophy and, given humor's capacity to make the most outrageous incidents more tolerable, we encounter a spirit of sexual permissiveness that extends the boundaries of seduction. Compare, for instance, the 1959 comedy *Pillow Talk* with the less humorous *Thief Of Hearts*. Can the case be made that, by today's standards, a rather chaste comedy possesses the wherewithal to be as sexually provocative as the erotic drama just described? Yes, although this answer depends on our definition of "sexually provocative," and on how much guardianship we accord to the forces of sexual censorship in 1959.

Jan Morrow (Doris Day) and Brad Allen (Rock Hudson) share a party line. Neither party knows the other, but since playboy/songwriter Brad monopolizes the line with sexual chatter, Jan finds herself upset over his conduct. She accuses him of behaving as a sexual libertine, and he retorts that she should stop living vicariously: "There are plenty of warm rolls in the bakery. Stop pressing your nose against the window."

Jonathan Forbes (Tony Randall) knows both Jan and Brad, but does not realize they share a phone line. What Jonathan does realize is that he's hot for Jan, although viewers know in this kind of film he may as well try to spit across the Atlantic. That, and the fact of Jonathan's three ex-wives tell us quickly about his purpose in the story: He's a reluctant pawn in the strategy to bring Jan and Brad together.

Through Jonathan, Brad learns accidentally of Jan's identity. And like Scott Muller in *Thief Of Hearts*, Brad harbors this information to his sexual advantage. He hides his plans from Jonathan, but in one exchange, he does expound on marriage and its Hereafter of Hell: "Jonathan, before a man gets married he's like a tree in the forest. He--He stands there independent, an entity unto himself. And then he's chopped down. His branches are cut off, he's stripped of his bark, and he's thrown into the river with the rest of the logs. And then this tree is taken to the mill. And when it comes out, it's no longer a tree. It's the vanity table, the breakfast nook, the baby crib, and the newspapers that line the family garbage can." Brad, you see, has a problem with marriage.

He has no moral problem with his tactics to bed Jan, however. *Pillow Talk* uses the narration of each character and an occasional split screen to convey Brad's relish in pursuing Jan. His observations are as reliably devilish as her remarks are innocent and hopeful. The relationship Jan foresees is not with Brad Allen, whom she despises, but with Brad's impersonation of a tumbleweed cowboy from Texas named Stetson. Stetson proves a perfect partner for Jan, since Brad plays the character as naive and overly respectful of women.

Brad tinkers with Jan's sexual anxieties. He phones her as the obnoxious Brad, warning her not to trust Stetson and his sneaky games. Then, as Stetson, he proceeds to play these games to the letter, departing from each scenario at the last instant. Jan, at first thinking that Stetson will move on her as other men have, is disappointed when he appears to do so, delighted when he doesn't, and finally perplexed as to WHY he doesn't. Is he, possibly, a Mama's boy (a 1950's euphemism for a gay male)?

Two scenes highlight the 1950's skittishness about sex before marriage. One split screen shows Jan and "Stetson" in their respective bathtubs, talking "pillow talk" to each other on the phone. Jan sensuously places her foot on the tile wall (where the screen splits), and Brad subsequently does the same--whereupon Jan quickly draws her foot back, offering viewers a bit of cinematic footsie. Later, when Brad (as Stetson) entices Jan to Jonathan's Connecticut retreat, they embrace in a passionate kiss. Jan suddenly pulls away with a look on her face that suggests she is one baby step from bed, and that maybe she should move a little slower.

Graphically, it's no contest between *Pillow Talk* and *Thief Of Hearts*. The latter film shows nudity and intercourse in what has become a perfunctory stint of sweat-and-groan calisthenics. The former film, by contrast, fails to place Jan and Brad (or Stetson) in the same bed, period. But *Pillow Talk* set a comic precedent for sexual frankness with its witty, erotically teasing dialogue. Screenwriters Stanley Shapiro and Maurice Richlin won academy awards for their work, giving *Pillow Talk* the distinction of inspiring a string of "sex comedies" (*Lover Come Back*, 1961; *The Thrill Of It All*, 1963; *Man's Favorite Sport?*, 1964; *Send Me No Flowers*, 1964).

If the sexual innuendoes of *Pillow Talk* hardly raise an eyebrow today, consider the willingness of wholesome stars like Doris Day and Rock Hudson to play this seduction of sexual mischief in 1959. The risks were made less risky by mounting *Pillow Talk* as a slick, expensive production (nice clothes, nice sets). Remember, too, that nothing really nasty or unseemly ever appears very grim in a movie that looks good. But, most of all, remember that the entire project became more palatable because of its use of **humor** (see Lesson Six). We tend to forget Brad's original game, namely, a guy who tries to get a girl in the sack under false pretenses. Now, imagine that Brad doesn't fall in love with Jan. Imagine, instead, that he talks her in the sack, and, after making love, he tells her his true identity. This outcome, even with humor, does not seem so nice, does it?

Pillow Talk, of course, cannot permit this consequence of seduction. Rather, one hour and 20 minutes into the story, Jan discovers Brad's secret. This discovery affords her precious little time for revenge--and the revenge, when it happens, amounts to nothing more than a garish redecoration of his apartment. But, ultimately, the two lovers stumble to a common understanding, as they must. Thus, a cavalier plan of deceit, a comic comeuppance for the deceiver, and a happy ending serve to dampen any thoughts of Brad's questionable conduct. All's forgiven because now they're together, they're in love, and Jan's pregnant. Pregnant, that is, after marriage.

Thief Of Hearts and *Pillow Talk*, each in their quirky fashion, demonstrate the sighting, stalking, and capturing of one sex by the other. Contemplate viewer reactions, nonetheless, if both films had reversed expectations and showed Mickey stalking Scott, and Jan plotting to finesse Brad into bed. These reversals possess dramatic and comic potential, yet they do not represent mainstream thinking about seduction. Males pursue, and females monitor these pursuits. Boys hunt girls as a generic pastime, although sometimes digressions and dating informalities blur the distinctiveness of who's hunting whom. But when a female takes up the reins to search and conquer, she provokes adversity for her "masculine" efforts. The pursued male, conversely, feels the pinch on his machismo and the need to redeem his usurped manhood.

Sighting, stalking, and capturing become more the male's social prerogative (see Lesson Seven). The rewards of this prerogative include allowances for male manipulation, such as keeping the female in doubt as to his next move, or whether he will move at all. But the male prerogative also has its drawbacks, as with the fellow who hunts, and hunts, yet never feels in command. His quarry remains elusive, largely because she doesn't give a fly's frosty eye about him.

Movies like *Thief Of Hearts* and *Pillow Talk* embellish the male initiative by using secrecy and humor to charm viewers into accepting the male's predatory pursuits. If you're handsome and crafty, you can make seduction appear quite enchanting. Secrecy works. Clearly, if Scott Muller and Brad Allen reveal themselves honestly to the women concerned, their quest ends on the spot. Secrecy keeps both males in the hunt and provides suspense for the viewers.

Humor also works. The sly antics of Brad Allen never permit us to mull the alternative of an above-board relationship (here, such honesty equals no movie). Instead, Brad's devious maneuvers depict a comic setup. We keep wondering when Jan will learn of his secrecy, and what hilarious antic she will perform to get even. By default, we wonder less about the shady premise that Brad devises to initiate his actions. Guys, after all, are guys. We do not expect males to play fair at every turn, at least not in the same spirit that we expect of females.

Intellectualizing Lust

There's lust, and, in movies, there's LUST with a snoot n' snicker. There's lots of both in *Basic Instinct* (1992), a manipulative film with a message that rough sex is the only sex worth having. It certainly intensifies the Oz experience since this sex includes not only bondage, but the added attraction of a lethal climax: According to the mentality of *Basic Instinct*, when you come you also may go, especially if your lover has a fetish for using ice picks.

The Oz of rough sex clearly has little in common with the more domestic love life that many of us enjoy; but, then, no one expects these characters to be very domestic. Nick Curran (Michael Douglas) certainly isn't. He's a San Francisco detective with the moniker of "Shooter," so labeled because of a past haunted by questionable killings. Nick's skirting a violent edge, and meets exactly the wrong person to tease him over that edge, a cool, blond novelist named Catherine Tramell (Sharon Stone). Catherine's sex partner, a rock-and-roll magnate, is murdered, found with his hands tied to the bed frame. Thus tied, the victim's body exhibits repeated stab wounds to the neck, made by an ice pick. Stabbed by Catherine, perhaps? Maybe so, maybe not, mostly just maybe.

The lust begins quickly when Catherine targets Nick as her new playmate. Indeed, Catherine delights in provoking males like Nick as a libidinous game of superiority. The infamous interrogation scene shows her center stage, defying convention by wearing a revealing, virginal white dress, sans underwear; and by exuding an arrogant confidence that unsettles her captive male audience. She has nothing to hide because Catherine knows that she's more than a match for the males she confronts.

Nick, taunted and incensed that Catherine appears to possess confidential information from his therapy file, vents his anger on Beth Garner (Jeanne Tripplehorn), a sometime lover. He slams Beth against the wall, then drapes her over a sofa, sunny-side up. After Nick finishes, Beth, shaken, tells him, "You weren't making love to me." The fact that Beth also serves as Dr. Garner, Nick's police therapist, apparently suggests no breach of professional ethics to Beth and Nick, or to the San Francisco Police Department.

Perhaps that summation sets the tone for the erotic games played in *Basic Instinct*. The film stacks contrivance upon contrivance by making Beth a police therapist, an ex-lover still longing for her patient, and a murder suspect because of her previous association with Catherine. More to the point, the film delivers a despairing note on the human condition: Neither Nick nor Catherine enjoys lovemaking for the purer sake of an affectionate relationship. Instead, their "love" gives way to physical anguish, a kind of erotic desperation that requires an element of risk. And there's only one risk that bent characters like Catherine and Nick find exciting.

Nick's flirt with death occurs in exchange for a torrid sexual liaison with Catherine. She straddles him, ties him to the bed frame, and commences a wave of violent thrusting. Then, provocatively, her hand flies out--but no, not to an ice pick...at least, not yet. Afterward, strolling on the beach, Catherine wants to know if their lovemaking frightened Nick. Nick rises to the bait and admits that he finds the game dangerous. That danger, he contends, is the point: to play the game and keep the stakes high. Catherine thinks otherwise: "Not going to confess all my secrets, Nick--just because I have an orgasm, you won't learn anything I don't want you to know." Nick disagrees, oddly, by admitting he's in love with her, yet insists she will lose, anyway.

The scene offers a strange dialogue of endearments between lovers, sculpted out of the bleakness they hold toward normal relationships, and from their failure to transform intimacy to a higher level of trust. Catherine and Nick share the passion, but they possess little else of substance. Nick finds himself plagued by a volatile past; and Catherine, in a moment of tortured irony, berates the fact that everyone she cares for, dies.

Circumstantial evidence guides Nick, not to Catherine, but to Beth as the true murderer. This evidence and a confrontation with Beth causes "Shooter" to kill the therapist in apparent self-defense. What Beth went for in her coat pocket, however, was Nick's apartment key, not a gun as Nick thought. He has killed again, and realizes, too late, that Catherine now materializes as the masterful architect of his downward path. The physical evidence suggests Beth as the murderer, except that Nick, and Nick alone, knows better.

So, what does he do? What would **you** do? Return to the lair for another go at your nemesis? Well, that's what Nick the gambler decides. He rejoins Catherine for a final(?) evening of pleasure. But once the passion subsides, Catherine asks him the ultimate question: "What do we do now, Nick?" Nick replies with a pat answer, which is to give no answer at all. Then, they turn and look at each other. A steady, searching look, full of import, full of destiny. The passion resumes as the camera slowly pans to the floor, and to the ice pick resting within Catherine's ready reach.

The characters of *Basic Instinct* speak of sex in lurid, cynical expressions. Sex becomes an arena, a contest of erotic wills, a rough-and-ready sport that aims for the stratosphere. What intelligence--what rationale--arises to give such lovemaking a sense of affectionate purpose? Sadly, none; none that includes the virtues of a thoughtful pursuit. *Basic Instinct*, although boasting slicker production values than most exploitation films, offers little nourishment for the complete sexual experience. To the contrary, thinking about sex with Nick and Catherine assumes the hue and cry of a slovenly game.

Lust and love are not strangers (Updike, 1993). **Lust** can represent the germ of a physical love, which, in time, may evolve to a more appreciable relationship between intimates (Lesser, 1980). Or, as with Nick and Catherine, lust may designate no deeper ties than that found through physical passion. Sometimes, unfortunately, the passion is a one-way street: Lust in the service of sexual assault, for instance, seems unlikely to include feelings of genuine love.

Love, as in **romantic love**, depicts a higher echelon of affection and attachment, compared to the gut-level, physical desire evidenced through lust. But **love**, in its complexity, harbors the potential of characterizing quite cruel acts: the scorned lover, for instance, who erupts sadistically in vengeful rage. **Cruel love**, indeed, need not even involve lust. Instead, it may resemble nothing warmer than the calculation and cold-heartedness of a possessive tyrant, free of any earthy passion normally associated with lust.

Lust and love, then, sometimes touch base, and sometimes go their separate ways. Our concern rests with the strategy or **intellectualization** that lust brings into play. Sex comedies like *Pillow Talk* demonstrate little more than the predatory male's recreational lust for the female, which, of course, usually ends with lust opening the door to greater affection. This strategy begins simply--How can He get Her in the sack?--and stays at that elementary level of intrigue.

Complications arise in *Thief Of Hearts* and *Basic Instinct* because the reasoning of the male characters goes beyond a mere game of sexual conquest. The game for Scott Muller and Nick Curran pertains to the female's tempting presence. For Scott, he wishes to possess Mickey and bring her closer to the image of what he believes she can become as a woman (Michelle). For Nick, he desires the formidable Catherine as does a moth to a flame: She's dangerous, and he likes the danger. Both males, unfortunately, pursue their quarry with a measure of male bullheadedness that dooms their chances to triumph. Scott underestimates the toll that secrecy will cost him when he reveals his manipulative scheme to Mickey. And Nick finds that Catherine's skill in protecting her monumental secrets keeps him from anticipating her lethal maneuvers. Secrecy, once again, looms darkly as a factor to swing the outcome away from one party and toward the other.

The practice of intellectualizing lust takes a softer turn in *sex, lies, and videotape* (1989). Ann (Andie MacDowell) is married faithfully to John (Peter Gallagher); John is conducting a vigorous affair with Ann's sister, Cynthia (Laura San Giacomo); and Cynthia finds John's old college buddy, Graham (James Spader), intriguing. Why intriguing? Because Graham, who appears to have meandered away his post-college existence for the past nine years, videotapes women who are willing to tell him of their thoughts on sex.

Each member of the foursome offers a different perspective on intellectualizing lust: For John, he's a yuppie lawyer with yuppie tastes, including the energy and cunning to tell

lies and do whatever he deems expedient to keep his yuppie
world in perpetual motion--at work, and in bed. Ann's
fashioned a sexual crutch by discounting masturbation as silly,
and by dispatching sex in general as overrated. Translation:
She and John are not having sex for reasons disturbing to Ann.
Cynthia attacks sex with a passion, enthralled by the pleasure,
and by the discovery of that pleasure. As for Graham, his lust
becomes the most intellectual. He uses videotaped confessions
to dreamily savor the power of having such intimate access to
women, while allowing his own erotic life to languish.

None of these entangling personalities can change without
affecting the others. The first wave of reform finds Ann
charmed by Graham's holistic philosophy. He tells Ann, "I
remember reading somewhere that men learn to love the
person that they're attracted to, and that women become more
and more attracted to the person they love." This thought
proves sufficiently benign to comfort Ann and encourage her
attempts to emphasize security and to keep her sexual concerns
at bay. But when she learns of Graham's videotape collection,
his invasion of female intimacy becomes too much for her to
bear. Ann retreats to a faltering marriage, feeling less and less
at ease with husband John and his false claims of fidelity.

Predictably, Ann's disenchantment with Graham's hobby
becomes sister Cynthia's fascination. She reads Graham
quickly as someone she can trust, and decides to make a
videotape. She relates to Graham her first time, at age 14, to
see a penis: "...I thought it would be smooth like a test
tube...When he finally pulled it out and I could look at it and
touch it, I completely forgot that there was a guy attached to
it..." (Note the difference in Cynthia's reaction to her first
penile viewing compared to Eugenia's scream in *Till Marriage
Do Us Part*, described earlier.)[6]

Cynthia even masturbates while Graham is taping, an act
of sexual confidence that Ann finds appalling. But later,
when Ann acquires evidence to confirm her suspicions that
John and Cynthia are lovers, she returns to Graham with a
different attitude: She wants to be videotaped. Graham
gently tries to dissuade her, but Ann remains adamant. He

then admits to her that he wondered how she would look when having an orgasm.[7]

Graham's admission opens the door to a challenge by Ann, a challenge that he tries to evade. Graham grows increasingly uncomfortable when she takes the camera and points it at him. Like Ann, he's been hiding from the obligations of a genuine relationship. Graham's shadowy existence of peering at the intimacy of others has kept his own problems conveniently in limbo. Now, however, Graham changes Ann's life, and she makes it clear that he, too, must reform. The change includes a fulfillment of their sexual attraction: for him, a dismantling of his videotapes, and, for her, a Dear John letter to John, Ann's wayward husband.

Cynthia, to her credit, has already departed her duplicitous relationship with John, and now seeks a more honest sisterhood with Ann. And John, to everyone else's credit, finds himself without Ann, without Cynthia, and, possibly, without a career--surely one of the worst fates to befall a yuppie in lust.

Lust, therefore, depicts not only feeling but logic. If the logic is not always so rational--as with Nick's fatalistic romp to Catherine's lethal tune--lust still attaches itself to a strategy.[8] Risky sex may be the only sex that "lovers" like Nick and Catherine find arousing in *Basic Instinct* (Pinkerton & Abramson, 1992). Consequently, lust may lead nowhere except to the big question: Will Nick survive Catherine? Or, lust may build eventually to a wholesome love, as with Graham and Ann in *sex, lies, and videotapes*. Clearly lust retains the power to make sex both taboo and irresistible.

A method joins this madness, telling us that, even in the movies, lust does not exist in a vacuum. Lust goes "somewhere" and creates certain repercussions. Moviegoers, in turn, are quite willing to fork over a few bucks, pamper Oz, and ride along for the trip. Without realizing it perhaps, we are intellectualizing lust. We want to see where the strategy leads and what the passion provokes. We quite willingly accept the irrationality of it all at times, as long as we gain some closure in our thoughts concerning whether Catherine will, or will not reach for that ice pick.

The First Time

The movies' propensity to give sexual practices a lurid, even lethal twist indicates that these practices customarily assume a sardonic orientation, via films like *Basic Instinct*. Virginal experiences, however, carry their own dramatic weight. Filmmakers recognize the value of characters whose lack of cynicism about sexuality offer a refreshing attitude in adapting to the rules of lovemaking. These "rules" become familiar because what viewers see on screen likely harks back to their personal trial-and-error exposure in attempting the same sexual practices.

William Simon and John Gagnon (1984) organize these developmental practices according to **sexual scripts**, a metaphor to describe the individual's acquisition of sexual experiences over time. Note that the metaphor is plural, indicating differences in sexual preferences among ourselves as individuals, and as a changing orientation in how we conduct ourselves sexually from childhood through the adult years. Contrasting cultures will produce strikingly different scripts for proscribing the sexual conduct that societal institutions choose to endorse. It should not surprise you, therefore, if the practice of sexual freedom varies a wee bit when comparing, say, America to Saudi Arabia.

Even within our culture, differences abound. One reason for these differences concerns the conflict that **cultural scripts** proclaim on sexual conduct: Our society pays lip service to a code of sexual caution with warnings of "safer sex"; yet our society undermines this formal finger waving by condoning a liberal exhibition of erotic practices.

We respond to these confusing dictates by creating and addressing **interpersonal scripts**, and, more privately, by entertaining ourselves with **intrapsychic scripts**. Interpersonal scripts open the door for ideas about sexual conduct when we fraternize with parents, siblings, and, for adolescents, the almighty peer group. Our peers, at a given time and place, suggest by their "suggestions" (and sometimes, their actions) what they deem acceptable or not acceptable, sexually.

Intrapsychic scripts concern our fantasies about sexual practices. These fantasies may bring us close to reality--to acting out--or they may prove more idealistic and remote from reality. Regardless, individual sexual scripts bear the stamp of a common culture, some more, some less; and the individual, though perhaps a solitary soul, feels the breath of influential peers who respond collectively to this culture. No one throws you in prison for violating the code, although banishment from the mainstream of adolescent conduct becomes a possibility.

One interesting feature of Simon and Gagnon's sexual scripts involves the **sequence**. Today, it's not rare for a first date to culminate in sexual intercourse. But the assumption holds forth that most first dates will not lead to such intimacies (see the introduction to Lesson Six). Moreover, for adolescents who contemplate their virginal status (i.e., when it will end), the sexual scripts that they follow may occur at an earlier age today, although the integrity of the sequence--what comes before what--stays intact, as in the past.

Stacy (Jennifer Jason Leigh), an enterprising character from *Fast Times At Ridgemont High* (1982), churns with sexual curiosity. She's had a few experiences, and wants more. Her most likely target for practice becomes Mike Damone (Robert Romanus), a kid with a pronounced swagger, but a swagger that Stacy suspects is a smokescreen for his virginal status. The couple's chance occurs in Stacy's bathhouse on the pretext of going swimming. Their tryst on film captures the spirit of a high-school student's account of the episode, reported to undercover journalist Cameron Crowe (1981, pp. 161-162):

> She reached over and grabbed his erection. She began pulling on it. The feeling of a penis was still new to her. She wanted to ask him about it. Why did it hurt if you just touched it one place, and not at all at another...but later she would ask him that. For now, she just yanked on it. Damone didn't seem to mind.
>
> "I want you to know," said Stacy, "that it's *your* final decision if we should continue or not."
>
> "Let's continue," said Damone.

As Mike Damone lost his virginity, his first thought was of his brother, Art. Art had said, "You gotta *overpower* a girl. Make her feel helpless."

Damone began pumping so hard, so fast--his eyes were shut tight-- that he didn't notice he was banging the sofa, and Stacy's head, against the wall.

"Hey Mike," she whispered.

"What? Are you all right?"

"I think we're making a lot of noise."

"I'm sorry. I'm really sorry." He continued, slower.

What a considerate guy, Stacy thought. He was kind of loud and always joking around other people, but when you got him alone...he was so nice.

Then Damone stopped. He had a strange look on his face.

"What's wrong?"

"I think I came," said Damone. "Didn't you feel it?"

He had taken a minute and a half.

They were unusual feelings, these thoughts pooling in Mike Damone's head as he lay on the red couch with Stacy. He was a little embarrassed, a little guilty...mostly he just wanted to be alone. He wanted to get the hell out of there.

"I've got to go home," said Damone. "I've really got to go."

Stacy, unfortunately, has reason to rethink her thoughts on Mike Damone as a "nice guy." Along with the excitement of learning about sex here and there, comes the price of having sex without protection. Stacy's innocent experimenting leaves her pregnant, courtesy of Mike. Damone, prickly and evasive, promises to drive her to an abortion clinic, but fails to keep his word. Stacy, accepting her responsibility for the pregnancy and the abortion, adds another lesson to her growing file on males, and on who's accountable to whom.

Travel now from 1981 back to 1942 and imagine adolescent sexual scripts as attended to in a culture less familiar with premarital sex. Consider 1942, a year of victory gardens, of paper and metal drives, of women moving into the industrial work force, the first full year of America at war. These changes cloud families and home-front activities in the *Summer Of '42* (1971). They flicker in the background of Hermie's life, a 15-year-old lad who resides for the summer at a New England beach with his family. He has an older brother in the war, but Hermie finds himself otherwise engaged: Hermie, Oscy, and Benjie (Gary Grimes, Jerry Houser, Oliver Conant), best buddies, obsess themselves with sex--how you do it, with whom you do it, and, most pressingly, **when**.[9]

Their obsession, punctuated by "attacks" on the coast guard station for recreational relief, converge to a common need for sexual information. Benjie reluctantly supplies a medical book, complete with photographs that say something about how you do it, and with whom. Benjie can't believe his parents performed the acts shown, despite affirmations from Oscy and Hermie. Oscy, the most assertive and most desperate for his "first lay," engineers a pairing off at the theatre: He matches Hermie with Aggie (Katherine Allentuck) because they're both intellectual; he pairs himself with Miriam (Christopher Norris) because she's the flashiest looker; and he couples Benjie with a third girl because both are leftovers. Or he tries, only to see Benjie dash off like a frightened gazelle, overwhelmed by the terrors of a first date.

The individual sexual scripts, even with a shared cause, show marked differences. The two couples watch a romantic movie that inspires the males, as if they needed encourage-ment, to execute their approach for capturing female companionship. (The theatre plays a 1942 film, *Now, Voyager*, which shows the famous scene whereby Paul Henreid lights two cigarettes in his mouth, then gives one to Bette Davis. A nice starry-eyed touch, depicting a suave gesture that is light years removed from the boys' adolescent maneuvers as they watch the screen.)

Oscy, always the bulldog, tries every scheme imaginable to bring Miriam into his "comfort zone," but Miriam knows the tactics and rebuffs him. Meanwhile, Hermie proceeds more cautiously. Slowly, in hushed suspense, he creeps his hand around Aggie's shoulder and down to what he perceives as her breast. Only later does Oscy inform him that Hermie's triumph of ecstasy came from his mistakenly gripping Aggie's arm, not her breast. Hermie reacts angrily at first, then mopes into reality. He can't distinguish an arm from a breast in the dark, so how, pray tell, will he ever master the rudiments of lovemaking?

The next opportunity involves a double date at the beach to "roast marshmallows." To prepare for this fine evening, Oscy borrows Benjie's medical book to write out a 12-point plan of sexual conquest (with a copy for Hermie). Oscy then persuades Hermie to go to the pharmacy for rubbers.

This excruciating episode begins with False Start #1: Hermie enters the store, looks around nervously, and leaves because a woman is present. False Start #2 places Hermie inside the store again (with Oscy's support, outside). Hermie gags and jitters, working up the gumption to ask for...an ice cream. False Start #3 sees him trying to regroup, but he manages only to solicit a napkin and sprinkles for his ice cream. Finally, in dire need of closure--and knowing that Oscy awaits outside--Hermie croaks out the Big Question: "How about some rubbers?" In fact, seeking lamely to appear cavalier, he asks for three dozen rubbers, prompting a few sly inquiries from the druggist, played by Lou Frizzell. Amused at Hermie's tortuous effort, and perhaps remembering his own "first time," Frizzell eventually sells the boy a box of three condoms.[10]

The marshmallow party proves a boon for Oscy, a bust for Hermie. Oscy and Miriam depart to a more discreet spot on the beach, whereupon Oscy learns that Miriam knows his 12-point plan and apparently a lot more. He borrows one, then two, then three of Hermie's hard-earned rubbers, leaving Hermie frustrated and at an impasse with Aggie. Aggie checks on Miriam before Hermie can stop her, and she is shocked to see Miriam and Oscy in action. She leaves disenchanted, and Hermie feels as far removed from THE ACT as an adolescent can get.

Miriam and Aggie epitomize interesting contrasts in teenage sexuality. Miriam fills the role of an early-maturing girl, possibly someone who joins with friends likely to smoke, drink, and have intercourse (Brooks-Gunn & Furstenberg, Jr., 1989). Miriam also appears a stronger candidate to prepare herself for "the first time." She may have a greater interest in sex than Aggie, and proves more likely to plan for intercourse and to expect and use birth control before marriage.

Sharon Thompson (1990), in gathering together 400 in-depth interviews about teenage girls' first-intercourse experiences, concluded that girls who **prepare** for intercourse recounted more early sexual activities (masturbation, child sex play) and more advice from their mother than girls who failed to prepare. Prepared girls told a richer story of their first experience, one that involved greater pleasure, compared to unprepared girls who simply didn't know what was happening, and who often found the intercourse painful, even boring. Miriam in the 1940s, however, wears the label of a "fast" girl. Aggie, on the other hand, comes closer to reflecting the norm. She adopts a different script for premarital sex than Miriam, possibly one that does not include intercourse until marriage.

Hermie's sexual awakening occurs unexpectedly, and, for a teenager, unconventionally. He admires an attractive young wife, Dorothy (Jennifer O'Neill), who sees her soldier husband off to war. Dorothy lives on a bluff overlooking the ocean, and Hermie helps her carry groceries home one day. Hermie, taken with someone so beautiful and nice, takes pains to leave his adolescent jargon behind and attempts to cultivate a labored adult prose, such as "You make exquisite coffee."

One evening Hermie visits Dorothy, only to find her living room in disarray. He spots a crumbled telegram which reads "We regret to inform you..." Dorothy enters, greets Hermie, and absently begins to straighten up the room. She is now a very different woman, not the chipper Dorothy that Hermie has learned to adore. Her mood becomes his mood. Hermie says softly, "I'm sorry." Those words are the last words spoken for over 10 minutes in the film.

What follows is a sad dance of grief and loneliness, and of grief and loneliness to come. Dorothy leans on Hermie, not as a substitute for her lost love, but as a friend who shares her despair. And Hermie shares it. The movie's theme song plays, telling of the seasons and their inevitable change. Hermie, no longer the tentative adolescent, spills a tear as he moves quietly with a stricken young widow. The war, through Dorothy, touches him at last.

We know almost nothing of Dorothy until this moment. She has remained little more than an enchanting figure to us, as to Hermie. But now Dorothy looms as a poignant casualty of another senseless conflict. She guides Hermie into her bedroom and into her bed. They disrobe solemnly to engage in a fragile bond of pleasure, Dorothy's gift to Hermie for his friendship, and, perhaps, a gift to herself as one last farewell to a love that might have been.

Afterward, they lie side by side, saying nothing. Hermie slowly looks at Dorothy, and she returns his gaze with a slight, ever so slight, smile. Then she puts on her bathrobe and walks to the porch. Hermie dresses, pauses on the porch, and Dorothy says "Goodnight, Hermie." He never sees Dorothy again.

A later meeting between Oscy and Hermie highlights the difference in their sexual experiences. Oscy accomplishes his avowed purpose to get laid. He gets laid, an introduction that he will use to become more proficient with the opposite sex, but not an experience that changes him dramatically. The more sensitive Hermie, however, has changed. His "first time" goes beyond a quiet seduction. He recognizes, where Oscy does not, that sex as intercourse represents more than a physical happening. He knows that what makes the happening special are the lovers themselves, what they mean to one another. Unlike Oscy, Hermie loses Hermie, and finds Herman.

No one can say with authority when adolescence ends. Hermie does not suddenly become a man because of Dorothy. But he steps closer to manhood, and marvels at the capacity of someone like Dorothy to help him grow. Sexual scripts differ to the extent that some youths actually find their teenage years a stretch of learning, joy, and camaraderie. Good times more than bad times, and good friendships not forgotten. Sexual practices may play an integral role in recalling the good times, but these practices are not a requirement. Virginity claims a special status for some adolescents (like Aggie), and not always a status that they feel compelled to overthrow.

Movies do not exhibit much of this positive philosophy, or at least find little entertainment value in promoting virginity's wholesomeness. What movies do capture, better than novels, is the visual immediacy of presenting sexual practices vividly through character and context. Sexual practices, in turn, prove memorable and less exploitative when they express a genuine affection between lovers: when they surpass the original intent of the seduction, when they surpass the lust, when they surpass the simple mechanics of thrusting bodies.

After all, the moans, the acrobatics, and the Grand Climax, we can do ourselves. The movies must do more. They need to indulge us and build constructively on our imagination. They need to make us wonder, make us empathize, make us think about our emotions.

Notes

1. Use narration intrusively, however, and it becomes awkward. Robert Mitchum, in a *Saturday Night Live* skit, spoofed the private eye's penchant for narration by showing the absurdity of bringing an off-camera technique into the scene. Mitchum narrates his thoughts to the audience as a client looks on, baffled by the private eye's behavior. The skit proceeds with Mitchum retreating to his bathroom for privacy as he continues his soliloquy. By this time, the client is seriously questioning the private eye's sanity.

2. *The Crying Game* (1992) represents a marvelous exception in the customary use of ribald humor to showcase a gender switch. Because of the movie's extensive publicity, it arrives as no revelation to note that the female character, Dil (Jaye Davidson), is really a male. Her lover, Fergus (Stephen Rea), once he knows the truth, overcomes his revulsion and learns--awkwardly to be sure--to "love" her for what she is. The notoriety surrounding the film's "secret" overshadows its true achievement: The sensitivity of one man to accept another man's natural propensity to be a woman. Given the sly and restrained conduct of Dil and Fergus, their discovery of a shared tenderness outshines any number of lesser male/female love stories on the market.

3. Movies exaggerate the male's carnal compulsions in the name of entertainment, but a modest amount of research does document a difference between males and females in perceiving social cues. Males become more

likely to interpret a female's friendly behavior as communicating sexual overtures. This proclivity suggests that males sport a stronger sexual orientation to the opposite sex than the opposite sex seems inclined to share (Shotland & Craig, 1988; Abbey, 1982). Occasionally, of course, the male's interpretation will be correct.

4. The mass media enjoy a capacity for bringing teenagers in touch with other teenagers and their sexual problems. One approach combined a book, *Sex And The American Teenager*, based on 1067 nationally distributed questionnaires and 50,000 pages of transcribed interviews, with an HBO documentary derived from the book's findings (Coles & Stokes, 1985). Television reaches more teenagers than books, and the best television can provide adolescents with sensitive portrayals of how their peers cope with common sexual practices.

5. Cameron Crowe (1981), a journalist, accepted an assignment to return to high school for a year. His job as an undercover reporter was to write about what teenagers were thinking, doing, and hoping as they neared graduation. Crowe, at age 22, passed the litmus test as a student, enabling him to chronicle the activities of a select group of youths. He admits to making superficial changes concerning identity and location, but contends that the incidents are true. His chronicle inspired the movie *Fast Times At Ridgemont High*, although it remains unclear if all the film's exaggerations stem from Crowe's observations--observations, incidentally, that we must accept at face value in terms of what he saw and what his student friends, like Brad, told him.

Nonetheless, according to pages 151-152 in Crowe's book, Brad (or whomever) apparently did suffer the embarrassing moment described. In counterargument, the actual Ridgemont High students, at their 10-year reunion, claim that fiction entered into Crowe's description of certain characters and happenings more so than the author suggests (Reno, 1989). If in doubt as to who or what to believe, remember our axiom from Lesson One: We must never, ever, under any circumstance, accept what a movie tells us at face value.

6. Females can look upon the penis as a weapon. Lorena and John Bobbitt made national headlines in 1993 when Lorena, using a 12-inch kitchen steak knife, decided to have John and his penis part company while he slept. Lorena then drove off, penis in hand, and subsequently threw the offending organ out the window. Fortunately for John, police located the penis, and, after a lengthy surgical procedure, John had his organ back, somewhat the worse for wear. The full extent of his sexual recovery probably won't be known for two or three years.

John, meanwhile, faced charges of marital rape, charges for which a jury eventually found him not guilty. Lorena, charged with malicious wounding, found herself a folk heroine to many women. Characterized as a "victim/offender," she spent a brief stay under psychiatric care before her release. Naturally, the Bobbitts' tragedy became the humorous focus of many one-liners, some of which were derived from movie titles: to wit, *Bye Bye Birdie, Farewell My Lovely, Divorce American Style, Pee-wee's Big Adventure, You Can't Take It With You,* and *Free Willie* (The Final Cut, 1993). Considering the many ways in which females and males find to humiliate one another, it is surprising that Lorena's revenge qualifies as a novel practice. The males' nervous twitter suggests that they hope the practice will remain just that-- a novelty.

7. **Orgasm** invites several definitions, not to mention a grand awakening for filmmakers to portray. **Physiologically**, orgasm becomes the culmination of organ contractions, neural impulses to the brain, and other anatomical agitation. This Climax benefits from previous stages involving excitement, more excitement, and finally, Bingo! Bingo occurs more reliably for males than females, although gifted females have refined the art of **faking an orgasm**. Sally (Meg Ryan) in *When Harry Met Sally* (1989) gives a solo rendition that, for men, proves uncomfortably difficult to divine from the real thing. And Bree (Jane Fonda) in *Klute* (1971) provides an amorous dash of ecstasy while making love; then, before continuing the oohs and yahoos, she glances surreptitiously at her watch to check her next appointment as a prostitute. Faking an orgasm to assuage the male's tender ego does not represent a sound idea, because (1) it's a lie, and (2) the lie may return as a hurtful revelation should the two lovers become less lovely together.

Psychologically, females and males under mutual consent display a common exuberance in reaching the Promised land. This exuberance creates a bond between intimates, temporary to be sure for partners in movies like *Basic Instinct*, but more lasting for lovers in movies like *Coming Home* (1978). Filmmakers, however, prefer to spend a lion's share of celluloid space in leading to the orgasm, than in showing the orgasm proper. Considering the real experience, this idea makes sense in cinematic time. Possibly the first, or one of the first, films to prolong lovemaking through mood music and a montage of graceful positions, happened in a little-known yet well-crafted horror film, *Don't Look Now* (1973). The lovers, Julie Christie and Donald Sutherland (and the camera of course), give ecstasy a surreal vision of what physical love can achieve.

8. The better filmmakers exercise a strategy in portraying sexual intercourse. This strategy involves a twist to the usual passion, something extra besides the moaning, groaning, and pumping away of two lovers. Faye

Dunaway, for example, plays a supremely ambitious television executive in *Network* (1976), who, even as she engages in lovemaking with William Holden, cannot stop babbling about her career. Here, Dunaway blends two passions--power and sex--into the ultimate orgasm. The filmmaker's logic, however, does not always succeed. The fierce sexual encounter between Jessica Lange and Jack Nicholson on a kitchen table in the 1981 film, *The Postman Always Rings Twice*, does not serve the story or characters as well as the sex imagined but **not shown** in the 1946 *Postman*, starring John Garfield and Lana Turner. Sometimes what you don't see can drive your imagination crackers.

9. An uncommon artistic endeavor occurred with *Summer Of '42*. Herman Raucher wrote the screenplay in less than two weeks, then later wrote the novel. He based the story on his recollections as a teenager when he summered at the beach, and claimed that he used real names for the lead characters (Nash & Ross, 1987, pp. 3201-3202).

10. A 1987 movie, *Amazon Women On The Moon*, consists of a collection of stories, one of which concerns a girl urging her boyfriend to go into a pharmacy for contraceptives. She won't have sex without protection, and the boy, eager to please, seeks to make the transaction as normal as possible. He fails because every horrible event you can envision "conspires" to embarrass him. The druggist knows him as such a good boy, then announces the boy's intentions to everyone in the store that he wants a box of condoms. This special purchase sparks a promotional stunt that shows an individual dressed as a giant condom, complete with television cameras, all focused on the boy. The final woe reveals his girl, leaving in mortification. All those condoms and no place to go. This humorous segment gives the boy less a sense of innocence than that realized by Hermie, but the practice of buying condoms still has a shiver to it. Perhaps that shiver is one reason why girls are just as likely, and possibly more likely than boys, to purchase this protection.

Lesson 3

Life And Death

Imagine your origin as a human sperm. There you are, one of 500 million human sperm, evolved over millions of years, yet relatively new at the game--and programmed to survive for only X-number of hours. Your trek of traveling six to seven inches appears simple, but will require arduous effort. This effort can involve a voyage of less than one hour or up to many hours, depending on environmental hospitality and your swimming speed (Nilsson, 1990, p. 42).

Many cohorts fall behind, too weak to compete. But you forge ahead, perhaps in pursuit of an attractive signal that compels your cylindrical self onward. You thread a hairline path, hampered on either side by the resistance of cervical mucus. Chemicals bathe you during the swim, fortifying your body with the capacity to fertilize. Your tail propels you forward and your body advances again to complete the uphill journey in order to enter a slender tube. There, you and a company of about 100 (100!) wriggling, swirling survivors encounter a massive sphere, the only one of four daughter cells to survive (Hubbard & Wald, 1993, p. 47).

You circle, you juke, you joust, you seek entry. Timing is crucial. The company, some of whose members perish in their final invasion, work to prune away nutrient cells that surround the sphere. You probe, your competitors probe, and suddenly, "something" happens. YOU succeed in piercing the sphere's chemical guard, its zona barrier. PENETRATION. You survive, triggering a chemical reaction that blocks further access (Fackelmann, 1990; Nilsson, 1990, p. 50). Now you must complete the fertilization process, (1) by losing your tail and (2) by laboring another 24 hours (or so), burrowing to the sphere's inner layer (Tribe, 1990, p. 123). Fertilization occurs once your chromosomes intermingle with the sphere's chromosomes. So, congratulations. You scored. You triumphed. You fused. You are the chosen one...for now.

The chosen one who survives against overwhelming odds. You are here because of chance. Chance in that you contested with millions of entities to ultimately achieve your singular status. Chance in that, upon fertilization, you could have emerged an armadillo, a platypus, or your pet hound, Baskerville. Chance in that the odds favored you not surviving at all, whatever your life form.

Hooray and hooray. You are more blessed than you know. Aside from kudos for your *coup de maître*, you also successfully weathered nine months of complex development. Since only 25 to 35 percent of embryos do so, you hurdled yet another host of barriers to defy the odds against survival (Morowitz & Trefil, 1992, p. 50; Fackelmann, 1990; Tribe, 1990, p. 123).

It's a miracle of life, but a miracle still shrouded in mystery: The mystery of why only a modest percentage of embryos continue to develop without undue complications; and the mystery of why the birth we know remains a mystery to many people today.[1] Thus, a **mystery** can arise out of the presently unknowable, such as why only a minority of embryos survive; and out of secrecy, as in suppressing the accurate information about birth that we do know. Either way, the idea of a mystery tantalizes the imagination. Mysteries fascinate people, scientists and filmmakers alike.

The **mystery of wonder** represents a genuine challenge. Life and death denote universal mysteries, of which the frailty of birth is a part. Filmmakers enjoy doing movies about grand mysteries (for example, the 1968 film, *2001: A Space Odyssey*), and they don't come much grander than the puzzle of why we're here, why we can't stay longer, and what happens to us thereafter.

The **mystery born of secrecy**, by contrast, details another matter. Secrecy realizes a certain benevolence, such as planning a surprise party for Dad; or keeping a round of bad news graciously to yourself; or even the necessity of staying mum about an attack strategy that can shorten a war. But secrecy commonly bears the reputation of harboring a darker side. Concealment coupled with propaganda can muddle, slant, and sometimes usurp what all of us have a right to know. Among secrecy's sadder faces is the kind of concealment that perpetuates a needless mystery. A mystery, not of wonder, not of what remains unknown, but a mystery steeped in secrecy. A mystery that exists to "protect" certain people from "too much knowledge" (Bok, 1982, p. 32).

When we think of what people should and should not know, we think usually of children. The problem for secret bearers is that children wonder where they come from and where they're going, as do adults. Adults hold back useful information about sex, perhaps to feel superior or to avoid embarrassment; possibly because they feel the child will benefit more from an uncluttered mind: "They'll learn about the vagina and penis soon enough, so why not wait?"

The bugaboo that undermines this protective strategy is **curiosity**. The desire to know, a desire that pulsates even stronger when children encounter "something" they are not supposed to know. Secrecy feeds on curiosity, and curiosity returns the favor. With sex, the curiosity of children (and adults) can reach a state not only of the need to learn, but of an imperative to learn.

Markets materialize for curiosity. Markets that seek to satisfy what people want to know about what they're not supposed to know. Markets that breach secrecy, some for the purpose of education, and others for the honored tradition of making a buck. Imagine what happens, therefore, when we translate our grand mysteries of life and death into the more concrete problems of birth and abortion. Imagine, further, how the mystery of secrecy fares in movies that take on birth and abortion as marketable issues. And imagine, finally, not just the movies of today, but movies as they were at the very beginning.

The Old Silents

The first three decades of the twentieth century became the lifeline of **silent films**. Movie fans know little of these pioneer pictures, other than assuming that the performers and stories remain best classified for their crude attempts at entertainment. The actors' flamboyant dramatics, and the movies' transparent plots and ubiquitous subtitles appear to doom silent films as quaint curiosities.

Young moviegoers today, generations removed from the old silents, associate these vehicles with an era of callow youth and sexual prudery--if they think of this period at all. Surely the themes of such films prove too dated to warrant much consideration. Surely, too, the old silents played as genteel works that dared not entertain issues like sex education, nudity, rape, divorce, child custody, contraception, abortion, prostitution, pornography, and sexually transmitted diseases.

And surely, movie fans disdainful of the old silents would be wrong. All the aforementioned topics found their way into silent movies, and all provoked the kind of consternation from censoring bodies that guardians of these topics profess today. If silent films drenched the controversial issue with excessive sentiment and slipshod special effects, behind each effort stood a filmmaker willing to risk criticism in dramatizing a sexual taboo. The willingness, of course, involved profit as much as (and perhaps more than) social conscience, but the critics behaved real enough and appeared quite prepared to pounce on the silents' liberal messages.

The cinematic tug of war, particularly for women, became an all-or-nothing duel between **commercialized virtue** and

commercialized vice (Brownlow, 1990, p. 10). The Pennsylvania censorship board, for instance, pursued virtue to an extreme by protecting moviegoers against scandalous glimpses of childbirth. These glimpses included any signals of pregnancy, such as a mother making clothes for her unborn child. The board justified its secretive stance with this reply: "The movies are patronized by thousands of children who believe that babies are brought by the stork, and it would be criminal to undeceive them" (Brownlow, 1990, p. 9).

Sexual innocence comprised the standard of virtue, more for females than males, even at the expense of a woeful ignorance regarding anatomical functions. Unfortunately, the idea that commercialized virtue denotes a positive value, yet a virtue that exists through ignorance, resulted in a contradiction of interests (Kuhn, 1988, p. 111). How could sexual innocence bridge the dilemma of serving as a virtue **and** a fault?

How, indeed? *Where Are My Children?*, a 1916 silent film advocating birth control but condemning abortion, attempted to resolve virtue's dual role (Brownlow, 1990, p. 50; Kuhn, 1988, p. 28). Lois Weber, a rare woman director, and rarer still for focusing on "thought" pictures, wanted to show the need for guidance in birth control, although not at the sacrifice of losing a child through abortion. Among its daring episodes, the film portrays a housekeeper's daughter, Lillian (Rene Rogers), as seduced, impregnated, and in need of an abortion. The film depicts pregnancy, not realistically with the swollen abdomen, but by showing the potential child as an angel, perched on the girl's shoulder.

The film's abortions, consequently, are symbolized by children with wings who return to earth, unwanted, morally and physically deficient, and "bearing the sign of the serpent" (Brownlow, 1990, p. 51). Lillian, paying the piper for succumbing to sexual temptation, dies in a botched abortion. The bumbling doctor suffers his transgression by going to prison for 15 years of hard labor. The movie's moral message seeks to maintain virtue's status with an asterisk: A little guidance (but not too much) about the dangers of seductive

sex will preserve the female's virginity and help her to bear
children who are wanted.

Commercialized vice, contrary to its virtuous counterpart,
entertained no dilemmas and no ambiguities. Besmirched was
besmirched. The silent film heroine begins as an innocent
creature, though a creature vulnerable to the sins of adultery
and susceptible to adultery's punishment. When she sins, she
sins BIG and she pays BIG. The disgraced heroine faces
humiliation for loss of her virtue (and her virginity), with a
dash of venereal disease thrown in for good measure. Her fall
from grace proves decisive and irrevocable (Kuhn, 1988, p.
63). For the woman who naively gives herself to active sex,
the road to perdition is clearly marked.

Nor will sexual ignorance save her from the Great Fall,
even if she portrays an unwitting victim. *End Of The Road*,
drawn from true cases of syphilis, represented a 1919 film
designed to show the value of a sex education for children.
The film's theme encouraged mothers to tell their daughters
the truth about impulsive sex, and to gird them morally against
wanton affairs. Girls so girded are forewarned of sexual
temptation and rely on chastity to direct them to the right
fellow. Girls not so girded are in big trouble. They pay the
price for a mother's failure to bolster her child's "character"
through sexual guidance. One moral slip-up and, as the "bad
girl" of *End Of The Road* demonstrates, wayward daughters
find themselves not only disgraced, but afflicted with
advanced syphilis (Kuhn, 1988, p. 52).[2]

And the male? Well, the male hardly claims a gentleman's
role if he leads an innocent female asunder. He may pay the
female's price and contact syphilis for his sexual iniquities.
But a male is a male is a male. His dominance and social status
permit him to weather such sexual improprieties with less
disgrace than that thrust upon the more virginal female.

The old silents, despite their sometimes stricken presentations of social themes, made commercialized virtue a matter of
public morality (Kuhn, 1988, p. 103). Venereal disease in
films like *End Of The Road* and *Fit To Win* (1919) reflected a
public concern that syphilis and other communicable sexual
diseases were a menace to the populace. Moviegoers and even

some performers working in these films shared a naiveté about sexually transmitted diseases that the films brought to public awareness (Brownlow, 1990, p. 66). If prevention meant a hard-nosed position on chastity, this philosophy seemed quite acceptable considering the dark consequences of sexual indulgence.

Today And Yesterday

Filmmakers, today, take what I call a **Heaven or Hell** approach to portraying conception and birth. These artists are capable, although frequently in absurd fashion, of dramatizing our life process for the precious miracle that it is, as in *Look Who's Talking* (1989) and *She's Having A Baby* (1989). But filmmakers also can make the life process a clever bit of horror. This horror ranges from Carrie's (Sissy Spacek) fright and inexperience over her first menstruation, made painfully public in the girls' high-school shower (*Carrie*, 1976); to Kate Miller's (Angie Dickinson) shocking realization that she has indulged in a reckless sexual encounter with a man who knew he had contracted a venereal disease, but failed to tell her (*Dressed To Kill*, 1980).

It should not surprise us, therefore, that filmmakers find ways to make the mysteries of birth work to their aesthetic advantage, using these mysteries to concoct fanciful tales of reproductive weirdness. *The Demon Seed* (1977), for instance, shows Susan Harris (Julie Christie) impregnated by a computer, no less. The machine figures all the necessities in advance, including a study of Susan's reproductive system, the method of conception, and the need to keep her a prisoner until she completes the gestation period and gives birth to her "child."

Another lauded effort involves *Rosemary's Baby* (1968), a story of devil worship and of a young woman, Rosemary (Mia Farrow), who becomes the receptacle of a new Antichrist (see Fischer, 1992). Rosemary is duped and drugged, recalling only a hazy dream of intercourse with a "creature." The deception continues and Rosemary gives birth...to something.

Viewers witness Rosemary's initial look of horror as she gazes upon her creation--a reaction that must pique the moviegoers' imagination since they never see the baby. What they do see, however, is Rosemary recovering from her shock and responding to the child with a lullaby, determined to give it a mother's love. A less worthy sequel, *Look What's Happened To Rosemary's Baby*, appeared in 1976. This sequel and other exploitative films (*It's Alive!*, 1968; *The Terror Within*, 1989; *The Unborn*, 1991) treat the life process with a heavy hand. These movies diligently avoid cleverness and wallow in gore best left to the viewer's fantasy.

Considering what we know today, and what we imagine happened during the Silent era of yesterday, let's play a little game of juxtaposition. For fun, compare what logically makes no sense to compare: today's cavalier treatment of sexual matters, but viewed by a silent audience of yesteryear. What would silent moviegoers think about today's commercialization of reproduction? If we define **Oz** as the magical connection between our imagination and the movie's fanciful fare, can you wonder what silent viewers might conclude about the sexual content in contemporary films?

Conjure up, if you will, how these movie fans would react to the "race" for fertilization depicted in *Look Who's Talking?* The opening and closing credits of this 1989 film offer a stylized interpretation of conception: You see sperm churning frantically for the egg, accompanied by the voice of Bruce Willis encouraging his cohorts to stay the course. Since the egg's zona barrier permits only one member to penetrate, Mikey, the sperm, surmounts overwhelming odds to emerge (or submerge) a "winner." Can you envision the uproar over this scenario during the Silent era, with Willis's comments translated to subtitles? An outrage, critics would say. Surely that's not the way it happens, patrons might exclaim.

Silent moviegoers would feel more comfortable with Woody Allen's version of the big "lift off." His final segment of *Everything You Wanted To Know About Sex, But Were Afraid To Ask* (1972), entitled "What Happens During Ejaculation?", provides a rare peek at the human male's Mission Control Center. Silent patrons, disturbed at seeing real sperm plow their way excitedly to a real egg in *Look Who's Talking*, could relax upon viewing Woody in a white sperm suit (complete with tail) as he nervously prepares for launching.

Woody's anxious, as always, about his chances to succeed: Maybe she's on the pill, he worries, and it's all for nothing; maybe what awaits him is a "wall of hard rubber"; maybe it's a homosexual tryst; or, maybe the host is masturbating and he, Woody, will "wind up on the ceiling." The odds, Woody decides, are against him: "I'm not going out there! I'm not going to get shot out of that thing!" But he does, and, with his companion sperm, leaps out to a fate unknown.

The anthropomorphism of little men in sperm suits (but, alas, no little women shown) would seem daring to silent filmgoers, although not especially outrageous. Certainly what happens in Woody Allen's mechanical reproduction of reproduction does not divulge much of the real mystery of secrecy that surrounds conception.

We see burly workers cranking up a wheel to give the human host--named Sidney--an erection. We see them standing in fluid, presumably semen, although the fluid is not named. We see several neural functions related to penile erection in action, except that none is identifiable as the real process. A change in some dialogue, and, of course, no mention of "ejaculation," should make Woody's satire acceptably remote from the actual chain of reproductive events. Oz, under these restrictions, would appear an enjoyable experience.

Suppose, however, we present a birth trauma to silent patrons that truly creates a gasping experience. Suppose, for a bit of sadistic pleasure, we transport to the past this jarring image: a silent film's rendition of the "birth" in *Alien* (1979). Mention *Alien* and viewers tend to think first of the scene that graphically depicts how the predator comes aboard the crew's spacecraft. Unknown to Kane (John Hurt), an organism incubates within him. He and other members of an outer-space scow are eating when the bloody mini-predator arrives. Reportedly, director Ridley Scott splashed his actors with movie blood, doing so without warning. Their expressions of genuine shock and surprise complement the gruesome,

gurgling emergence of the baby alien. The creature bursts
forth through Kane's chest and scoots away making little
gremlin noises.[3]

Kane, it appears, is the worse for wear. You don't have
your chest and tummy blown open and tend to survive, and
Kane doesn't. So, even without the sound effects of birth,
how would all this eruption play to a silent audience? Whether
you speak of movie fans in the early decades of this century,
or of movie fans today, you can find a select group who thrive
on breaking the barrier. Granted, the *Alien* birth might
convey too much horror for most viewers of silent films, but
a certain number would relish the experience. For others of
that period, seeing birth dramatized as a fountain of blood and
guts--even black-and-white blood and guts--could provoke
a solemn promise. The ladies might vow never, ever, to
become pregnant. The vow, naturally, would depend on them
knowing how **not** to become pregnant.

Those silent ladies, nonetheless, might respond positively
to one valiant feature of *Alien*: The portrayal of a heroine
who courted no flak from anyone, especially males. Sigourney
Weaver's Ripley, with the resilience and resourcefulness of a
woman hellbent on survival, might well appeal to female
viewers, particularly after World War I. Silent films did not
march in lockstep with Victorian values during the entire
period. The first great war brought a number of social
changes, changes that worked their way into the movies'
treatment of women. Specifically, middle-class women
behaved with greater emancipation, and the later silents
flattered this emancipation.

Sexual overtures became more animated, females more
spirited, and men more befuddled during the Jazz Age of 1918
to 1929 (Higashi, 1990, p. 365). The sexuality of contrasts--
the virgin and the vamp--found competition from real-life,
middle-class women who pursued a democratic lifestyle, and
who didn't mind if that lifestyle escalated into wealth and a
finery of fashions and jewels. Unspeakably, these Jazz-Age
belles might even know about contraception--and actually use
such devices.

What the frisky females didn't do, still, was to depart wholeheartedly from traditional sexual conduct. Sumiko Higashi (1990, p. 367), discussing this period of silent films, argues that "...Social preoccupation with female conduct remained inordinate, however. Sex had become more playful, but the 'new woman' had to walk a fine line. As a pal who sported boyish fashions and bobbed hair, she exerted sex appeal but was not quite as abandoned as she might appear."

The female, in other words, could be a tad vampish without sacrificing her girlish appeal--she just couldn't be too vampish. A finer analysis of cinematic change involved not so much an explicit exhibition of sexual taboos as an upbeat tempo in female characterization and conduct to make femininity more vital. More vital, incidentally, at the expense of the male's masculine image of derring-do.

When Does Life Begin?

The old silents and their merry presentations of sexual issues suggest a primeval world to contemporary moviegoers. But the silents asked questions about life and death still asked today. Children then and children now want to know: When does life begin? Where do babies come from? And how does life make a choice between female babies and male babies? Inquiring minds expressed an ardent curiosity about these questions in the Silent era as they do in our so-called Modern age.

Recurring controversies over conception and abortion reflect the power of life-and-death mysteries to bestow strong emotions. Both phenomena inspire a cavalcade of mutterings and exhortations. Attempts to engineer conception artificially provoke a conflict of whether to tinker with the natural spontaneity of fertilization. Selective breeding (tinkering) arouses a potful of discordant emotions over humans who become the subjects of experimentation. Abortion controversies exist along several fronts, although these disputes center on the woman's right to her sexual freedom versus the unborn's right to go full term.

The mystery of wonder, of not knowing all we need to know, keeps birth a marvel and the debates that surround it in a state of flux. But the mystery of secrecy, the idea of not sharing what we **do** know, wobbles along more tenuously today than in the Silent period. The silents marked a culture whereby guarded beliefs about sexual revelations helped to explain the secrecy. Knowing more than you should know about sexual matters sparked concerns of debauchery. But now, with the movies' cumulative freedom to illuminate sexual taboos, the mystery of secrecy proves less comprehensible, though still a reckoning force (see Schwarzbaum, 1994).

Therefore, since filmmakers currently enjoy a greater liberty to create sexual entertainment, what do they practice presently that they did not practice in silent movies? Interestingly, filmmakers of both periods cultivate a fair patch of common ground. Silent and sound histories of movies include documentaries on a number of sexual issues, such as birth control and venereal disease. Documentaries, then and now, deliver intellectual discourses about these puzzles, whereas mainstream movies opt for an emotional emphasis in pursuing dissertations on life and death.[4]

Today, aside from better technical resources, filmmakers bear a freer privilege of cinematic speech, although a speech still tinged with caution. One class of movies, usually television movies, falls in the purview of **educational melodramas** (also called **docudramas**). These message-centered vehicles use surrogate mothers (*Baby M*, 1988), spouse abuse (*The Burning Bed*, 1984), sexual assault (*A Case Of Rape*, 1974), abortion (*Roe vs. Wade*, 1989), AIDS (*And The Band Played On*, 1993), and other sexuality topics as dramatic themes of life and death. Viewers receive a crash course on these issues, and, more pointedly, acquire a quick recognition of who's on which side and why.

Viewers, however, may or may not receive an accurate accounting of events, since these events have a way of succumbing to dramatic license. Also, the events portrayed typically involve strong emotional confrontations, both personal and legal. Other true-life instances of surrogate mothers, spouse abuse, sexual assault, abortion, and AIDS comprise a different, less tumultuous course of action. These quieter, lower-profile instances of life and death usually do not surface in dramatic form because they lack the ingredients that filmmakers seek for entertainment.[5]

Let us ponder the one question that links conception and abortion in a Gordian knot: the question of "When does life begin?" Our inquiry proves deceptive since, at first glance, no reason arises as to why adults and children should not have a chance to find the answer. The initial problem emerges when we learn that no single answer passes muster for everyone. This disagreement supplies the first crescendo of a gnashing of teeth that accompanies the abortion controversies. (Abortion represents a media industry, and, as such, produces a network of entangling arguments over sexual matters.) One argument involves the assumption that youngsters are better served to retain the mystery of secrecy about reproduction than to know of the options available.

What are the options? The zygote-to-embryo-to-fetus's biological development provides a narrow tolerance of time as to when certain organs and functions develop, but the **sequence** of how they develop offers a seamless pattern to observe (Morowitz & Trefil, 1992, p. 43). Suppose we borrow from the remarks of Clifford Grobstein, a specialist on embryology, and itemize a scorecard for when life begins (Hall, 1989):

(1) **Genetic individuality** starts at conception, typically involving an XX chromosome for females and an XY chromosome for males.

(2) **Developmental individuality** occurs approximately one to two weeks after conception, when the fertilized egg implants on the wall of the uterus. Cells are not orchestrated to become an embryo until this implantation results. A cell that breaks away before implantation may develop into a separate embryo (twins, for example).

(3) **Functional individuality** arises about the fourth week, distinguished by a beating, two-chambered heart. The organism remains passive otherwise, still an embryo, not yet a fetus.

(4) **Behavioral individuality** in the form of movement can arrive as soon as six weeks. But the beginning of this early fetal stage involves simple reflex actions; probably, as Grobstein speculates, actions managed neurally at the level of the spinal cord.

(5) **Psychic individuality** allows for sufficient neural connections in the brain to demonstrate a pain experience. But to assume a threshold of what Grobstein calls "minimal awareness" normally requires 26 to 30 weeks of development. Brain waves show a semblance of order, including patterns that may suggest waking and sleeping.

(6) **Social individuality** assumes the cumulative presence of all other states and likely does not occur until after birth. Grobstein defines social individuality as recognized communication between two humans.

Knowing this information suggests the complexity of answering a question about when life begins. Moreover, as essayist Roger Rosenblatt (1992, p. 49) describes, the history of this question involves not only biology, but religion, politics, philosophy, and other forces that give abortion a truly contradictory presence over the centuries.

Creativity's sliver of light shines forth when the filmmaker finds a way to make this substantive controversy informative, entertaining, and commercial. A documentary might proceed to spell out the six orientations to life just summarized, narrated, say, by talking heads and supplemented with animation. A movie of entertainment, however, must search for a different format. The six orientations probably would surface emotionally, with the filmmaker invoking a dramatic scheme that may or may not best serve the question, "When does life begin?" The key rests with how adroitly the filmmaker attempts to meet the challenge of an educational drama.

Abortion And Secrecy

Eleven years before Roe and before Wade we have the ordeal of Sherri Chessen Finkbine. Sherri became the center of a media storm in Arizona and across the country when she made the private matter of abortion public. Moviemakers who hasten to translate a notable tragedy to the screen today were nowhere to be found during Sherri's crisis in 1962. What this mother of four children did find, regrettably, amounted to a circus of media hounds outside her home, and an onslaught of hate mail and nasty phone calls that labeled her a "baby killer."

A Private Matter (1992) dramatizes Sherri's story 30 years after the fact, with Sissy Spacek as Sherri and Aidan Quinn as Bob, her husband. Bob, touring with his high school students in Europe, returns carrying a tranquilizer called Thalidomide. He took the drug to help him sleep, and Sherri does the same, not knowing, as so many pregnant women did not know, that Thalidomide's side effects would prove responsible for approximately 7,000 babies entering the world without arms or legs (Rosenblatt, 1992, p. 90; Lipton & Armstrong, 1992).

A Private Matter conveys American society's longstanding reluctance to explain openly the Hows and Wherefores of sexual matters, including reproduction. A reluctance, incidentally, not that removed in spirit from the silents' secretive treatment of conception and birth. Sherri's plight becomes more sensitive because she hosts a children's TV program called "Romper Room." Her boss, reflecting on her pregnancy, cautions Sherri that she must take a hiatus from the program before she starts to "show": "We wouldn't want the little darlings to find out where they come from now, would we?" Later, he's not so lighthearted when Sherri tells him of her desire to abort, and her hope to continue with the program. Nervously, he retreats from his earlier convivial spirit, and reaffirms the prevailing convictions regarding abortion: "We can't even say the word 'pregnant' on TV..."

If Sherri's condition of carrying a deformed fetus had remained private, she probably would have obtained an abortion in a local hospital. She meets with a psychiatrist who goes through the formality of making abortion legally acceptable by casually coaching her to say the "right" words. The right words include Sherri's guided admission that the stress over her pregnancy may endanger her life. This admission is what the psychiatrist wants to hear. He, in turn, gives his endorsement to the hospital board and all signals appear go--until her private matter becomes public.

Sherri not only loses her job, she finds that her decision to abort rests with males who hold the power to say Yea or Nay. Her doctor takes Bob aside to discuss the options, leaving Sherri out of the loop. Subsequently, an all-male hospital board votes not to endanger the hospital's image, thereby reviving Sherri's guilt over a physical problem that deserves no guilt, and forcing her to look elsewhere. Ultimately, the Finkbines fly to Sweden for, as Sherri calls it, the "operation" in her 12th week of pregnancy.

This closing scene hardly speaks of victory or of nobility for a woman who pursues her bodily rights to privacy. We see, instead, a couple badgered publicly over a moral dilemma; a dilemma that, to many outspoken individuals, incurs only one outcome: birth, not death. We see in Bob a caring husband, but also a husband who does not grasp Sherri's anger when the doctor excludes her from his confidence. (Bob admits to the doctor, "I don't know, sometimes I think women are a different species altogether, you know".) And we see Sherri, not a saint, but a woman who reacts badly at times to the sudden blight on her world.

We remember best, however, a poignant interlude when the Finkbine's oldest son and daughter ask about the trouble. Sherri, gently, quietly, tells them of the "bad pills" and why a life must go to sleep. The children seem to understand, a feat that places them several leagues ahead of the truly fractious parties in this sad story.

Roe Vs. Wade

The cultural winds of the early 1970s sweep forward, bolstered by a cacophony of assassinations and social movements from the 1960s. A change in the Zeitgeist asserts itself--a change in the spirit of the times--to permit a window of reproductive control for Jane Roe that so haunted Sherri Finkbine a decade earlier.

The challenge of dramatizing *Roe vs. Wade* (1989) offers an example of how History and Hollywood manage to tango, mostly to the same tune. The "Wade" in question is Henry Wade, the Dallas District Attorney invested with the legal power to enforce an 1857 Texas statute that prohibits medical doctors from performing abortions except to save the mother's life. But the "Roe" in question proves less straightforward. Jane Roe depicts a pseudonym for Norma McCorvey in real life, and for Ellen Russell in the drama (played by Holly Hunter).

We first see Russell as a carnival barker, hawking patrons to move inside and view, among her menagerie, a five-legged cow and a two-headed snake. Ellen emanates the free spirit who's been a bit too free with her sexual favors, and more than a bit negligent in confronting the consequences. The consequences include one child, born in wedlock, but now cared for by Ellen's mother; and a second, unwanted child that she conceives out of wedlock. It is her second pregnancy that ultimately permits legal counsel to establish their arguments over a woman's right to choose her motherhood.

More by happenstance than design, Ellen Russell meets an attorney, Sarah Weddington (Amy Madigan), who seeks a plaintiff for a test case that can bring the Texas abortion law before the courts. Ellen, prior to meeting Sarah, wrestles with the prospect of an illegal abortion. Indeed, she visits a back-alley room, gazing at its musty setting and the room's collection of horror-shop paraphernalia used to end a life. Ellen finds the savvy to recognize a butcher shop when she sees one. She backs away, subsequently to place her faith in Sarah and in an unlikely course of events: changing the Texas law to favor abortion rights for women.

This option becomes the sword wielded by Sarah, Ellen's champion. Ellen, herself, finds neither the law's elegance nor the law's pace comprehensible. Time will not wait for the life she bears, and, eventually, Ellen chooses to carry her baby full term and to surrender it for adoption. (The scene in which Ellen gives birth is pitched emotionally to show the rigors of childbirth, and to record Ellen's anguish in not being allowed to hold the baby, or to know its sex.) For Ellen, the law comprises another world, a white-collar clambake of legal maneuvers that fails to ease her plight.

For Sarah, the white-collar clambake represents her life. She and her associates persevere to see *Roe v. Wade* work its path to the United States Supreme Court. Sarah's counterpart, Assistant District Attorney Jay Floyd (Terry O'Quinn), displays a benevolent devotion to citing the evils of abortion; a devotion that rivals Sarah's desire to propound the issue's

virtues. So, the scene is set. The counsel are ready. The
justices file in. The mystery of life--when it begins and when
it ends--hangs elusively in the balance.

The shame is that no compromise can ease the pain felt by
either side. And the travesty is that the Court allots each
counsel a mere 30 minutes to present the controversy. Thirty
minutes to engage the mystifying arguments of legal, moral,
and emotional portance that concern the right to choice versus
the right to life. Thirty minutes interrupted by questions from
the justices. Thirty minutes of exhibition that harbor months
of legal preparation and years of gestation to do battle. Thirty
minutes from each party that will affect the lives of millions
of individuals, women and men.

Thirty minutes. Perhaps the drama's most stirring moments
arrive in these time-precious pleas that capture the pinnacle of
a lawyer's career: to argue before the Supreme Court. During
their final arguments, both counsel blend emotion and intellect
as they search for that faint truth to swing the judgments of
those justices who can be swung. Recalling the six orientations to life summarized earlier, you can appreciate the
difficulty of each counsel's task.

Roe vs. Wade proves more a pro-choice drama than a right-
to-life advocatory. It proves so because the movie centers on
Ellen Russell as a woman in need, although she creates that
need; and on Sarah Weddington as a woman dedicated to
giving women like Ellen a choice heretofore denied them.
You can say that *Roe v. Wade* becomes law because women
have a right to privacy; because legal protection applies
naturally to infants after birth, and less naturally to fetuses
before birth; because a majority of the justices already
favored the woman's right to choose; because one counsel
makes a more effective presentation than the other counsel; or
maybe, just maybe, because time and sentiment--the
Zeitgeist--is right.

What freedom does *Roe v. Wade* actually grant women?
The U. S. Constitution does not specify a woman's right to
abortion. This assumed right relies on interpretation, and the
interpretation bears on the **liberty clause** of the Fourteenth
Amendment. Laurence Tribe (1990, p. 83), author of

Abortion: The Clash Of Absolutes, describes the problem this way: "...'No State shall...deprive any person of life, liberty, or property, without due process of law.' It is the guarantee of 'liberty' contained in the due process clause, sometimes also called the liberty clause, of the Fourteenth Amendment that provides protection of our rights from infringement by the state governments. And the word 'liberty' simply is not self-defining." The liberty clause depicts a broad provision of the Constitution that pro-choice advocates view as supportive of a woman's right to control her body, whereas pro-life advocates do not (also see Alderman & Kennedy, 1992, pp. 321-322).

Practically speaking, the freedom or right of privacy, a fundamental right, permits the pregnant woman to exercise her choice of abortion during the first trimester (the first three months). Thereafter, the government can intervene, but under certain restrictions. These restrictions in the second trimester concern the woman's health, since an abortion becomes more hazardous later in pregnancy. And in the third trimester, the restrictions prove more severe because health concerns are now shared with protection of the fetus as it becomes viable, that is, capable of living outside the womb (Morowitz & Trefil, 1992, p. 131; Tribe, 1990, pp. 11-12).

No legal victory, however, need remain absolute or etched in stone, even when adjudicated by the Supreme Court. *Roe v. Wade* continues to face opposition, and continues to fall under the scrutiny of a changed composition of Supreme Court justices--changed in philosophy, at least, from the Court that declared *Roe v. Wade* a law in 1973.

The *Webster* case in 1989, for example, enacts a change in how some states can now choose to interpret *Roe*. The *Webster* decision appears to suggest that (1) the fetus deserves protection **before and after** viability, which means protection throughout pregnancy; but that (2) this protection cannot impose an **undue burden** on a woman who decides to abort during her first trimester (Tribe, 1990, p. 23). The Supreme Court's *Webster* decision does not overturn the earlier *Roe* judgment, but *Webster* allows the states to concoct their own restrictions that, in effect, make it more difficult for women to control their right of choice. The question, it seems, relates to the basic decision of what is and is not an "undue burden" on the woman. And, in time, this question relates further to the possibility that the states will finally govern a woman's right to reproductive privacy.

Does the movie *Roe vs. Wade* depict accurately the people and events that made the case a landmark legal decision? The parties who lived it, both for and against, say "Yes" for the most part (Zurawik, 1989a, 1989b, 1989c). But, as with any movie, *Roe vs. Wade* sports an accuracy dependent on highlights, and on compressed dialogue and happenings. The drudgery, the legwork, the sense of cumulative progress in gathering popular support for the woman's right to choose-- these qualities do not portray a clear representation in the drama.

Sarah Weddington (1992, pp. 258-260) comments on the movie, noting that the docudrama would have been made even without her cooperation. She participated to try and ensure the legal accuracy of presenting *Roe vs. Wade*, but became disenchanted upon viewing other scenes. Scenes, for instance, detailing an argument between herself and her husband over time spent on the case, and an admission by her colleague, Linda Coffee, that she cannot continue with the work. The viewing experience became disenchanting because these exchanges never happened in reality, yet apparently found inclusion to create dramatic tension. Moviemakers, you must remember, hate a void.

Nor, adds Weddington, does she know what truly happened in the episodes claimed by Jane Roe. Weddington does not know, for example, if Jane Roe never held the baby born to her, as the movie indicates. What Sarah Weddington does know, and what the movie slights, is that the case of Jane Roe was not just for the person of Jane Roe as a plaintiff, but a class action suit on behalf of all women who found themselves in Jane Roe's predicament (Weddington, p. 260).

One telling inaccuracy involves Ellen's declaration of rape that led to her second pregnancy (Rosenblatt, 1992, p. 94). She admits to Sarah Weddington that the rape never happened, although in the movie her admission occurs while the *Roe* case remains unresolved. But Norma McCorvey, the real Jane Roe, did not reveal her false assertion of rape until over 10 years later (Tribe, 1990, p. 5; Zurawik, 1989a, 1989b, 1989c).

Why worry over the difference in time? Well, rape denotes a special set of circumstances to pro-choice and pro-life advocates alike. Laurence Tribe (1990, p. 233) speculates that many pro-life devotees make a distinction between **consensual** and **nonconsensual** sexual relations. Abortion, say the pro-lifers, indicates murder, but a murder in which they hold the female responsible because of her willingness to engage in lovemaking. She chooses to have sex, and thus should pay the consequences of her actions by carrying the life she holds to birth. This sentiment, moreover, calls forth an old-fashioned morality about sexual conduct that we witnessed during the Silent era of movies: If you succumb to sexual temptation, you pay for your transgression. And if you're a woman, you pay more.

When a rapist or incestuous father forces the female to acquiesce, the picture of murder, at least to the less fanatical pro-life activists, becomes more complicated. Abortion under this rationale does not always constitute murder, despite the glaring fact that when the fetus dies, the fetus dies. The rape exception simply points to one more dilemma concerning life and death. We need a checklist to ascertain what conditions benefit the pregnant woman's rights, and what conditions do not. Rape and incest and jeopardizing the mother's health, yes, at least for the more tolerant pro-lifers and for many fence-straddlers. But refusing to use birth control, or a birth control device that fails, even accidentally, produces a "no" response regarding the woman's rights. Again, the distinction between the yeses and nos traces to nonconsensual versus consensual sex.

Perhaps it seems more forthcoming to have Ellen confess her false rape earlier than it actually happened. Perhaps, too, rape becomes a better rallying cry for pro-choice advocates to justify the need for abortion rights, both before and after *Roe* became law. You must decide for yourself if this alteration of "real reality" to "cinematic reality" commits a grave disservice to the pro-life position, as illustrated in the movie.

The liberal leanings that many movies espouse affect the Oz experience. Clearly, if you agree with *Roe*'s pro-choice message, you will find more to like about the characters and the story's outcome. But what you believe and what you experience in seeing the movie need not enjoin a straight-forward connection. If you prefer pro-life, your adversarial reaction does not have to assume a flat declaration, such as "I don't agree with the pro-choice position, so I know that this damn movie will be a cesspool of propaganda!"

Rather, you may place your pro-life sentiments aside momentarily to appreciate a dramatization of conflicting beliefs and intense emotions. Then again, you may not. What Oz becomes will relate to (1) what you expect from the movie, (2) what you **get** from the movie, and (3) the mood that you bring to your viewing experience. If you find *Roe vs. Wade* fairer than you anticipated, your Oz process will acknowledge the drama as achieving a more fastidious nature. You need not care for the movie's resolution, but you can respect those attempts to bolster the pro-life position in an essentially pro-choice story.

Whatever your value judgment, the cinematic closure of *Roe vs. Wade* leaves an impression of finality: The idea that this legal victory shall achieve a lasting testimony to the female's right to reproductive privacy. Possibly, the real participants in the 1973 decision may have thought likewise. But the law is not immutable. Social movements are not sustained indefinitely, countermovements arise with the ferocity of an underdog, and the Zeitgeist changes once again.

Three stormy considerations now arise that give pro-choice and pro-life advocates pause to contemplate the future. First, the 2000 plus physicians who perform abortions in the U. S. must find the practice sufficiently worthwhile and lucrative to tolerate the abuse directed at them (Blow, 1992a, 1992b). Should they not, you can use your imagination as to what a desperate woman might do to solve her problem. Second, if the abortion pill developed in France, RU 486, becomes available to American women, the process of abortion will assume a lower profile, more difficult for pro-lifers to detect and to protest (Biema, 1993). But third, if restrictions ultimately reach the first trimester of pregnancy--the period during which most abortions occur--then a different era of reproductive privacy shall emerge, and the ruling of *Roe v. Wade* will be dust.

What remains enduring is the daring of those filmmakers, past and present, who found a way to make sexual taboos entertaining and informative. Telling a cinematic story silently, or with sound and sense, possesses the potential (though not always realized) to underscore a sexual issue and its complexities. Telling the story, for example, of two women, unlikely allies, who share precious little in lifestyle and temperament. What they do share congeals into a directive that goes against the establishment, an establishment armed with reasons strongly felt. For one ally, the personal right to make a choice; for the other, the legal right to forge a fundamental freedom. For this story, at least, we have an ending.

Notes

1. Henry Bauer (1992, pp. 74-75), a chemist and philosopher of science, argues that scientists rationalize an understanding of scientific phenomena, even if the needed information is not in evidence. The "unknown unknown" and the "known unknown" refer to mysterious phenomena that constitute our total ignorance or our partial ignorance. Scientists propose principles to explain such scientific puzzles, assuming (1) that the crucial guidelines are known and valid, and (2) that only the details require discovery. Bauer contends, however, that even "The known comprises not what we know but what we believe, what we *think* we know" (p. 74). Our interest in this current lesson focuses on the "known," specifically on the scientific and cinematic treatment of what we "think" we know about reproduction and abortion.

2. The morality campaign continued beyond the old silents. A 1937 film, *They Must Be Told!*, melodramatically tells of a girl, Millicent, who wins a beauty contest, leaves her boy friend (Wendel), goes to the big city, gives herself to the wrong man, and returns home...with syphilis. She receives treatment from a quack doctor, and, thinking herself cured, marries the boy friend, has a baby, and appears on the road to happiness. She's not, of course.

Her husband contacts syphilis, her baby contacts syphilis, and the road looks rather grim for Millicent. Wendel forgives her for leaving him, and forgives her again for giving him syphilis. Wendel's almost too good to be true, but his goodness has a purpose: *They Must Be Told!* describes a morality tale in which the main plot uses Millicent as the woman who falls from grace and receives her punishment.

3.   An Associated Press item appeared about a lady who experienced stomach pains after a generous meal of tacos. What she assumed as indigestion turned into an unforgettable evening at home: labor pains, followed by birth. Unforgettable, not just for the miracle of birth, but because she did not know of her pregnancy, and because her husband had undergone a vasectomy two years earlier (with a 1 in 1000 probability of fathering a child). Unforgettable, too, because the delivery happened while the mother was watching...yes, *Alien* (Indigestion turns..., 1984).

4.   If you believe that the old silents proved overly cautious in dramatizing sexual matters such as birth control, consider the tardiness of modern movies. A **1988** film, *Cross My Heart*, designates the first major, American movie whereby two lovers, Cathy and David (Annette O'Toole and Martin Short), make an issue of birth control in the service of safer sex (Ebert, 1988, p. 144; Nash & Ross, 1988, p. 54). After the usual awkwardness of new partners disrobing, David prepares to slip on a condom when Cathy intervenes and provides a sheep-gut condom that she prefers him to wear. This request adds humor to the bedroom scene, as well as a lighthearted testimony on the changes in sexual frankness. The point remains, however, that birth control must offer a potential for entertainment to become useful to filmmakers.

5.   Amy Heckerling's direction of *Fast Times At Ridgemont High* (1982) presents an interesting exception. The movie received mixed reviews, perhaps because the film offers a bewildering slice of life about teenagers. One criticism concerns the character of Stacy (played by Jennifer Jason Leigh). This concern rests with Stacy's abortion in the story and the belief that she simply shrugs off the experience (Nash & Ross, 1986, p. 821). A different interpretation, viewing Stacy as an understated character, suggests that she does not panic but keeps the abortion quiet to spare her parents and to escape notoriety. Stacy indulges her curiosity and experiments with sex, although she dutifully accepts her pregnancy as a consequence of this indulgence. Thus, rather than throw a tantrum, Stacy remains calm and controlled even when the boy who impregnated her shows a reluctance to help. This latter evaluation indicates Stacy's placid, sensitive nature, and offers a stronger justification of integrity for her character than does the first interpretation.

Lesson 4

Macho Machos

What's wrong with this scene?

John gurgles his piteous moans, strapped to the cross ties of a railroad track. Faintly but surely he feels the bars come alive. A burring sound vibrates his well-secured body. Ohmigod, ohmigod, ohmigod, he knows what that means. The hum of an approaching train. The hum jumps to a buzz. Ohmigod, ohmigod, ohmigod. IT'S COMING. The monster engine looms into sight, as does a figure in black leather, riding a pale, wild-eyed stallion. The figure dismounts, kicking up a swirl of cinders. "Hello, John," she says calmly. "Marsha," John screams, "quick, quick, untie me!" Marsha sighs. "John, you're such a wimp." Quietly, deftly, she releases John and pulls him aside just as the 4:40 roars past. Marsha pauses and looks at the man she saved. He shakes, he trembles, he clasps his hands in a prayer of thankfulness. "Why John," Marsha says, "I do believe you've wet your pants."

Really, John, not a manly thing to do. And Marsha, not a womanly thing to say. What's wrong here? Ask a male and he will say "Everything!" Ask a female and she will say "Alright!" Given the customary genderisms in our society, this scene between John and Marsha plays most credibly for humor, not drama.

Moviegoers search for a measure of trust in their character of choice. Considering all the dangers of an adventure epic-- the snakes, the natives, the beguiling lover, the awesome perils still ahead--the viewers' character must prove someone special. HE requires a daunting stamina, a cavalier sense of calculation, a cynical humor; whereas SHE requires only modest capabilities: a dash of spunk, a droplet of foresight, a sprinkle of humor, compensated, of course, by an abundance of beauty.

Why does HE carry the load? The male presides in films as the "main man" for humor, for tragedy, for action. This explanation indicates that the male shoulders the responsibility of doing what must be done. Or, as the movielore surrounding a manly male like John Wayne commands, "A man's gotta do (pause) what a man's gotta do." Since we seldom hear about a "main woman," the female appears to play her usual supporting role to the Big Guy. Filmmakers, moreover, rarely wish to lose the Big Guy, unless the movie's almost over.

Genderisms

Gender, for our purposes, refers to a cultural emphasis, an abstraction used to evaluate sexuality (see Lesson 2, p. 36). How you assess your masculinity, your femininity, your bisexuality, how you comport yourself sexually--these inclinations reflect gender. Gender concentrates on females and males playing their appropriate roles. Segregation demonstrates the norm for the sexes, apparently even into adolescence.

Boys hang around with boys, gaining experience in competitiveness, in dominance, and, generally, in the male vernacular called "roughing it." Girls hang around with girls too, except that "hang around" seems the wrong expression. Girls "join" other girls, fostering cooperation more than competition. Boys and girls express themselves differently when segregated, and these disparities become evident when the two sexes intermingle. The outcome appears to place girls at a disadvantage in persuasiveness. They do not exert much influence, at least not direct influence, over boys when the two sexes work together (Maccoby, 1990).

The sexes satisfy gender stereotypes called **genderisms** when boys commonly fulfill one set of expectations and girls another set. Genderisms refer to words and acts that simplify, and sometimes oversimplify the sexes. Such stereotypes make it convenient for us to classify people according to appearances, beliefs, and backgrounds. Genderisms denote well-worn labels that we attach to feminine and masculine conduct. If John whines, screams, and cries, these behaviors go against the genderisms established for masculinity in our culture. If Marsha belches, chews tobacco, and swears like a sailor, these behaviors, too, run contrary to the genderisms that we associate with feminine conduct.

Genderisms represent a proving ground for identifying and reinforcing the roles played by males and females in many (read that "most") movies. A man and woman walk into a room and they see a body, presumably dead. The woman screams, but the man says "Hush!" and instructs her to stand back and calm down. He checks the body for signs of life (somehow knowing how to do this), and informs the woman that the body is, indeed, dead. He then issues the standard orders: "Go to a phone and call the police. And, for god's sake, get control of yourself, okay?" The female, in turn, finds herself playing a familiar supporting role. She takes instructions, she follows instructions, she obeys. The male assumes command because males usually assume command. You do this, you do that, and you don't touch anything, okay?

Genderisms abound. So much so that their definition becomes part of the problem (recall the "dichotomous" and "relatedness" camps used to distinguish sex and gender in Lesson 2). **Sex** denotes a biological emphasis, an abstraction that reminds us of our anatomical parts and functions. The problem arises in how we perceive these anatomical parts. Males possess a penis, a truly prominent creation, out front and upstanding; females, by contrast, harbor a vagina, a creation mostly hidden and passive by comparison. The penis

penetrates, an aggressive description if ever one existed, whereas the vagina **accommodates**, helping the penis with its penetration. The penis acts, the vagina submits. The penis thrusts, the vagina expands to receive these thrusts.

Genderisms extend right down to our private parts. To wit, sexually exploitative films cast male and female characters so unimaginatively for commercial gain that they seem little more than penises and vaginas in action. Filmmakers in a position to challenge this inequality, usually shy away. Instead, they provide us with a preponderance of cinematic genderisms that spells out male/female inequality in big, bold strokes.

Bawdy Awful Words

Consider this claim: Swearing is the male's province because he must swear. A woman swears, and does so publicly with fewer inhibitions today, but she has no need to swear. Why should men believe that obscenities belong more to them than to females? And why should dirty words naturally fit and sometimes enhance the male's masculine stature, when the same dirty words tend to diminish the female's femininity?

Why should spewing out a string of blue words work better for one gender than the other? A look at tradition and how males harness their emotionality suggest that men need a few well-chosen utterances to vent their feelings (women in labor also can use a few, of course). The broad-shouldered male, carrying the weight of history on his shoulders, demands a little affective slack; a release from his emotional straight-jacket, a way to blow off the world. He's dominant, but he's put up with a lot. He can't always kill somebody, drink himself into a stupor, or have sex when he desires, therefore swearing becomes an "acceptable" way for the male to keep in touch with his emotional self. And, too, swearing gives him a sense of power, however illusory.

So, "Frankly, my dear, I don't give a damn" echoes the line whose context requires little explanation. Rhett Butler says goodbye to Scarlett O'Hara his way in *Gone With The Wind*

(1939). If we change Rhett's farewell to "Frankly, my dear, I don't give a darn" or a "hoot" or a "dang," it just doesn't work. The remark demands a "damn" to reflect Rhett's years of coping romantically with Scarlett. "Damn," in this instance, spells the difference between a parting epithet, sharp with candor, and a parting that fails to acknowledge the tumultuous events already experienced in the saga between Rhett and Scarlett.[1]

The male's emotional moments are allowable under stress and in a crisis. But in movies the macho male tends not to cry, bare his soul, or touch strangers in a familiar way. He can swear, however. He can swear if he sees a beautiful sunset ("Damn beautiful sunset"); he can swear if he misses his mother ("Damn beautiful Mom, I miss her"); he can swear if he's bored ("Shit, nothin' to do around here"); he can swear if he wins or loses a contest ("Dammit to hell, not again?"). Obscenities constitute the macho male's emotional currency for saying what he truly feels. Swearing gives him the continuity of feeling to express what he must for release, and to assert himself. Females, well, females can cry and touch anytime they wish. They are, after all, females.

Obscenities depend on discretion to retain their vitality. Used tragically or hilariously, obscenities supply intensity. They enliven language, foster explicit communication, and realize their proper expression through intimacy. Yet violate this convention by vocalizing forbidden words carelessly, and the violator--the swearer--finds himself to blame for misconduct (see May, 1972, p. 73).[2] Thus, the cinematic hero will refrain from using a dirty word too often, perhaps at all, although the villain may indulge freely. Do you recall this pithy challenge from a macho hero to a would-be-macho villain who's trying to decide on his chances for retaliation?

I know what you're thinking. Did he fire six shots or only five? Well, to tell you the truth, in all this excitement I've kinda lost track myself. But being this is a .44 magnum, the most powerful handgun in the world, and would blow your head clean off--you've got to ask yourself one question: do I feel lucky? Well, do ya, punk? (Haun, 1986, p. 129).

Harry from *Dirty Harry* (1971) reeks with macho recklessness. Harry's so machismo that he doesn't need an expression stronger than "punk" to register his hpermasculinity. The tall, silent hero says little and swears even less. Instead, characters who curse vociferously in movies tend to represent (1) nasty individuals, (2) individuals placed in a stressful environment, (3) individuals for whom swearing becomes a defining key to their personality--or (4) some combination of all three.

Timothy Jay (1992, pp. 231-234; also see Callahan, 1990), a psychology professor, examined the number of obscenities used in certain movies. We can match Jay's tally to each of the three film characters just labeled: (1) **The nasty character** or **villain** proves a likely candidate for a dirty mouth. A count from *Scarface* (1983) resulted in 299 swear words, or one every 34 seconds, most of which are uttered by Al Pacino's character: A vile-speaking megalomaniac who gives "dirt" a new name. (2) **The stressed character**, however, may swear profusely to mask his fear, and to release his frustration and anger. *Platoon* (1986), the line soldier's view of Vietnam and a rich source of profanity, produced 243 obscenities or about one every 30 seconds.

Finally, we have (3) **The defining character** who swears as a feature of his personality. He can range from President Harry S. Truman, portrayed by James Whitmore in *Give 'Em Hell, Harry* (1975), to the CIA agent played by Roy Scheider in *The Russia House* (1991), to a crusty old man on the brink of mortality. The latter character appears in *On Golden Pond* (1981), a film that makes Jay's list with an obscenity every 81 seconds, primarily through the courtesy of Henry Fonda's cantankerous character, Norman Thayer, Jr.[3]

Roger Ebert (1993, pp. 810-811) suggests that the use of dirty words in movies provokes two trains of thought. One, the honesty of a player's character may demand hearing obscenities, thereby bolstering the film's artistic integrity. But two, dirty words hardly constitute the essence of a literate script. The train of thought pursued depends on the natural use of blue language in conjunction with characters and story. Put another way, would Norman Thayer, Jr. have communicated such a feisty presence if he had been prevented from mouthing his off-color expressions?

The movie version of a macho male seems to say that if our hero has the authority, the physical strength, the sexual appeal, the sense of humor, and the skill to survive, then he has less need of swearwords than those males who are a little short in the machismo department. Or, like an aging Norman Thayer, Jr., the declining male finds his once-robust masculinity a fading memory. Cursing gives the flawed macho a chance to realize emotional release, and compensates him-- more or less--for his masculine inadequacies. Consequently, if he believes that swearing makes him appear more macho, he will swear.

Females, therefore, become the uninvited. Surveys and polls do not offer a clean sweep favoring males, but findings show that males know and use more obscenities than females in most of the contexts tested (Selnow, 1985; Wilson, 1981; Jay, 1980). Thomas Thompson (1976, p. 46) highlights this disparity when he reconstructs the famous murder of Joan Robinson Hill, allegedly killed by her husband, plastic surgeon John Hill, into a study of contrarious characters. The author's work led to a television movie called *Murder In Texas* (1981). Thompson uses Joan's incongruous but frequent *goddamns* to heighten the personality differences between Joan and John Hill--two lovers, ideally unsuited:

> As she watched the mating dance, Maggie Foster thought to herself: this is a terrible mismatch. These two people have nothing whatsoever in common except they are both beautiful. She is rich, spoiled, bored, looking for a new husband. She knows horses and night clubs and where Pa keeps his checkbook. John Hill knows how to play the trombone and make sutures. He is a mama's boy who winces every time Joan says "god damn," which is often....She was the kind of woman indigenous to Texas--intensely feminine for one moment, and then, spitting out an obscenity, becoming one of the boys. John Hill was cleaved by lightning. He told Maggie Foster in a bread-and-butter telephone call early the next morning, "She's the most incredible girl I ever met."

A man may resent a woman who curses because he feels that the female's blue vocabulary detracts from her femininity. A stronger suspicion, nonetheless, concerns the possibility that he doesn't like a woman to curse because he feels intimidated by her, especially since HE'S the one who should be intimidating. Besides, if she swears like a sailor, she may usurp him in other respects, too: for instance, when they're in bed, having sex, and he discovers that she's bored.

Heaven forbid, he shudders, that such a sexual nightmare should occur. This insult hardly bolsters the fond hopes of a masculine wonderland. What's a macho fellow to do? Well, in such dire moments of masculine insecurity, he can always go to the movies and search for macho inspiration.

Classic Machos

The movies profit from male bonding, particularly the "Buddy" films that offer a variety of male/male relationships, from roustabouts like Spencer Tracy and Clark Gable (*Boom Town*, 1940), to meandering cowpokes like Paul Newman and Robert Redford (*Butch Cassidy And The Sundance Kid*, 1969), to hustlers like Dustin Hoffman and Jon Voight (*Midnight Cowboy*, 1969), to adventurers like Michael Caine and Sean Connery (*The Man Who Would Be King*, 1975) (Champlin, 1981, p. 144). If you're macho you have moxie, and males who show moxie can do quite well on the big screen. Females, except for a rare film like *Thelma And Louise* (1991), need not apply.

Macho reflects a genderism, one that, positively, encourages males to show self-confidence and a strong sense of independence: a sort of Clint Eastwood primer in aloofness and sexual savvy.[4] **Classic machos** get things done, and rely on rugged looks and a world-weary cynicism to attract their women. The women, in turn, appear mesmerized by the macho's maverick image. His masculine eminence promises not only protection, but also a terrific evening in the sack.

Negatively, the classic macho code of conduct exhorts males to foolish exhibitions of bravado against challengers, and demonstrations of callousness toward females (see Joan Mellen's harsh interpretation of Classic Macho personalities in *Big Bad Wolves*, 1977). Because the macho idea represents an exaggeration of masculine conduct, recognized even by macho males themselves, the image caters to a strange, dual role.

One feature of the macho guise promotes a role model for "real men" to emulate; but the other feature nurtures a spoof of the macho strut. Macho males joke about the "John Wayne" syndrome--be tough, be independent, and don't cry--even as they subscribe to the image in their own personal way. John Wayne parodied his career of classic macho figures when he became Rooster Cogburn in *True Grit* (1969), playing a one-eyed, two-fisted fighter, who, in one scene, holds the reins in his mouth as he gallops toward the bad guys with both weapons blazing. Wayne did well enough with his touch of farce to win an academy award, possibly as much for making a profession out of macho machos, as for his portrayal of Rooster Cogburn.[5]

Machismo, nevertheless, constitutes serious business. Jack Nicholson as Jake Gittes in *The Two Jakes* (1990) finds himself harassed by a snot-nosed detective named Loach (David Keith). When Loach pushes a disgruntled Gittes too far in one scene, Gittes gets the drop on him and shoves a revolver in the detective's mouth. The confrontation involves a comeuppance for Loach, complete with a little puddle of urine as he suffers every macho's nightmare of wetting his pants in public. Not only is Loach's handling of fear "un-macho," he allows colleagues to witness this insult to his manhood. Interestingly, we do not see Loach again in the film, as if the director (Nicholson) decided that the man had served his cinematic purpose. Truly, what humiliation could top a supposedly tough detective dribbling through his drawers?

The classic macho image plays strongly in westerns, where men are men and women must usually stay clear of harm's way. In *Hombre* (1967), Paul Newman portrays John Russell, a white man raised by Apaches. Circumstances lead to a standoff in an old mine where Russell and his companions possess goods that the villain, Grimes (Richard Boone),

desires.   Grimes climbs a hill to palaver at a distance with
Russell, seeking to trade his hostage, a woman, for the goods.
Russell asks Grimes how he figures to get back down that hill.
Grimes, realizing that Russell intends to kill him, runs for his
life.   Russell attempts to shoot Grimes, but Russell's
companions interfere, claiming that Grimes came in good
faith.

The simple fact that Russell wants to kill his adversary in
this unheroic fashion demands justification (Wilson, 1991, p.
10). Cinematic rules governing the Old West are romanticized.
The bigger the odds against our lone Western hero, such as
Gary Cooper in *High Noon* (1952), the more fulfilling the tale.
Russell's ungentlemanly behavior goes against this tradition.
What gives?

The answer lies in Russell's character as a stoic, practical
man of Indian ways. He knows better than his companions
that Grimes will try to kill everyone. He also knows that
Grimes, alone on the hill, offers Russell and his party perhaps
their only chance for survival. Russell's apparently "unfair"
behavior retains artistic integrity because his behavior derives
logically from the man's hard-edged experiences as an Indian.
If you know a man plans to kill you, use surprise, use
whatever it takes, but kill him first. Ironically, Russell saves
the party but dies doing so at the movie's end. Had his
companions allowed him to kill Grimes earlier, Russell would
have benefitted from **his** code of the West.

The Old West brings into focus the male's most virile, most
manly moment: a squaring off for that macho of macho tests,
the gunfight. The classic western *Shane* (1953) illustrates how
the familiar territory of a gunfight can still carry the
poignancy and pathos of high drama. The contest of interest,
sadly, represents no contest at all. Torrey (Elisha Cook, Jr.)
plays a homesteader and harmless braggart devoted to the
Confederacy. He crosses a muddy street and approaches the
saloon, only to meet his nemesis, a man dressed in black who
has positioned himself to call Torrey out.   Jack Palance
portrays Wilson, a gunfighter hired to frighten the homesteaders and to drive them away from their beautiful valley, nestled
in the Grand Tetons.

Wilson, grinning, stands on the saloon porch, clear of the mud, walking parallel with Torrey, who must step through the grime as he looks up at Wilson:

WILSON: They tell me they call you Stonewall.
TORREY: Anything wrong with that?
WILSON: That's just funny. Guess they named a lot of that
    (pause) Southern trash after old Stonewall.
TORREY: (frighten but game) Who'd they name you after? Or do
    you know?
WILSON: (slowly putting on a black glove) I'm saying that
    Stonewall Jackson was trash himself. Him and Lee and all
    the rest of them Rebs. (pause) You too.
TORREY: You're a lowdown, lying Yankee.
WILSON: Prove it.

End of dialogue. Torrey reaches for his gun in a lame draw that finds his weapon pointed no higher than the ground. Wilson has already drawn and waits, savoring the moment. An onlooker shouts "No, Torrey!" Torrey freezes, head almost bowed, gun still pointed down, when Wilson fires. The bullet's impact slings him backward into the mud. End of Torrey. (Elisha Cook, Jr., who enjoyed a long career of playing the victim, emphatically found himself sailing backward. The director, George Stevens, attached wires to Cook and launched him accordingly to enhance the scene's grim reality.)

Torrey, the amateur, scared and outclassed, forced by his manhood into a death match against Wilson, the cool professional. And the screen has produced no cooler, more enigmatic gunfighter than the whispery evil figure portrayed by Jack Palance. He is the classic macho evil that Torrey faces, as Torrey, trembling and alone, waits to die. The killing of Torrey alarms the homesteaders and sets a collision course between Shane (Alan Ladd) and Wilson. The murder, eloquent in its cinematic execution, does not exist for mere show. It heightens tension and gives meaning to the volatile events that follow.

Across time and place, this principle of classic macho foolishness finds continuity. Young males use violence as a status tool to affirm their manhood. They bluster, they maim, they kill, and are killed in return, to declare their masculine legacy. *Boyz N The Hood* (1991) brings us an atypical movie about blacks in the inner city, and an atypical father, Furious Styles (Larry Fishburne), who wants to raise his son, Tre (Cuba Gooding, Jr.), above the violence. The father proves a scarce and significant force in guiding Tre through the neighborhood's maze of drugs and murders, particularly in contrast to Tre's two best friends who are fatherless (Cardwell, Coto, Matzer, Pearlman, & Thompson, 1991; Diamond, 1991).

One scene finds Tre and his father on a rocky beach. Furious asks his son what he knows about sex. Tre, with a sly smile, says he knows a little bit: "I know that I take a girl, stick my thing in it, and nine months later a baby comes out." Furious laughs, perhaps remembering his own naiveté in learning about babies. Then, serious, he adds: "Well, remember this: Any fool with a dick can make a baby but only a real man can raise his children."

Boyz N The Hood underscores this point in flesh and blood. The macho theme in East L. A. becomes the only badge of honor for many blacks without fathers like Furious Styles. Rick (Morris Chestnut), one of Tre's friends, has a slim window of opportunity through a football scholarship to escape the streets. But the window closes when he's gunned down, and, in the programmed world of macho honor, Rick's brother, Doughboy (Ice Cube), retaliates by killing his brother's killers. Just before he fires to finish the final assassin, Doughboy gives us the pained look of a youth trapped by his wayward masculinity in time and place. He's weary of this "shit" but he has nowhere to go.

Indeed, Doughboy talks quietly with Tre in the film's closing scene, urging him to make it out. They embrace and Doughboy walks across the street--then fades from our view, as if by magic. Sadly, this cinematic magic merely foretells his future: Two weeks later, we are told, Doughboy is murdered.

Shane and *Boyz N The Hood* tell us how ardently some males carry their manhood. Back down from a challenge and you occupy a lower rung in macho society; or, in a volatile neighborhood, you hit rock bottom. Torrey could not live with himself on that lower rung, so he chose not to live at all. His narrow orientation denotes macho to the nth degree. A code of conduct that permits no consideration of equal footing for women, a code where men stomp their stuff, swagger through their cynicism, and, bereft of positive male leadership, generally play out a stark hand as the lone pilgrim.

Certainly the lone pilgrim has never played a better hand than in those characters given life by John Wayne. The quintessential film that illuminates this loneliness, *The Searchers* (1956), finds Wayne portraying Ethan Edwards, a bitter soldier on the losing side of the Civil War, and a wandering man who needs his mission in life. Ethan's mission arrives, tragically, when he learns that Indians have slaughtered his brother, his brother's wife whom Ethan loved, and the remaining family members, save one. Comanches have taken a daughter, Debbie (Natalie Wood), captive for use as a squaw. Ethan's values are the classic macho's values: He hates Indians, he hates their ways, he hates sharing the country with them, and, frankly, he needs the vengeance to give his life some purpose (Solomon, 1976, p. 44). He must find Debbie, and he must kill her.

Ethan's convictions tell him that Debbie cannot return to a white society after experiencing Comanche traditions (see Kolodny, 1993; Slotkin, 1992, p. 461). Vengeance invests in Ethan a long-lasting fire, a burning desire to right his version of a wrong. He searches for five years before finding Debbie, a discovery that leads to still another revelation: He cannot kill her. Ethan changes, not readily, not even willingly, but he rises above his hard-earned experiences during the search to salvage what remains of a lost family.

The classic macho tradition, contrary to popular beliefs, is not a simple tradition. True, the macho hero or villain can prove one-dimensional in lesser films, with no allowance for change in character. But Ethan does change, and his shift in philosophy reflects a gruff sensitivity to spare Debbie and to return her safely.

A closing scene shows Ethan bringing Debbie home to other family members. The camera is positioned inside,

looking out through a doorway. Debbie and the other parties
enter the house, but Ethan stays on the porch, outside.
Outside, and ever the outsider. He pauses, gazing inside:
"...Wayne stands alone--looking in--holding his left elbow
with his right hand. He then breaks this stance, turns around,
and walks back into the wilderness. The door closes, leaving
the viewer in darkness" (Nash & Ross, 1987, p. 2790).

Ethan's choice not to enter appears less a choice than a
resigned destiny. Long ago, he chose a life without close
companionship, and his devotion to that life will not allow him
to forsake it and enter another world. Ethan's machismo does
not permit much change--enough to save Debbie, but not
himself. The searcher has rearranged his values, yet cannot
escape the isolation that his dark past commands. The classic
macho code, for all its cinematic glamour, exacts a high price
in the sacrifice of love, comfort, and fatherhood.

Will Penny (1968), another western, offers a stronger case
of cinematic reality. Charlton Heston as Will Penny shows us
the tenuous working life of the cowboy, a man wedded to the
trail. Will is getting older, and he knows that a serious injury
can threaten his livelihood, indeed his very survival. The
movie's storyline gives him an opening to change his life. He
receives that rare opportunity to join a family with a good
woman, Catherine (Joan Hackett), and her son. Will stands a
better chance than Alan Ladd's Shane to relinquish the
haphazard hardships of wandering the range for the more
predictable hardships of farming. But Will casts his fortune
with what he feels is right. He has spent many dusty years as
a cowboy. It's what he knows, what he does, and the men that
he works with on the trail.

Will can't change, or he won't change to accommodate a
different life. A life with a family, in fact, that proves more
sensible for an aging cowpoke. Instead, Will Penny chooses to
stay on the move, despite the likelihood of a desolate end.
Thinking of Will's plight and considering everyday reality, the
classic macho does not make much sense. He distinguishes his
persona with crustiness and lonely forbearance; he pursues--
on his terms--a clearly defined philosophy of masculine rights
and wrongs. He can change a little, as Ethan Edwards did,

and become more than a vacuous stereotype. But the classic macho, for all his mystique and erotic allure, fails to muster much hope as a male committed to long-term relationships.

He seems unlikely to benefit from an accumulation of shared experiences that may permit a closer intimacy with his loved ones. When the change does not materialize and the classic macho retains his frosty demeanor, the social distance can foster a masculinity that disparages intimacy. Garth Brooks's video, *The Thunder Rolls* (1991), requires only 4 minutes and 26 seconds of music to tell a story of the classic macho philanderer who abuses his wife and holds other women in contempt. The abuser (Brooks disguised in glasses and a beard) uses his mistress for self-gratification, nothing more. He leaves her to arrive home amid a torrent of rain. Unknown to the womanizer, his scorned mistress calls the wife and reveals the husband's adultery. We see his wife, her face bruised from a previous beating, anxiously awaiting him. They argue, he strikes her, then spots his little daughter on the stairway.

He moves toward the daughter...to do what? Strike her? Molest her? Or simply carry her upstairs? We aren't sure, but his wife's reaction suggests a dreadful outcome. The wife decides to end his reign of terror. She reaches for a revolver and challenges him to cease and desist; he beckons with his hands, daring her to fire. She does. Her action accompanies the crash of a tree through the window, adding to the tumultuous storm. The aggressor, the classic macho of unreserved disdain for women, meets the classic macho's death, triggered by a contemptuous dare and a swagger.

What a waste: The promise of familial affection, lost; the promise of teaching a child the positive virtues of life, lost; the promise of tenderness and dedication to render the male a responsible parent, all lost. The classic macho dies not fit easily into a world of family values.

Modern Machos

Contemplating movie reality, the modern macho comes closer
to everyday performance than the classic macho. Cinematically, **modern machos** are less easily classified by genderisms,
and more likely to engage in sensitive partnerships.

A message on the emptiness of the lone macho theme
occurs in *Man In The Wilderness* (1971). Zachary Bass
(Richard Harris), suffering severe wounds from a grizzly
attack and left for dead by his male compatriots, somehow
ekes out a solitary existence. Zachary deals with the basics of
life: How to stay alive at any cost, and then, when he is
stronger, how to elude hostile Indians. At one point, weak but
hidden, Zachary observes an Indian squaw dismount and
position herself to give birth. The father, her escort in this
venture, gazes patiently, quietly waiting for the miracle of a
newborn. Life is faint in the wilderness, but tenacity and an
incentive to survive give life a chance. For Zachary, the
incentive rests with a son who waits for him (the mother has
died). Zachary's silence and endurance go beyond the classic
macho stereotype. He makes a commitment to fatherhood, the
kind of commitment that John Wayne's character of Ethan
denies himself. The modern macho seeks a connection with
others, whereas the classic macho can do without--or he **does**
do without, whatever his true preferences.

Modern machos with the trappings of a classic macho
mentality, like Zachary, desire a caring relationship. Clouding
this sensitivity, however, is the macho's penchant to jockey for
the male advantage, particularly the kind of leverage that
helps him to advance himself. This male savvy strikes home
through the feisty alliance of a boozy reporter, Peter Warne
(Clark Gable), and a spoiled heiress, Ellie Andrews (Claudette
Colbert), in *It Happened One Night* (1934) (see Kendall, 1990,
p. 26; and Cavell, 1981, p. 71). Ellie's fleeing from her tycoon
father who wants to isolate his daughter from her insipid
husband. Ellie has married more to spite her father than for
true love. This spite places a confused and unhappy Ellie in
the novel position of traveling incognito to New York by bus
to reach her "beloved."

Peter and Ellie, by cinematic coincidence, happen on the same bus. Love and humor become an equalizer in their sparring, softening Peter's macho posturing on those few occasions when Ellie gains the upper hand. One famous scene, in which Ellie proves that "the limb is mightier than the thumb," finds Ellie's shapely legs more productive than Peter's frantic thumbing in gaining the two wayfarers a ride.

Peter's a classic macho in attitude, but a modern macho at heart. He's more worldly than she, wiser in the ways of the common folk, and knows better the value of a dollar. Yet Peter's love for Ellie brings his mercenary, macho ambitions crashing down. He's a reporter and she's a story, so the scoop on her flight from daddy should come first. Every viewer expects, nonetheless, that as a modern macho, Peter will succumb to love. He does so reluctantly, expressing sarcasm and amazement over his need for Ellie and her screwball ways...but succumb he does.

Still, the prevalent problem for most modern machos concerns, not a softening of their classic machismo stance, but the apprehension that they are not macho enough. Their desire to assume a classic masculinity creates despair for them and loved ones who must weather the modern machos' tempest-tossed episodes. Physical strength, once of practical import in work, now realizes only specialized exhibitions. One such exhibition is the **cosmetic response** in which bodybuilding helps the modern macho to look strong, even if he finds few relevant outlets to utilize his weight-lifted physique (Gagnon, 1971). The loss of physical strength as a useful, outward manifestation of manliness complements the inward insecurities of the beached male. He's macho but not genuinely macho, inside or out.

How does he work through this problem and embrace the classic macho demeanor? One way, if he has money, is to become a cowboy, just like the "old" days. Return to the land of classic macho lore and make physical strength and endurance count for something again. *City Slickers* (1991) offers that solution to three disenchanted males of the urban maze. Phil (Daniel Stern) agonizes under the cross of his shrewish wife, a woman who holds the family wealth and who calls the shots on Phil, including how much time he can spend at a party. Phil diddles sexually on the side, an indiscretion that blows a gasket in his marriage when the diddlee comes to the party and publicly proclaims her pregnancy. Becoming a cowboy seems a smooth escape for Phil, considering his turmoil at home and his ineptness at asserting himself.

Ed (Bruno Kirby) presents a contrasting figure. He craves adventure, indulging himself to live a carefree lifestyle as he talks the others into crazy vacations that risk life and limb. Ed portrays a stud on the run, seeking his machismo through excitement. He makes a surprising move and marries, but his responsibilities do not extend to children. Ed sees the cowboy caper as simply another diversion, a way to confirm the freedom that he feels compelled to pursue.

Mitch (Billy Crystal) gives us the balanced portrait of a man with a family, a marketing executive whose product jingles have gone flat, and whose marriage is following suit. Mitch doesn't know if he can "find himself"; he doesn't know if two weeks as a cowboy will help; nor does his wife know if she can continue to abide a hapless husband. This depression reaches a humorous peak as Mitch, called upon to tell his son's grade-school class about his work, conjures up such a lackluster description that he leaves the entire class feeling melancholy.

Knowing about movies that dramatize men who seek to resurrect their manhood, both with a laugh and a tear, you know that the three spiritually impoverished males find their masculine niche in life. Phil goes a little crazy, but it's a macho kind of crazy that ultimately allows him to pull his spirits up by the bootstraps. Ed remains the least likeable character, and the one who takes longest to admit his need for a family. Mitch, however, personifies the film's centerpiece. He's the wiseacre yet troubled male who finds an unexpected friend in a brusque ranch foreman, Curley (Jack Palance), a true throwback to the classic machos of yore.

Curley says little, befitting the classic macho figure, but he lives by a simple philosophy, one that he conveys to Mitch. Curley is unattached, a classic macho state, although he does recount the story of his most memorable love. The love concerns a girl that Curley sees from afar, a full-figured woman in a field who leaves an indelible impression on the lone cowpoke. Mitch does not understand at first. He asks Curley why he left, why he chose not to approach her. Curley replies cryptically that simply gazing upon this special woman inspired a moment without comparison. A moment that Curley knew he could not surpass by further action on his part. Romance, marriage, family--these obligations did not square with his life. If you knew the vision was exquisite, if you savored it, that sensation should be enough. Curley's elementary code suits the classic macho, and Mitch manages to adapt the experience to ease his own masculine worries.

Physical confrontations and hardships contribute to changes in how the three males think of their masculinity. But the most intriguing change occurs for Mitch through his fleeting rapport with Curley. When Curley dies, sitting upright as if etched in stone, Mitch realizes that Curley's philosophy, for him, either will bear fruit or turn to dust. Mitch, Phil, and Ed must drive the cattle themselves. Naturally, they succeed. And naturally they return to civilization as modern machos more assured and in control of their desires. The women in their lives, all secondary to the story's masculine quest, benefit from lovers who bring to them a renewed appreciation of intimacy. (Renewed, that is, except for Phil and his wife. She's out, and a female cowpoke that Phil meets in his adventurous West, is in.)

Machos And Authority

The two male types, though not independent of one another's concerns, do respond differently to **authority**. The classic macho often portrays a self-proclaimed authority, or, at best, affects a disdainful attitude regarding the top echelon.

Rick (Humphrey Bogart) behaves as the classic macho personality in *Casablanca* (1942) and operates under a regime of Nazi oppression, but remains quietly scornful of his "superiors." Paul Henreid's Victor Laszlo, the French patriot and a modern macho character, wears his emotions more boldly. He openly defies his adversaries, as in the famous scene in which the Nazis tauntingly sing a war song, only to be challenged by Laszlo and his allies who drown them out with the French national anthem, "La Marseillaise!".

Authority denotes a central entity in defining the macho personality. The classic macho and the reigning authority figure are either united, or they represent grave enemies, with no quarter given. Authority describes the essence of the classic macho's sexuality. If he surrenders weakly to another power, he diminishes himself sexually by sacrificing his character's masculine strength.

The modern macho's masculinity proves more ambivalent because he may not have the resourcefulness to accomplish the deeds of a classic macho, or because he feels less inclined to give loyalty and honor high prestige. For Henreid's Laszlo, he believes in his cause and is a leader, but he must rely on Rick to ensure his freedom. Laszlo, moreover, must depend on Rick to relinquish Illa (Ingrid Bergman), a sacrifice that Rick honors in the grand tradition of the classic macho's ability to live a life of self-reliance.

How far will a classic macho go to retain his self-reliance in the face of daunting odds? Well, consider two movies that appear similar in setting and plot, yet strike a different intent concerning the classic macho's confrontation with authority. *Mister Roberts* (1955) offers a wartime look at a naval ship, the U.S.S. Reluctant, a supply vessel whose officers and crew are low on morale and essentially out of the war. Henry Fonda plays the classic protagonist, Mr. Roberts, and James Cagney the antagonist, a petty captain who runs the supply ship like a self-indulgent Napoleon. Roberts has no respect for the Captain, and the Captain, knowing he needs Roberts to maintain morale, resents his executive officer's attempts to transfer out and get into the war.

Mister Roberts enjoys the basic thrust of a comedy, despite the coarse animosity between the two central characters. The film, as did the play, communicates the importance of humor among men "pitched" to fight, but unable to fight because of circumstance. Humor means release, and the men must find release to tolerate the Captain and the ship's tedious routine.

The movie carries forth a comedic arsenal of pranks and sexual shenanigans, darkened by periods of despair and resignation.

A series of events finally permits Mr. Roberts to transfer out. Later, however, the men learn that he loses his life in action. This solemn moment leads to the film's humorous climax. Ensign Pulver (Jack Lemmon) blusters and struts throughout the film, yet never demonstrates sufficient macho courage to defy the Captain. Roberts' death gives Pulver that courage. In a fit of comic rage, Pulver grabs the Captain's precious palm trees and throws them overboard. The closing scene shows the Captain placing his hand over his face, realizing that he must now cope with another Mr. Roberts.

One Flew Over The Cuckoo's Nest (1975) presents an interesting parallel in that the classic anti-hero, McMurphy (Jack Nicholson), squares off against the mental health establishment, coldly personified by Nurse Ratched (Louise Fletcher). McMurphy is not really crazy, he's just macho wild and unruly, an opportunist. His leadership over the other mental inmates, most of whom are not crazy, permits the film its humorous episodes. But this movie is not a comedy at heart. This film is a tragedy, a sad testimony to the human dignity that slips away in a sanitized setting of boredom and routine--not unlike the U.S.S. Reluctant.

McMurphy cannot prevail, of course. Nurse Ratched's sanctimonious authority must remain inviolate, even to the point of authorizing a lobotomy on McMurphy and reducing this robust character to a vegetative state. An Indian, Chief Bromden (Will Sampson), cushions the tragedy by responding to the vital McMurphy that he remembers. Bromden commits two acts of freedom: First, he smothers McMurphy to death, giving the rebel a release that he knows McMurphy would appreciate. And second, Bromden frees himself by escaping the institution, preferring to tackle the world outside than remain in a timeless ward.[6]

Roberts and *Cuckoo* appear, on the surface, to constitute comparable films. Both movies involve a demoralized group of individuals--sailors and patients--caught in the tedium of life's baser moments; both movies elevate a scheming spoilsport to the status of frightening authority; and both movies introduce classic nemeses, Roberts and McMurphy, whom the antagonists cannot defeat in a fair contest. Ratched fails to rival McMurphy's leadership and decides to preserve her rule by taking him, and his disturbing macho intrusiveness, out of the scene. The Captain, too, finds himself unable to match Mr. Roberts' superior leadership, and, losing face, finally permits him to transfer away.

So, why is *Roberts* a comedy at heart, and *Cuckoo* a tragedy? The artistic integrity of a comedy or tragedy encompasses the entire film (see Lesson 6), but let's simplify this approach and concentrate on the repercussions of Roberts' and McMurphy's death. The ship's captain commands absolute authority, a status that the Reluctance's Captain uses to vain advantage. Still, the Captain keeps losing, and losing humorously, during the movie. He loses when he fails to realize, for a considerable time, that Ensign Pulver is aboard his vessel; he loses when Roberts gains his freedom to depart; and he loses when a revitalized Pulver indicates the friction will continue. A captain should be a captain, but Cagney's Captain remains too handicapped and too vulnerable to turn the U.S.S. Reluctance into a tragedy.

Not so with Nurse Ratched. She is a slick automaton in starched white garb. Her vulnerability lies in having her authority usurped, and no one, not even McMurphy, can disarm that authority indefinitely. Nurse Ratched represents the system, indeed, she **is** the system. The most visible instrument of a bureaucracy that narcotizes its inhabitants and maintains life at a tranquil, low hum of efficiency. Day in, day out, the mental ward encapsulates a constancy of drabness, dullness, a pall of inactivity. Ratched is a tragedy unto herself because she personifies the disparaging philosophy of treating her patients as nonentities. Chief Bromden's escape may strike a personal mark against her, but his disappearance will not unseat the woman. Nurse Ratched possesses a greater power to persevere than the Captain. She is a villain of reckoning for any classic macho. The Captain is not.

Gay Machos

If an antithesis exists to the cinematic macho, it rests with the characterizations of gays on film. A **gay macho** seems a contradiction in terms. Macho denotes a genderism that indicates an exaggeration of masculine conduct. But the popular conception of gays focuses less on masculinity and more on discovering the proper gender niche. Any assumption, therefore, that gays somehow depict the opposite of machismo denotes a genderism in reverse: Genderism in this instance is equated with sexual bias, the kind of bias that tees off against the gay posture.

Sexual bias arises because individuals interpret information given to them according to predetermined beliefs about sexuality. The bias may prove positive or negative, but whatever the value judgment, it constitutes an individual's inclination to hold a certain conception about sexuality. Let's assume that you harbor a modest bias against homosexuals. A **homosexual bias** includes prejudice against gays, expressed mostly through a passive desire to disavow their sexual orientation. **Homophobia**, by contrast, signals a strong irrational reaction to anyone and anything that smacks of homosexuality (Gramick, 1983; Fyfe, 1983; Basow, 1980, p. 215). The homophobic, possibly to convince himself that he possesses no drop of homosexual empathy, may resort to an active persecution of gays, even invoking the pathetic practice of "gay bashing."

Is this sexual bias, modest or extreme, a reasonable profile of how gay characters appear in movies? Vito Russo, author of *The Celluloid Closet* (1981, 1987), chronicles an annotated bibliography of almost 500 films that bear on male and female homosexuality. The films are not all mainstream vehicles, and the homosexuality in question refers to the presence and sometimes the mere suggestion of gay figures and themes. Some instances, moreover, depict gays and ideas about gays in the original work, such as a novel, but are absent in the movie.

Russo's bibliography carries its history back to silent films where comedian Fatty Arbuckle paraded in drag in *Miss Fatty's Seaside Lovers* (1915), and where director Cecil B. De

Mille displayed two lesbians kissing during an orgy scene in *Manslaughter* (1922). But the earliest expression using **gay** as a homosexual reference does not surface, apparently, until Cary Grant ad-libs a line in *Bringing Up Baby* (1938): "When Katherine Hepburn's Aunt Elizabeth (May Robson) discovers Cary Grant in a lace nightgown, she asks him if he dresses like that all the time. Grant leaps in the air and shouts hysterically, 'No! I've just gone *gay*...all of a sudden!' This exchange appears in no version of the published script" (Russo, 1987, p. 47; also see Boswell, 1980, p. 43).

Alas, it requires another 23 years to shake free of the Hay's censorship code before the makers of *Victim* in 1961 bare sufficient moxie to use the word **homosexual**, and to permit one man to say "I love you" to another man (Phillips, 1975, p. 159; Russo, 1987, p. 126).[7] The film centers on a respected lawyer who jeopardizes his career as he attempts to avenge the death of a former male lover. The creators of *Victim* engaged in a daring venture, made all the more impressive by their sympathetic portrayal of gays.

Most movies do not offer such sympathetic fare, as Vito Russo reiterates throughout his history of homosexual films. Too many films reinforce gay stereotypes via a cornucopia of ridicule, violence, and victimization. These sexual traps tell uninformed viewers that gays are hapless people who lead hopeless lives, especially when compared to the sacred "rightness" of heterosexual relationships. Gay males and females on the screen come across as losers, BIG losers, particularly when their characters and stories are compromised by the practices of cinematic timidity and cinematic abnormality (Adair, 1981, p. 300; Phillips, 1975, p. 157).

Cinematic timidity refers to movies that abandon or neutralize the possibility of a homosexual theme. Alfred Hitchcock's *Strangers On A Train* (1951), for example, does not explore the mutual masculine attraction of presumably dissimilar personalities--namely, the sexual appeal of Farley Granger as an ambitious tennis star, coupled with Robert Walker's pathological charm as a spoiled playboy. The screen version of *Cat On A Hot Tin Roof* (1958) also plays down the hero's latent homosexuality, a feature the stage play develops.

Midnight Cowboy (1969) denies any gay relationship uniting the characters portrayed by Dustin Hoffman and Jon Voight, and buttresses this denial by leaning on gay characters in the film as guilt-ridden faggots. *Midnight Express* (1978) chooses to depart from its true story by skirting a gay relationship that transpires between the lead character and a prisoner, whereas *The Color Purple* (1985) prefers to ignore a lesbian relationship in the film that occurs in the novel (Smith, 1991; Russo, 1987, p. 80).

Arguably an admission of homosexuality would have made certain "timid" films more comprehensible in character motivation and storyline (Sayre, 1982, p. 141; Mellen, 1977, p. 286). Timidity, furthermore, imposes stronger limitations on gay males than gay females. Lesbian portrayals of intimacy appear easier for an audience to accept than to witness two males kissing on screen (Bell-Metereau, 1985, p. 118).

The alternative judgment, sometimes difficult to distinguish, concerns the caution not to imagine a homosexual relationship where none exists. This possibility generalizes to the idea that assuming a homosexual bond between two characters is guesswork at times. Such guesswork may depend as much on the viewer's homosexual bias--and its effect on the viewer's Oz process--as on actual happenings in the movie. Therefore, certain relationships, say, in *Butch Cassidy And The Sundance Kid* (1969) and that between Rick and Renault in *Casablanca* (1942), appear a straightforward depiction of close friendships that are nonsexual (Mellen, 1977, p. 285; Greenberg, 1975, p. 89). But, then, from the gay perspective, perhaps not...

Cinematic abnormality contrasts with timidity by vividly illustrating the oppression and degradation of living a gay life (see Simpson, 1993). The constant fear of discovery, from others and from one's self, leads ultimately to suicide for a politician in *Advise And Consent* (1962); and to the masking of an intricate plan between gay lovers who are intent on terminating the wife of one of the lovers in the 1982 film, *Deathtrap* (see Smith, 1991; and Phillips, 1975, p. 159).

Viciousness also plays a paramount role in showing the dark nature of a gay murderer who stalks females. This negative portrayal receives melodramatic emphasis in *The Silence Of The Lambs* (1991). Ted Levine's gay serial murderer--complete with a dog named Precious--tells us that we should expect gay males to display hostility toward women, and that a few misbegotten souls will even murder them for their skin. We should expect further that some males, realizing the deep-rooted fear of homosexual attraction, will engage in an adverse reaction and behave violently to bolster their heterosexual defenses against gays. Al Pacino portrays one such homophobic male in *Cruising* (1980), a movie that views other gays as dead meat and the murderer as a sadomasochistic misanthrope.

Attractive gay males occasionally come to life on screen. The long-married, gay lovers of *La Cage aux Folles* (birds of a feather) (1979) encounter hilarious complications when the son of one of the lovers from an early marriage comes home to marry...a woman. Likewise, Robert Preston's exuberant gay character in *Victor / Victoria* (1982) breezes through a comedy of misunderstandings and mixed-up genders. And John Malkovich's thoughtful gay figure in *Queen's Logic* (1991) becomes the one male to maintain a perceptive steadfastness in a group where the heterosexual males appear off-center and out of control.

One of the most positive treatments of gay masculinity derives, ironically, from a kaleidoscope of loving relationships in *Longtime Companion* (1990). Ironic because this comedy/drama tells of gay love in a 1980's decade of hope, marred indelibly by the quiet invasion of microscopic intruders called the AIDS viruses. Ironic, too, because the AIDS decade inspires gut-level acts of male compassion and sacrifice that give the title **gay machos** its finest expression.

AIDS, an acronym for **Acquired Immune Deficiency**, technically refers to the last stage of full-blown symptoms as the immune system verges on collapse (Bateson & Goldsby, 1988, p. xv). But a casual interpretation of this acronym during its prominence in the 1980s broadens the disease's medical usage, and, additionally, burdens the affliction with semantic baggage that carries political, economic, philosophical, and social consequences. It is the social consequences that *Longtime Companion* chooses to explore.[8]

The expression "longtime companion" can mean a person of either gender who has weathered a goodly number of years in some devoted capacity to another individual, also of either gender. But this idea translates uniquely to "lover" in the homosexual community. Thus, "longtime companion" denotes a heterosexual affectation for publicly acknowledging the private business of gay sexuality (Ebert, 1993, p. 393). The movie *Longtime Companion* presents a chronology of this private business, beginning with the news announcement on July 3, 1981 of a baffling cancer that appears concentrated among members of the community.

This toll seems distant to the microcosm of gay lovers and friends who we come to know casually during the AIDS onset of the eighties. Our particular group of gay buddies cavort at the beach, bantering and posturing their joy in the effusiveness of a bonding companionship. Two lovers, David (Bruce Davison) and Sean (Mark Lamos), the longest of the longtime companions, sit in beach chairs, side by side, facing the sea. Momentarily, a hunk of a hunk comes prancing into their panoramic view, and, deftly counting a beat, both heads turn in unison to appraise this masculine doll--a familiar practice at beaches, but performed here with unfamiliar players.

The film offers snippets of gay life: A prelude to sex here, a squabble between lovers there. Nothing so earthshaking as to undermine the movie's relentless journey through ordinary relationships set adrift by the killer AIDS. April 30, 1982 offers up the first casualty, John (Dermot Mulroney), shown with the camera peering from above, tethered to a network of life-support machines. He's young--the youngest-looking of the group--and, oh, so helpless. We never see John having sex to know the virus's origins, but we know he's doomed, put to earth by his own passion. A killer of the cruelest kind since the virus stalks the very physical sexuality that gays have paid a price of misunderstanding and prejudice to enjoy.

June 17, 1983 brings a growing paranoia of symptoms, imagined and real. Sean feels that his body is not right. David reassures him that he has remained faithful since that affair at

Key West in 1980. Surely, Sean has no reason for concern. And surely, as we know now that having sex with someone is having sex with all who went before, the unpredictable incubation period of AIDS begins its assault on another victim.

Sean regresses to a simpler and simpler state. By March 22, 1985, Sean's job as a scriptwriter is in jeopardy when the boss calls about changes in the script. David, who is ghost-writing Sean's work, must coach his now childlike lover on what to say. Sean, glazed with incomprehension, says "No" when he should say "I'll think about it," and "I'll think about it" when he should say "No," thoroughly confusing his boss and causing David to go into a windmill of frantic gestures as he seeks to salvage Sean's job.

A later scene depicts David and Sean outside, taking in a fine day. Sean wanders away as David sits on a bench and reads. David looks up to see a woman smiling, and hesitantly he smiles back; then the woman gazes past him and David sees her smile fade to puzzlement: Sean, blissfully unaware of his surroundings, is peeing in public. An intelligent, creative, loving man has, through **AIDS dementia** (infection of the brain tissue), been transformed into a child of need, a bare whisper of his former self.

January 4, 1986 sees a bedridden Sean, struggling to speak as David and a friend change his disposable diaper. Finally, the time of gracious release arrives. Sean mutters "Let go" and David takes up the appeal, encouraging him to leave the pain. David, urging him away through soft utterances, eases his longtime companion's exit with Sean's own words of "Let go," repeated tenderly to cushion the victim's last breaths. Sean departs, merely another statistic on the AIDS list, another "good riddance" from the hate clan of homophobes, possibly another "God's retribution" from the fundamentalists' sect-- but an immeasurable loss to David.

Longtime Companion, nonetheless, reflects an ensemble piece. Other players grieve and die as AIDS savages their once halcyon days and delivers them to a new, sobering reality. If David and Sean personify the group's center of stability, then Willy (Campbell Scott) embodies the group's conscience. Willy comes to visit early in Sean's illness, spooked by the virus and by his concern that he will be next. When he leans down for Sean to greet him with a kiss, Willy nervously turns his lips away so that the kiss lands on Sean's cheek. His maneuver is slight but noticeable to us.

Afterward, excusing himself to use the bathroom, Willy earnestly scrubs his face and hands, willing this act to cleanse himself of Sean's contamination. His dialogue with the others remains superficial, although no one indicates an awareness of Willy's discomfort. We know, however, that he is at a loss to reconcile his conflicting desires. Friends are friends, but the virus...well, the virus looms like an invisible leech, threatening his very existence.

Willy demonstrates the finality of his conflict at David's house. Friends arrive to console David and to view Sean before his removal. Willy touches Sean tentatively and remarks shyly to David that "He's still warm." Alone with Sean, Willy reaches a decision and grasps Sean's hand more firmly. The decision, long in development, finds resolution through Willy's action, and his determination to confront the disease as a fighter.

July 19, 1989 sees three figures walking the beach. Willy, Willy's lover, Fuzzy (Stephen Caffrey), and a longstanding friend to the group, Lisa (Mary-Louise Parker), stroll the sands and reminisce about the group and the good times. They remain. And of the three, Fuzzy, seen for the first time without his trademark beard, has the disease. He does not yet resemble another Sean, but the formula is well known by now.

They fantasize about the group's reunion, indeed, about the reunion of all those they knew who left them. Fuzzy says, "Can you imagine what it would be like?" Lisa speculates that it would be "Like the end of World War II." Willy asserts, "I just want to be there." And, magically, they are. A boisterous horde comes thundering down the walkway and onto the beach. They're back. Alive and alive before the death knell of AIDS, before the decimation. Friends greet friends, and lovers find lovers. Willy, Fuzzy, and Lisa run with the spirit of their imagination, realizing for a fleeting moment the wonder of the group's affection and bonhomie. A virility of manhood before the fall.

The moment passes, and they are alone again. But the spirit remains, the happy thought that one day such a reunion will happen: AIDS, defeated; and life, resurrected.

The male's "Achilles heel" concerns his deceptively robust presence. His cinematic masculinity, whether invested of a classic, modern, or gay bearing, depends on a guardianship of bravado and ferocity. A guardianship too fraught with risk and sadness to accord the macho male much chance to persevere. The classic macho wraps himself in loneliness and austerity. The modern macho quietly yearns for a manhood beyond his awkward reach. The gay macho struggles to overcome the stigma of his peculiar masculinity in a heterosexual society. Given these darker appraisals, none of the three cinematic portrayals provides a manhood of confidence that stays the course in sexual commitment. Each male must learn to tend his personal gremlins and earn a masculinity that creates the intimacy, sharing, and blessings of a blossoming relationship.

The cinematic ease with which macho machos find their pomp and circumstance usurped occurs dramatically in a scene from *The Big Country* (1958). Gregory Peck plays a retired sea captain and Charlton Heston a ranch foreman. The two men dislike each other for sundry reasons, including their competition for a certain young lady, so it's no surprise that they ultimately fight to decide who's the most macho macho. Their bare-knuckles contest happens privately, at night, in the middle of a large field. But the director, William Wyler, placed his camera at a considerable distance from the actors.

Heston, in a television interview, admitted that he first thought Wyler had made a mistake. Does it make sense to show two tall men as diminutive figures whom the viewer can hardly see? Wyler thought so, perhaps because showing two hefty males dwarfed by a "Big Country" helped to emphasize the insignificance of the men and their dispute. The characters and the fight gain an added dimension because of this distance. No matter how dominant the males appear, the land overwhelms them in its sweeping grandeur.

Two men, churning up dust, settling their differences in manly fashion...Two shadowy figures, groping and poking in the throes of another senseless scuffle...Two specks, flailing away, inching their way toward oblivion.

Notes

1. One Hollywood story concerns the claim that David Selznick, producer of *Gone With The Wind*, had to pay a $5000 fine in 1939 for permitting the "damn" to be said. Furthermore, according to Timothy Jay's (1992, p. 219) study of the subject, Rhett Butler's original line was "Frankly, my dear, I don't care." David Selznick argued persuasively that "damn" was essential to Rhett's parting from Scarlett. However, surveying the tussle between David Selznick and the Hays Office of censorship, film historians Leonard Leff and Jerold Simmons (1990, p. 105) comment on the fine as legend rather than fact: "...As one critic quipped, the real shock was not that Rhett Butler cursed Scarlett but that he took so long to do so" (p. 106).

2. Swear words enjoy a varied sexual history in that the passing centuries do not lock a word in place. A few words--a precious few--retain considerable intensity over time, although their application becomes more expansive. One clearly comprehends that *fuck* refers to sexual intercourse, but a *good fuck, bad fuck, easy fuck,* and so forth serve to qualify the act of intercourse and give it a coarse breath of subtlety. *Fuck*, moreover, can relate to almost anything **besides** sexual intercourse, depending on the swearer's delivery and reason for swearing (e.g., a *fucking* fine morning...) (Montagu, 1967, pp. 314-315). Inevitably, cultural attitudes change, occasionally accelerated through the dramatic revisions of rebellion and revolution, so that blue words shift to reflect these revisions (see Hughes, 1992, p. 206; and Gass, 1976, p.25).

3. The connection between a male's chronic swearing and his sexual forays remains elusive. Harry Truman's public epithets failed to compromise his adversity to improper sexual behavior. The man's blue language did not trespass upon his sexual standards (Miller, 1973, p. 356). And, despite the knowledge that Richard Nixon used invectives freely, perhaps the one accusation not made against him concerns any attempt to associate his verbal improprieties with questionable sexual conduct. Conversely, a few presidents not singled out for their dirty language have let their standards slip to become sexual Romeos.

4. Academically, **macho** opens the door to certain semantic kinfolk, including **machismo, hypermasculinity**, a **man's man**, a **ladies' man**, and other related terms awash in the vicissitudes of sex and gender (Mosher, 1991; Glass, 1984; Pleck, 1981, p. 95). The distinctions made about these labels can be academic indeed, too elegant for us to pursue with our movie heroes.

From a cinematic perspective, **macho, machismo**, and **hypermasculinity** serve to acknowledge the male's exaggerated bearing and conduct. A bearing and conduct that underscore his masculinity, but do so as a stereotype, a genderism. The drawback to this perspective is that **macho** as a cinematic genderism does not permit much subtlety in personality, and leads easily to a blanket distortion of masculinity running amok (Guilbault, 1989). The filmmaker's creativity, then, begins with an artistic revision of the macho stereotype. This revision occurs by awarding masculinity an added dimension of vulnerability or tenderness or humor or change that transcends the expected machismo image.

5. Macho's latest innovation, however, appears to represent the ultimate parody. Robots, cyborgs, argonauts--whatever--offer us a new wave of classic macho characters. You can't become much more macho than to be a robot willing to face anything, and to keep coming back until every screw is loose. Arnold Schwarzenegger's bad robot in *The Terminator* (1984) and his return as a good robot in *Terminator 2* (1991) give forth a stark macho presence, complete with dark sunglasses and cryptic lines like "I'll be back." Arnold's character captures all the distant features needed to drive a classic macho personality except for sex...and even there, who knows?

6. Considerable searching occurred to find the exact words for Bromden to say when he "releases" McMurphy. After much trial and error in discarding different lines, Bromden finally utters just two words as he leans over McMurphy: "Let's go."

7. The gay male and the male who engages in homosexual behavior are not interchangeable souls. **Homosexual** as a label originated in the late 19th century (the Ancient Greeks had no word for homosexuality), but the term remains vague and suggestive of pathology. All in all, the use of "homosexual" as a noun to identify character carries a negative connotation to gay males (Schwartz, 1985, p. 150; Altman, 1982, p. 70; Bardis, 1980; Boswell, 1980, p. 42). "Homosexual" indicates greater usefulness as an adjective, such as describing a "homosexual marriage," so that the reference denotes an activity rather than a person (McWhirter & Mattison, 1984, p. 146; Altman, 1982, p. 42; Boswell, 1980, p. 44).

Gay depicts an older term, dating to the 13th century and the period of courtly love, although its early usage remains cloudy (Boswell, 1980, p. 43;

Schwartz, 1985, p. 150). Reinhold Aman (1979) proposes that the word **gay** developed from the Old English (Anglo-Saxon) **gal**, and that **gal** relates to merriment, pride, and lasciviousness. So gays prefer **gay** not only because of its positive connotation, but because it's more explicit than **homosexual**. "Gay" designates an erotic attachment of one male for another male, or of one male for the cultural expressions (poetry, art) of males who share his sexual philosophy (Boswell, 1980, p. 44). "Gay" of course serves other meanings, except that its nonsexual references to fun and frolic are overshadowed by the word's homosexual monopoly. Adversaries who decry gay's homosexual ownership and who find themselves hoping to change the word's meaning have pressed for a revision. The odds, however, do not look favorable (see Zorn's comments in *Newsweek*, November 5, 1990; and see replies to Zorn's plea for the return of **gay** to heterosexual usage in *Newsweek*, November 26, 1990).

8. A flu virus makes its uninvited presence known quickly, and in so doing triggers a complex chemical process of search-and-destroy activity from the host's immune system. Part of this chemical process involves **helper T cells** that "recognize" the intruding virus. These cells help by orchestrating, among other events, **killer T cells** to attack and eliminate the alien virus. Finally, a third cadre of T cells, known as **suppressor cells**, works to diminish the immune system's reaction when the invaders are vanquished. Further, should the same flu virus force its unwelcome presence at a later time, a population of helper and killer T cells will exhibit an immunological "memory" to recognize and attack the virus more quickly (unfortunately, we cannot count on the same flu bug arriving season after season).

What happens, therefore, when a "smarter" virus comes along? A virus, say, that has the capacity to quietly compromise the all-important helper T cells? Mary Catherine Bateson and Richard Goldsby, in their little book *Thinking AIDS* (1988, pp. 51-52), note that the AIDS family of viruses follows this deceptive strategy of stealth: "By contrast, Human Immunodeficiency Virus (HIV), the virus family that causes AIDS, tackles the immune system head-on. It actually takes up residence in the immune system and uses its reactions as a vehicle of its own multiplication. HIV infection results in a catastrophic loss of the helper T cell population....Once established, the virus makes another smart move. Unlike smallpox or polio, it does not immediately make the host gravely ill. Typically, after a brief episode of relatively mild illness, there is a latent period of seven to ten years which are virtually symptom-free. These apparently healthy carriers continue their normal patterns of life at full vigor, and hence are ideal vectors for spreading the disease." The backward puzzle of AIDS, where and how it began, remains a mystery. Possibly a less virulent virus existed that underwent mutation to a more lethal agent for humans. Actually, the bafflement of medical researchers as they attempt to sort out the disease's causative agents during the early 1980s is reflected in *Longtime Companion* by showing the gay characters' occasional erroneous conclusions about the disease.

AIDS, for all its devastation, constitutes a platform for making the homosexual lifestyle more visible in film. A small number of independent films and TV movies dealt with AIDS during the 1980s and 1990s, dramatizing a social range of reactions to the HIV virus (Pilipp & Shull, 1993). Still, what about Hollywood's hutzpah in presenting AIDS as an issue for a mainstream film? *Philadelphia* (1993) illustrates one such possibility, detailing the plight of a lawyer (Tom Hanks) fired from his firm because of the disease. But marketing for this movie involves a tremulous undertaking since, as journalist Mark Miller (1993, p. 99) observes, "...the film is the first major production to simultaneously take on two Hollywood taboos: AIDS and homosexuality." Therefore, how much legitimacy and how much mileage a disease like AIDS can lend to the gay cause on screen remain speculative (see Rosenberg, Miller, & Leland, 1994; and Corliss, 1994).

Lesson 5

B-B-Beauty

Jennifer rushes up and thrusts the color photo of a face (front view) in Susie's hand. "This is Dinky," whispers Jennifer. "He's seen you and wants to go out. I got the picture from his sister." Susie analyzes Dinky, or at least his face. Light blond hair, broad forehead, blue eyes (maybe), weak chin though, and he's not smiling. Susie computes, imagining how Dinky (Dinky!) would look if he were smiling, and how she would look with him. "How tall is he," Susie wants to know. "No problem," Jennifer assures her. "He's got a nice build and even if you're in heels, it's okay." Jennifer leans forward expectantly. Susie rocks back and forth, staring at the photo. "All right. Tell me more."

We normally judge sex appeal using better information than that invested in a snapshot. Upon meeting someone, you combine several channels of communication, such as speech, demeanor, posture, and gestures. This practice tends to lessen the face's importance in determining who is physically likeable (Ekman, Friesen, O'Sullivan, & Scherer, 1980). Susie's impressions of Dinky go beyond what the photo really tells her. Fortunately for her, she has Jennifer's appraisal of Dinky to fill in the blanks.

The face, however, translates into the performer's fame and fortune. The beauty need not be classic in the image of Elizabeth Taylor, guileless in the spirit of Julia Roberts, striking in the intrigue of Cher, sassy and volatile in the guise of Madonna, or starkly honest in the openness of Debra Winger. Beauty can drift to cover other characterizations too, but the limits beyond which snow turns to slush are unforgiving. Either the camera "loves" the face, or it doesn't.

That Wonderful Face...

Speaking summarily, SHE must be **photogenic** and **charismatic** in appearance. Photogenic? Well, that requirement includes numerous pretty faces and figures but also a sampling of imperfect faces and figures, some of which are concealed and some of which the imperfections leave a pleasing impression: Barbra's Streisand's nose, for instance. Charismatic? A mystery more difficult to solve except to say that most women either fail to project such appeal on the screen, or they possess a mere droplet of this visual magic.

How about males? Don't they suffer the same requirements? Yes, but only in approximation. Eye wrinkles, a busted nose, and pug ears may grace the male face to suggest toughness and maturity. Similar cryptic blemishes on the female face conjure up a bag lady or Witch Hazel. Beauty relaxes its stiff demands of males, but lowers the almighty boom on petrified females (Lakoff & Scherr, 1984, p. 282). Beauty is a tyrant to her, a pest to him.

The paradox of the face is that it projects **stability**, yet reflects **change** (Landau, 1989, pp. 59 & 221; Cross & Cross, 1971). Researchers, studying female infants and girls of grade-school age, suggest that facial attractiveness can become apparent early in life, and that the facial configuration (high cheekbones, for example) remains relatively stable compared to other features, such as hair style and cosmetic changes

(Hilderbrandt, 1983; Sussman, Muesuer, Grau, & Yarnold, 1983).

Individual differences, of course, create a range of possibilities between a face's stability and its capacity to change. Could you, for instance, recognize snapshots of your mother and father when they were children? Pictures of celebrities as children reveal a clear continuity of looks in some faces, but a disruption of this continuity in other examples. Still, whether a beauty reveals her attractiveness as a child or poses as an ugly duckling until that beauty blossoms forth, she needs an extraordinary "something" about her face to make her a commercial success. A "something" that the "ordinary woman" does not possess.

Physical appearance represents one branch of beauty's domain, a branch concerned with body image. **Body image** indicates an idea sufficiently abstract to foster numerous complications about how a female thinks of her physical appearance, and how she believes others think of her (Martin, 1987, p. 71; Korabik & Pitt, 1980; Bersheid & Walster, 1974). The woman of "average" looks, if such a woman exists, lacks a dimension of body image that the exceptionally beautiful woman imbues and obsesses over, notably an **ideal image**. An image of attractiveness particularly fetching to sell perfume, lawnmowers, sweatsuits, hard liquor, soft drinks, and, for a few chosen faces and figures, the lady Herself (Glassner, 1988, p. 22; Freedman, 1986, p. 43).

Beautiful women abound in the mass media where competition runs tight. An ideal image that demonstrates marketability relies on finding the proper look for the right product. Looks are specialized, not generic in this game. A female with beautiful hands does hand modeling; a female with trim legs or exquisite feet does leg or feet closeups; a female with lovely alabaster skin does...well, you get the idea.

A movie star whose physique fails to measure up on certain shots, or who refuses to appear nude in a scene, hires a body double. The double must resemble the star proportionally, and usually not much is said or promoted regarding the model's discreet substitution. Even models who present a fitting image, say, comparable to a swimmer (broad shoulders) or a dancer (lean and lithe), must undergo extensive makeup and subject themselves to the correct camera angles to appear "perfect" in face and form (Glassner, 1988, p. 41).

Arlo of the comic strip *Arlo & Janis* (Johnson, January 10, 1994) puts Hollywood's engineering of beauty most succinctly when he observes that "Hollywood's idea of an ugly woman is a pretty woman with glasses." For the movie industry, even an ugly duckling must secretly be a beauty in disguise.

Defining Beauty

So, what is this "something" that the cinematic beauty must offer the camera? To assume any kind of answer, the first requirement concerns reaching an orientation on defining beauty. For our purposes, imagine beauty according to three perspectives: the perceptual, the pragmatic, and the cinematic.

Perceptually, beauty registers early. Early enough for two-month-old infants to indicate a preference without the benefit of extensive cultural experience. Infants who gaze longer at female and male faces, already declared attractive by society's norms, may do so because they prefer the curves and vertical symmetry that attractive faces represent (Langlois, Roggman, Casey, Ritter, Rieser-Danner, & Jenkins, 1987).

This early preference facilitates more complex and subjective choices as society and peers indoctrinate youngsters into beliefs about what beauty is and is not.[1] Still, the perceptual strategies that define beauty also must accommodate a personal bent or twist that shades the viewer's unique assessment of physical attractiveness. A response to beauty does not invoke a pat formula, despite the mass media's apparent dogma of prerequisites and dimensions.[2]

John Liggett (1974, p. 140) in his book, *The Human Face*, recalls how medieval artists created a formula for the "perfect face" by dividing it into sevenths: the hair (one-seventh), forehead (two-sevenths), nose (also two-sevenths), nose to mouth (one-seventh), and mouth to chin (one-seventh). A certain comfort must exist in applying numbers to perfection and beauty, but, fortunately, the standards for these abstractions do not remain invariant.

Liggett supports the opposing view, namely, that we **impart** beauty **to** a face, and that we are more likely to do so when the face holds a pleasing ambiguity for us. He notes that film stars like Ingrid Bergman and Greta Garbo have faces which lack strong definition, thereby permitting observers latitude to draw their own conceptions of beauty from each face (Liggett, p. 156; also see Lakoff & Scherr, 1984, p. 83).

Pragmatically, beauty does not float passively in a vacuum (Patzer, 1985, p. 225). Beauty connects. Beauty works. Beauty creates a self-perpetuating image that makes the exceptionally attractive woman a different individual in self-concept, body image, career, and personal opportunities. Murray Webster and James Driskell (1983; also see Barthel, 1988, p. 87) argue that we should associate beauty with status. These researchers contend that a favorable status occurs for beauty; so favorable, they say, that beauty assumes the privilege of a **diffuse status characteristic**. This bit of jargon merely indicates the widespread belief that beautiful people are recognized more positively than people deemed less attractive (Barocas & Karoly, 1972).

One key in assessing beauty's pragmatic value involves **congruence**, the correspondence between attractiveness and usefulness. Congruence represents a means of putting beauty to the test. If attractiveness is not suitably matched to the task or product at hand, the quality becomes a handicap. A beautiful woman can prove too beautiful for a conservative firm's managerial position, too distracting for an advertisement selling recreational vehicles, or too flashy for casting in the role of a mousy housewife (Glassner, 1988, p. 29; Jackson, 1983a; Jackson, 1983b; Heilman & Saruwatari, 1979; Baker & Churchill, Jr., 1977). Practical constraints on the usefulness of beauty vary, but they are there (see Feingold, 1992; Eagly, Ashmore, Makhijani, & Longo, 1991).

Cinematically, beauty becomes sexuality. A first impression suggests that how a woman looks establishes her destiny in film. Thus, "What you see is what you get." A more apt expression, however, suggests defining cinematic beauty according to the dynamics of the Oz process: "What you see is what you **think** you get."

Recall that in Lesson 2 we met Shirley (Pauline Collins) of *Shirley Valentine* (1989), a Liverpool housewife who dreams her dreams by talking to herself as she seeks to enliven her humdrum existence.   Shirley lives a comfortable life, though she realizes little emotional connection with the family, especially her husband, Joe (Bernard Hill). Joe's a faithful and regular husband who immerses himself in his business. The part that bothers Shirley is Joe's regularity: his predictability, his drifting away from Shirley so that their earlier years of intimacy whisper only faintly to her.   Joe's past due and Shirley decides to rock the boat by leaving for the Greek resort island of Mykonos.

Whether a disenchanted woman like Shirley can become enraptured once more by having a lightly regarded affair with an Italian waiter, and by becoming a waitress herself, indicate a transition that seems more fantasy than reality. But what remains provocative about *Shirley Valentine* is the ending. Joe and Shirley's son, Brian (Gareth Jefferson), the one family member who understands his mother's need for reformation, accuses his father of being frightened of change and encourages him to go to Greece.   Joe, chastised, travels to Mykonos with the thought of convincing Shirley to return home.   Before his visit, Shirley offers her soliloquy to the audience. She's hopeful that Joe will stay, but her hope seems distant, almost a formality.

Upon his arrival, Joe walks up a pathway leading to the hotel where he expects to find Shirley. But Shirley, wearing sunglasses and dressed casually yet smartly, sits at a small table along the pathway--and Joe passes her as if she's a stranger. He gives her a glance, smiles briefly, and continues walking ahead.

Shirley has altered her appearance, not markedly, but in a womanly way. The setting helps, of course, although Shirley's look and attire differ compared to her Liverpool presence. Her posture and demeanor reflect a serene woman, someone richer in feeling, someone more content. You may assume that Joe just doesn't expect to see her there, at the table. You can accord him a little slack on that count, yet his single-mindedness betrays such tolerance. Joe searches for his Shirley, the comfortable "old-shoe" image that he's locked in place all these years. He hasn't bothered to see, or perhaps wanted to see, a different image.

Shirley calls to Joe, who turns, and with a glazed expression on his face, says "I didn't recognize you." Shirley replies, "I know. I used to be the mother. I used to be the wife. But now I'm Shirley Valentine again." Sexually, Shirley does not seek to regain her youth, but she does desire an image that permits her to experience more of life.

She invites Joe to sit and drink. Her tone and attitude suggest a relationship on trial. Shirley's changed. Can Joe? We don't know, and we aren't told. The movie closes with Shirley and Joe at their table by the sea. They talk, hesitantly it seems, as the credits roll. Their moment together can mark the beginning of something new, or merely the end of something old. Shirley, remember, has lived on Joe's terms for many years. Now she wonders if he can honor her convictions.

Perceptually, beauty depends on a compromise between consensus and personal appraisal. Pragmatically, beauty needs a function, a congruence of appearance and task. And cinematically, beauty must come alive through a mesmerizing grace. B-B-Beauty envelops the capacity to swell into a breathtaking, heart-pounding flash. The kind of photogenic beauty radiated by statuesque Miss Americas or by those lithesome women of the fashion world's "supermodel" elite.

One eminently photogenic beauty who exudes her share of breathtaking glamour remarked that she encountered males who, shocked by her sudden arrival, could only tremble and gape. Although this claim may stem merely from a case of lofty narcissism, the lady may, truthfully, have confirmed beauty's prowess as a magnetic presence.

Regardless, is this B-B-Beauty the stuff of cinematic magic? Can beauty, finely defined, sell tickets? If so, we should see numerous Miss Americas and even more super models on the big screen. But no, whatever photogenic delights a beauty brings to the camera, the viewers' Oz asks for something more: Beauty must realize, too, a dash of charisma. Something special must happen with the camera's eye that permits the beauty's face and good fortune to become more than picturesque.

Perhaps that specialty relates to a face not fully understood. A face in repose, teasing us with a hint of mystery. A face beyond our ready comprehension, yet a face we feel compelled to watch. A durable beauty that pragmatically tells us of earthiness, or gaiety, or innocence, or dangerousness. A beauty that makes us think.

Cinematic beauty depicts a visible sensuality in flux. Beauty may appear frozen in time, but beauty has a story to tell, a story that must convey the character's development. Beauty, as Shirley Valentine illustrates, is not static on screen; beauty endorses movement and mystique. Visible sensuality cannot lie untouched by a character's tribulations. What a character experiences, beauty imparts. Cinematic sexuality, more so for women than men, graces beauty as **the** priority in transmitting femininity's appeal. Gazing at the big screen, you engage in a discourse with the fluid beauty you see. It's what you think you get that allows the Oz process to flourish.

Alpha Roles

Indeed, the Oz process in our society draws on a beauty that, as an image, finds itself orchestrated largely by male directors, male producers, and male writers.[3] The cinematic beauty you know augers a beauty favoring youthful vulnerability over seasoned charm; a beauty adorning male prerogatives rather than female sovereignty; a beauty wicked as it is foolish; a beauty with its manifesto seemingly designed to keep Marsha saying, "John, please be careful," and John replying, "Now Marsha, don't you worry your pretty little head about it."

John's declaration pictures Marsha as **ornamental**. She's decorative. She's desirable. She looks terrific. Ergo, her beauty adorns the background and occasionally the foreground of numerous films. She portrays an **Alpha role** that permits her to do little more than function as a sounding board.[4] Her presence shows what the male has to lose, to gain, or to pursue. He acts, she reacts; he decides, she agrees; he leaves, she stays.

Sexually she's a dud in cinematic terms. No color to her cheeks, no wit to her personality, no oomph to her uumph. She's not Scarlett O'Hara (*Gone With The Wind*, 1939), not Rose Sayer (*The African Queen*, 1951), not Juliet (*Romeo And Juliet*, 1968), not Ripley (*Alien*, 1979), not Thelma or Louise (*Thelma & Louise*, 1991).

What she is, essentially, is someone who tiptoes around. She may appear for no other reason than to portray a convenient sexual partner--as Janet Leigh does for her ex-husband, Paul Newman, who plays a private detective in *Harper* (1966). Janet's character is pretty, but a bland prettiness, the kind of pretty that competently qualifies her for an Alpha role. She may display a dash of vim and vigor to tell us we have a spunky lady here, but the vim and vigor are perfunctory, exhibited sparingly to give her personality a little polish. Thereafter, she relaxes into a ho-hum supporting portrayal and shows only a ripple or two of initiative. After a rough day in *Harper*, Newman wants a little comfort with his bed and board, which Leigh reluctantly supplies. But by morning he's gone, and she's left in the lurch, again.

The Alpha role's most admirable qualities become the female's good heart, her fidelity to ladylike femininity, and her perspicacity in doing the right thing. The purest in heart were the serial queens, durable female roles like Kay Aldridge enjoyed as Nyoka in *Nyoka And The Tigermen* (1942), and Linda Stirling pursued as the Tiger Woman in *Perils Of The Darkest Jungle* (1944). Stirling's Tiger Woman (in a leopard outfit) even sits on a throne and gives orders, but not to the hero, played by Allan Rocky Lane. Tiger Woman exercises her athletic ability in riding a galloping horse, jumping from trees, and, in one scene, spinning a villain around on her shoulders before dumping him. Still, in other episodes her spunk submerges and she's captured and tied up with such frequency that Rocky Lane spends most of his free time rescuing her. Given the chaste principles of the serial genre, she neither kisses the hero nor suffers lewd overtures from her captors. She does, from time to time, show a little leg.[5]

Perhaps the greatest fault of a beauty playing an Alpha role concerns her failure at individuality. She's too good, too true, too transparent to convince us that we are viewing a lady with an intriguing past. She's a straightforward personality and not too exciting in her own right. Therefore, the story must "make" the lady interesting by placing her innocence in jeopardy. This tactic proves useful since, all too often, the Alpha character comes across as hapless and helpless, anyway (Mrs. Peel excepted; see End Note #5, page 162).

The **pristine sexuality** of an Alpha role denotes a cinematic setup. An Alpha character plays a more enticing victim because of her virginal allure and vulnerability. Hence, the beauty in an Alpha portrayal finds herself sexually strapped: screaming in the shower, screaming in her car, screaming almost anywhere as a victim of sex and violence. She communicates to the audience that her character cannot overcome, cannot persevere, cannot muster the smarts to defend herself against the lusty male: A generic plight that profitably drives many exploitation films.

Should we hold the Alpha character in contempt for her sheltered sexual existence? Pity her for an inability to ward off evil? Laugh at her for such naiveté? We can, of course. Snickers and smirks probably arise when a virginal beauty bites the dust, or when she gives herself selflessly to the man she loves. But there's a special dimension to pristine sexuality. A fascination, possibly a grudging respect for the woman who cherishes her sexual ethics. Alpha characters play by traditional rules and wish to give love and marriage a lasting relationship. Pristine sexuality carries a brief yet precious life: that threshold of young womanhood in which an Alpha screen personality finds her beauty (her sexuality) budding forth.

On rare occasions, this budding beauty becomes the focus of an absorbing story. Transport yourself back in time and imagine a group of finishing-school ladies enjoying a St. Valentine's Day picnic at Hanging Rock in Australia. A lurking strangeness pervades the picnic atmosphere. Then, something unexplainable happens. The official account indicates that on February 14, 1900, three girls disappear from this group, none of whom are ever found.

The film, *Picnic At Hanging Rock* (1975), reconstructs this disappearance but does so by adding a few dramatic touches, such as having one of the teachers also vanish, last seen running about in her "drawers," a Victorian no-no. And, later, the film has a young man discover one of the three missing girls still alive on the rock, although the girl cannot remember anything that happened--or so she says.

Peter Weir, the director, assumes a mystical approach that refuses to seek an answer regarding the girls' true disappearance. Instead, he uses the film as a projective device to inspire different interpretations. One of the girls, before she vanishes, prophetically (?) remarks that "Everything begins and ends at exactly the right time and place." Did she and the other girls plan a collective suicide? Did they find their present life meaningless and the possibility of an afterlife more enchanting? Or did the girls' disappearance point to three cases of murder? We have no way of knowing. Moreover, unlike the penchant of American films to tell all, *Picnic At Hanging Rock* ends without any final revelation.

Weir prefers to make the camera his star, using it to move lazily up and down the spires and crags of the Hanging Rock formation, and around and amid his ensemble of characters. The film is a pursuit of ambiance, showing lizards, ants, swans, and even plants at work, sometimes accompanied only by environmental sounds. He provocatively yet leisurely mingles nature's mysterious ways with the enigmatic titillations of Victorian school girls, alive and awash in their curiosities about sexuality and youth. Curiosities, however, shackled by the social limiting world of a girl's college in 1900. Truly, the correct dress and formal social customs of Australia's rural communities in 1900 play an important role in how the remaining girls and townspeople react to the survivor, and to her inability or refusal to tell them what happened at Hanging Rock.

Weir's film teases with the fantasy that we are vicariously viewing young women who crave to gratify a growing sexual inquisitiveness. A craving that, subsequently, moves them to seek release from the suppression of their erotic wishes. This sexual tension arises as a palpable force in the story, a force that sets both teachers and students on edge. These girls of Alpha character are on the threshold of becoming women and preparing for a straitlaced life, publicly; whereas, privately, their preparation reveals an obsession with the passion of knowing themselves sexually.

For every imaginative *Picnic At Hanging Rock*, unfortunately, beauties in Alpha roles find themselves relegated to less memorable portrayals and more mundane happenings. The decorative female, save for an interlude of giving herself up to sex and violence, normally exercises little bearing on characters or story. She's upstanding though not outstanding. She's there to remind us that a man needs a good woman, and that she's available in her pristine glory.

Beta Roles

If an Alpha portrayal appears mostly ornamental, what about Beta performances? A Beta character brings us closer to what passes for cinematic reality because this personality taps into the pain and pleasure of a passionate relationship. She's not perfect. She may be a hooker (*Some Came Running*, 1958), or a drinker (*Days Of Wine And Roses*, 1962), or an abused wife who kills her ex-husband (*The Burning Bed*, 1984). She may be willing to tear apart a marriage (*Fatal Attraction*, 1987). She may be contemplating an abortion (*Roe vs. Wade*, 1989). Or, she may be too erotic for her own good, like the animated Jessica when she purrs, "I'm not bad, I'm just drawn that way" in *Who Framed Roger Rabbit?* (1988).

Whatever, she's well beyond any thought of pristine sexuality. Her philosophy permits less sunlight than that which luxuriates the Alpha character's mental outlook. The beauty in an Alpha role pays a price for her sexual allegiance. Passion engulfs her, proving volatile and sometimes dangerous for female and male.

The Beta character feels, and feels deeply. She cannot assume Alpha's sleek, uncluttered outlook on proper sexuality.

The Beta personality is not proper, though she wants to be. What she desires seems a mere eyelash away at times, and a galaxy afar on other pursuits. Her sexual hopes soar, then plummet. She will not win all the time, but passionate encounters with males encourage the Beta character to continue her forays of intense attachments. Attachments can spell trouble for her and trouble for him. The portrayal of a Beta's sexual life rumbles along, cockeyed and nervy, but seldom dull.

Beta characters come into sharp focus even as they transcend flesh-and-blood personalities. An MGM musical, *The Band Wagon* (1953), climaxes with "The Girl Hunt," a 12-minute jazz ballet that spoofs the private-eye mystery (see Harvey, 1989, p. 123). Fred Astaire (Rod Riley, private eye) faces a frenetic profusion of beatings, shootings, and bombings, and a tempting confusion of two graceful creatures: the Girl in White and the Girl in Red, both played by Cyd Charisse.

Rod Riley dances with his mysterious partners, one of whom he wants to protect (Girl in White) and the other of whom he does not trust (Girl in Red). The musical story tunes itself to a resolution amid the eerie, warning notes of a trumpet. This mournful sound signals the presence of "Mr. Big." Riley wins his shootout and Mr. Big collapses in his arms, the villain exposing "himself" as the supposedly vulnerable Woman in White.

And the Woman in Red, what of her? Rod completes his case, puts a cigarette in his mouth, and searches for a match. Slithering like a well-bred snake, a dark-gloved hand enters the frame to give him a light. She's there if he wants to take the chance. Rod muses, "She was bad, she was dangerous. I wouldn't trust her any farther than I could throw her. But...she was my kind of woman." A Beta character either does not hanker for, or realizes little chance of, sedate companionship. Rather, she represents a woman for whom a long-lasting, secure companionship appears elusive. A Beta personality like the Woman in Red can play the game with a passion as genuine as her heart is fickle.

Beta doesn't win in *Dick Tracy* (1990), however. This stylized film presents Breathless Mahoney (Madonna) as a saloon singer who defies her treacherous possessor, Big Boy Caprice (Al Pacino), to pitch her passion at the movie's square-jawed hero, Dick Tracy (Warren Beatty). Breathless tempts Tracy but she fails to overcome two obstacles: (1) Tracy's bulldog devotion to law and order, and (2) Tracy's sweetie pie, Tess Trueheart (Glenne Headly), an Alpha character par excellence. Given the myriad circumstances in which a love triangle can flourish, any confrontation between Beta and Alpha usually leaves only Alpha standing. Tess Trueheart isn't named Tess Trueheart for nothing.

Betas As Prostitutes

Tess, for instance, glows too wholesomely with an Alpha character's conviction of right and wrong to consider such a tattered profession as prostitution. **Prostitution** depicts a commercial exchange of resources: Sex for money, sex for stock options, or sex for whatever the female deems of value. Beta personalities, unlike Alpha portrayals, find prostitution a comfortable cinematic image.

Indeed, the image they depict appears so comfortable and so sympathetic that viewers are likely to express greater concern for them as fallen women than to consider why and how they entered the profession. Tussles over sexual morality only get in the way. What counts in the Oz process is whether the prostitute has a good heart, and in the movies, most of them do.

This good-heartedness extends through two scenarios that filmmakers favor in presenting prostitution as entertainment. The **Dawn scenario** emphasizes a fantasy of prostitutes trolling as free spirits, sampling the good life, and imagining prosperous times ahead. Another day is beginning, rich in promise. Dwelling on the morality of sexual conduct when surrounded by such gaiety seems an intrusion. Morality figures only lightly, for instance, in the plans of professional ladies like Shirley MacLaine and Dolly Parton in the comic vehicles *Irma La Douce* (1963) and *The Best Little Whorehouse In Texas* (1982). Thus, Dolly Parton as Mona Strangely sings and dances with her girls, although neither Mona nor her girls look like losers. They look just fine in fact, and the closing of their whorehouse seems patently unfair. After all, there are still riotous shindigs to celebrate, lovely gowns and lingerie to exhibit, handsome tricks to turn, and, um, well, maybe we've lost a little perspective here.

Pretty Woman (1990) doesn't offer much reality either. Julia Roberts as Vivian Ward, like Dolly's Mona, portrays a sharp lady. Too sharp, you would think, to chance her existence with AIDS and other assorted maladies. But *Pretty Woman* caters to a light fable, a Cinderella story in which the anointed Princess, full of grace and graciousness, stumbles fortuitously into her Prince Charming, played with bemused detachment by Richard Gere (Edward Lewis).

Vivian's Dawn will brighten, of that we are sure. She encounters sly putdowns regarding her chosen work, and we are hurt as she is over such prejudice. Still, Vivian will prevail; we know so even if she doesn't. The Dawn philosophy presents a vision of good will and happy trails. Our Beta character may not match Alpha for purity and lofty standards, but she's operating in an accommodating world that remains manageable for her. She likes the action and the risk.

The **Dusk scenario,** by contrast, unleashes an ominous wind against Beta personalities who eke out an existence with their bodies. No rosy promises to cherish here, just a slew of exploitation movies that shout the same, recurring message: The prostitute is fair game. Harlots are shot, beaten, drugged, butchered, diseased, and otherwise delivered to a death commensurate with their life. They constitute good victims because they are sexually sullied and find themselves less deserving of survival than women in Alpha roles. Or, if they do survive, Beta characters show us the blemishes, the blisters, the boredom of prostitution at Dusk.

Working Girls (1986) grinds away at this boredom, punctuated by brief interludes of caring, anger, and frustration. We see monotony providing the prostitute's most insidious despair, a tedium that creeps upon her bones as the

"Routine." The routine of phony pleasantries with a client before getting down to business. The routine of popping out the condom, which the prostitute does automatically, a gesture not lost on her John. The routine of intercourse, the mechanics and pretend emotions of which sap sexual intimacy of its intended passion. The routine, finally, of waiting for the next routine to commence. With few exceptions, the interludes between these grooves permit those moments of fakery to wash away and reveal a glimpse of the real Beta woman catching her breath.

Lizzie Borden, the director of *Working Girls*, actually required her unknown actresses to seek a job with a brothel (to seek only) (Nash & Ross, 1987, p. 311). This initiation and Borden's research on middle-class prostitutes produced a spirit of Janes serving Johns that mark a different world from the likes of *Pretty Woman*. The film begins as a routine, with Molly (Louise Smith) awakened by her alarm clock and reluctantly leaving her lesbian companion to spend another day at a Manhattan brothel. The job is a job and one we must presume that Molly would not pursue except for the money.

The movie ends, unlike most American movies, with a sigh rather than a firm resolution. Yes, Molly decides against returning to the brothel, but her decision does not free her. She chooses instead to lock herself into another relationship, servicing an older gentleman on an exclusive basis. Molly exchanges one regimen for another. Whatever her hopes and those of her sisters in the brothel, their chances of fulfillment seem as bleak as the fantasies entertained by the male clients who saunter in and out. Not much eroticism here, though a lot of what it takes to recognize prostitution as a business (Haskell, 1987, p. 386; Jaehne, 1987; Hobson, 1987, p. 235).

Occasionally, a Dusk character threads her way to a sliver of light and leaves the audience with an arresting question: Will she stay or will she leave? Jane Fonda's Bree Daniels in *Klute* (1971) portrays an ambitious woman who aspires to act and model, both intensely competitive professions that force her to turn tricks to finance her auditions. She hardly endears herself as a warm, positive figure, although Bree does illustrate the incongruities of a career-minded woman who seeks to guide her fortunes. Bree, in therapy and in trouble, gets caught in a whirlwind of events that causes her to trust and rely on a private detective, John Klute, played by Donald Sutherland.

They blend in an odd pairing, she, sexually used up and in need of genuine affection, and he, quiet, passive, almost stoic in his attitude about life. The closing scene scans Bree's empty apartment, leaving open the suggestion that she chooses to go with Klute and build on their relationship. Does this possibility sound too optimistic for a driving spirit like Bree, that she will relinquish her dreams? Perhaps a Duskier version becomes more appropriate: Bree's leaving proves temporary and her affection for Klute too inadequate to accept him or his lifestyle. She finds her ambitions reviving and feels compelled to return to her old haunts. We don't know, of course, but a Dusk scenario does not show much tolerance for slivers of light.

Cinematic females who beat the odds and manage to maintain a Hollywood career may make the shift from Alpha to Beta roles. They possess the talent to put their Alpha image to contrary use in a different role. Shirley Jones, who established herself as an Alpha character in musicals like *Oklahoma!* (1955) and *Carousel* (1956), did a turnabout by appearing as a revenge-minded prostitute in *Elmer Gantry* (1960). Departing from one's physical appearance to play an unexpected role proves a difficult task in an industry that pays homage to the creed of "How you look is what you are." For Shirley Jones, the switch won her an Oscar as best supporting actress.

Deborah Kerr and Donna Reed, both typecast as projecting the "nice girl" image of Alpha roles, created Beta characters against that image in the pre-World War II melodrama, *From Here To Eternity* (1953). Kerr plays Karen Holmes, the unfaithful wife of a mutually unfaithful company commander, Capt. Dana Holmes (Philip Ober). Karen, disabused of any loving relationship long ago, cavorts with numerous males, among them the captain's sergeant, Milton Warden (Burt Lancaster). She finds a fleeting, torrid passion with Warden, but their affair comes to a shattering end with the attack on Pearl Harbor.

Donna Reed's Alma Lorene holds forth as a "hostess" for the military guys in Hawaii, but, like Karen, Alma attaches herself to one military guy in particular, a classic macho figure by the name of Robert E. Lee Prewitt (Montgomery Clift). Alma's problem links to Karen's problem in that both women compete with the U.S. Army as their rival. Both lose.

They meet accidentally at the film's end, two strangers on a ship leaving Hawaii. Alma fabricates a story that her man was a pilot, killed by the attacking Japanese as he tried to take off. Prewitt, in truth, is AWOL when he learns of Pearl Harbor, and guards kill him by mistake as he attempts a return to his unit. Karen and Alma throw their leis on the water as the boat leaves Hawaii, the decorations a symbol of two drifting loves. The flower petals, so fresh and moist in the beginning, soon, all too soon, fade and wither.

The Beta character, cursed with sexual intimacies that complicate her life, discovers belatedly that her very passion becomes a cross. The same passion that launches her impulsively into another relationship, also depresses her with another failure, diminishing the female's hopes for an enduring love. Beta, the truth be told, appears less suited to the discipline and commitment of marriage, day by day. She's not Alpha with her unstinting loyalty through thick and thin. She's Beta. And the more she gives of her passion, her love, her warmth to still another male, the more she realizes that sexuality places an escalating price on these endearments.

Omega Roles

The most arcane role, though, has little in common with Alpha or Beta personalities. This role allows a beauty to channel her feelings selectively. She manipulates males, teasing, daring, beguiling them to do her bidding. She plays the game as a survivor; the calculating survivor, one whose sexuality becomes less a gift and more an instrument to accomplish the mastery she desires. She's someone to reckon with, someone who bears watching, someone whose beauty spells danger. She's the bane of all males who want her and can't have her. She's an **Omega character**, and if you get in her way--watch out.

Omega characters appear made to order for the movies. They flash glacially on the screen, captivating, bewitching, tantalizingly unattainable. Beauty, again, complements character. Sexuality breathes through the physiognomy and personality of its owner. Beta and Omega constitute different characters, different sexualities, different relationships with males.

Omega uses her sexuality selfishly, and, in doing so, spares herself the pain that Beta suffers when a relationship founders. Omega, nonetheless, lacks the wherewithal to express any depth of affection. She's awesome physically yet remains shallow emotionally, lacking Beta's passionate commitment to a more substantial partnership. To wit, with Omega what you see is what you *think* you get. But you don't, actually. Not by a lion's roar, a cat's meow, or a snake's hiss. What you get is a marvelously looking creature who can have you for breakfast.[6]

Ned (William Hurt) and Matty (Kathleen Turner) find themselves drawn to each other in *Body Heat* (1981). He, a lawyer of dubious skills, and she, a femme fatale of dubious reputation. She's married and affluent; he's neither, but these differences seem to enhance their torrid affair. Ned "pursues" Matty at an open-air concert, searching for an introduction. He conveniently makes himself available when she walks away from the concert for a breath of air, not realizing that Matty engineers his pursuit to spin her own entanglements of deceit. She even tells him, "You're not very smart. I like that in a man."

The lovers acquaint themselves in a rush of lustful passion: on the floor, across the bed, in a hot tub. These recreational activities depict the plot's nicer moments. Murder and deception follow. Ned and Matty conspire to kill Matty's husband, who's not a nice guy anyway. The conspiracy leads Ned to club the husband to death and transport his body elsewhere for arson. The lawyer in him tries to be careful but he's doomed because of Matty. She dupes him. Matty dupes him when she selects Ned as a lover; she dupes him into killing her husband; and she dupes him away from her embrace and into the arms of the law. Justly, Ned goes to prison. Unjustly, Matty goes to Hawaii. She stays free of Ned, of the police, and of any remorse over her duplicity.

Now, contrast Ned and Matty's slick melodrama with another gritty tale, *Dance With A Stranger* (1985). This story, based on a true British murder, concerns the volatile love affair between a working woman, Ruth Ellis (Miranda Richardson), and an upper-class playboy, David Blakely (Rupert Everett). The film chooses to weave its way through the futility of their attraction, and through a number of broken promises by David that ultimately prove too disillusioning for Ruth.

Her bitterness reaches its ragged edge, when, in a daze, she waits for Blakely to emerge from a London pub. When he appears, Ruth shoots and kills him, an act full of the lovers' torturous past. Ruth Ellis's emotional state and her public execution of David Blakely leave open the question of sanity. Due process, however, moves swiftly. She is convicted and executed in 1955, the last woman to receive the death penalty in Great Britain.

Ned and Matty clearly demonstrate a perpetration of murder against Matty's husband. But the character of Ruth Ellis inspires an arguable point: Does Ruth murder David Blakely in cold blood as an Omega, or does she kill in the disoriented, disturbed mind of a Beta? *Dance With A Stranger* fails to offer a firm answer. Her execution suggests that British law viewed Blakely's death as murder, simple and deliberate. Ruth Ellis, nonetheless, is no Matty Walker. Matty victimizes, but does not become a victim. She conveys a rare presence for women in film: A female who outwits her adversaries, including her sleazy husband, the husband's suspicious sister, the slow-footed lover (Ned), even the police.[7]

Ruth, by comparison, invests too much hope, too much feeling into her affection for David. She's hooked, as a Beta would be, struggling to make the mismatch work. Ruth behaves as a Beta character who chooses an Omega act to solve her problems: She kills David. But she commits the act in an unprotected state, with no master plan for escape. The killing does not transform Ruth to an Omega personality, although she leaves no doubt of her lethal intent. Earlier in the film we learn a little about Ruth, her young son, and of her not altogether respectable life. We know enough of Ruth Ellis to understand how a social history of ambition and bad judgment lead her to the final confrontation with David.

We know precious little of Matty Walker, however. Her previous experiences retain a dark and sketchy past, insufficient to tell us why she behaves with such detachment. We feel that Matty has always harbored her Omega ways, that she was never a person who felt genuinely about anyone. Her mystique of glamour, sexual intelligence, and callousness reflect the ideal Omega role.

The movies' film noir genre captures the Omega character on screen as a temptress who looks too good for any male's own good. **Classic film noir** concentrates on black-and-white films of the 1940s, films like *High Sierra* (1941), *Double Indemnity* (1944), *The Postman Always Rings Twice* (1946), and *Out Of The Past* (1947). These stories evoke a cynicism about life, and Omega personalities carry this cynicism to the point of sexual indulgence, jeopardizing their own lives in the process.

Omega women are smart and knowing in the classic film noir's shadowy world, although not smart and knowing enough to avoid the punishment that awaits them (Wilson, 1991, p. 171). The sexual relations in such films promise all the ardor that comes with lust and betrayal, except you must use your imagination. The graphic expressions of these physical passions could never find their way to the giant screen.

Modern film noir overcomes this barrier by bursting free of the censor's paddle. Lust and lasciviousness roam freely in *Body Heat*, and an attraction between two women complicate the pursuit of justice in another film noir story, *Black Widow* (1987). David Mamet's *House Of Games* (1987) even uses the sex act as a catalyst for an Omega female's determination to reassert her superiority. Margaret Ford (Lindsay Crouse), a workaholic psychiatrist, finds herself sexually and financially duped by Mike (Joe Mantagna), a con artist.

Margaret corners Mike and seeks to reaffirm her dominance by forcing him to beg for his life. When he refuses, she kills him. Not only does Margaret discover a way to rationalize the murder, she feels further vindicated when, like Matty Walker, the police are unable to arrest her. Thus, modern film noir relaxes the censorship on sexual portrayals, and on the rigid formula that every criminal must receive his or her due punishment.

The Omega philosophy goes beyond film noir treatments, however. Remember *All About Eve* (1950)? Recall that Margo Channing (Bette Davis), a Beta female who feels the creepy-crawlies of age upon her, still enjoys her status as a star of the theatre. Margo hospitably takes in Eve (Anne Baxter), a graciously modest individual on the surface, but secretly a conniving, young actress who fervently wishes to succeed. Hence, we have Beta versus Omega.

Margo, who has the sincere love of a longstanding suitor, Bill (Gary Merrill), almost loses his love with the fear that he will stop caring for her as she grows older. Fortunately, despite Eve's devious sallies at Bill, Margo realizes that it's time to act her age, a realization that includes marriage for Margo and Bill. Eve accomplishes her goal too, but she knowingly pays a price. Unlike Margo, Eve has no close friends. Her one ally is Addison DeWitt (George Sanders), a powerful but cynical gossip columnist who takes "charge" of the star's career, a coup that includes the star as well. Will Eve adapt to this intrusion in her life? We don't know, except to say that it is never wise to anger an Omega woman.[8]

Beta/Omega Entanglements

The Alpha, Beta, and Omega roles comprise a cinematic formula. Alpha, a decorative fixture too wholesome to be true; Beta, a hapless pawn of love who must work for her felicity; Omega, a siren whose self-interests overshadow her sexual attachments. These roles frequently surrender to stereotypes in exploitation movies, becoming a predictable presence that leaves little to the viewers' imagination.

More imaginative are the efforts of filmmakers to develop female roles so that beauty undergoes change. Change, of course, must dance to a certain logic. You would not expect a true Omega character to somehow travel "backward" and become a Beta character. Such a reversal appears to occur in *La Femme Nikita* (1990), a violent film about the transformation of a female drug addict to a sober assassin with feelings. We first see Nikita (Anne Parillaud) and her motley crew steeped in drugs and out of control, as the police confront them during a reckless robbery. Dreamily, Nikita looks on as the battle rages; then, with little thought to her actions, she casually caps off the slaughter by killing a young officer.

We next see Nikita convicted of murder, but directed to a confidential training program for undercover agents. Haltingly, the woman without her drugs begins to show us a compassionate Nikita. Her desire for trust and affection surfaces when she meets a young worker in a grocery. They become live-in lovers, a domestic existence punctuated by Nikita's orders to secretly terminate selected targets.

The incongruity of her conduct proves difficult to justify logically. We first see a woman who, through substance abuse and a pathetic life, appears close to perdition. *La Femme Nikita* asks us to accept the fairy-tale prospect of redeeming an apparently incorrigible woman so that, once again, she feels and shows virtue. Perhaps Nikita portrays a Beta character who continues to conceal genuine feelings, yet masquerades as an Omega when we first meet her. Or, perhaps she truly reflects the Omega role, but possesses enough vulnerability to experience the genuine affection of a Beta in love.

Artistically, *Nikita* represents an interesting journey in how a woman regains her conscience. Logically, however, the Omega character does not easily abandon her self-absorption and embrace the male in a relationship of sexual faith. Nikita's new lease on life offers viewers a heart-warming story of someone who beats the odds, legally and psychologically, to stay alive and find a genuine love. So, in this instance, logic be hanged.

A more legitimate Beta/Omega variation arises in the vacillation of a female character who is sometimes Beta, sometimes Omega. Actresses can delight in such transformations, as does Michelle Pfeiffer in *Batman Returns* (1992). She's Selina Kyle, a Beta character, and also the bumbling secretary who wallows about as a klutz with a loser attitude. But she comes alive as Catwoman, an Omega on the prowl, a feline who meows her males into lowering their guard, then streaks through them with her claws, her whip, or whatever's handy.

The saving grace of this otherwise artificial duplicity is that Catwoman's heady behavior inspires Selina Kyle to show some spunk. And Catwoman, to her ambiguous credit, doesn't play her Omega role to the hilt (Gerosa, 1992). She's bad, but not all bad. She's deceitful, yet permits a twinkle of compassion to shine forth. She's Omega with a twist of lemon--exhibiting just enough virtuousness to make us wonder about redemption. That paradox, of course, is the cinematic catch: Catwoman with virtue is no longer Catwoman...and no longer a fascination of unpredictability.

The most prudent consideration of Beta/Omega entanglements involves a forward development of character. The buddy/buddy tale of *Thelma & Louise* (1991) gives us two Beta personalities as working women who seek relief from life's blue-collar drudgery (see The many faces of *Thelma & Louise*, 1991/1992). Both females play "ordinary women"--a housewife, a waitress--but they do so in the Hollywood tradition of using extraordinary physical appeal to make these women striking and sympathetic.

Thelma (Geena Davis), the younger and more impressionable partner, adapts herself to an oppressive husband who controls the minutes of her days. Louise (Susan Sarandon), more experienced in the valleys of life, waits numbly for her good-hearted yet uncommitted boyfriend to establish himself. Louise initiates the release for both women, deciding that too few precious moments remain to keep either of them in place.

The incident that catapults Thelma and Louise into a spree of risk-taking feats begins when Thelma innocently flirts and dances with a stranger in a bar. The unforeseen consequences of this encounter come to pass outside in a parking lot. She's woozy from drinking hard liquor too fast, and he moves in for the score. When she resists, his manly sweet talk ends and he punches her in the face, twice. Dazed, Thelma finds herself draped over a car's fender, rear end up.

Louise cannot stop this predatory male with her bare hands, but if one of those hands holds a .38-caliber revolver, she has a chance. Louise keeps the gun leveled at him as Thelma staggers away, then she backs off after a few parting words. But the male triggers something dark and dangerous in Louise's past. He stands sullenly, the glowering male deprived of his conquest. "Suck my dick," he says, the macho equivalent of sucking his thumb. Louise's face freezes in a death mask of hatred. She raises the revolver, she aims, she fires, a blood ring widening suddenly on the rapist's chest. He's dead, payment for her previous ills, although payment extracted through a primal reaction that solves nothing and only complicates Louise's moody outlook (Schickel, 1991).

Later, Thelma recalls the experience, half laughing, half crying: "Suck my dick," she echoes, and then gives a blasting sound with her mouth to mimic the shot. Thelma finally reaches a point of no return, a point Louise passed years ago. The two women have only each other. Thelma's husband is too infantile and uncaring to help; and Louise's boyfriend offers her, too late, another chance at marriage and commitment. Neither woman indicates that she has a home or family for refuge. So when Thelma makes an airhead mistake, Louise compensates. And when Louise sags from the despair of it all, Thelma picks up the slack. Together they accomplish an odyssey that neither could manage alone.

What concerns us, however, is how Thelma and Louise change. Louise, after killing the attacker, questions her actions and what lies ahead, an apprehensiveness that costs her her confidence as a leader. She's a Beta who shows remorse, and who knows better than Thelma that, in a man's world, their daring charge to female freedom permits no return.

Thelma, less perceptive but now more assertive, concludes--perhaps too quickly--that she has a knack for bamboozling the strident male. She pounces on this latent talent by leaving her Beta tentativeness behind, and by savoring a new-born zest for embracing an Omega philosophy of superiority. Thelma tastes power, a mesmerizing sensation that excites her sexually (Schickel, 1991).

Does this change indicate that Thelma matches the stereotypical bitch profile of an Omega character?   No, Thelma's personality conveys more mischievousness than coldness.   But she uses her feminine wiles as barter, as an edge, as a means to preserve her freedom and rejoice in her victories.   Thelma drifts toward the Omega sentiment, a movement away from her old acquiescing self and forward to untold excitement.   She finds herself a world apart from the prosaic life that she led under her smothering husband.

Indeed, neither woman can restore herself to what she was before, nor does either traveler wish to.   Two women on holiday, destined not to return.   Women have left before and not returned, although likely without experiencing the hazards invited by Thelma and Louise: Two road warriors who depart a treadmill past and who realize an exhilaration that transfigures their lives.   Now, Thelma and Louise appear as women who no longer need men, a truly threatening idea that marks them as misfits in a patriarchal society (Shapiro, Murr, & Springen, 1991).

The only way out, with gusto, is to take their grand leap in a grand canyon. *Thelma & Louise*, remember, is a movie of entertainment, not a documentary on role models for oppressed women to honor (Carlson, 1991). Women deserve their fair share of power, a share that is overdue, yet a share that does not rest with firearms and exploding diesel trucks (possibly symbolic in the film of...what? Penises?). Thelma and Louise, for all their exuberance, do little to endorse the generosity of a loving relationship between the sexes. The two women, instead, box themselves in a corner and rakishly commit to the only highway that celebrates their short-lived emancipation. They take the big leap.

Cinematically, the partners' denouement proves provocative yet fitting. We care about Thelma and Louise because their fetching looks complement their actions: Two women, each harnessing a singular attractiveness to invest her struggling character with a burst of feminine revelry in a flight to nowhere. Beauty and character fuse to ignite a verve for living, however brief.

The Ordinary Woman

Realistically, however, Thelma and Louise's grand leap nullifies the more abiding though disciplined path that women must pursue to make their contributions known. A woman of ordinary beauty does not enjoy the resources of an elite beauty. Movies are movies where B-B-Beauty reigns supreme. Hollywood's glamorized allure perpetuates a sexuality of youthfulness and masks a growing maturity. The high pitch of beauty in cinemaland creates a surrealistic atmosphere using as its norm a promenade of dazzling females.

Few beauties can claim distinction by projecting their physical allure so dramatically as do our adventurers in *Thelma & Louise*. The congruence of beauty and pretense comprises an artistic achievement, especially when these remarkable talents manage to portray ordinary women at heart, and portray them believably. The performer's physical virtues sashay their way into her pretend character and fashion a more conspicuous presence on screen. The actress entertains us by playing an ordinary woman, which, by contradiction, means that she's fascinating to watch: The ordinary made interesting.

Ordinary as in the **ordinary woman** implies no disrespect of females judged less attractive by society's vanguard. Ordinary denotes a label to include the many females who, regardless of the whys and wherefores, do not meet the image requirements of the marketable beauty. A vast number of women will never know that rarified image addressed by the modelmakers and filmmakers of Hollywood. **She** will be more than merely too knobby in the knees, too hippy in the thighs, or too flush of face. She and the camera simply will not affect that haunting vision to sell whatever the marketeers want her to sell.

B-B-Beauty, of course, has no specialty without the ordinary woman. An exceptional beauty is exceptional only because plainer variations exist, and exist in abundance. The ordinary beauty shall not draw on the fruits and flavors of the viewers' Oz process, but neither shall she suffer the travails that such beauty invites. What the ordinary beauty can do is live a life of consequence, allowing her natural attractiveness to make a continuing statement on her behalf. She's not pursing a formulaic Alpha, Beta, or (heaven forbid!) Omega role. She's not the cliché character that many screen beauties portray. A screen beauty must play against the odds to be otherwise; to play, say, a complex Beta character like Louise or a fledgling Omega personality like Thelma.

The ordinary woman, by contrast, represents a mass of contradictions. Her looks reflect her moods, and her moods may be legion. She can defy classification because her beauty, at variance with the poised declaration of a cinematic beauty, enhances **her** character with greater discretion. The Hollywood beauty usually needs a dynamic first impression to give her character a head start of acceptance with the audience--particularly if her personality falls short on substance.

The beauty of ordinary beauty, however, involves its cumulative appeal. First impression, second impression, third impression, "something" happens with the woman who permits it. Her beauty becomes indistinguishable from her conduct. A natural coalition of body and spirit occurs that gives the ordinary woman a growing presence in real time, a complex feat that seems unlikely to be mimicked in cinematic time.

Thus, the ordinary woman, though not immune to the privileges and pleasures visibly displayed by the B-B-Beauties of the cinema, gives the scope of beauty a greater dimension. She exists as a lesser beauty to the Hollywood eye, but her physical attractiveness retains a style and substance that provides sexuality with a wholesomeness unmatched by the glitz and glamour of orchestrated characterizations. The exploiters of beauty do not have a clue as to the ingredients of this splendid arrangement. The ordinary woman is not the straitjacketed personality of a routine Alpha, Beta, or Omega. She's much more.

Notes

1. One controversy, generated around the idea that viewers perceive the computer simulation of composite or "averaged" faces as more attractive than singular faces, has provoked some interesting comments. See, in order, Langlois & Roggman, 1990; Alley & Cunningham, 1991; Pittenger, 1991; Langlois, Roggman, Musselman, & Acton, 1991.

One diversity possessed by some females involves the dramatic changes that can occur when they tinker with hairstyle, makeup, and engage in a body language to complement these cosmetic variations. Model Cindy Crawford altered her appearance to become various personalities, including one transformation to a male that defied identification--despite public awareness of her attractive features.

2. Beauty and attractiveness do not express identical ideas, although experts have yet to agree on a working relationship (Machotka, 1979, p. 229; Liggett, 1974, p. 155). Nonetheless, let us consider **physical beauty** and **physical attractiveness** as interchangeable concepts, realizing that our references to beauty and attractiveness restrict these ideas to physical appearance. Defining beauty and attractiveness infers a common standard--a consensus of opinion--that arises through a vaguely perceived history of cultural consent (Patzer, 1985, p. 39; Adams, 1977; Bersheid & Walster, 1974). To wit, physical beauty depends on a communal standard in our society, however ill-defined that standard appears. But beauty also becomes personalized through the eye of the beholder. Therefore, we must make an allowance for the predilections of males and females to judge beauty. Put succinctly and no doubt too simply, beauty "intermingles" perceptually according to a process of (1) consensus and (2) personal preference.

3. What kind of commercial images have the male popularizers of beauty erected? (1) **Advertising images** that stereotype the sexes, engineered to portray the female consumer as a cleanliness freak: The female spokesperson as a role model, for example, who wears mostly flesh to pitch a product (Courtney & Whipple, 1983, pp. 73 & 103). (2) **Cosmetic demands** that

monopolize a woman's attention, including makeup and makeovers perpetrated to keep women in line; and to keep them cultivating their beauty for profit and pretense (Freedman, 1986, p. 47).   (3) **Sexual storytelling** that beguiles females, such as beauty rituals, endowed by marketing to soothe women with promises of purification and power (Barthel, 1988, p. 151).   (4) **Beauty alterations** that subordinate the female consumers, encouraging them to expend energy on thinness at the expense of more relevant feminist pursuits (Wolf, 1991, p. 179).

Whether you agree or disagree with these declarations, they do point to a common outcome of picturing the beautiful female as ornamental.   Consequently, if she spends considerable time prepping herself cosmetically, she has less time and possibly less interest to consider more worthy endeavors.

4.   I used the same Alpha/Beta/Omega format in an earlier book, *Good Murders And Bad Murders* (1991, p. 154).   My idea in *Murders* concerned classifying the differing relationships where women triumph as aggressors and men lose as victims.   Therefore, Alpha relationships depict females who engage in self-defense to survive; Beta relationships involve females who become both the cause and effect of a troubled partnership, finally killing to end a volatile period of their life; Omega relationships showcase detached females who kill for reasons of manipulation.   The spirit of this classification carries over to the current description, although Alpha, Beta, and Omega roles apply now to sexual relationships presented as entertainment.   But the underlying theme remains intact: namely, that females characteristically find their actions defined relative to male behavior.

5.   Emma Peel (Diana Rigg) pranced forth to assume the serial queen's banner in a 1960s' series, *The Avengers*.   Mrs. Peel, sexually provocative in svelte jump suits and more independent than her predecessors, nonetheless volunteered to accept directions from a male companion, John Steed (Patrick MacNee).   Steed, with his casual formality, referred to Emma as Mrs. Peel, their sexual relationship an ongoing mystery from week to week.   He uses her first name however, when the two say goodbye in a final episode.   Emma's husband, thought dead, returns and Emma, as an emancipated though loyal beauty, chooses to honor her Alpha role and join him.   We see Emma driving away, sitting next to her long-lost spouse, who, from behind, looks remarkably like...John Steed.

6.   If an Omega character who is charming, manipulative, and quite without remorse sounds suspiciously like that of a psychopath, score one for you. Researchers have not uncovered firm evidence to indicate how psychopaths miss out on that essential quality of empathy.   The answer does not always

include a logical development, such as a violent upbringing (see Hare, 1993, p. 155). Filmmakers, too, are frequently content to gives us a psychopath like Matty in *Body Heat* without worrying over how and why she became so cold and duplicitous.

7. The sister's daughter, who comes to visit Matty and her husband, almost blows the scheme apart. One evening, with the husband away, Ned and Matty engage in a reckless liaison. Ned, wandering about in the buff, encounters the little girl. Later, when the police ask the girl to look for a familiar face, she fails to identify Ned. Why? Well, social scientists speak of a "weapons focus effect" as one obstacle that hinders eyewitnesses from making an accurate identification. Eyewitnesses to a crime who see a weapon--pistol, rifle, rocket launcher, whatever--may fix on the weapon and find it difficult to remember the offender's physical appearance (DeAngelis, 1991). So when the girl observes Ned, the "weapons focus effect" principle comes into play. She sees his penis, and, presumably never having seen such a monster before in her brief life, she forgets everything else.

8. Nor can an Omega relax in the presence of other Omega personalities. At the close of *All About Eve*, an aspiring actress finesses her way into Eve's apartment and begins the cycle anew. Eve almost throws her out, but decides that the young girl is harmless. In the movie's final scene, the girl poses before a full-length mirror, dreaming--as Eve dreamed--of receiving a prestigious award. Barbara Bates, who plays Eve's would-be successor, never realized that dream in her own career. Years of personal and professional problems led her to a fateful judgment on March 18, 1969: the day she entered a sealed garage and committed suicide in her Volkswagon (Crivello, 1988, p. 104).

Lesson 6

Once Upon A Time...

Jerry knocks and Karen, pausing a moment to "shimmy" down her dress, answers the door. They exchange greetings.

He mentions the prospect of dinner (sushi) at a prestigious restaurant. Jerry knows the maître d', he says. Karen acts suitably impressed. Jerry also slips in an enticement: Meryl Streep, playing in *Sophie's Choice*. I'm so "in" to Meryl Streep, he murmurs. Ummm, says Karen, so am I.

Jerry expresses a little nervousness. He doesn't usually go out on blind dates, but tells Karen that she's not only beautiful but "someone he feels he can "open up to."

Karen smiles, prepares to leave, and then, oh, yes, she says, can I see a major credit card and a valid driver's license? Jerry's perplexed. Come again? Karen politely insists. It will only take a moment, she coos: I want to run a compatibility check.

Baffled, Jerry hands her his driver's license. Karen punches out a well-practiced routine on her computer keyboard, slides his card through the slot, and says it won't take long.

Jerry doesn't realize what a "compatibility check" means, but he'll soon learn. The machine spits forth several pages of printout, summarizing Jerry's demeanor as a gentleman and dating partner. Worse, the printout also chronicles his sexual history in the sack.

Uh oh, says Karen. She frowns, sends him an accusing look, and cites his sexual misdemeanors: (1) You had sex on a second date and never called the girl again. (2) Not only that, but you were selfish in bed eleven times, turning over to go to sleep after you finished. (3) Twelve times you ignored your date to flirt with a more beautiful woman. (4) One hundred sixty-nine times you feigned interest in a woman's career. And (5) seventeen times--make that eighteen times now--you lied to women with lines about how much you're "in" to Meryl Streep.

Jerry stammers, blusters, and denies, to no avail. He's failed Karen's compatibility test. Too bad, she says, but you're too selfish in bed. No date, no bedtime romantics.

Jerry storms out the door, exclaiming that maybe he'll get one of those machines and check **Her** out. The next scene shows Jerry in a phone booth talking to Beverly. He tells her he can be by in ten minutes. Beverly hesitates, finally says okay, and then adds, oh, yes, can you bring a major credit card and a valid driver's license?

Jerry stands frozen in time, a glazed smile on his face. The romancing Romeo, done in by technology and the female's campaign for sexual honesty. He knows that his gallivanting days (and nights) are numbered.

What's happening in the war between the sexes? The female's secret weapon--a compatibility check--portends the beginning of the end for sly jocks like Jerry. Karen (Rosanna Arquette) and Jerry (Steve Guttenberg) portray a pair of blind daters in this cautionary spoof on dating ethics from *Amazon Women On The Moon* (1987). Just imagine the wholesale changes needed in Jerry's tactics if, indeed, females gained access to his dating and sexual past. All those wonderful lines gone with the wind; all of his well-rehearsed ploys in need of serious repair. The entire business would prove too tragic to bear, were it not for humor's saving grace.

Laughter And Tears

You'd rather laugh than cry, right? Well, no, not always.
Crying has its devotees. Some people love to cry. Classic
operas, soap operas, torrid melodramas--these soulful
productions seem pitched emotionally for fans who don't mind
shedding a tear, or two, or three. Frequently you want this
escapism. To laugh, to cry, to sink pleasantly into the movie's
mood describes a comfortable Oz experience of make believe.

Comedy and **tragedy**--the cheerful face and tearful face--
constitute emotional experiences that only seem contrasting.
Actually, each experience complements the other, often
working in concert to give moviegoers a roller coaster ride of
emotive peaks and valleys.

Comedy, like tragedy, subscribes to logic and follows rules.
Consider, first, the dynamics of laughter. What makes a
shocked reaction, a pratfall, an insult, or two lovers quarrel-
ing, funny? A case in point: What makes Jerry's plight
humorous as Karen recounts his improprieties?[1] **Humor** defies
an exhaustive analysis, therefore let us focus on a lesser,
skeletal interpretation. This bare-bones approach includes
three ideas--salience, incongruity, and Factor X--that attend
most humorous gatherings.

Salience constitutes the most fundamental property, a
process that relates to familiarity. We sense more readily the
humor of people and topics that we know (Suls, 1975). A
hearty laugh becomes likelier when the President of the
United States commits a silly mistake than when Alvin T.
Poole does so. Who is Alvin T. Poole? We don't know. All we
can say is that if he makes the same mistake, it isn't as funny.
Likewise, Karen's ability to turn the tables on Jerry provokes
humor from the familiar dating protocol of "getting to know
you." Females having encountered the disenchantment of a
"bum date" will find it delicious to envision the leverage that
Karen exercises over Jerry. They empathize with her dismay,
and find salience in recognizing Karen's desire to retaliate.

Incongruity involves a surprise, an unexpected twist, the
proverbial "punch line" (Zillmann & Bryant, 1991, p. 268;
Cetola, 1988). Funny people behave a tad strangely, a tad off

center, a tad irrationally compared to people who behave seriously. But incongruity must count for more than nonsense. The twist, as Karen's revelation of Jerry's sexual history, needs to embrace meaning that permits a clever connection to the story. Moreover, any silly ending can offer a surprise, but if the ending lacks an insightful reappraisal of the story, it fails to offer substantive humor. Females who find humor in Jerry's distress do so possibly from a prickly sense of triumph in "putting it to" the opposite sex. Males, however, appear less likely to invest much humor in the male putdown, but can laugh, perhaps nervously, at Jerry's discomfort in the dating game.

The mystery of what makes humor funny becomes a mystery of how we register our abrupt comprehension and delight at the incongruity. This sudden comprehension--this connection of the surprise (incongruity) to the familiar (salience)--gives rise to **Factor X**. Factor X doesn't really explain the liftoff to humor. It does stand, nonetheless, as an example of the ignorance that plagues us when we try to understand why we find a story or character funny.

One probe of Factor X concerns a theory that conceptualizes verbal humor as **dispositional**, whereby one party (playfully?) victimizes another party (Zillmann & Bryant, 1991, p. 270). Given our state of Oz, we can laugh at this inequality, especially if the victimized party is a stinkeroo. We can even enjoy the comedy again by anticipating the more humorous scenes. But the same elementary principle prevails in both instances, namely, that we laugh when our expectation of what should happen, doesn't happen.

The expected outcome gets fancifully turned on its head to permit the unexpected. The word "fancifully" denotes the key, as well as the mystery of humor. The unexpected must not only make sense in a nonsensical sort of way, it must make the kind of sense that we interpret as funny. (Factor X, in other words.)

Consider this scene, described in Lesson 2: Jack Lemmon, who masquerades as a girl through most of *Some Like It Hot* (1959), must convince "her" boyfriend, Joe E. Brown, that "she" is really a "he." Lemmon strips off his wig and exclaims to Brown that it's all a mistake, that he, Lemmon, is a guy, not a girl. We expect the boyfriend to appear upset, angry, and generally hurt over this deception. Instead, Brown, displaying the mischievous, incandescent smile that was the actor's trademark, takes Lemmon's masquerade in stride. Benignly beaming on his "girl," Brown replies nonchalantly, "Well, nobody's perfect."

Brown's blithe response works as a last line because it echoes the naive ardor of his character. He truly likes women; he loves to pursue them, woo them, win them. Money cushions the bumps in his life, but wealthy or not, Brown plans to hanker after the fair sex until he can hanker no more.

Overall, *Some Like It Hot* works as a comedy of romance because the film relies on an axiom of humor that filmmakers have used successfully since the Silent era. The gimmick calls for taking creative advantage of the **performer's ignorance**. Viewers, in on the joke, laugh at the inequity of characters who rush about seeking to comprehend what the audience already knows. These romantic follies become fodder for hilarious moments of misdirection and misunderstanding in movies as diverse as *Topper* (1937), *Heaven Can Wait* (1943, 1978), *Bell, Book, And Candle* (1959), *What's Up Doc?* (1972), *Tootsie* (1982), *Splash* (1984), and *A Fish Called Wanda* (1988).

Comedic Sexual Parody

Humor, with its salience, its incongruity, and its indecipherable Factor X, permits words and deeds about sexuality that, under other circumstances, exhibits grounds for artistic bad taste. Certainly if a comedy fails to work, the bad taste escalates to a malodorous vehicle of ill repute. The movie faces condemnation twice over: first, for showcasing questionable sexual behavior, and, second, for presenting itself as a comedy that's not funny.

Good comedy, by contrast, functions as a grand equalizer. **Parody** refers to a mockery of serious intentions, and **sexual parody** denotes the ridicule of erotic practices and conduct.

Going to extremes with sexual humor permits a movie to slam reality in the chops and undertake, say, a fairy tale of romance. We suspend disbelief of the film's sensuous shenanigans by invoking Oz to accept that fairy tale if the characters and story have any chance to entertain us.

A sexual parody, therefore, calls for the viewers' Oz to **relax the bonds of sexual taboos**. A taboo reflects a prohibition, and a sexual taboo reflects, specifically, a prohibition of physical intimacy considered too risqué for public exposure (Davies, 1982). The outrageous scene made humorous encourages a release from such constraints. A sexual taboo that proves delicate and daring becomes more acceptably permissive when received humorously.

The absurdity of sexual parody has its comedic and tragic overtones. The comedic face is by far the safest, since viewers know that the darkest of deeds--even child pornography--will end well when the comedic face of sexual parody is in force. Imagine, for instance, the silliness of erotically offbeat characters and absurd incidents when these ingredients are thrown into the normally serious drama of bringing a "wounded" plane to safety.

Airplane! (1980) relies on the comedic sanctuary of inane humor to pursue these ingredients, revolving its zaniness around a troubled romance between Elaine (Julie Hagerty), a flight attendant, and Ted (Robert Hays), a former fighter pilot. Their romance becomes a tenuous thread that strings together the movie's onslaught of sexual sight gags and non sequiturs during the flight.

Keep in mind how these erotic references would fare without the creativity of absurd humor to give them approval: (1) Elaine reminds Ted how she used to sit on his face and wrinkle it. (2) An elderly lady describes Elaine to Ted as a woman with "supple, pouting breasts." (3) A sign flashes the silhouette of a male and female engaged in intercourse, prohibited during takeoffs and landings. (4) Dr. Rumack (Leslie Nielson) examines a woman passenger with her feet up in stirrups. (5) A small boy, acting very adult, asks a small girl how she likes her coffee--and the girl replies, "I take it black, like my men." (6) Elaine gives an apparent "blow job" to an inflated male doll that passes as an automatic pilot. (7) The "automatic pilot" subsequently positions "himself" behind Elaine and grabs hold of her "pouting breasts." (8) Captain Oveur (Peter Graves), who has a "thing" for boys, makes overtures to one boy by asking, "Joey, have you ever been in a Turkish prison?" (9) And the Captain's wife, not to be outdone, informs her bed partner that she has to go to the airport--whereupon her partner, a horse, whinnies his understanding.

Airplane! amounts to an agenda of controversial issues suggestive not only of sexual perversity in general, but of child/adult interracial sex, child/adult homosexual relations, oral sex, sexual molestation, and--oh, right--bestiality. Still, where is the controversy? Where is the outrage? Remember, the movie uses children for several of its sexual references. How can this taboo of taboos pass muster with an audience?

To do so, *Airplane!* must spoof the issues and render them harmless. It must make a potentially contentious moment sufficiently absurd to inspire laughter rather than anger. Absurd humor, performed aptly, accomplishes this feat. Such humor imposes new rules, conveying a crazed irreverence that spares no sexual taboo, including a child's eroticism.

The movie also ridicules other targets involving race, religion, drug addiction, airplane safety, and airplane movies. But the primary text that *Airplane!* uses to present its fragmented tale of off-color scenarios...is a love story. Elaine and Ted participate in various silly encounters, including a "seaweed" reprisal of the passionate scene between Burt Lancaster and Deborah Kerr in *From Here To Eternity* (1953). Elaine and Ted, like Deborah and Burt, embrace sensuously in the ocean turf, except that Elaine and Ted do so amid kelp and debris.

Young love, though, must keep its furnace stoked. The lovers falter and grow apart. Elaine leaves Ted because of his troubled past, and because his love now lacks that "seaweed ferocity" to keep them together. Ted wants Elaine back, but she refuses, exclaiming that she can't love him if she doesn't respect him. To Ted, her reaction is a "pisser" and he's determined to follow her. Consequently, we accompany him on the flight and sympathize with his attempts to win Elaine. Ted, of course, eventually gains her respect and flies the plane in safely.   More important, the lovers' reconciliation, no matter how bizarre, provides a warm ending and thus a positive glow to all those sexual titillations that went before.

Romance depicts a ripe object for comedic sexual parody because such parody thrives best on the **basics**.   The fundamental institutions of society contain a rich source of fads, foibles, and folderol, just waiting for a jolt of burlesque or satire to knock these inanities askew (for other examples see *Dragnet*, 1987, and *The Gods Must Be Crazy*, 1984).

Institutions like marriage offer a particularly long life for comedy.   Humorous views of marital problems in the early years of movies still find an audience today. Marital discord creates a strong salience, and it matters less if the male/female confrontation occurs in the 1990s or the 1920s.

Spite Marriage (1929), the last silent film by Buster Keaton, demonstrates infatuation, jealousy, commitment, rejection, and reconciliation: all the emotional qualities that lovers can package into a relationship. Buster Keaton portrays the one comic performer whose courtly presence makes him perfect as an ardent suitor, but whose disciplined demeanor never allows his character to succumb to pathos (Gilliatt, 1990, p. 9). Keaton's appeal invites the coupling of a master comic, exquisite in his command of physical humor, yet a figure capable of retaining his dignity to convey determination and grit. He personifies a rare combination of vulnerability and resilience - - two qualities that wear well in traversing the rocky road to romance.

Keaton plays Elmer, a pants presser, enamored of Trilby Drew (Dorothy Sebastian), a stage actress. She, in turn, finds herself enamored of her leading man (Edward Earle), an actor who remains enamored mostly of himself.   This triangle underscores one of the film's captions, that there are only two cures for love..."marriage and suicide."

A wandering plot shows Trilby marrying Elmer to spite her leading man. She doesn't care for Elmer, but uses him to make Earle jealous. The plan fails and leads to one of the classic Keaton sketches: his affectionate yet futile efforts to get a soused Trilby to bed. He can't figure how to undress her because her mystifying dress appears to have no buttons; nor can he keep Trilby's rubbery body on the bed for long. Finally, just as he succeeds and starts to walk away, the bed collapses.

Trilby leaves Elmer, convinced that she's made a mistake. But the magic of movie romance refuses to leave Elmer forsaken. After a haphazard sequence of comic capers, the two meet again on a yacht, with Elmer a deck hand and Trilby still vainly pursuing her leading man. A series of events isolate Elmer and Trilby on the yacht, until they are invaded by a crew of gangsters.

The finale has a bantam-sized Elmer squaring off against the head villain, a smiling menace who wants Trilby for his own dastardly designs. To add further insult, the Menace even takes a captain's cap that Elmer wears. Elmer, visibly upset, has accomplished some heroic deeds aboard the yacht and feels, for the first time in his subdued life, that he deserves to wear that cap.

Trilby's sexual safety and the cap become the impetus that drives Elmer over the edge. He bobs, he skitters, he dashes, he keeps resurfacing to hound the Menace one more time. Elmer, beside himself with masculine bravado, goes through a frenzy of acrobatics to physically overpower his adversary and win Trilby back. Upon dispatching the villain, he collapses, a panting figure of rapture and bravery. Trilby holds an exhausted Elmer in her arms and places the captain's cap on his head--where it belongs.

Comedic sexual parody gives the looniness of movies like *Airplane!* and *Spite Marriage* a welcome mat. No matter how spicy the sexual references or bizarre the hero's efforts to win his true love, the comedic spirit endorses these episodes with a warm, comforting glow. Nothing bad **really** happens, nothing tragic carries much sting. Viewers, secure in this knowledge, can cruise along with Oz and enjoy themselves.

Tragic Sexual Parody

Tragic sexual parody encompasses those films in which humor assumes a negative texture. Moviemakers know that moviegoers prefer their cinematic heroes and heroines to play positive stalwarts who persevere. Tragic sexual parody goes against this formula. No guarantee arises that viewers will see heroes triumph, love win out, or happy endings burst forth, flinging blossoms to and fro.

Filmmakers, with trepidation, embark on darker waters when they harness fantasy to a parody of grim chaos (Keough, 1990, p. xi; Fadiman, 1972). Consider those harsh pranks and cruel jokes that the medical personnel of *M*A*S*H* (1979) practice to cope with the insane business of treating Korean war casualties day after day. Or contemplate the "war room" circle of political and military leaders in *Dr. Strangelove* (1964) who bumble their way toward a nuclear holocaust. Or imagine the sheer comic abomination that erupts in *Ruthless People* (1986) between a scheming husband and his wife.

These movies ask viewers to find laughter from tears, humor from tragedy, relief from devastation, love from hate. To master this transformation, cinematic vehicles must create a solemn world moving out of control. The deterioration of this world communicates a sense of hopelessness that only humor can combat. Without the absurd humor of tragic parody as the viewers' life preserver, the bleak events that unfold simply become a relentless nightmare.

The Hospital (1971) delivers such a message. Here we witness an institution under siege: Protestors are clamoring outside for better health care; patients are misdiagnosed, mislaid, misidentified; and, as a final insult, a murderer walks the corridors knocking off a doctor here, a nurse there. Clearly, these agonizing events demonstrate the antithesis of what we expect from a profession dedicated to healing.

Capping off this madhouse is the chief surgeon, Herbert Bock (George C. Scott). He's a burnt-out soul who finds himself drifting slowly into drink and despair, and who ponders the prospect of suicide as an increasingly desirable option. A psychiatrist asks Bock, "Are you impotent?" and

Bock answers, "Intermittently." He then explains that "...I haven't tried in so long, I don't know." The Chief Surgeon perversely claims pride in his impotence, as if this sexual dysfunction embodies the price he pays for trying to do his job. Bock continues spiraling away from his responsibilities, overwhelmed by an inability to cope with himself, but mostly frustrated with a system of medical care that appears ready to self-destruct.

A missionary's daughter, Barbara (Diana Rigg), becomes his tormentor and his salvation. She's there because her mentally disturbed father has entered the hospital for a routine checkup, and, through a series of medical mistakes, now appears seemingly comatose. Barbara, however, is not accusatory. She has weathered her own hell and calmly draws on a spiritual strength to handle her adversities. Moreover, she's attracted to Herbert Bock and sees in the weary doctor one more adversity that needs a healing touch.

She shamelessly indicates her interest to Bock, and he responds by saying, "I admire your candor." Barbara replies, "You better admire a lot more than that." This provocative exchange leads Bock to unleash his pain in which he explains that, for him, impotence means more than the inability to achieve an erection and have sex: He's lost the desire to work, a more debilitating dysfunction for the doctor than his elusive passion to make love.

Psychologically, Bock reaches a suicidal state and prepares to inject himself with potassium. His saving grace, however, becomes Barbara, and the incident that catapults him beyond his pain begins as an act of rape. He storms at Barbara, throws her on a couch, rips her clothes, and has his way. Without embellishing the act, he assaults her sexually. Barbara, stunned, recovers and smiles when he achieves penetration. She pulls Bock back from the brink of surrendering to his despair, and offers him the passion of love as a way to reclaim his soul.

She does that much for him, now he must do something for her. Barbara wants to take her father from the hospital and back to the mountains, and she wants Bock to join them. She tells him, "I'm offering you green silence and solitude. The natural order of things. Mostly, I'm offering me. I think we're beautiful, Herb." Bock agrees, dumfounded over her attraction to him, and surprised at his own desire for her.

Regrettably, complications derail their quicksilver romance. Barbara's father, not really comatose, has waged his own Biblical war of retribution on the healing establishment, including the execution of a few medical staffers. The hospital, threatened on several fronts to implode, calls forth Herbert Bock's commitment to his profession. He explains to Barbara, "I'm middle class, and among us middle class love doesn't triumph over all. Responsibility does."

He stays, she leaves. The only marriage that truly captures Bock's passion--his attachment to the hospital--demands that he remain. The absurd humor of showing all that a hospital should not be offers the message that these dark happenings cannot gain ascendance. The humor of an orderly, life-and-death institution in disarray is a comic parody built on tragedy.

Death, made satirical, represents only part of the parody. The satire must harbor a substantive theme that transcends the exaggeration of medical mistreatment and chaos. If this theme is absent, *The Hospital*'s grim humor proves merely exploitative. Herbert Bock personifies the best that the hospital has to give. Barbara's love returns him to his true devotion, and that devotion concerns his mission to restore order and minister to the ill. We understand why Herbert Bock must stay.

Compare *The Hospital* and its higher purpose with *Pretty Maids All In A Row* (1971) and its lack of purpose. "Tiger" McDrew (Rock Hudson), a high-school counselor, also lays claim to success as a football coach, military hero, admirable family man, and a philosopher of love whose ideas fit nicely with the sexual freedom in vogue during the later 1960s. Tiger commands the eyes and ears of everyone, especially the girls. And there are lots of girls. Long-legged girls, mini-skirted girls, girls with bouncing breasts and swinging derrieres, girls advertising their I-know-what-I-want look. The girls, if not palpitating in the foreground of many scenes, populate the background leading cheers, engaging in calisthenics, and generally doing what comes naturally with their bodies.

Ponce de Leon Harper (John David Carson), a virginal youth, constitutes the story's centerpiece. Ponce finds the breasts, legs, and derrieres almost more than he can bear. Because of Tiger's savoir-faire, the boy admires the counselor and looks to him for help. The wily Tiger decides that Ponce needs someone mature to lift him over his virginity, so Tiger enlists the aid of Betty Smith (Angie Dickinson), a mini-skirted teacher. He falsely informs Betty that Ponce is "totally impotent" and suggests that she talk with the youth in her home. Ponce, of course, is not only not impotent, he finds himself going to the bathroom to do multiplication tables in a feeble attempt to vanquish his unwanted erections.

The tragic parody of *Pretty Maids All In A Row* resides in the movie's title. When Tiger's "testing" sign goes on, no one disturbs him. He's testing alright, testing out those exceptional females who find him irresistible. The examination occasionally gets interrupted with a killing when one of Tiger's girls decides that she wants to marry him or otherwise blow the whistle. Tiger, with beguiling equanimity, terminates the troublemakers, leaving them in the men's restroom, the boiler room, the football field, whatever locale proves handy.

The murders, all performed off camera so as not to disrupt the sexual gaiety, seldom alter Tiger's countenance or his relations with family and friends. He's a romantic at heart, believing that the value of love lies in the fact that it doesn't last. This convenient philosophy gives Tiger all the slack he needs to maintain his calm. He's genial, he's self-assured, he's...well...he's Tiger.

A parallel seduction scene shows the difference in mentor and pupil. Tiger, with another nubile prospect in his station wagon, abruptly turns the front seat into a horizontal bed, causing his adoring audience of one to squeal with delight. Ponce, by contrast, awkwardly attempts to kiss Betty and falls backward on a chocolate duck filled with booze. This embarrassing pratfall, nevertheless, leads to a bath, a bed, and Ponce's induction to the world of nonvirgins.

Alas, just as Ponce gains a visceral assurance about himself, he loses Tiger. The deaths become too distracting for the counselor to sidestep, and so, in an apparent suicide attempt, Tiger disappears. Later, at his funeral service, Tiger's wife accidentally drops an airline ticket to Brazil from her purse. A detective notices the ticket and makes plans to follow the wife. Whether he does, and whether he succeeds in locating Tiger, we never know.

The amoral conclusion of giving Tiger a chance to escape punishment denotes the unpredictability of tragic sexual parody. More disturbing, however, is Ponce's new direction in life. Once timid and unsure about girls, he now approaches, caresses, and advises them with confidence. Ponce appears ready to emulate Tiger in establishing himself as a model of male charm. He's cultivating a charisma...to do what? We have no indication that Ponce will improve on Tiger's shallow creed, thus we discover no redeeming message in the macabre humor of "loving" girls with an air of expendability. The best we can say is that Tiger's physical appearance and conduct symbolize the focus of his self-worth. The inner Tiger remains a penny-ante mystery, as do the minds of those light-headed girls he sends out to pasture.

Hence, we find few morsels of worth in *Pretty Maids All In A Row* to rival the charitable aims espoused in *The Hospital*. But the two films do share a plot of common ground. Aside from their absurd use of comedy and tragedy, both movies demonstrate a **bargaining relationship** between males and females: Someone wants togetherness and offers herself as the reward (Barbara, the missionary), and someone decides reluctantly against this companionship to pursue a different reward (Herbert Bock). Or, someone wants to marry and submits her body, hook, line, and sinker (insert any impressionable girl's name), and someone takes steps to ensure that the body doesn't become a liability (Tiger).

"Love" in such relationships enriches its prospects for comedy and tragedy, particularly when the parody concerns a bargaining of rewards and costs that ensues within the wonderful tradition of marriage. So, enter Henri Verdoux, also known as Monsieur Varney, Monsieur Bonheur, and

Monsieur Floray (Charlie Chaplin). The country is France, the time is the 1930s, and the Narrator, deceased in 1937, returns from the Great Beyond to relate his eventful life between 1930 and 1933 in *Monsieur Verdoux* (1947).

Henri Verdoux finds himself unemployed after 35 faithful years as a bank clerk. Economic times stutter up and down (mostly down), forcing Henri to put his creative skills to work in support of his invalid wife and little boy. Henri's fluid motions and quick recoveries after making a mistake help to finesse him into the arms of numerous women over a busy, busy three years. (Charlie Chaplin's masterly walk, sweeping gestures, and elevator eyebrows personalized his classic figures of Silent films and prove beneficial here.)

Henri, however, loves only one woman, his wife. He marries other women to obtain their money, and to obtain their money he must, well, dispose of them. Where Tiger McDrew merely indulges himself in lustful liaisons, Henri Verdoux considers his female prey inferior and minimizes physical contact as best he can. The bargain, known only to Henri of course, involves **his** tentative companionship weighed against **her** tangible assets.

This parody reaches its comic height when a "wife," Annabella (Martha Raye), continues to elude Henri's lethal plans. One attempt, that could have played as a silent skit, shows Henri preparing a special poison. He leaves it in the bathroom and searches for a corkscrew to open the bottle of wine, for which the poison is intended. While he searches, the maid finds the bottle of poison, one that resembles a bottle of peroxide. She pours a bit into a dish, then accidentally smashes the bottle. The maid replaces the poison with a real bottle of peroxide, just in time for Henri to return and pour it into the wine. The end result: A lucky Annabella stays alive, an unlucky maid watches her hair fall out, and a perplexed Henri wonders what he must do to get at Annabella's cash flow.

Conversely, the sexual parody of *Monsieur Verdoux* courses to a solemn depth when Henri meets a young woman (Marilyn Nash) just out of jail. He prepares a snack for her, but also plans to give his special poison a trial run with the wine. She's depressed about her life, and with an indulgence only the young can afford, states that she prefers suicide to a drab existence. The woman adds, "I suppose if the unborn knew of the approach of life, they would be just as terrified."

The young woman possesses one hope, however. She believes in the fullness of love: "Love is giving, sacrificing, the same thing a mother feels for her child." Henri disagrees, embittered by his slate in life. He says bluntly, "I love women, but I don't admire them." He explains that a woman will reject a man to marry another man of inferior status. A ruthless world dictates to Henri that only physical love can exist between a male and female, and that one must be unscrupulous to survive. Clearly, his philosophy mimics the many lives of duplicity that he leads.

The woman denies Henri's callous beliefs, and this denial leads to circumstances that spare her from death. She confides that life matters little since her invalid husband died. The woman loved him dearly, so dearly that she would have killed for him if necessary. Henri realizes a rare moment of empathy, recognizing a parallel with his own family. He changes wines, gives his guest money, and sends her away. They meet by chance twice again, and on both occasions she must remind Henri how they met. Henri's act of kindness represents such a departure from his accustomed guile that he selectively forgets his charity.

Their last encounter reveals a different, aging Henri. He even confesses that "Everyone needs love," prompting the woman to suggest that he has lost his zest for bitterness. Henri, indeed, has lost more than his zest to defy the odds: The market's collapse wipes him out financially, and he tells the woman that his wife and child have died. The words he chooses lead us to suspect that Henri may have helped them die, rather than force his loved ones to face the poverty of a bleak future. It is a credit to Henri's way with words that we do not know conclusively. Regardless, his mission of marriages and monies is finished. He has no reason to continue the quest.

He also has no reason to remain free. Meeting the woman enlightens this sad figure to reach a final decision: Henri allows the police to capture him so that he may "fulfill his destiny." This destiny includes a closing statement to the French court at a time when the shadow of the Nazi swastika looms nearby. Putting his Bluebeard murders in perspective, Henri warns, "As a mass killer I am an amateur by comparison....I shall see you all very soon, very soon."

What Henri sees as we leave him, nonetheless, is a long corridor that leads to the guillotine. This romantic man of pretense, so sensitive to the needs of the women he courted and killed, comes to realize the profundity of true love. But his realization occurs only after he has no one through which to experience the affection.

Bargaining, in one sense, seems at odds with the ideal of romantic love. Henri demonstrates this conflict when he cold-heartedly provides his companionship in return for whatever resources he can glean from his wifely victims. But a healthy marriage cannot subsist on romance alone. Tradeoffs between lovers must occur, spats demand compromise and acquiescence, and the lingering of hurtful feelings needs assuaging.

When this bargaining does not find a voice, we encounter a hollow marriage: The kind of feuding relationship that Oliver and Barbara Rose (Michael Douglas and Kathleen Turner) live in *The War Of The Roses* (1989). Oliver and Barbara certainly meet romantically, two college students who happen upon an auction during a rainy day on the island of Nantucket. She outbids him for a Shinto goddess figurine that sets the tone for their sparring engagements.

The sparring assumes less priority at first, giving way naturally to the partners' thirst for great sex. Oliver's hot for her, and Barbara's a gymnast--a combination that gives the couple more thrills in bed than in the remainder of their marriage. On one occasion she murmurs "I'm sorry," presumably embarrassed at enjoying the sex so much. Oliver, enraptured, admonishes her to "...never apologize for being multi-orgasmic."

Warning signals disrupt their serenity and involve, as they often do, little skirmishes that widen the gap between lovers. Oliver's consumed with building a career as a lawyer, leaving Barbara to select and furnish the house of their dreams. He dislikes her inability to tell a story at social gatherings, and reads Barbara's decision to enter the catering business as a nuisance. In truth, however, Oliver senses a disconcerting preference on Barbara's part to rival his growing professional status.

What Oliver fails to realize, regrettably, is that Barbara dislikes him more than he dislikes her. She finds his phony laugh annoying, and observes that he nods his head like a bird when he eats. Moreover, she detests his snoring and enjoys inserting her fingers up his nostrils to gag him awake. To worsen the brew, Barbara's a cat person and Oliver's a dog person. Barbara fakes out the dog by pretending to throw tidbits, then, leaving the dog thoroughly frustrated, she feeds the tidbits to her cat.

Oliver, baffled, asks the inevitable question: "What the hell is wrong with you?" Eventually, he receives his answer. Stricken with an apparent heart attack that results in a false alarm, Oliver bitterly takes the train home when Barbara fails to come for him. Upon confronting Barbara, she admits that she was scared of losing him--but scared because "I felt happy." Oliver, finally, senses something of the hatred that awaits him.

The house becomes their sad Waterloo. Barbara has worked years to furnish it with loving, l-o-v-i-n-g care. The house is her house, she wants it. Oliver views the house as being there because he paid for it. The house is his house, he wants it. Objectively, the house represents years of social investment accumulated by two people who find themselves oriented differently to life. Oliver deserves the first round of stones because of his insensitivity to Barbara's needs during their early years together. But both partners make mistakes, and a common, obsessive desire to keep the house proves their ultimate misfortune.

Oliver enlists Gavin (Danny DeVito) as his lawyer, and Gavin uncovers an obscure legal arrangement that allows Oliver to maintain "separate" residence in the house. Gavin comes to regret his discovery. He watches his friend sink slowly into a demented state, daft to the point of Oliver showing Gavin a blueprint of the house with "his" and "her" designations, followed by Oliver's fiendish boast that he has "more square footage." Gavin, recognizing that Oliver is losing it, seeks to dissuade him: "Oliver, my father used to say that a man could never outdo a woman when it came to love or revenge." Alas, Gavin's advice arrives too late.

Barbara also visits Gavin, intending to seduce him to her advantage. Gavin, with considerable will power, rebuffs her advances but resumes smoking, a vice he had successfully overcome until the Roses. Later, Oliver pointedly asks him if he "banged" Barbara. Gavin says no, truthfully. Oliver, momentarily distracted, wistfully recalls Barbara's lovemaking powers and admits, "She was great. She was a gymnast."

The hostilities escalate: Oliver deliberately intrudes on a party given by Barbara for her catering clients. He sneezes on her display of delicacies and urinates on the fish; in retaliation, she destroys his Morgan sports car. Afterward, they reduce their conflict to a physical struggle in the attic. Oliver gasps, "Well, I guess I'm on top now" and finds himself duly aroused. Barbara plays along, even to the point of pretending to give Oliver a "blow job" that turns into a "bite job," allowing Barbara to use her sexual prowess to good purpose.

The Shinto goddess, the tie that began their romance, poses as the final icon of no return. Oliver shatters the figurine, and, in a pause of comedic madness, he and Barbara find themselves perched on a wobbly chandelier looking down from a considerable height. Cables pull out slowly, wires snap, all the symbols of a marriage long in decay. The final break plummets the chandelier and the Roses to the floor below, snuffing out candles along the way.

The lovers lie peacefully amid the debris of their lives. Oliver painfully reaches over to touch Barbara. Barbara, in response, covers his hand with hers--then abruptly flings his hand away in a final gesture of disdain. Oliver, wanting to love her, cannot love her enough; and Barbara, wanting to rid herself of him, refuses his last overture of togetherness.

The moral? Gavin, who narrates the story to a prospective divorce client, gives the client a choice that he knows the Roses should have taken. Either prepare to give the wife all she wants and avoid untold misery, or, "...or you can get up and go home and try to find some shred of what you once loved about the sweetheart of your youth." Sad to say, but for the Roses, Nantucket never seemed so far away.

The Velvet Touch

The movies, as we have seen, defy hard-nosed reality by supplying preposterous humor to parody the usual conventions about sex and love. Sometimes the parody is absurdly comedic to unleash the zaniness of love in bloom, and sometimes absurdly tragic to comment on love's darker corners.

The movies, in venturing to satisfy our Oz of fables and farces, rely on still another process, that of **sheer fantasy.** Sheer fantasy involves breathing some timeless passion into our pale illusions. A "compatibility check" does not exist, but what if it did? Could Jerry turn honest in his dating relationships? Imagine the scenario where technology compels Jerry to walk the fine line, knowing that his natural propensity to selfishness can deny him the "goodies" he seeks. There's humor and tragedy in this predicament, and sheer fantasy, too.

The movies give fantasy a commanding role, whatever its exact contribution. We don't gaze at the big screen to assimilate another dose of everyday reality. We wish for fantasy to reign, to prescribe a more pleasing appearance. Apart from the movies, we entertain this pleasing appearance only fleetingly in our daydreams. Consequently, we depend on Oz to give ourselves a world of fantasy. Movies can concoct sheer pretense with such panache. They can make romance something special, and, in exquisite moments, something memorable.

Sheer fantasy softens reality, content to embroider the facts with a little spiritual glow, a little ethereal kiss. *Local Hero* (1983) offers us a modest subplot that illustrates fantasy's **velvet touch.** The main story details an American oil company that wishes to buy the little fishing village of Ferness in Scotland. This storyline proves less important than the film's numerous diversions. Among them, a gangling Scottish lad, Danny (Peter Capaldi), who's smitten with Marina (Jenny

Seagrove), a mysterious, self-assured Scottish lass. Marina, true to her name, appears more natural in the water than out. The revealing instant arrives when Danny, lavishing kisses on Marina's anatomy, discovers a hitherto unknown fact about his beloved's fetching feet--namely, that she possesses webbed toes. The director, Bill Forsyth, wisely leaves the fantasy at that, affording his audience a little space to wonder about Marina and her mermaidish ways.

Another velvet touch occurs in the artistry of Steve Martin's eye-stopping proboscis: the architecture of his marvelously extended nose in *Roxanne* (1987). Martin plays C. D. Bales, a fire chief who harbors romance in his heart, but who's saddled with a nose that simply can't be ignored.[2] Bales and Chris (Rick Rossovich), a newcomer to the firehouse, find themselves at the mercy of a beautiful blond astronomer, Roxanne (Daryl Hannah). Both males suffer a romantic handicap: Bales, sensitive about his prominent appendage, assumes that Roxanne could not overlook the Mother of all noses; and Chris, physically a superb specimen of manhood, falls apart verbally when he attempts to speak with her.

Fortunately, *Roxanne* delivers more than a one-nose story. Bales, sacrificing his prospects, attempts to help Chris conquer the hunk's verbal nonsense in order to win the fair Roxanne, leaving C. D. to his melancholy dreams of a smaller nose. But the movie allows sheer fantasy to gather momentum and work its delicate magic: The velvet touch arrives just in time to give reality a shot in the snoot. Fantasy's perspective permits love's mesmerizing spell to draw C. D. and Roxanne together, the fire chief's wondrous nose notwithstanding.

The velvet touch, however, does not require the props of a damsel's webbed toes or a fireman's extended nose to cast its charms. The touch may simply require a firm faith in the power of love's attraction. *Sleepless In Seattle* (1993) conjures up a love-at-first sight experience between Sam Baldwin (Tom Hanks) and Annie Reed (Meg Ryan), finessed in the wings by Sam's small son, Jonah (Ross Malinger). Sam's wife dies unexpectedly and the widower finds himself unable to steer free of his grief. Jonah, therefore, searches as much for a wife to ease his father's mourning, as he does a mother to fulfill his own needs.

Annie, settled into an engagement with a nice chap who makes the word "bland" seem tumultuous, gradually realizes that she wants out. Indeed, she really wants Sam, although the two have never met. The odds do not appear favorable. Geography (Annie's in Baltimore and Sam's in Seattle) and Annie's apprehensiveness over the prospects of a love-smitten relationship hold her back. Annie's mother tells of the magic in her very first date with Annie's father, but the daughter doesn't understand. She fails to comprehend because nothing of the sort has ever happened to her. Annie begins to feel something "special yet confusing" only when she hears about Sam and his loss on a radio talk show.

Slowly, inevitably, the velvet touch assumes control. Neither geography nor the proposition of loving a virtual stranger will stay Annie from her course. *Sleepless In Seattle* gains inspiration from old ballads that create the appropriate mood swings for its fated lovers. Anne also realizes inspiration from a 1957 melodrama, *An Affair To Remember*, starring Cary Grant and Deborah Kerr. *Affair*, notes Roger Ebert (1993, p. 613), acts as a "romantic compass" to guide the lovers through perilous detours so that they may safely manifest their destiny.

Jonah manages some tenuous arrangements to gather Annie, Sam, and himself on the observation platform of the Empire State Building in New York. Cinematic reality suggests that these arrangements should never materialize. But the velvet touch says otherwise. The parties **almost** don't meet, but "almost" does not belong in Once Upon A Time's vocabulary. Jonah and Sam leave before Annie arrives, but Jonah forgets his backpack (decreed by fate) and he and Sam return to the platform. Surprise! Annie's there, Sam's there, and Jonah couldn't be happier. Kismet: There's magic in the air.

The lovers who have never touched introduce themselves, although these amenities prove superfluous. Annie and Sam gaze upon one another, humbled by the intensity of their attraction. The two are immeasurably grateful that in a world of grief, distance, and pedestrian affections, they enjoy the good fortune of discovering their special romance.

Thus, when Sam offers his hand and Annie accepts, it's difficult for the viewer not to tingle a bit. You don't worry about the practicality of whether Baltimore will move to Seattle or Seattle to Baltimore. You don't wonder about the labor to keep a partnership going, day by day. The velvet touch, true to its amorous ways, refuses to bother with such grit and grime. You just know that Sam and Annie are meant to be, ordained by whatever providence blesses their togetherness.

The Velvet Clout

The velvet touch of movies like *Local Hero, Roxanne,* and *Sleepless In Seattle* denotes an exception to the rule of sheer fantasy. More commonly, cinematic fantasy chooses to march forth, strident and challenging, willfully breaking traditional customs to carry moviegoers into another dimension. Wholehearted fantasy gives itself over to timeless passion. The movies know how to unleash intense feelings, and how to make these feelings the breakfast, lunch, and dinner of lovers.

The velvet touch, therefore, accelerates more frequently to the **velvet clout** in love stories: A paradoxical combination of romance spiced with a rousing dose of the supernatural. Compare, for example, Marina, our feminist mermaid of *Local Hero*, to Madison (Daryl Hannah), the naive though adventurous mermaid of *Splash* (1984). Marina's an environmentalist and easily as concerned with the ocean's resources as with the possibility of acquiring a Scottish lover. Consequently, we wonder about her "naturalness" in the water. Did Danny see a fishtail flash and disappear oh so briefly in the bay...or did the youth's obsession with Marina trick his imagination? The director teases us with the likelihood of a transformation, but we aren't sure.

Splash, by comparison, leaves no doubt. Madison's truly a mermaid and she's madly in love with Allen (Tom Hanks), a Manhattan gadabout who wheels and deals in vegetables.

Their fable imposes rules to give the fantasy greater urgency: Madison can stay only a short time, and once she goes back to the ocean, she can't return. To wit, the velvet clout of *Splash* raises a searching question about commitment: Does Allen love Madison enough to return with her?

The sheer fantasy of *Splash* demands that we suspend reality, indeed that we hang it high and dry. Allen must juggle the comfort of familiar surroundings against the prospect of relinquishing his material and social trappings to accompany Madison. He stutters and stammers at the pier's end, first deciding "No" and waving goodbye to Madison, who tearfully understands. But sheer fantasy is "go-for-broke" fantasy, and love's too precious to squander halfheartedly on a city life he already dislikes. So, Allen dives in. The viewer's Oz process compels it, so in he goes. Forget that our hero enters an underwater kingdom, complete with a new agenda for adapting to Madison's watery life. You can forget such problems because in a full-blown fantasy only the passion of romance really matters.

Interestingly, *Splash* relates the happening of a male who exchanges his world for the female's world. This grand illusion works fine in fable since we can freeze the romantic finale of Allen and Madison, evermore. The velvet clout knows no boundaries for expressing love's magic spell since neither distance, time, nor death shall deter the lovers. The sheer fantasy of romance sees to it that all lovers triumph, or at least that the lovers' fascination will not perish.

A favorite theme of the velvet clout involves resurrection and the finagling of time. A **Timeless Romance**, in its most literal interpretation, concerns a mastery over death. Once you accept this mastery, all other events fall into place. Heavenly spirits can experience a love they never felt on earth (*Defending Your Life*, 1991), and other spirits can enter new bodies to discover romance and success previously denied them (*Here Comes Mr. Jordan* in 1941, and its remake *Heaven Can Wait* in 1978).

Or, if a story dictates that the transformation become less facile, spirits can labor more diligently to convey the love felt from one world to another, as Sam (Patrick Swayze) does for

Molly (Demi Moore) in *Ghost* (1990). The newly departed Sam works not only to communicate his presence and love through an addled psychic (Whoopi Goldberg), he finds it necessary to thwart the devious designs of a supposed best friend who lusts after Molly.

Rest assured that Sam's fantasy love shall triumph, but note that the lovers--and the viewers--must struggle for their "happily ever after." We pay money to enthrall Oz with love's indomitable spirit, and we expect such a love to confront and transcend insurmountable obstacles. "Indomitable" and "insurmountable" constitute the absolutes that give romantic love its glorious fantasy, and make our captivation worth the price of admission.[3]

Perhaps the purest love to defy time and death becomes a love that obliterates all other persons, passions, and priorities. *Somewhere In Time* (1980) embraces this quality with its simple tale of romance, but does so, first, through an intriguing prelude: An elderly woman approaches Richard Collier (Christopher Reeve), a promising playwright, and presses a pocket watch in his hand as she murmurs, "Come back to me." He's baffled, but eight years pass before Richard, now soured on his talent, drives to a beautiful hotel on Mackinac Island in Michigan. His promise as a writer began there, and he feels the urge to return.

The velvet clout of love leaves little to chance. Richard's arrival sets in motion a series of encounters, reminders, and puzzlements that convince him he not only lived a previous life at the hotel, but that he did so with a lovely actress, Elise McKenna (Jane Seymour). Richard wills himself back to June 27, 1912, the day he meets Elise for the first time. Indeed, when she gazes upon him, Elise poses the question: "Is it you?"

The actress, it seems, searches for the man of her dreams, an image that the males in her life have not gratified. Richard brings Elise's dreams to harvest, although once together, people and events intervene to keep the lovers apart. But the barriers foster only delays at best, and cannot rival the single-mindedness of two people who hunger for romance. This hunger ensures that love is too potent and ascendant to waver, no matter what catastrophes await...including death.

Wrenched back to the present just as he and Elise had countered all resistance, Richard pines for his lost love. He embraces her portrait; he refuses to eat; he sits by the window and sees nothing. Attempts to revive him fail for he does not wish to survive. Through death and beyond, Richard rejoins Elise, united at last in defiance of time, distance, and the finality of life.

Somewhere In Time dramatizes an unrelenting story of romance, accompanied by Rachmaninov's haunting "Variations on a Theme by Paganini." The movie's palpable force-- Richard and Elise's unabashed affection--visually and melodiously transports viewers above the angst of time's twists and distractions to savor the lovers' determined resurrection. The actors' understated portrayals give a quiet life to their love. Elise and Richard capture a solemn declaration that does not falter, even as they recognize the need to surpass time and death.

Resurrection presents a majestic cinematic tool for glorifying romance. Its definition, moreover, travels beyond the mastery of death to encompass the idea of **Renewal**. A Timeless Romance can revitalize life, repair lost hope, and, most importantly, create a rebirth of love.

Imagine these cinematic possibilities: A witch, who cannot cry or fall in love as a witch, loses her powers (and her cat) when she experiences love's enchantment for the first time (*Bell, Book, And Candle,* 1958); a young widow falls in love with an alien...who assumes the appearance of her late husband (*Starman*, 1984); a fearsome beast realizes love through the charms of a fair young beauty (*King Kong,* 1933/1976; *Mighty Joe Young*, 1949; *Beauty And The Beast*, 1991); and, borrowing from the classic love story of *Casablanca*, a neurotic (Woody Allen) relies on the help of Humphrey Bogart to learn about love and how to sacrifice that love like a man (*Play It Again, Sam*, 1972).

A rich concoction of love and the supernatural draws on the good magic and black magic of 13th century France. Two lovers travel together, wandering in despair, forever trapped because of an evil bishop's vengeful curse. By dawn, he transforms to a handsome knight, Navarre (Rutger Hauer), and his ladylove to a noble hawk; by twilight, she materializes as the lovely Isabeau (Michelle Pfeiffer), and he becomes the nocturnal prowler, a wolf restlessly awaiting the curse's endless cycle.

Ladyhawke (1985) thus unfolds the story of two tormented souls, bonded in spirit, yet physically apart. For one brief, tantalizing moment, during the metamorphosis, Navarre and Isabeau can glimpse themselves as human: A vanishing, bittersweet glimpse filled with all the longing and agony than an evil spell can command.

Curses, damnation, and malediction! How forever is forever? Will the lovers find no relief? Portentously for them they encounter a young runaway, Phillipe (Matthew Broderick), who becomes their messenger, their guardian, and their ticket out of the hinterlands. Phillipe not only helps each lover stay alive, he proves instrumental in arranging the decisive confrontation between good and evil.

Resurrection empowers its lovers to dare nature. But the lovers' rebirth does not concern a triumph over death. Rather, Isabeau and Navarre wish a harmonious rebirth to human form; a Renewal of human existence that will give substance to their attachment. The answer comes through a natural geological event--an eclipse of the sun, turning day into night--a happening that appears quite frightening and supernatural to the inhabitants of medieval France. Here, for a few precious minutes, Navarre and Isabeau can confront the wretched Bishop and stare down his curse. They have in their grasp a rare opportunity to break the cycle of "forevermore" and give themselves the gift of renaissance.

Navarre, thinking Isabeau dead, fights in the cathedral as the last desperate act of a man condemned to die without love's fulfillment. He struggles to the alter, facing the Bishop: two men who desire the same woman, although for reasons as contrary as night and day.

Navarre prepares to slay the Bishop and die himself, but he hears a voice, Isabeau's voice. The Bishop, assured of the curse's success with only Navarre present, now cringes in terror as Isabeau approaches. A final, dastardly attempt to kill her fails, culminating in the Bishop's demise. Isabeau and

Navarre embrace, bathed in a shaft of soft light. They cling
to each other with an exuberance that only resurrected lovers
possess: "Isabeau!" "Navarre!" The words speak volumes for
two lost souls who have earned their happiness.

A Timeless Romance, then, can remove curses and
rejuvenate Navarre and Isabeau's tortured attachment by
conquering the forces of darkness. The practice of cinematic
resurrection can even take a movie within a movie and tease
this fantasy/fantasy into a happy confusion of wish fulfillment.

Imagine a young woman who realizes little love in her life.
She's married to a man who treats her indifferently. She
works as a waitress in a cramped cafe. To worsen her plight,
she loses her job because she can't stay on top of the patrons'
orders, drops dishes, and talks too much to her sister, the other
waitress. She talks too much because she's distracted, and
she's distracted because her desired existence is not with the
cafe or her loutish husband. She fantasizes, instead, about her
sanctuary. The one haven she frequents to escape broken
plateware, rude customers, and a philandering spouse--the
movie theatre.

Violating the sacred canon that segregates fiction from
flesh-and-blood reality, a matinee idol steps from the silver
screen, still in character, to learn about love and real life from
his adoring young fan. The fan is Cecilia (Mia Farrow); the
fictional character is Tom Baxter (Jeff Daniels); the actor who
creates Tom is an ego-ridden performer, Gil Shepherd (also
Jeff Daniels); and Cecilia's thoroughly perplexed husband is
Monk (Danny Aiello), a man without vision who wants her
back to take care of his needs.

Woody Allen's *The Purple Rose Of Cairo* (1985) develops
this mismatch into an unlikely love story. Cecilia, feeling
unloved and unappreciated, suddenly finds herself torn in
three directions. Monk wants her back as she was, to prepare
his meat loaf and give him money to play craps. Gil becomes
enamored of her because she lavishes him with praise. But
Tom, the fictional character, wants her for herself. He's a
romantic, a figure who knows and does only what his

character should know and do (he can drive a car, though not start a car).

Tom's a poetic idealist, and a wee bit naive. Emma (Diane Weiss), a prostitute, brings him to her bordello and tries to explain the difference between being "in love" and "making love." Tom, however, remains committed to Cecilia, and decides to induct her into his world on the screen. This decision relieves his fellow actors who have squabbled among themselves and complained to the management that they can't continue the story until Tom returns. *The Purple Rose Of Cairo* tells us as much of the one-dimensionality of actors-- people so wafer thin that they seem right at home on the screen--as of the moviegoers' drudgery off the screen during the Great Depression of the 1930s.

Woody Allen, using the characters in the movie/movie and in the film proper, takes his potshots at the wavering line between fantasy and reality. The movie/movie (also called *The Purple Rose Of Cairo*) represents a B-vehicle, and the actors constitute B-actors. The players, waiting for Tom Baxter to return, bicker at the audience, and the audience, tired of the players doing nothing, bicker back.

One actor, irritated, notes that maybe "We're a reality, they're a dream," a dash of wishful thinking. Earlier in the film, a moviegoer rushes to the manager with her own complaint: "I want what happened in the movie last week to happen this week, otherwise what's life all about?" No one is satisfied with the unexpected merger of fantasy and reality. Tom, the fictional character, leaves fantasy behind to discover his freedom and the reality of reality, whereas moviegoers attend the theatre to leave the Great Depression behind and lose themselves in sheer fantasy.

The focus of this tug-of-war between fantasy and reality is Cecilia, and Cecilia must make her choice. Tom offers her his simple philosophy on togetherness ("We'll live on love"). Gil professes his affection and wants the two of them to fly to Hollywood, the headquarters of all her dreams. And Monk, well, Monk just wants her back. Cecilia chooses Gil, telling a heartbroken Tom not to worry because "In your world things

have a way of always working out right." Tom, understanding, returns to the screen.

Cecilia rushes to her dingy apartment to pack, then returns
to the theatre only to find that the moguls, including Gil, have
gone. Gil flies back to Hollywood, reflective of deserting
Cecilia, but not so remorseful as to allow her into his life and,
more critically, to become part of his career. With Tom back
on the screen, Gil can resume his work again, the only pursuit
that truly matters to him.

And what of Cecilia? Her modest, cardboard suitcase in
hand, she goes, not home, but to the theatre. Cecilia gazes
forlornly at her dream world--Fred Astaire and Ginger Rogers
are dancing cheek to cheek--a fantasy so near, yet so far. It
was almost her world, surely a moment so unlikely that it must
be treasured. Haltingly, a small smile lights her face. Reality
dims and she loses herself once more to the luster of the giant
screen. Astaire and Rogers...now that's real magic.

The crazed humor of lovers in love, the magic of sheer
fantasies that soar above reality, these qualities allow the
cinema to present its fare with a flourish. Such irreverences
spite convention and permit Oz to experience cinematic
illusions at their pinnacle. Illusions that strut their stuff,
parody the usual bonds of daily existence, and resurrect love's
ardor to circumvent death and overcome a curse or two. A
velvet touch or a velvet clout on the viewer's nose that does
marvels for a droopy disposition. Love's funny that way.

Movies excel in glamorizing romance. Given the movies'
penchant for dramatizing love's spellbinding attraction, it's not
surprising that passion receives the most cinematic attention
via absurd humor and sheer fantasy. Elaine and Ted, Trilby
and Elmer, Annie and Sam, Madison and Allen, Elise and
Richard, Isabeau and Navarre: These lovers embark on
different excursions of fantasy, yet all share the spontaneity
and intensity of love's passion. Intervene to disrupt lovers in
heat and you'll rue the day. Passion proves a force unto itself;
an emotional blunderbuss that charges in high gear against all
barriers, illuminating the kind of ferocity that translates so
well to the big screen.

Still, love encompasses much more than passion. Love also brings forth soft-spoken blessings like intimacy and commitment: blessings that give passion a chance for substance and longevity. Absurd humor and sheer fantasy say little of such blessings, but there are stories to follow in which intimacy and commitment become paramount. Stories that show young lovers and mature lovers struggling for the same paradise. Struggling, in essence, to discover **the** relationship, and, this time, to get it right.

Notes

1. I conducted a study to examine the humor in Jerry and Karen's tango of the sexes. I used a convenience sample of students from a frosh Human Sexuality class and a junior-level Psychology of Aggression offering. A convenience sample represents one of the less random forms of selecting subjects. You simply access students who are available, usually students willing to lend themselves for extra credit. Excluding four males and two females who had viewed the Jerry/Karen scenario before, and after determining that no appreciable differences prevailed between students in the two courses, I obtained humor ratings using a 0-to-9 scale.

My descriptive results yielded the following values, drawn from 49 females and 26 males: Females: Arithmetic Mean = 6.61, Standard Deviation = 1.497; Males: Arithmetic Mean = 5.65, Standard Deviation = 1.495. The Standard Deviation values indicate that males and females provided about the same consistency of ratings. The Mean values suggest that females found Jerry's predicament funnier, although males might have judged the scenario just as funny but, since they portrayed the "goat" in the piece, felt obliged to rate it more conservatively.

When I asked students for reasons concerning the skit's humor, four possibilities surfaced: (1) Reasons related to **salience** arose in which females recalled trying to assess the honesty of lines like those given by Jerry, and in which males admitted to the familiarity of attempting comparable lines on girls. (2) Reasons favoring **control** emerged whereby females enjoyed the idea of gaining an upper hand via the machine, and males acknowledged that females would find pleasure in knowing the male's sexual history. (3) Reasons based on **expressiveness** occurred when females and even males experienced humor from Jerry's stunned reactions. (4) And reasons devoted to **character** came forth when females painted a despairing picture of males as slime, and when males confirmed that some females prefer to disparage males in general.

Thus, in keeping with the humorous caliber of Jerry and Karen's blind date--and with the kind of cinematic humor that the sexes frequently display--most of the "blind-date" funniness stems from a negative rationale.

2. Humor, as noted, thrives on the unconventional response. Bales could yell in despair when someone reminds him of his curse. Instead, he learns to poke fun at himself, while ridiculing others. The movie's opening scene shows C. D. walking and swinging his tennis racquet, when he encounters three "studs" who begin delivering cracks about his nose. Bales, borrowing from his character's predecessor, Cyrano de Bergerac, uses his racquet to duel the three bumpkins, foiling them in a flourish of grace and wit. Later, a bar-room adversary derides Bales's nose, only to find himself upstaged: C. D. bounces around and uncorks a series of clever one-liners to disparage his nose, a tactic that makes his adversary the bigger fool. Bales, however, cannot protect himself from romance, nor from the lovely charms of Roxanne. He tries to laugh away the hurt, but he can't.

3. *The Ghost And Mrs. Muir* (1947), an earlier story of love in limbo, offers a thoughtful comparison to the Swayze/Moore *Ghost* story. The former film presents Captain Daniel Gregg (Rex Harrison), a discontented ghost who wants to set the record straight about his death, and attempts to do so through the kindness of Mrs. Muir (Gene Tierney). The extended relationship between the Captain and Mrs. Muir develops through a mingling of reality and fantasy (Johnson, 1993). Subsequently you begin to question just how ghostly the Captain really is, since his ethereal love for this woman shows all the agony of an earthly affection. A reminder becomes necessary to keep the Captain a ghost, namely, that his love for Mrs. Muir overcomes the dilemma of two souls caught awkwardly in time and space.

Time passes and Mrs. Muir, now an elderly lady, dies, becomes young again, and finds herself reunited with the Captain--on equal terms at last. This **Timeless Romance** proves a happier ending for viewers than the Swayze/Moore parting in *Ghost*, but the principle in both films remains inviolate: Love harbors the power to conquer death and to renew the spirit toward an eternal intimacy.

Lesson 7

Getting It Right

"**T**he difference between the right word and the almost right word is the difference between lightning and the lightning bug" (Winokur, 1986, p. 89).

People who consider writing essential to life will recognize Mark Twain's pithy comment about discovering the right word. The prosateur, the songwriter, the playwright, the screenwriter, surely the poet, search for the best word, the word that "feels" right, the only word that matters. Laurence Perrine (1956, p. 4), author of *Sound And Sense*, explains that the common use of language is to inform. But for Perrine, experience offers a nobler aim because it transcends the mere assemblage of facts.

Writing for experience demands a judicious selection of words. The best word becomes an exercise worth examining. Challenge yourself, therefore, to discover the most apt word in the poem to follow. Challenge yourself to experience one woman's reminiscence of a missed desire. This thoughtful memory, entitled *The Look*, seems not so much composed as **felt** by the poet, Sara Teasdale (Fairfax & Moat, 1981, p. 27).

Choose the word you believe best captures the spirit of Teasdale's verse and place that word in the space provided (we shall return to Teasdale and her poem later in the lesson):

> Strephon kissed me in the spring,
>   Robin in the fall,
> But Colin only looked at me
>   And never kissed at all.
> Strephon's kiss was lost in jest,
>   Robin's lost in play,
> But the _____ in Colin's eyes
>   Haunts me night and day.

Experiencing the language takes a bit of practice. What you feel for someone, or for an idea, can enhance your understanding. Oz, as stated before, primes you to assume certain emotional expectations about a film. But feelings also mislead. An exciting movie will intensify the emotions, and coping with these emotions can color the conclusions you draw.

Recall from Lesson 2 that a movie's **lurking intelligence** becomes manifest when the viewer's emotional experiences permit insight into the filmmaker's theme. Feelings complement thinking so that the viewer becomes emotionally primed to consider nuances about a movie's message heretofore not realized. Put succinctly, The emotive experience unlimbers the intellect.

Love, for example, addresses a special meaning in the world of illusion and glamour. This awesome emotion, as an experience, moves beyond the trappings of academic curiosity to assume a favorite target of the moviegoer's Oz process. Surely the lessons are legion in how, and how not to, negotiate amorous relationships. Surely, too, considerable intelligence lurks in the many ways that we, as viewers, choose to decipher this experience.

Experience is what love **does** to people: to their physical desires, their willingness to compromise, their normally common sense, to their very being. Robert Sternberg (Sternberg & Whitney, 1991, pp. 65-86) speaks of experiencing the most **consummate love** through a fulfillment of passion, intimacy, and commitment. Passion calls forth intensity, intimacy encourages emotional closeness, and commitment gives the relationship continuity.

Our previous lesson emphasized that movies entertain most lavishly when they present love as passion. Absurd humor and sheer fantasy dote on passion and accord this strong emotion the heights (and depths) through which lovers chart their course. But Sternberg contends that a rich orchestration of all three experiences becomes essential for a consummate love to occur. Love expressed merely by passion, or intimacy, or commitment, denotes a flawed attachment.

If you equate love with **passion**, what do you feel? You feel infatuation, a rousing sense of physical desire, perhaps a "rush" to satisfy your sexual urges. But you feel this sensual gratification without the pull of intimacy and without the obligation of personal commitment. Passion alone carries you to a sexual relationship, a playfully erotic relationship, although not a relationship that leads to a deeper love--despite what the movies of sheer fantasy enjoy proposing.

By contrast, **intimacy** and **commitment** characterize a companionship free of passion's fire, offering instead a bond of friendship. Portraying lengthy heterosexual friendships excites neither moviemakers nor moviegoers. How many films do you know where a female and male partner remain friends rather than lovers? This elite category allows for an occasional entry, such as the book lovers (Anne Bancroft and Anthony Hopkins) who find themselves allies in *84 Charing Cross Road* (1987). But mainstream movies pay homage to the belief that lovers prove a more marketable commodity than friends.

Romantic love arrives on screen sporting a staple prerequisite. A consummate love in real life defines a dull love in movie life. Something must happen to the lovers; something troublesome to disrupt happiness, something entangling to forestall contentment, something ominous to mount the odds against a romance serene and secure. Filmmakers know that couples in ecstasy are too vulnerable to be left unsullied.

Cinematic complications sally forth to muddle the lovers' brew. These complications depend on the maturity of the romantics and other attending problems: Lovers trying to "get it right," lovers trying to "keep it right," lovers wondering what "went wrong," lovers trying to "start over," and, the most perilous undertaking, lovers trying to be lovers for the "first time."

Love's Big Question

Peyton Place harbors the usual gossip regarding its citizens and their nefarious pursuits. The most delicious gossip centers on on the town's sexual proclivities, a pastime that Peyton Place pursues with zeal, if not aplomb. The community tingles of tales hinting at adultery, abortion, illegitimate offspring, nude swimming, and who's making out with whom. The film *Peyton Place* (1957) relates these stories in fine, soap-opera tradition: Stories that teem with the secrets of small-town America, laid against New England's changing seasons of beauty of despair.

Allison MacKenzie (Diane Varsi) prepares to graduate high school, yet admits to only two kisses during her senior year. Her second kiss comes awkwardly from Norman Page (Russ Tamblyn), a boy so mousy and mother-dominated that Allison must give him several green lights before he acts. Indeed, the youths of Peyton Place show us such prim and proper behavior that necking in the dark becomes one of their more daring escapades.

The necking, incidentally, occurs at Allison's birthday party. A party that her mother, Constance (Lana Turner), was reluctant to allow. True to form, Constance walks into her darkened house to surprise several teenage couples in action, although the lovers are fully clothed, lightly smooching, and-- zounds!--not a drop of alcohol is in evidence (Allison refused to spike the punch).

Certainly, even today, a mother could walk into this precarious situation and launch a tirade. Constance, however, has more at stake: She's burdened herself with memories of an unhappy sexual past, fostering a guilt that draws her tighter than a steel guitar. She yells for everyone to leave. Rodney Harrington (Barry Coe) lamely tires to salvage a bad scene by claiming that they were just playing "photography"--you turn the lights out and see what develops. What develops, unfortunately, is that all parties depart and Allison finds another reason to rail and wail at her mother.

A new high-school principal, Michael Rossi (Lee Philips), enters the fray and forces Constance to reexamine her lifestyle. They begin, however, at opposite poles. Rossi wants to institute a course in sex education at the school. Constance reacts in horror, noting as so many adults have noted, that young people will learn about "that" when they marry. What she doesn't know is that Allison and mousy Norman have already whet their sexual curiosity by ordering the "book" in its proverbial brown wrapper. A book that contains information, naturally, about what kids are "not supposed to know."

You realize upon viewing *Peyton Place* that the girls appear better at the game, that they know more than the boys. Betty Anderson (Terry Moore) summarizes this advantage in a memorable line as she notes, perceptively, that "We can see much better than they can think." To underscore her point, when Betty's real love, Rodney, reluctantly follows his father's wishes and attends the prom with Allison, Betty gains her revenge. She entices Rodney to his new car, then charms him into making lustful overtures. She asks Rodney if he really, really, loves her. He replies that he really, really does--at which point Betty slams his head with her purse and stalks away.

Constance creates an unhealthy tension as she seeks to constrain Allison's budding interests in what it means to be a woman. Across town, Nellie Cross (Betty White), winning the award as Peyton Place's most mournful figure, finds that she cannot control her worthless, drunken husband, Lucas (Arthur Kennedy). Nellie's problem is not to ward off his unwanted affections, but to keep Lucas from ravishing Selena (Hope Lange), his stepdaughter. Selena's a good girl, like most of Peyton Place's youth, but she risks her virginity each time a smashed Lucas enters the frame.

Honoring the soap opera in all its passion, four events transpire to galvanize the inhabitants of Peyton Place into action. Event 1 gives us the awaited rape, with Lucas finally overpowering Selena. Considering the delicacy of dramatizing a sexual assault in the 1950s, viewers do not witness the full attack.   Rather, as the invasion commences, the camera discreetly focuses on Selena's hands gripping the bed's headboard.

Lucas commits this taboo of familial intimacy at his peril. Matthew Swain (Lloyd Nolan), the town M.D., informs Selena she's pregnant, but refuses to abort the new life. She tells him of the tragedy, and Swain forces Lucas to sign a confession and take a hike. But if you believe that Selena has finally freed herself of the sneering Lucas, you don't know your soap operas.

Event 2 serves as a wake-up slap when Allison discovers that she's illegitimate. Allison has made a hero of the father she never knew. Take this hero image away, add a heavy dose of mother hatred, and you have an unhappy daughter. Unhappy enough to leave home? Yes, and with the music swelling, unhappy enough to answer an inquiry of "How will you live?" by telling her mother, "I'll live off some man the way you did." Love (sigh) loses its first layer of innocence.

Event 3 brings us Pearl Harbor, a minor episode in the history of Peyton Place, but necessary because the crisis prompts Norman Page to enlist in the paratroopers. (Norman decides that either he'll get blasted to eternity or he'll become a man.) Rodney, against his father's wishes, has married Betty. The war changes this equation and Rodney joins the call, leaving his father and Betty in an uncomfortable relationship. Regrettably, Rodney does not return, a tragedy that ends positively by uniting the two survivors.

That's the good news. The bad news is that Lucas Cross returns to Peyton Place. He's in the navy, he's on leave, and he's still a creep. Event 4 stages a replay of Lucas seeking to double his pleasure with Selena, but she gains an advantage in their struggle and beats Lucas senseless with a piece of firewood. Her mistake, in the confusion of what to do, arises when Selena fears that the decadent Lucas's relationship with her will tarnish the reputation of her boyfriend, Ted Carter (David Nelson), who wishes to become a lawyer.   Selena deduces that the people of Peyton Place will never accept Ted if knowledge of her misfortune surfaces.

Selena's actions are revealed so that her trial and, oh yes, the close of World War II, bring all the characters together. Fascinating, isn't it, that all the stories of Peyton Place display a vested interest in sexual relations. Constance's pain at loving a married man, Michael Rossi's pain as he works to win Constance, Allison's pain at her illegitimacy, Norman's pain in falling so short of manhood, Betty's pain in wanting Rodney, Selena's pain borne of rape, Nellie's pain in the shame of having a husband like Lucas, and Lucas's pain, well, in just being Lucas.

Norman, now a man, meets Allison by cinematic accident on the train back to Peyton Place. He's coming home to stay, she's coming home for Selena's trial, but not stay, or so she thinks. The film's denouement occurs in the courtroom. Matthew Swain, the conscience of Peyton Place, breaks a vow of silence to Selena and tells everyone of Lucas's vile actions. But more important, he gives the townspeople of Peyton Place a lesson in morality. Swain reminds them of their constant gossip, and of the belief by youngsters like Selena that the people will not support her or Ted if they know the truth. It's time, Swain says in effect, to change our ways and encourage the youth of Peyton Place to stay and prosper.

The people respond warmly, Selena realizes a new life, and Allison a new love. From her first blush when Norman gazes at her in her bathing suit, to the forgiveness of her mother, Allison grows from a detached romantic to a young woman of selfless affection. Pain seems the avenue, often, for building such a bridge.

Allison, who narrates the changing seasons in the movie, observes a new season nested in the beauty of Peyton Place's surrounds: "We finally discovered that season of love. It is only found in someone else's heart. Right now someone you know is looking everywhere for it--and it's in you."

Allison's sentiments hark the usual melodrama of cinematic romance: Lovers must earn their happiness. **Adversity** becomes the process for testing love to make it stronger, or send it crashing against the rocks. We, the audience, know what the characters need to achieve, so Oz dictates that we wait, more or less patiently, for them to catch up. Moviegoers never seem to tire of what adversity can do to a good romance.

Young romantics during the era of films like *Peyton Place* give love's awakening a flattering innocence, despite the pain. Merritt Andrews (Dolores Hart) of *Where The Boys Are* (1960) courts trouble, for instance, when she tells her college Courtship-and-Marriage teacher that "playing house" before marriage seems a sensible arrangement. The teacher, taken aback, tells Merritt to rethink her priorities. Cohabitation represents a common practice today, although not the logical preparation for marriage that young people may believe. But in Merritt's generation, her espousal of the idea proves too suggestive of sexual irresponsibility.

She needs to ponder her academic problems, so, with college chums Tuggle (Paula Prentiss), Melanie (Yvette Mimieux), and Angie (Connie Francis) in tow, Merritt heads to Fort Lauderdale for a spring break that will foster sun and relaxation. Sun, yes. Relaxation, hardly. Thousands of students jam the streets and sands of Lauderdale, among them our four girls, each with a love to nurture and consequences to suffer.

Matchups conveniently arise as Merritt jousts wits with a wealthy student, Ryder (George Hamilton); Tuggle finds a gangly free spirit in TV Thompson (Jim Hutton); and Angie encounters a myopic musician, Basil (Frank Gorshin). Melanie, however, breaks the mold and travels a different route, a mistake that ultimately carries the girl/boy game of sexual commitment to a solemn test.

So, what about these relationships? They unfold in the film as lightheartedly adversarial, yet unfailingly stereotyped by gender. Merritt, wise in the ways of male overtures, tells Ryder that guys are either "sweepers," "stokers," or "subtles." Whichever one you are, she contends, the end result is to make a good girl forget she's a good girl. Ryder rebuts her argument by spelling out his philosophy that sex is a friendly experience, like shaking hands, and that love comes later. First you get acquainted, then you love.

The lines of demarcation are clearly, if naively, drawn.
Merritt, Tuggle, and Angie intend to protect their pristine
sexuality, pressing the males (Ryder, TV, Basil) to move
beyond physical passion and face that frightening experience
of commitment. Ryder and TV, talking it over, commiserate
by concluding that boys and girls don't play for the same
stakes. Girls simply can't comprehend the risks attached to
marriage. Ryder and TV decide, without mentioning the fear
specifically, that commitment compromises their male
freedom.

Also threatening, nonetheless, is the thought of sacrificing
a promising relationship. What to do? The gals try to
influence the guys, yet guard those resources that the guys
desire. The guys, in turn, fidget and fumble about, searching
for a way to love and leave. True love, naturally, says that the
guys don't really wish to leave, they just need to convince
themselves to embrace an obligation to stay. We don't expect
Sternberg's umbrella of passion, intimacy, and commitment to
burst forth in the full flush of spring here. But we know from
the girls' philosophy that commitment rules the day. They
must have the boys' assurance, however fragile, that there
exists something more than a genital-level entanglement.

Cinematic fencing between the sexes involves a contest of
cautious invitations and jocular testing, although these
inquiries derive from a one-sided skirmish: She defends, He
attacks. Tuggle remarks that TV keeps "knocking on the
door," a euphemism for the pressure a girl feels when the boy
desires sexual intercourse and the girl chooses to fend off his
advances, verbal or otherwise.

Early in their relationship, TV asks Tuggle if she's a "good
girl" and Tuggle answers "Yes." TV leans back, deflated. But,
later, had he been privy to Tuggle's other remarks, TV might
have absconded for parts unknown. Tuggle admits to the girls
that she was never meant for higher education. Instead, girls
like her were built to have babies. Her wish, in fact, is to be
a "walking, talking baby machine."

Melanie, meanwhile, longs to fall in love, preferably with
an Ivy Leaguer, particularly with a Yalie. She meets Dill
(John Brennan), who tells Melanie what she wants to hear, and

a romance begins. Then Dill becomes unavailable and Melanie is passed to Frank (Rory Harrity), whose intentions are no more honorable. Melanie quickly--too quickly--fabricates a romance with Frank, hesitantly mentioning a couple that met in Ft. Lauderdale and later married. Frank dances around Melanie's queries, giving the distressed girl nothing to construe as a commitment and leaving her confused and increasingly dependent upon him.

Unlike the other girls, Melanie steers herself into treacherous territory. First, Dill seduces her. Then, knowing that she may have gone too far too soon, Melanie shyly asks him not to tell anyone (a promise not likely kept). Later, she becomes Frank's "girl," seduced again, and now desperate to resolve her risqué behavior through the sanctity of marriage. Frank agrees to meet at their "spot," a motel, after he finishes partying with the guys. Only when she opens the door, it's Dill, not Frank, and the emotional switch becomes more than Melanie can handle. Dill, quietly but firmly, forces her back into the room, fully prepared to have his way. Melanie protests weakly, but she finds herself too numb to resist him. What happens, happens off camera, yet the circumstances exhibit all the accouterments of today's date rape.

Melanie leaves the motel in a daze, walking the highway's center stripe, no longer able to keep her battered defenses intact. A car deals her a glancing blow, just before Ryder and Merritt rescue her. Later, in the hospital, Melanie mumbles to Merritt, "I feel so old, so old." Whatever the promises of love's awakening once meant to Melanie, she can never recapture that romance. Dill and Frank have wrung this idealism from her, and now we wonder if Melanie will ever embrace a true love (see Paglia, 1992, p. 52).

Merritt, under stress from Melanie's ordeal, blames all boys, including Ryder, for what they'll do to get what they want. Her bitterness stems not just from Melanie's tragedy, but out of feelings that tap the fundamental adversity a female must overcome to gain the male's commitment.

Where The Boys Are maintains the genderism of girls who play a passive game of search-and-win, waiting for the boys to commit.[1] The girl cannot be too forceful, show too much

interest, or become too available, lest the boy feels cornered
and beats a hasty retreat. This traditional scenario means that
the girl must walk a fine path of reticence to land her fellow.
The notion that **she** could behave as a guy, and simply date for
fun with no intention of securing a mate, does not figure in
the cinematic game of romance.

Merritt relents, of course. Movies like *Where The Boys Are*
dare not let Ryder and Merritt part company. The closing
scene finds them on the beach, now deserted, ready to admit
to their vulnerability and their desire. Ryder tells Merritt that
she's strong and capable, although Merritt finds love, or what
she thinks is love, too challenging to really feel in control.
Merritt asks Ryder how you know the difference, how do you
know real love? Ryder has no answer. Merritt decides to ask
the searching question: "Ryder, do you love me?" Ryder says
he thinks so. Then, surprising herself, Merritt asks the more
thoughtful question: "Ryder, do I love you?" Ryder, pausing,
answers fervently, "I hope so."

Why ask such a question? You can argue logically that
Merritt merely seeks Ryder's assurance of her commitment.
But love hurtles forth as an **experience**. Love's awakening is
surely as much an experience as a logical choice. And Merritt
wonders if the feeling she experiences...is the right feeling.

Love's Rude Awakening

Merritt and Ryder earn their commitment by achieving an
intimacy that permits the asking of hard questions without
flinching. (Remember that Melanie searched for this same
honesty, but Frank refused to match her sincerity.) Romance
in the 1950s presents chastity as an admirable quality for
females like Allison and Merritt, despite having chastity
succumb to so many prudently melodramatic interpretations.

The formula worked well in its time, but such formulas do
not remain indelible. Lovers like Allison and Norman, and
Merritt and Ryder, characterize the closing of an era.
Romantics began to ride a cultural wave of change in the
1960s: The Zeitgeist--the spirit of the times--relaxed sexual

restraint and indulged lovers to behave more publicly with their amorous desires. Partners in passion subscribed to a more tolerant climate upon pursuing their new-found romance. Love's awakening became destined for some radical surgery.

Imagine, again, that you are immersed in the 1950s. Eisenhower guides the country with a prosperous hand, and you sway gently to soulful melodies like *Cold Cold Heart* (Hank Williams), *The Tennessee Waltz* (Patti Page), and *Anytime* (Eddie Fisher). Are you once again visiting Peyton Place and Ft. Lauderdale, ferreting out the subterranean flow of love's awakening? No, you've returned to the 1950s alright, but the rules of chastity hardly apply. Now, you find yourself in the Florida Everglades, joining a group of teenagers who plan a quick trip to Porky's. The teenagers, moreover, pass themselves off as '50's adolescents, yet in no way resemble the modest characters of *Peyton Place* and *Where The Boys Are*.

The teenagers in *Porky's* (1981) exhibit a language and behavior that would overwhelm our chaste couples and their virtuous talk of promiscuity. What a difference a generation makes. The time period stays the same on screen, but the antics graphically portrayed in *Porky's* appear to have transpired on another planet. The film, most generously described as one long, sexual romp, demonstrates that sexual crassness can translate into big business at the box office.

Pristine sexuality becomes a laugh with these youngsters, as if chastity and innocence exist only for ridicule. Porky's denotes a tavern on the water, a place to hustle, and get hustled. Our boys from across the county line go there to hire a Porky's prostitute, someone who can relieve one group member of his virginity. The boys' bravado antics work against them: They are duped, dunked, and sent back with their tails limp in humiliation. Ultimately, the guys realize their revenge, and, without further ado, that's the story.

The story, however, constitutes *Porky's* least essential element. A more relevant focus is simply the boys' behavior in gazing upon and outwitting the girls through a series of schemes and pranks. The passion to score proves so paramount that desire rules the kingdom, leaving little in the cupboard for intimacy or commitment. Boys tease their buddies with lines like "Fuck you and the horse you rode in on," but the true adversity remains a male/female conflict. Girls are "pussies" and "bitches," labels that reflect the selfishness in force as males seek to maneuver females into compromising positions.

Porky's dispels the mystery of sexual attraction. The movie concerns itself with mechanics by humorously portraying the down-and-dirty deeds of males as they callously relate to females, and by laughing with females as they play their raunchy games in return. The relationship is physical; a matter of sex by the numbers, lacking any thought of the mutual respect and longevity that derive from intimacy and commitment.

The movie entertains us by promoting a carnal love, swooping forth out of playfulness, yet offering little in substance. A ludic affection bound by the sexual act, and dependent thereafter on the ability of one gender to finesse the other into self-serving liaisons. A myopic sexuality that speaks of tremendous ignorance regarding the adolescents' capacity to know and earn a mature love.

Sooner or later, the sexual frolics must give way to a sober calculation of the future. Love's rude awakening also pertains to the thought that, somehow, intimacy and commitment must figure into the mystery of sexual attraction.

Getting It Right

Luckily, other films manage to move beyond teenage orgies to consider Merritt's more pertinent question in *Where The Boys Are*: "Ryder, do I love you?" The changes in sexual freedom impose a new complexion on the business of love in bloom, although the same puzzle continues in force. When do you find your true love?

Yes, if you desire intercourse, it's prudent to prepare for sex, use a condom, feel physical pleasure, and use your bodily functions as a natural resource. If you wish to retain your virginity, no stigma need be attached to the desire of waiting for that experience of lovemaking. But, the physical prospects aside, what makes a relationship last? What about the vagaries of getting married and staying married? After all the promise and pain, How do you "get it right"?

The consequences for Gavin Lamb (Jesse Birdsall) boil down to finding the proper girl and the proper time. Gavin's lame rationalization of distancing himself from the fearsome opposite sex serves to idealize his sexual fantasies, and keeps him, at age 31, a virgin. Confused and despairing of discovering his perfect woman, Gavin seeks to unravel the mysteries of femininity in one of those modest English comedies, aptly entitled *Getting It Right* (1989). The mysteries, he learns, arrive in markedly different guises, personified by the uniquely feminine wiles of three women: Joan (Lynn Redgrave), Minerva (Helena Bonham Carter), and Jenny (Jane Horrocks).

Gavin's a hairdresser who possesses a genuine feeling as he caters to the anxieties of older ladies. Fortunately for him, his deflowering occurs gently and seductively at the invitation of an older woman, Joan. She's perceptive and kindhearted, someone who continues a vain search for her own dream lover, but, in the meantime, Joan willingly plays a game called "Secrets" with Gavin. The youth, much to his surprise, quickly discloses his innermost feelings, including the fantasy of inventing girls to love him. You suspect that Joan pursues the same fantasy, except that she can bring her invented lover to life, for a breath or two, because of her wealth.[2]

Joan has a true devotee in Gavin, but refuses to return his calls. Gavin, perplexed, runs afoul of Minerva, whose first appearance, complete with coal-black bushy eyebrows and porcelain complexion, reminds viewers of the ghost of Christmas Past. Minerva is appealingly neurotic, bulimic, impulsive, distraught, and desperate to marry.

She's certainly more than Gavin cares to handle, although he realizes that Minerva needs mostly a steadying hand to assure her that life can suffice somewhere between her emotional crescendos. At one point Gavin tells Minerva that he doesn't love her. When she asks if he's in love with someone else, Gavin admits "I don't know." Minerva, puzzled, says "How funny not to know." These two disparate souls demonstrate how vast the conceptions of finding a mate. But, undoubtedly, if Gavin plans to "get it right," it won't be with Minerva.

So, we come to Jenny. She's a "junior" assisting Gavin in the beauty salon, and he sees her only as a helper, not a person who figures in his romantic fantasies. But one day he spots, from the back, a golden-haired young lady in the park. His daydreams swirl into action and he wonders about her, until she turns to face him and...it's Jenny. Jenny, shy yet forthright; Jenny with her little Chaplinesque walk; Jenny who shocks Gavin into the revelation that he's known her for two years, yet never really seen her. This belated recognition tells you something about Gavin's grip on reality.

They don't seem a match at first. Jenny knows of life, but not art. She has quietly yet readily assumed responsibility for raising her son, born out of wedlock a few years earlier. Gavin knows art, although the realities of life elude him. Jenny wants to learn about art, and Gavin is willing to teach. He brings her to his parents' house, where he still lives. Gavin tells Jenny that they will go upstairs to his room. Jenny, who begins to shrug out of her wrap, pauses. Slowly, she puts the wrap back on, a bit of body language that says all you need to know about her conduct. Gavin reassures her that his classical records and art books are in the room, that he respects her, and that his intentions are honorable. Thus, upstairs they go. No sex, no passes, no flirtations really. Just the beginning of a relationship between two guileless people.

Left to his timetable, Gavin may have dilly-dallied the relationship to death. But two crises intervene to force his hand. Crisis #1 involves Gavin's gay friend, Harry (Richard Huw), who suffers a turbulent companionship with his indifferent lover, Winthrope (Kevin Drinkwater). Earlier, when Harry and Gavin discuss relationships, Harry advises him: "If you counted up all the things you could or couldn't stand before you started living with someone, then there would be no one left to live with."

Gavin's not so sure, and he's even less certain when he arrives just in time to witness Winthrope leaving Harry.

Harry, who did more than his share of conciliation to pacify his lover, tells Gavin that Winthrope is leaving for America with Joan. Gavin tries to persuade Joan not to take Winthrope as her "cosmetic" companion, but, instead, Joan gives Gavin some additional advice: "Don't worry about being loved. Worry about loving. It's far more important." Gavin, again not so sure, wonders how well the love philosophies of Joan and Harry have helped **them**. Both are unhappy because the other person did not love them back. Consequently, mired in these pressing intrusions of reality, Gavin feels the urge to see Jenny.

He encounters crisis #2 when he finds Jenny in the park and she tells him of her reluctant decision to leave for Germany with her mother, and her mother's soldier lover. Gavin, out of options, tells Jenny that he loves her, that he wants her to stay. Jenny, waiting the wait that females often endure, says "Yes." Softly, Gavin removes her glasses to reveal a face radiant in happiness, so radiant that you wonder how Gavin could have missed this woman for two years. Is love really **that** elusive? True, he finally gets it right, but only because of Jenny's enticing temperament and her long-suffering patience.

What strikes moviegoers as particularly inviting about cinematic love is that (1) it never runs smooth, and (2) it usually ends handsomely. "1" occurs because viewers need to experience an **emotional investment** in the lovers' adversities. Our Oz process wants them to realize happiness, but not too soon or too easily. "2" depends on "1" in the sense that a happy ending seems more satisfying if the lovers (and Oz) work to achieve it. Smitten souls who gracefully overcome reality's burdens, by contrast, do not merit a cheering section.

The wait comes established with a set of rules. The male behaves more actively, the female more passively. He initiates and she defends. Any reversal of roles in this one-sided foray creates consternation for the male and a risk of rejection for the female. You want to fall in love? Fine. But play by the rules, or else...

The Manifesto And The Pledge

One reason for the lovers' shifting sands concerns the psychology of what **she** expects, wants, and needs, and what **he** expects, wants, and needs. Frequently, female and male expectations reflect different agendas. Deborah Tannen (1990, p. 26) opens her book, *You Just Don't Understand*, by noting that women play to intimacy and men to independence:

> *Intimacy* is key in a world of connection where individuals negotiate complex networks of friendship, minimize differences, try to reach consensus, and avoid the appearance of superiority, which would highlight differences. In a world of status, *independence* is the key, because a primary means of establishing status is to tell others what to do, and taking orders is a marker of low status. Though all humans need both intimacy and independence, women tend to focus on the first and men on the second. It is as if their lifeblood ran in different directions.

Take heed of the last line. The issue is not to rehash that old bromide of sex differences, but to acknowledge the self-serving orientations that males and females bring to matters of intimacy. **Intimacy** concerns a sharing of confidences, a sensitive process of each lover learning to understand the whims, whispers, and woes of the other. Intimacy spells affectionate closeness, grounded in psychological and physical understanding.

Men and women, as Deborah Tannen comments, do not customarily spell this affectionate closeness with the same letters. Rather, the genders appear to fly their sexual kites in separate corridors.[3] They appear to, although the idiosyncrasies of human nature allow for assertive women and timid men, prosperous women and deprived men, depraved women and virtuous men, carnally enthusiastic women and sexually closeted men. The **societal focus**, however, suggests a blanket image of passive women and active men. Jenny of *Getting It Right* notices Gavin hovering near her, tense and unsure, so she shocks him by saying, "Are you going to ask me to go out with you?" He is, but she knew. Jenny's a patient and knowing lass; after all, she's been waiting two years.

Movies supply the prejudices that wedge males and females apart, but the movies accomplish this feat with more glamour and bite than we recognize in real life. The **Male Manifesto** dictates, cinematically, that masculine stakes are high: The male must search, conquer, and control the female. This practice represents the Manifesto's generic plan of action that Ryder, TV, and the other males embody in *Where The Boys Are.*

The plan, though, enjoys variations. Gavin hardly fulfills all the conditions in the macho style of manly pursuit. He does go through the motions to actively search and conquer, whereas Jenny's intentions remain low profile and her selection, once made, depends on Gavin coming to his senses. Thus, in modern fashion, Gavin completes his Manifesto by engaging in a halting search, and by "conquering" Jenny primarily because she wishes him as a lover. Regarding the Manifesto's third stipulation--controlling Jenny--Gavin's chances of managing this trick rival winning a trip to Venus.

If the male has his Manifesto, the female has her **Pledge**. She pledges solemnly, as Merritt and Tuggle do, to rebuff premature or unwanted sexual advances. She pledges to preserve the integrity of her femininity in the game of "getting it right". And, most important, she pledges to carve out as equal a status as she can against the male juggernaut.

She falters on occasion and sometimes releases herself of the Pledge, as happens to Melanie in *Where The Boys Are.* But she knows that the vow underscores her only hope of reaching a finer purpose. When Jenny regretfully shrugs back into her wrap, before comprehending Gavin's benevolent intentions, she jeopardizes a rare chance at happiness. But Jenny willingly risks this jeopardy because, truly, if Gavin only wants a quick bonk in the sack upstairs, she cannot find him an attractive prospect.

Picture this Pledge in action during the turn of the century. Imagine chin-to-ankle fashions for women, imagine the pressing formalities of social and sexual niceties, imagine the mannered ways of an affluent class in their leisure, their gossip, their engagements to marry. Imagine this culture and you have tapped into the life stream of James Ivory and Ismail

Merchant's *A Room With A View* (1985), adapted from E. M. Forster's novel.

Lucy Honeychurch (Helena Bonham Carter), a young lady who dares to address the passion of Beethoven at the piano, lives an otherwise cloistered existence. We meet Lucy and her chaperon, Charlotte Bartlett (Maggie Smith), touring Florence as they passively experience the temptations of erotica through Italy's brooding sculpture and art. Each lady could stand a dash of spirit in her travels, particularly Charlotte who has spent her years retreating from life's more adventurous prospects. Bluntly stated, she has permitted too many such prospects to evade her, leaving in their wake a tremulous character who squabbles over the fact that she and Lucy do not have a room with a view.

The disconcerting chivalry of Mr. Emerson (Denholm Elliott) and his son, George (Julian Sands)--who enjoy a room with a view--move father and son to exchange rooms with Charlotte and Lucy. Even here, Charlotte's Victorian oppressiveness takes charge as she says to Lucy, "I would have given the larger room to you, but I happen to know it was the young man's." A stolid Victorian attitude to be sure, since any hint of eroticism, such as a young lady occupying a young man's room, proves too uncomfortable a hint for Charlotte.

Love, however, is love. When it happens, it happens. George and Lucy probably spend less time together as lovers than have almost any other lovers on the big screen. Their first encounter of note occurs in the piazza where Lucy witnesses the lethal stabbing of a youth. She faints and George carries her to safety. Lucy attempts to dismiss the incident, but he tells her that "Something's happened to me, and to you." Lucy should listen to George, but she simply does not understand this strange chap. He baffles her with his fervor for life, and frightens her with his disarming presence. Lucy senses a fulfillment in George's search for adventure that she desires, yet the boldness of it drives her away from him.

The pivotal scene that gives Lucy her romantic memory occurs just outside of Florence. The tourists travel by coach for a holiday in the countryside.[4] George, full of himself, climbs a tree and shouts to the glories of nature, a celebration

that his father understands, but others do not. It is amid
nature's glories, in a field alive with poppies and golden rods,
that Lucy happens upon George. Without Victorian ado, he
runs to her, wraps her in a no-nonsense embrace, and plants
what is likely the first real kiss of Lucy Honeyworth's budding
life. Charlotte intrudes and the moment ends, but the kiss
lingers.[5]

When George first sees Lucy across a dining table, he
forms his food into a question mark and shows it to her (oddly
enough, Ryder does the same with Merritt in *Where The Boys
Are*, except that Ryder fashions his question marks in the
sand). Lucy's puzzled. What's happening here? When George
changes rooms, he turns a picture to the wall and Lucy sees
another question mark on the back of the frame. She's still
puzzled. But neither this conundrum nor his unsettling kiss
prevents her from leaving George and returning to her pastoral
home in England.

In time, to the disenchantment of her mother (Rosemary
Leach), her brother, Freddie (Rupert Graves), and her
warmhearted vicar, the Reverend Beebe (Simon Callow), Lucy
becomes engaged to Cecil Vyse (Daniel Day Lewis), an effete
gentleman of little wit. Cecil, perched precariously atop his
own slender niche in life, harbors little empathy for the
opposite sex, the same sex, or for the world at large.

The engagement party, formally held on a trim green lawn
with a tent for shelter and a band of parasols bobbing here and
there, allows Cecil to explain his attitude on life. Holding
forth with a small cluster of admirers, Cecil diffidently
proclaims his philosophy: "It is as long as I'm no trouble to
anyone, I have a right to do as I like. It is, I daresay, an
example of my decadence."

Cecil represents, I daresay, a polarized example of what
Lucy has drifted to in her flight from George and his
perturbing thirst for excitement. The contrast appears most
divine during a stroll to a pond when Lucy, displaying a rare
burst of perceptiveness, tells Cecil, "I somehow think that you
feel more at home with me in a room, never in the real
country like this." Cecil agrees, and then asks what George
deigned not to ask: "Up to now I have never kissed you....May

I now?" Lucy replies, "Well, of course you may, Cecil. You might before. I can't run at you, you know."

True, as a proper Victorian lady, Lucy must toe the Pledge and wait for Cecil to muster his Manifesto and kiss her. The kiss, alas, proves hardly worth the wait. Cecil pecks instead, and then dislodges his glasses in the ungainly attempt. He's embarrassed, she's embarrassed, and, for the first time, you begin to feel a tinge of sympathy for Cecil. He appears as another Ichabod Crane doomed to disappointment. Cecil can never do what George did, and he can never be what Lucy needs him to be. Their relationship would have commitment, but no passion and precious little intimacy--not the best prospects for a good marriage.

George and his father, ensconced in a nearby cottage, are back in the picture. George returns to Lucy's life, although she continues to backpedal furiously to keep him from sweeping her away. Finally, George confronts Lucy about Cecil: "He's the sort who cannot know anyone intimately, least of all a woman...You understand how lucky people are when they find what's right for them. It's such a blessing, don't you see?"

Yes, Lucy appreciates the blessing (getting it right), but she still doesn't surrender. She needs to relax her Pledge and go with George, but she can't.[6] What Lucy manages, however, is to tell Cecil that she must end their engagement. Cecil's response is not the response you may expect. Accepting her rejection quietly, he thanks her "For showing me what I really am. I admire your courage." Cecil then asks Lucy to shake hands, which she does. How many suitors can take their disengagement so graciously? Not many I suspect, not even in the mainstream of Victorian manners.

Charlotte, in a slapdash arrangement, leaves Lucy with Mr. Emerson so that he can learn of her freedom and make his pitch to bring Lucy and George together. He pitches, Lucy catches, and finally--finally--she pledges her love to his son. Previously, Lucy's mother accused her of becoming more like Charlotte, a comparison not at all pleasing to Lucy. This revelation and her encounter with Mr. Emerson lift Lucy over the last obstacle. And Charlotte, who has done her part in not allowing Lucy to shy away from the risks of loving, must belatedly examine her own choices: the sheltering of herself from love's prospects for so many years. She acknowledges more frankly now the seclusiveness of a timorous woman who has imposed upon herself a room with very little view.

The film closes as it began, this time with Lucy and George on holiday in Florence, at the same rooming house and the same dining table. Across from them a young girl complains to her chaperon that she does not have a room with a view. Lucy and George smile, and George says softly, "We have a room with a view." He says more than the young girl can possibly understand, since, for George and Lucy, their view extends well beyond the window and into the mysteries of love itself.

The sexual scripts for "getting it right" change as the years pass, but the male's Manifesto and the female's Pledge carry on in principle: He's invested, biologically and socially, with the task to search, conquer, and control the female. She's endowed with the defensive aim of ensuring intimacy and commitment from her partner. This principle even withstands the cultural shock of traveling from merry old England to the rowdy avenues of Manhattan. The essence of male pursuit and the female's guarded response to this pursuit retains a certain timelessness. Now, however, his Manifesto and her Pledge simply find a different arena.

Sally (Meg Ryan), sampling from the fruits of a more tolerant sexual script than that which prevailed during Lucy Honeychurch's day, nonetheless cherishes her Pledge of sexual fulfillment in *When Harry Met Sally* (1989). She meets Harry (Billy Crystal) when, as college students, they share the driving chores in traveling from Chicago to New York.

Sally shows us that she's orderly and pragmatic. She believes, moreover, that males and females can be friends without lustful overtones. Harry blows grape seeds out the window to suggest he's not so orderly or so tidy. He's convinced, furthermore, that males and females can never be friends because "...the sex part always gets in the way." The two even differ on *Casablanca* and how Ilsa feels about leaving Rick. Sally thinks Ilsa finds happiness with Victor Lazlo; Harry doesn't.

Sally's Pledge and Harry's Manifesto clash five years later when they meet by chance on a flight. She recognizes him before he recognizes her, which says something, perhaps, for the male's slacker memory in recalling personal encounters. Anyway, the argument turns to sexual etiquette. Sally feels that it's rude for a guy to make love and not stay around to sustain the warmth. (Can you imagine Lucy and Cecil discussing this subject in Victorian England?) Harry, this time, gets practical: "How long do I have to be here to hold her before I can get up and go home? Is 30 seconds enough?"

Clearly, Harry's answer, and Harry himself, do little for Sally. She cannot see him as being "right" for anyone, least of all her.[7] (For a look at how certain ideas and dialogue found their way into the film, consult Nora Ephron's preface to her screenplay, 1991, p. vii.)

Another five years pass, and Sally and Harry meet fortuitously in a book store. They find themselves talking and staking out common ground, not because the two prove so matching in temperament, but because each party suffers a shared pain: Sally's lover has left her, and Harry's marriage is falling apart. They walk, they chat, and Harry reaches a conclusion he could not have accepted five years earlier: that he and Sally are friends. "You know," Harry says, "you may be the most attractive woman I've not wanted to sleep with in my entire life." Sally's wry response to this remark sets in motion a new course for their lives. A friendship develops, giving passion a back seat and permitting intimacy to prosper between two independent people.

A two-year period of grace chronicles the friendship: Harry and Sally meeting for companion dates, talking frequently on the phone (still disagreeing about *Casablanca*), and learning to do what best friends do best--commiserate with each other's woes and indulge each other's faults. Glimmers of more than friendship flash by on occasion, but Harry and Sally, without consciously admitting the problem, fear that making love will shatter their relationship.

And it almost does. Sally, upset when she learns that her old boyfriend plans to marry, sees this loss in a brutal light: He's marrying someone else because he didn't want to marry **her**. Harry rushes over to give comfort. A vulnerable Sally reaches out...and an overwhelmed Harry receives her. We next see Sally cuddled with Harry, a sweet, salutary smile sweeping her face. But Harry stares at the ceiling, dumbfounded. What has **he** done? What have **they** done?

Harry leaves awkwardly, and both meet later to blurt out their apologies. Harry rationalizes that "Maybe you get to a certain point in your relationship where it's too late to have sex." The act, however, intrudes on their friendship and they part company. True, if Harry had behaved differently after making love, if he had sustained the closeness, Sally would have accepted him then and there. She was ready; he was not.

Both companions pay the price of missing their togetherness. Sally, though emotional, honors her Pledge by trusting Harry and loving him. Harry bruises that trust when he pulls back after their physical intimacy, and when he fails to follow through with a commitment to match her own.

Harry is the one with the Manifesto, and he's the one who must set the record straight. He wanders the streets on New Year's Eve, miserably telling himself how happy he feels. Finally, his misery propels him to Sally, and prompts him to itemize his love for her; a list that says as much about intimacy and commitment as about the passion that Harry now accepts.

Harry's observations of "Why I love you" derive, not from a few dates, but from years of **emotional investment** in learning about one special individual of the opposite sex. This investment of shared experiences, especially the positive experiences, constitutes the **equity** of a long-standing relationship. It moves Harry to weigh his independence of not being with Sally, and to recognize her absence as too great a loss. Their emotional investment swings the pendulum to send him searching for her. Sometimes the emotion of love demands patience to get it right. For Harry and Sally, his search and her acceptance takes them 12 years and 3 months.

The Marriage Ceremony

The trappings of a marriage ceremony afford us a clue about what to expect next...and it's not much of a romantic fantasy. The **ceremony proper** radiates a democratic air, which means that if you find the right two people, the right authority, and the right place--any two lovers can "marry." The lovers can do so ceremonially, if not legally, even though they're of the same sex, the minister represents the Worldwide Church of Ultimate Togetherness, and the locale is a picnic site atop Yaller Dog Hill.

Lovers marry while jogging, water skiing, on a Ferris Wheel, on horseback, on a tightrope, "on" a computer, underwater, in a hot tub, an airplane, a bowling alley, a tattoo parlor, in their birthday suits, and at the site of a car wreck where they first "met." Lovers advertise to marry by billboard, the classifieds, and by offering money. Lovers have trouble getting together because a mother locks her son in the bathroom to stop a wedding, or because parents kidnap their daughter to prevent a marriage from continuing.

Lovers of all ages find common ground, however, even when he's 100 and she's 14, or she's 44 and he's 14. Lovers marry (sort of) when he's on death row, when the groom is already dead, and when both bride and groom are deceased. Lovers can marry frequently (26 times for one man), and occasionally without bothering to divorce the current Mr. or Ms. The bride marries in rare instances believing her guy is a guy...when he's not. And the blissful couple may find, as one couple did, that the wedding reception lasts longer than the marriage.

These happenings denote, not the movies, but quirky slices of real life. Perhaps lovers work harder to make their wedding vows memorable because they remain uncertain about the longevity of marital jubilation. Ruth Benedict (1938) speculated on the value of the ceremony as a **discontinuity** in culture. Discontinuities in primitive cultures, she noted, realize expression through important rituals, such as the "Making of Man" ceremony, a child-to-adult rite practiced in Australian and Papuan societies. The "Making of Man" is just what it suggests: A striking change imposed on boys to drop one life for another, once they complete the ritual.

Such a dramatic turnabout proves more difficult to attain in advanced societies. The wedding ceremony possesses symbols rich in folklore, including the ring, the kiss, the bridal veil, the gown, even the cake (Chesser, 1980). But pragmatically, the ceremony has little "teeth" to it. Modern rituals do not proclaim the gravity of holy matrimony sufficiently to sober its lovers for a different life ahead.

The acrobatic variations in getting married do not weaken the ceremony's solemnity so much as they compromise the lovers' sense of what the ceremony is supposed to accomplish. The wedding ritual gets them married, usually in the eyes of religion and society, but lacks the far-reaching clout of more primitive ceremonies to keep them married. Family support, shared interests, physical health, a decent income, good will, fortuitous happenings, and a continuing romance facilitate the durability of a happy marriage.

None of these qualities matter much to the filmmaker. What does matter is that movies use the marriage ceremony as a platform to explore **diversions from normality**, diversions that may have little to do with the bride and groom. *Lovers And Other Strangers* (1970), for instance, presents us with a bride, Susan (Bonnie Bedelia), and groom, Mike (Michael Brandon). The bride and groom behave as two of the more stable characters amid an odd assortment of family members and friends in search of resolutions.

One of the busiest members is Susan's father, Hal (Gig Young), who devotes himself to keeping everybody happy, including his wife, Bernice (Cloris Leachman), and his mistress, Cathy (Anne Jackson). Cathy, just a whisker from collapsing emotionally, feels her biological clock ticking. She's there, yet not really there. The family toasts Susan's forthcoming nuptials but inadvertently leave Cathy out. Later, Cathy catches the bouquet thrown by Susan, an irony that proves too much for her, and she runs crying from the room - - a reaction that only Hal understands.

He understands because his whimsical logic of happiness now seems in jeopardy. We find Hal and Cathy in their favorite sanctuary, the bathroom, with Hal seated on the only seat, and Cathy on his knee. He offers her his latest commode philosophy for continuing their relationship without telling his wife: "Now I love you and I want you to be happy, and I don't love Bernice but I want her to be happy, and I do love my children and I want them to be happy, but I don't want my wanting Bernice to be happy to take away from my love for you, but by wanting my children to be happy while not taking away from my love for you will make Bernice happy, and, therefore, make the children happy. I want everyone to be happy..."

If you're puzzled, you should see the look on Cathy's face. Yes, Hal's verbal meanderings do make sense, it just takes a while. Being obtuse can sometimes allow one to avoid a ticklish situation, but Hal doesn't engage in these tactics deliberately. He **really** wants all his loved ones to be happy.

Unfortunately, Hal's happiness eludes everyone except the bride and groom. Mike's older brother, Riche (Joseph Hindy), plans to divorce his wife, Joan (Diane Keaton), whereupon Richie's parents, Frank and Bea Vecchio (Richard Castellano and Bea Arthur), desperately seek to salvage their son's union. During the reception, Frank and Bea chronicle for Joan the marital woes of different couples they know at the party, ending each sad tale with a lamely upbeat ending of, "But they're still together." Frank and Bea's school of togetherness seems to have borrowed a page from Hal's book of happiness.

Meanwhile, the bride's sister, Wilma (Anne Meara), has volatile verbal fests with Johnny (Harry Guardino), her macho-strutting husband. Johnny's trouble is that his strut fails to match is sexual output: Wilma wants more, and Johnny just doesn't feel he has more to give. He refers to her as "Willie," his "equal-time orgasmic fanatic." Johnny's real problem, however, concerns Wilma's assertive ways. He's the boss; at least he's supposed to be the boss, but Wilma challenges his manhood. After all, he's an ex-marine, by god! Why should an ex-marine feel threatened by a woman on sexual overdrive?

Finally, the groom's best friend, Jerry (Robert Dishy), goes on a blind date with the bride's best friend, Brenda (Marian

Hailey). A blind date, according to movie logic, cannot go smoothly. Jerry's a guy who doesn't like to gamble (translation: When he's with a girl, he wants the certainty of "scoring"). But Jerry finds himself unprepared to deal with a transcendental Brenda who reads *The Prophet* among other soul-searching literature, and who declares to him, "I am you, you are me, and we are one." Mostly, Jerry wants to be "one" with Brenda, though not for eternity. His catering to Brenda's mystic moods denotes one of the longest-running acts of sexual foreplay in movie history.

What to make of these couples? The most sensitive dialogue comes from Frank Vecchio, Mike and Richie's father. Frank tells Richie a deep secret, namely, that he's always felt he was more intelligent than his wife, Bea. Before committing himself to Bea, Frank speaks of a bright girl, Mary Rose, who wouldn't go out with him. He wonders that if marrying Mary Rose, someone of the same intellectual level, would have made him, Frank, a different person. Someone who doesn't yell so much, someone who realizes an opportunity to appreciate the finer moments of life. Frank wistfully considers the possibilities because he knows that the question shall remain unresolved for him, the path he could not take.

Bea fails to recognize the prospect of Frank's intellectual superiority, commenting to the effect that, with Frank, there's not much there. What she has never accustomed herself to, nonetheless, is Frank's sexual desires. Bea perceives these desires as a rude surprise, a glimpse of the "animal" in Frank. She knows his good qualities, yet the "sex thing" goes beyond her comprehension.

Thus we have two people, understandably different in many respects, although layered with the common pursuits of a long marriage. Bea and Frank's solidarity appears to represent contentment more than happiness, and commitment more than passion, yet both would be quick to say, "But we're still together."

Lovers And Other Strangers closes with Mike, the groom, in bed watching one of his favorite movies, Alfred Hitchcock's *Spellbound*.[8] Earlier in the film, we find Johnny, the ex-marine, watching the same movie and refusing to turn it off, even at Wilma's sexual urgings. Susan makes the same request of Mike, who teases and refuses at first, then hands her the remote. A different ending for them and perhaps one expected of newlyweds...but you wonder. How long will Mike be content to graciously hand Susan that remote? Hmmm.

An impending wedding, then, becomes prime fodder for creating diversions from normalcy: throwing order into disorder, array into disarray, and stateliness into a litany of catastrophes. Entertainment relies on making the ordinary, extraordinary; and with a forthcoming marriage, entertainment takes usually well-centered individuals and casts them off-center. Just ask Stanley Banks (Spencer Tracy) or George Banks (Steve Martin) as each gentleman recalls the organized mess and revolting responsibilities that overwhelmed him in *Father Of The Bride* (1950/1991).

The original *Bride*, shot in black and white, opens with a weary Stanley Banks, rubbing his feet and reflecting on the aftermath of a wedding from hell.[9] Hell includes a barrage of demands that comes rushing at Stanley in the fandango of rules called wedding etiquette. When Kay (Elizabeth Taylor) casually mentions that she will probably marry Buckley (Don Taylor), Stanley and his wife, Ellie (Joan Bennett), find the surprise a **real** surprise.

Stanley cannot recall Buckley and wonders if he's the one with the "teeth," the "porcupine hair," the "poopedoop" English teacher, the muscle-bound ham with the "shoulders," the "musical bebopper," the "genius" who's supposed to fix his radio, or the "radical" who never seems to picket. When Stanley peers out the window to see which candidate comes up the walk, it turns out to be "shoulders," and a pained Stanley puts his hand over his face. The trial has begun, as has his hurt at losing Kay: "From here on, her love would be doled out like a farmer's wife tossing scraps to a family rooster."

Meeting and trading bald-faced lies with the "in-laws"; dueling with a snobbish caterer, Mr. Massoula (Leo G. Carroll); shoring up an unexpected rift between Kay and Buckley; and accumulating the wedding bills--especially the bills--send Stanley into a stratosphere of consternation. He

asks Ellie in disbelief, "What does Buckley's family give? Just
Buckley?" And Ellie answers, "Just Buckley."

The cost of a wedding offers an instructive contrast
between the 1950 and 1991 versions of *Bride*. Stanley's upset
when he learns that the cake will go for $400, and that 280
guests will attend the wedding reception in his home, priced
at $3.75 a head. Stanley even suggests slyly to Kay that he will
give her $1500 to elope, then covers his tail quickly when she
finds the idea unattractive.

Stanley, nonetheless, would turn ashen if he had to pay the
1991 prices of George Banks (Steve Martin), in which the cake
inflates to more than a thousand dollars, and the price per
head soars from $3.75 to $250. George, for example, knows
he's in trouble when his caterer tells him that the house must
be color-coordinated with the swans. Swans? What swans?
Romance (sigh) has grown expensive over the past 40 years.[10]

The heart of both *Brides* remains much the same, however.
The two fathers work through the pain of losing a daughter,
forgetting until later that each man has a loving wife at his
side. Stanley and George seem a bit piggish about love,
actually.   Joan Bennett's Ellie pops up with an acerbic
comment at the appropriate time to keep Stanley in line,
whereas Diane Keaton's Nina plays a softer role, feathering
George's nest when he needs feathering. But both women are
supportive, and neither Stanley nor George need worry about
"losing" the love of a daughter. Each man continues to bask in
the love of a fine woman.

Stanley and George share another point in that they show
their vulnerability to the wedding game. When Steve Martin's
George first meets his daughter's beau, he assumes a perpetual
scowl, particularly when the beau places his hand possessively
on the daughter's knee. By contrast, Nina projects a delighted
if dazed grin at what lies ahead. The women in both stories
take over, leaving Stanley and George in the dust. The men
are the last to know what's happening, and the last to
understand. George, for instance, can't interpret a word that
the caterer says, but the women have no trouble. The caterer,
Franck (Martin Short), sports his own zesty lingo (a cake is a
kake) and generally seems to belong in Oz.

Differences arise, though, in character and expression. Tracy's Stanley calls forth a bear-like presence, a curmudgeon where Buckley is concerned, yet a curmudgeon who growls softly. Martin's George doesn't growl as effectively, but enjoys a freedom of sexual phrasing not possible in 1950. Just as his daughter and his "adversary" are leaving, George, still befuddled over the engagement, tells them to "Drive carefully and don't forget to fasten your condom." His daughter's exclamation brings George back to reality, and, squirming with embarrassment, he adds, "Seat belt! I meant--I meant seat belt."

Stanley and George see themselves in life's passage, viewing the departure of their daughter as the underscoring of a sexual cycle. This message finds easier expression in the 1991 film as George muses over his daughter's life: "You worry about her going out with the wrong kind of guys, the kind of guys who only want one thing--and you know exactly what that one thing is because it's the same thing you wanted when you were their age."

The wedding ceremony marks the beginning for new lovers, yet also strikes a chord of memories for the parents, blessed with the emotional investment that comes from a long, happy marriage. The Banks in both movies end their story by dancing amid the remnants of a wedding past and present. Their daughter's wedding ceremony preserves a rewarding continuity of stability and happiness.

Keeping It Right

The ceremony, regrettably, marks a poignantly different memory for those marital partners who founder. A beginning steeped in passion, and perhaps intimacy as well, deteriorates to a marriage that ultimately lacks the discipline of commitment. Two partners, rife with promise and good will, learn that they cannot sustain their marriage.

A marriage ceremony, sporting all the best intentions imaginable, does not command that sobering change of life to prepare lovers for the day-in, day-out trials of living together.

Some grit and substance also figure into the equation. Lovers, to make the love work, must commit themselves to persevere.

When sex poops out, the marriage may soon follow. The difference between a vigorous relationship and one beyond resuscitation concerns a difference that movies find easiest to demonstrate through the presence and absence of sexual behavior.

A Fish Called Wanda (1988) distinguishes, in parallel fashion, two couples in a bedroom. Wanda (Jamie Lee Curtis) and Otto (Kevin Kline) prepare for action with an enthusiasm born of impatient anticipation. He speaks Italian, a gimmick that arouses her; she lifts her legs for him to remove her boots; he takes a healthy sniff of the boots and of her undies; then he launches himself upon her, crooning in Italian and pumping away as if hammering for oil. Wanda and Otto are not just having sex, they're making a grand production of it. Their enjoyment is infectious: two otherwise mismatched souls find common ground in a passion for physical pleasure.

Now, intersperse this sexual gaiety with the bedroom routine of a staid married couple, Archie (John Cleese) and Wendy (Maria Aitken). As Otto hoots his sexual prowess in Wanda's eager arms, Archie slowly and silently undresses, clips his toenails, and settles into his twin bed. Wendy goes through her perfunctory ritual, silently disrobing, spraying beneath her arms, and settles into her twin bed. He glances at a paper, yawns, and mistakenly calls her Wanda in his absentminded-ness.

The outcome for Archie and Wendy is not surprising when we consider their paucity of communication, and the likelihood that sex, for them, poses at best a faint memory. Communication between marital partners proves more important than any mandatory decree to have sex, but if a marriage has neither, then "getting it wrong" exercises an edge over "keeping it right."

Keeping it right sometimes means receiving a **second chance.** The opening scene of *The Philadelphia Story* (1940) shows the dissolution of a marriage. Tracy Lord (Katharine Hepburn) cracks her husband's golf club over her knee, and the husband, C. K. Dexter Haven (Cary Grant), responds by putting his hand to her face and pushing her down through a doorway. End of marriage, and beginning of story.

Tracy Lord finds herself referred to as a "goddess," a woman who possesses beautiful "purity," someone who is "lit" from within. But these superlatives suffer competition from a negative camp consisting specifically of her ex-husband, Dexter, and her wayward father, Seth (John Halliday). Dexter reads Tracy as "The young, rich, rapacious female" (where else in the history of movie dialogue will you discover the expression "rapacious female"?). Seth Lord, though, conjures up the most telling insight. Accused by Tracy of embarrassing her mother and the family because of his scandalous affair with a dancer, Seth replies: "What most wives fail to realize is that their husband's philandering has nothing whatever to do with them." The true reason that older men have affairs, Seth adds, is "a reluctance to grow old..."

Tracy is rich, about to marry a pompous ass ill-suited to her, and must contend with a writer, Macauley Connor (James Stewart), and a photographer, Elizabeth Imbrie (Ruth Hussey). Macauley and Elizabeth, against their better judgment, arrive to exploit Tracy's wedding on orders from the magazine's opportunistic boss. These contrivances spark witty exchanges ranging from sharp to brittle to blunt. The central theme, however, tags a deeper pain than that customarily found in the sophisticated comedies of the '30s and '40s (see Cavell, 1981, and a response to his views by Thomson, 1982).

Dexter develops a problem with alcohol during the marriage, a problem that Tracy chooses to view as human frailty. Instead of understanding, Tracy retreats to her "ice queen" sanctuary and condemns his weakness. Thus, Dexter's numerous pot shots at Tracy stem from his bitterness at her inability to tolerate imperfection. The humor, laced with a stinger here and a barb there, affords only thin insulation in masking the kind of miscommunication that can embroil an ex-wife and an ex-husband. The consequence of this misplaced love is that Dexter's on the wagon, but he gets there by self-reliance and not by Tracy's helping hand.

So, Dexter must work to stay sober, and Tracy must admit her own frailties and learn to be human. Real life does not provide much opportunity for rapid change when spouses differ in how they perceive faults. But in *The Philadelphia Story* Tracy adjusts her thinking radically during a 24-hour period, and she appears to make the transformation more because of her father's pointed assessment than because of Dexter.

A diversion, an affair between a smitten, inebriated Macauley (the writer) and a thoroughly plastered Tracy, isn't much of a diversion at all, although Tracy can't remember what transpires...and fears the worst. Naturally, her groom does not understand, and, naturally, Dexter does. He's lightened up and relaxed his verbal assaults on Tracy for the most obvious of reasons. Dexter wants her back, especially now that she's behaving more like a human being than a goddess. Thus, the marriage that crashes in the first scene renews itself in the film's finale. Tracy and Dexter, together again, this time for better **and** worse. And, this time, perhaps both lovers can handle the downside of wedded bliss.

The downside seems inevitable, even in the happiest of relationships. *Adam's Rib* (1949) denotes an early, humorous look at how feminist issues can rock a stable marriage. The movie begins with Doris Attinger (Judy Holliday) tailing her wayfaring husband, Warren (Tom Ewell), as he walks jauntily to his mistress's apartment, whistling "You Are My Lucky Star." His luck runs out when Doris enters brandishing a .32 caliber revolver, and starts firing wildly about the room. Her head down and eyes closed, a hysterical Doris misses the mistress but wings her hubby. Warren, caught barefaced, nonetheless decides to file assault charges.

These charges draw Adam and Amanda Bonner (Spencer Tracy and Katharine Hepburn) into the fray. He's an assistant district attorney who views the law conservatively, and she's a defense attorney who favors more liberal interpretations, particularly interpretations that concern gender inequality. The Bonners reflect a happily-married couple, although the lawyers' professional differences keep their wedded merriment on the brink of guerilla warfare. Domestically, they're harmonious; professionally, they've learned to dance lightly around their disagreements. But the Attinger case will require more than a soft-shoe shuffle to calm the stormy seas ahead.

Women are supportive of Doris Attinger shooting her husband, including the Bonner's maid, who, seeing the story in the paper, says enthusiastically, "Attagirl!" Amanda unwittingly prefaces the trouble to come when she explains to Adam that "All I'm trying to say is there are lots of things a man can do, and in society's eyes it's all hunky-dory. A woman does the same thing--the same mind you--and she's an outcast." Arguably, Amanda's words still carry sufficient provocation today to gird the sexes in keeping a wary eye on each other.

Amanda, at one point, questions the mistress, Beryl Caighn (Jean Hagen), about her relationship with Warren Attinger: "Mr. Attinger had never touched you before this time?" Beryl pauses and answers, "Sure." Amanda feigns her amazement with an "Ahhh." Beryl then smiles and adds, "We used to shake hands quite a lot." Amanda, disgusted, asks her rhetorically, "Did you enjoy it?"

The turning point between the Bonners arrives one evening as Amanda takes her turn for a massage. Adam, smoldering over her courtroom shenanigans, gives Amanda a robust slap on the rump. Amanda leaps off the table, a stunned look of growing comprehension: "I'm not so sure I care to expose myself to typical instinctive, masculine brutality." Adam attempts to make amends but Amanda reaches another, more startling conclusion: "And it felt not only as if you meant it but as though you felt you had a right to." Amanda breaks into tears, provoking Adam into scoffing, "Here we go, the old juice." But the juice is effective, and as Adam comes close to her, Amanda kicks him in the shin, adding triumphantly, "Let's all be manly!"

Adam sees their professional differences as too fundamental to allow them to stay together. He packs as Amanda seeks an answer for his leaving. Finally, Adam responds by giving Amanda a soliloquy on marriage: "It's a contract. It's the law. Are you going to outsmart that the way you've outsmarted all other laws--that's clever. That's very clever. You've outsmarted yourself, and you've outsmarted me, and

you've outsmarted everything...I'm old fashion. I like two
sexes...all of a sudden I don't like being married to what is
known as a new woman. I want a wife, not a competitor..."

Adam wins his point but Amanda wins the case. She
devises an ingenious scheme of asking the jurors to view Doris
Attinger as a man, and Warren Attinger as a woman, and then
to contemplate how this switch in masculinity and femininity
changes the complexion of the shooting. She successfully
defends Doris Attinger, but the reconciliation with Adam
demands further labor.

They meet at the tax attorney's office to review old
receipts, and the receipts lead to recollections of money spent,
and where, and why. The receipts, in effect, spur memories
of happy times, and of a marriage that works in spite of
differences between the two feuding partners about what it
means to be female and male. The Bonner's emotional
investment in each other supports a happy history, a history
too satisfying to dismiss in the face of professional differences. Adam and Amanda Bonner give themselves a second
chance.

Perhaps the truest test of keeping a marriage right is when
that marriage serves as a linchpin to **survival**. Discontent over
real and imagined inequalities between genders hardly rivals
the struggle that many families suffer, and have suffered, to
maintain human dignity. *Sounder* (1972) recounts the
uplifting experiences of a black family during the Depression
in rural Louisiana. Nathan and Rebecca (Paul Winfield and
Cicely Tyson) are married to each other and to the land. They
sharecrop a sugar cane field for the owner, a man who
reminds the family that he does them a favor each time he
gives them credit for their grocery purchases. The prejudice,
always lurking, dribbles forth like a Chinese water torture, one
drop at a time, but drops that seemingly have no end.

Sounder, the family dog, becomes a metaphor for the black
family's philosophy of life: When matters get worse, you must
do whatever it takes to persevere. Nathan obtains a ham he
shouldn't have obtained, to place meat on the table for his
wife and children. Sheriff Young (James Best) comes for him

and, as he's taken away, Sounder is shot and wounded by a deputy who becomes irritated at the dog's vocalizing.

Sounder leaves, to heal on his own, just as Nathan, taken away, must come to terms with his punishment. Sheriff Young, moreover, refuses Rebecca permission to see her husband in jail. He chides her, saying that she knows the "rules," and the rules dictate that a woman (make that a black woman) cannot visit her husband in jail, *anytime*.

A husband who leaves his family forces an adjustment and, possibly, a lower standard of living. But Nathan leaving Rebecca places her and her children in dire straits to work the crops, take in laundry, and handle a host of other chores just to stay a family. Under a regimen of daily drudgery, the marriage of Rebecca and Nathan sustains a spirit of commitment that gives the family its reserve of strength. This commitment fulfills the essence of a mature love--the robustness of a yearning to cling together, even in spirit, and to prevail.

Sounder and Nathan return, almost new. Nathan's lame in one leg from an explosion, but he's back and they're a complete family again. The father, wanting his oldest boy to gain an education, tells him, "Son, don't get too used to this place." Nathan knows that there's more for his son than a homestead always in need of repair, and a land that, for them, surrenders its resources only through primitive tools and the back-breaking efforts of bodies bent to the earth. Rebecca and Nathan find their joy in living, not from the land, but from a partnership of love that helps them transcend a world not of their making.

Remembering It Right

John Gottman (1994, Chapter Three) has spent over 20 years studying why some marriages succeed and others fail. His summary of the whys and wherefores concerns "The Four Horseman Of The Apocalypse." The four horseman-- criticism, contempt, defensiveness, and stonewalling--

constitute directives and reactions that spell trouble for a married couple.

How much trouble, Gottman notes, depends on how readily and how pointedly a husband and wife proceed through the four warning stages. **Criticism** becomes, not specific, but more general and fundamental: "You used to care for me, now you don't." Such criticism, without intervention, can lead to **contempt**, a devaluing of each partner: "No, I don't care for you because you're not worth caring about."

Once the marriage has reached this juncture, positive communication seems unlikely. **Defensiveness** substitutes for listening and the partners expend considerable energy shoring up their self-esteem, whatever the cost. The cost, regrettably, can prove overwhelming, psychologically. The final warning sign, **stonewalling**, realizes numerous expressions, but the devilment of stonewalling concerns one partner who shuts out the other partner. It goes beyond a mere refusal to listen or respond; in essence, stonewalling involves distancing oneself emotionally from the other person. Without help, without a radical reconstruction of giving and compromise to dispel these four grievances, the marriage teeters dangerously close to going *kaput*.

Recalling the turbulence associated with Tracy and Dexter's adversarial relationship in *The Philadelphia Story*, and the sharp exchanges between Adam and Amanda in *Adam's Rib*, you can recognize Gottman's four warning signals in all their ominous glory. When a marriage rocks and shutters from a shower of criticism, contempt, and defensiveness, what can partners do to keep their union from drifting apart? What can they do to avoid the ultimate consequence that stonewalling represents? One possibility, as Adam and Amanda discovered, concerns remembering the good times, remembering what brought the lovers together, originally.

"They don't look very happy," says Joanna. "Why should they? They just got married," replies Mark. This gloomy observation comes from Mark Wallace (Albert Finney) as he and his wife, Joanna (Audrey Hepburn), sit in their Mercedes-Benz and watch a wedding party.

The Wallaces have been married 12 years, and keeping it right has proved, well, not so easy. Mark evokes a dour and flinty disposition about life in general, whereas Joanna's temperament proves softer and more compliant, but just as stubborn as to what their marriage should be.

We learn, in slapdash fashion, of their high notes and low notes in *Two For The Road* (1967), a comedy/drama of getting in and out of cars, in and out of spats, in and out of relationships. The relationships, excepting the brief dalliances indulged in by each partner, are **their** relationships. The lovers find their thoughts and feelings altered through time and circumstance, spanning the spectrum of emotions from joyful to pensive to hurtful.

Joanna and Mark meet while traveling across Europe, he a student of architecture, she a student of music. The viewer needs a scorecard, however, to monitor the shifting sands of time in their story. Early moments cascade into older interludes, and older interludes abruptly change course to become midlife confrontations, illustrating how a few years can rearrange the fervor and expectations of two lovers.

Early, as acquaintances-about-to-become-lovers, they see a couple sitting silently at a table. Mark comments lightly, "What kind of people would just sit like that without a word to say to each other?" And Joanna responds lightly, "Married people?" The question gets asked again, sometimes by Mark, sometimes by Joanna, but not so lightly. The lovers gradually shoulder a heavy-eyed dose of disillusionment as they experience that marital silence for themselves.

Since every marriage that ever was has had to face a certain reality to continue, the Wallace's problems are not unusual. The fact that they have somehow held together for 12 years indicates promise. But rather than build on that promise, Joanna and Mark rummage about in their past to sort out where it all "went wrong." Was it the mishaps on the road with the MG? Was it Mark's success as an architect that made him less attentive to the marriage? Was it this, was it that?

The sex, Joanna tells Mark, is not personal anymore. Mark doesn't understand. Joanna explains that sex stopped being fun once they married. This dissenting viewpoint of males and females to sex and marriage holds forth in the story as Joanna accuses Mark of not knowing what love is. Mark has lapsed into seeing sex as "sex" with no particular connection to marriage or any other state of affairs. Joanna, however, views passion as integral to marriage, made special because of the lovers' intimacy and commitment. When it no longer seems special, then, for Joanna, the loss becomes a harbinger of grave proportions.

The one constant for these partners has been Mark's passport. He's forgetful and, more than once, Joanna bails him out by retrieving his passport (occasionally, too, she will hide it from him). So, what does the passport really mean? For Mark it means that he needs Joanna, an admission he finds difficult to accept in his manly way, but accept it he does. Mark once told her, "If there's one thing I really despise, it's an indispensable woman."

Fortunately, Mark recognizes this truth in the front seat of his Mercedes-Benz. He has always been more brusque about admitting his feelings, and more reluctant than Joanna to accept the obligations of a permanent relationship. Fortunately for him again, Joanna has weathered the rough winds and choppy seas to keep their marriage afloat. What both lovers now realize in their mellower mood is what too many tortured lovers fail to realize: Mark and Joanna allow their 12 years of cherished memories to work a cumulative wisdom that tells both partners they **have** a marriage. A marriage worth saving and worth remembering.

Should partners ignore the consequences and salvage their marriage at any cost? Surely not. Moviemakers, in lockstep with the commercial philosophy of "Happy Endings," usually seek to avoid such a bleak conclusion. But the criticism, the contempt, the defensiveness, and the stonewalling can inflict psychological damage because, in reality, there's nothing there for some couples to salvage. The four warning signs become more than mere warning signals, they mandate the inevitable outcome of a love that has nowhere to go. Partners, possibly right for each other in the past, have grown apart.

Love runs its course, partners change partners, and relationships begin anew (see *The Way We Were*, 1973, and

Rich In Love, 1993, as examples). The new prospects may fare no better than the old, but the need for change becomes a paramount force. Put another way, to **remember it right** the partners must recall enough happiness to make staying together a realistic option. But if it ain't there, it ain't there.

Love's Commitment

Marriage exists less as a traditional institution and more as a **chameleon**, assuming the complexions of its partners. Myrna Loy, a versatile actress who excelled in light comedy and in drama, offers us two final salvos at this chameleon-like bond.

Loy played Nora Charles to William Powell's Nick Charles in six *Thin Man* films (1934 to 1947). The Charles's had a partnership made in cinematic heaven: precious little reality, but a generous serving of style, wit, and verve. Their affection never sagged, never wandered. Their zest for togetherness never faltered because the lovers reckoned themselves as newlyweds, day after day. Whatever disparaging words might be heard, were words bantered to and fro with a mischievous smile. Moviegoers **liked** Nick and Nora. They also liked the idea that such a marriage could prevail, at least in cinemaland.

Later in her career, Myrna Loy played her most memorable role in *The Best Years Of Our Lives* (1946), a story of families and lovers reunited after World War II. A classic scene begins with her husband, Fredric March, returning home and quietly shushing his son and daughter as he waits to surprise his wife. Loy, in another room, hears something unusual, pauses, then she **knows**. She hasn't seen him yet, but the wisdom of a durable, loving relationship tells her that he has arrived.

Their first sighting and embrace carries with it years of affection. A subsequent scene adds to this impression. The daughter (Teresa Wright), going through a troubled relationship, tells her parents that she can't expect a perfect marriage as they have had. She feels, despairingly, that she will never be so fortunate. The revealing glances between Loy and March reflect a discernment that the daughter has yet to comprehend. Loy, quietly yet knowledgeably, informs her daughter of the ups and downs of their own partnership, and of their struggles to stay together.

Myrna Loy becomes a touchstone to show how far movies can range in portraying the vicissitudes of marriage. Whether light and fanciful in *The Thin Man* capers, or dramatic and cinematically true in *The Best Years Of Our Lives*, she symbolizes the marital spirit as a cosmopolitan mystery of love and commitment.

Therefore, in keeping with this mystery, how do you Get It Right, Keep It Right, and Remember It Right? We have pursued the odyssey by eavesdropping on startlingly different characters, living in dramatically different worlds. Try to compare the chaste lovers of *Where The Boys Are* with the sexually experienced lovers of *When Harry Met Sally*. Or, more markedly, compare either of these relationships with the bedrock love that Rebecca and Nathan of *Sounder* draw upon to give their earthy existence the dignity it deserves. The currents of love flow in peculiar formations, making the prospect of a simple formula for happiness quite absurd.

Compare a time, for instance, when the Manifesto and the Pledge cross swords in a simple declaration of adversity, against a time when lovers eschew the simple declarations for a more tolerant and reckless view of male/female adversity. Were the 1950s really that simple, and that chaste? No, the 1950s were not, although the movies made in those years teased viewers with the prospect that "chastity in jeopardy" could be entertaining (Breines, 1992, p. 108).

Stephanie Coontz (1992, p. 185), author of *The Way We Never Were*, opts for a more balanced appraisal:

> ...the 1950s were hardly asexual. My modern students, who accept premarital sex between affectionate partners quite matter-of-factly, are profoundly shocked when they read about panty raids and the groups of college boys who sometimes roamed through a campus chanting, "We want girls! We want sex!" Much of the modern sexual revolution, indeed, consists merely of a decline in the double standard, with the girls adopting sexual behaviors that were pioneered much earlier by boys.

The male's Manifesto continues in force, but the female's Pledge undergoes more than a cosmetic overhaul. Women, flushed with greater independence, better career opportunities, and a stronger sense of what it takes to kick butt for gender equality, have streamlined the Pledge to meet their current needs. *About Last Night* (1986), for example, introduces us to Danny (Rob Lowe) and Debbie (Demi Moore), two attractive people who exchange knowing looks across a crowded room. Debbie can't help herself: A first date and she's in the sack with Danny; a second date, and, her protests to the contrary, she's back in the sack. The only awkwardness either lover experiences is when Debbie must find a way to leave Danny the next morning.

Or, consider *Cross My Heart* (1988): We meet Cathy (Annette O'Toole), a single mother who has a smoking habit and who finds herself weary of the dating game. Thus, when Cathy encounters a promising chap named David (Martin Short), she decides that she must like him since "I'm shaving above the knee." Cathy's preparing for that crucial third date when "things" are supposed to happen.

The "third-daters" go to David's apartment (not really his apartment, but that's another story) where Cathy anguishes over how earnestly she plans to honor her Pledge. Earlier she tells a friend that she doesn't intend to have sex, whereupon her friend asks Cathy why, then, is she carrying her diaphragm? When David begins some clumsy hinting about going to bed, Cathy wants to be careful, but not too careful. She tells David, "I could fall for a guy like you and I just want to make sure you are a guy like you."

The lovers in *Peyton Place* and *Where The Boys Are* appear to move at a mere turtle's pace, whereas the timetable for passion in today's films accelerates to Mach One. True, the movies' chronicle of the female's sexual emergence retains a more legitimate interpretation now, compared to the cautious sexual excursions of the 1950s. But this legitimacy concerns a popular culture of sexuality, not the more diverse and less colorful **private practices** that represent reality. Indeed, this private agenda of personalized likes and dislikes encompasses a subterranean sexuality that harks back even to the professed prudery of Victorian times (see Freedman & Hellerstein, 1981, p. 124; and Foucault, 1978, Chapter One).

What has not changed, however, is the spirit of Getting It Right. Popular expressions of sexual etiquette may have evolved from courtship (*A Room With A View*) to dating (*Where The Boys Are*) to "let's meet somewhere" (*When Harry Met Sally*). But, for romance, Getting It Right and Keeping It Right still pose the same hoary puzzle: How can lovers discover the complete joys of that fragile package called passion, intimacy, and commitment?

The movies have never made it easy to discover, and, for once, Oz and reality agree. The most fruitful message, nonetheless, remains the message vested in reality: Marriage is compromise. Marriage is an earned livelihood. Marriage is work. Marriage is commitment. Marriage is, for all its imperfections, a bond that blesses its intimates with a stability and affection that the movies can never match.

Notes

1. Earlier, when Merritt and Ryder start to cross the line and involve themselves in some heavy necking, Ryder pulls back. Merritt expresses surprise because she knows that Ryder has her where he wants her, yet stops. Ryder replies that maybe he's "feeling charitable." An interesting choice of words, and probably considered more chauvinistic today than in 1960. What Ryder implies is that he's doing Merritt a favor by being a "good guy."

2. Wealth and secrecy play another role in *Metropolitan* (1990), a film about privileged adolescents and their games away from the formalities of pomp and circumstance. The youngsters' coming-of-age diversions etch out a presence even amid decorous settees and finely-woven rugs. Strip poker occupies one pastime, but does so without the raucous demeanor of blue-collar entertainment. Pants and skirts come off with ease, giving more credence to what is said than what is shown. One girl decides to remove a garment even when her cards don't require it, prompting another participant to note wryly that "Playing strip poker with an exhibitionist somehow takes the challenge away."

A more dangerous wager, the Truth game, demands fearlessly honest answers to even the most intimate questions. Tom Townsend (Edward Clements), a newcomer to the group, loses such a wager and must confess his romantic involvement. He responds openly about his commitment to a girl, an airy beauty who first leaves him and then resumes the relationship. Tom, sensitive to his outside status, remains painfully insensitive to the girl who yearns for him, Audrey Rouget (Carolyn Farina). She sits next to Tom as he offers his juvenile sentiments about love, her lowered gaze disclosing all we need to know about her hurt and the distance between them. The Truth game results in the pressured revelations of youthful passions, some of which are better left unstated.

3.   One virtue of intimacy concerns its capacity to tolerate different orientations to sexuality, and to work out compromises for those lustful interludes that arrive, sometimes, at the oddest moments. Jimmy Johnson's (July 19, 1991) cartoon strip, *Arlo & Janice*, shows the married couple on a blanket at the beach. Arlo says, "Lying around on the beach does wonders for my appetite!" Janice replies, "Here, have an apple." She offers him the apple, but he doesn't accept it. He just looks at her with a smile...and she says, "Oh." Oh, indeed.

4.   Victorian morality rears its prudish head during this ride when a vicar demonstrates his straitlaced upbringing. The driver has his girl beside him and the two are enjoying a cuddling of *passione*. Their shameless affection overwhelms the vicar's sense of modesty, and he orders the girl off the coach, much to the lovers' dismay. Later, when the tourists are scattered about the countryside, Lucy asks the driver to direct her to a friend. The driver, wise in the ways of romance, takes her to George instead.

5.   Remember Sara Teasdale's poem at the beginning of the lesson? Considering the kiss that George just delivered to a bewildered Lucy, imagine our damsel in Teasdale's portrait who wonders about the kiss not given. I asked a class of Human Sexuality students to ponder the right word, and the students most commonly chose "look," although other choices like "lust" and "hurt" also surfaced.

Sara Teasdale's selection, and the selection of a relatively small number of students, was *kiss: But the kiss in Colin's eyes/Haunts me night and day.* The right word is unusual, unlikely, unexpected. Such empathy in *The Look* permits a nobler sentiment because "kiss" commands a stronger, more concrete sensation than "look" in Teasdale's scheme. "Kiss" brings you closer to the felt experience of what the poem embraces (Fairfax & Moat, 1981, p. 27).

6. Interestingly, Charlotte hears George's plea as she gazes out the window to see Cecil awkwardly batting away an insect. Cecil, it seems, has absolutely no communal spirit with nature. The contrast that Charlotte witnesses between George and Cecil, and a searching look at her own timid existence, compel

Charlotte to engage later in one of the few decisive actions of her life.

7. Sally's friend, Marie (Carrie Fisher), stumbles across her "right guy." She sighs and says to him, "Tell me I never have to be out there again." "Out there" refers to a war zone where dating assumes an adversarial relationship: the male's Manifesto versus the female's Pledge. Dating partners behave guardedly, wondering how readily they can trust their "significant other," and mulling over the uncertainty of whether they will know the truth if they hear it.

8. Mike and Susan, unknown to their parents, engaged in a developing trend of the 1960s and 1970s called **cohabitation**. They lived together for a year-and-a-half, a practice that Mike's brother, Richie, labeled a wise move. What better way to learn about your future spouse than to become roommates? Subsequent surveys on cohabitation, however, suggest that this premarital abode does not ensure longevity in marriage (Renshaw, 1990; Hall, 1988; Newcomb, 1986). One reason concerns the possibility that lovers who cohabit shy more from commitment and its responsibilities than do lovers who accept this commitment on faith and delay their living arrangements until marriage. But cohabitation also may save a warring couple from the mistake of taking their turbulent relationship into the legalities and obligations of a marital state.

9. Vincent Minnelli directed the 1950 *Father Of The Bride*, a movie that, at first glance, appears as another MGM lightweight comedy. But Stephen Harvey (1989, p. 162), in a retrospective of Vincent Minnelli's work, notes that "While allowing ample space for the movie's comic set pieces, at every opportunity Minnelli gives a disquieting undertone to the script with two elements banished from most movie comedies--darkness and silence."
Harvey adds that much of the story occurs at night as Stanley contemplates the worthiness of Buckley (the groom), the expense of a big wedding, and other marital tribulations. The film, moreover, complements these dire proceedings with very little music, and even includes a nightmare sequence in which Stanley's grotesque attempts to fulfill his role as father of the bride become a little exercise in horror.

10. Wedding presents become the one dividend for a father of the bride. Both film versions of *Bride* use the very same present as the most garish gift of the lot: a chalky white, female statue with a clock for a pelvis. A wedding present also becomes the reason for an argument between the 1991 prospective bride and groom. The fiancé gives his fiancée a blender, a gift she interprets as a 1950's sexist symbol, suggesting that the female belongs in the kitchen.

Lesson 8

Sex And Censorship

The guardians of sexual innocence encountered their own dilemma during the advent of motion pictures. Some guardians could see the value of sexual foreknowledge as a guide to proper conduct (Kuhn, 1988, p. 109). Forewarned is forearmed. But the other temptation also intruded: The longstanding conviction that nudity and adultery and prostitution, no matter if presented negatively in the movies, would encourage impressionable youth to favor sexual promiscuity.

Pursuing its desire to present sexuality as entertainment despite the dangers of censorship, Hollywood became proficient at two practices, both of which recur throughout its history. Paying homage to **Practice #1**, the film moguls, apprehensive that congress and the states might intervene to regulate their industry, opted to establish an office of censorship themselves. Far better that Hollywood police Hollywood than to tolerate "outside" interference.

Thus, Will Hays, a politician who enjoyed a "clean image," and, more important, a politician who actually liked the movie industry, became the moguls' choice to command a board of censorship in 1922. The **Hays Office**, although it would gain more influence than it manifested initially, temporarily deterred the carping critics who wanted movies ruled with a chaste hand.

Will Hays, however, never controlled Hollywood's second practice. **Practice #2** involved filmmakers who cleverly managed to circumvent the censor's guidelines. Film historian Kevin Brownlow (1990, pp. 20-21) notes how both parties crossed swords to parry and thrust:

> Hays admitted that the dozens of ways of injecting sex into films led to games of hide-and-seek. Directors, having to cope with Hays *and* the state boards, became adept at signaling to the audience over the heads of the censors. Of course, it depended on the censor; the type who saw sin in sandwiches would let nothing through. But others were more literal. A shot of a girl dusting foot powder into her shoes would indicate to them merely that she suffered from tired feet. A more sophisticated audience, trained to watch for the smallest hint, would realize at once that the girl was a streetwalker.

The Ratings Game

Today, Hollywood pursues the same two practices, albeit with different players and different rules. Concerning Practice #1, neither the U. S. Government nor other censorship groups do much to fetter the industry artistically. Movie executives continue to wriggle free of any sweeping content restrictions on its craft.

This wriggling has resulted in a rather soft ratings system that depends on compliance from theatre owners who exhibit the industry's product. Likewise, regarding Practice #2, filmmakers still seek the most moderate rating for their work, coupled with the least editing of controversial scenes.

The censor's judgment falls in the vicinity of **G, PG, PG-13, R, NC-17**, and **X**. **G** refers to movies for General Audiences, although few films appear suitable for kids, adults, and pets alike. **PG** stands for Parental Guidance whereby Mom and Dad decide on movie attendance. **PG-13** requires youngsters under the age of thirteen to attend with an adult.

NC-17 indicates that no children under seventeen can view the movie. And **X**? Well, **X** symbolizes an "adults only" film, the kind of entertainment that loiters on the bottom rung of any ladder that proclaims a hierarchy of artistic taste.

If we see silhouettes of two lovers in the nude, or if we glimpse a shot of female breasts, then the movie probably inspires a **PG** or **PG-13** rating. But if the camera probes more intimately, say, by making discreet use of the lovers' nude bodies in a simulated act of intercourse, viewers will likely be watching an **R**-rated film (Kawin, 1987, p. 483).

Should the act become less simulated and more graphic to illuminate some "profound theme," the film moves closer to the **NC-17** proscription of excluding youngsters under the age of seventeen. Finally, should the lovers exhibit the stamina to make love throughout the film--just to make love--they will earn an **X** rating for their sexual marathon. The lovers' thoughts in **X**-rated films remain at loin-level and therefore depict pornography, at least as decreed by the Motion Picture Association of America (MPAA).

The distinction between **NC-17** and **X** seems elusive at first glance, and some say at second glance, too (Abramson, 1991). The intended use of **NC-17** concerns sexually graphic yet substantive movies, such as *Henry And June* (1990), a film about the erotic interludes of novelist Henry Miller. This sexually suggestive vehicle and others of assumed merit benefit from the qualifying designation of **NC-17** because, without **NC-17**, such movies likely will receive the revenue-limiting **X** rating. The consequences of **NC-17** and **X** labels indicate that (1) few filmmakers will accept the **NC-17** rating for their expensive films and risk losing most of the teenage audience; and (2) pornographers, in turn, will try to elevate their "works of art" occasionally with the **NC-17** designation (Horn, 1991; Gerosa & Thompson, 1990).

The crux of the ratings game, however, remains the **R** movie. **R** movies harbor the potential for broad theatrical distribution, and prompt only slight editing of risqué scenes. This artistic latitude allows these films to retreat from the abyss of receiving an **NC-17** or **X** rating (Harris, 1993). Moreover, given the greater permissiveness to exhibit cinematic violence, the appropriate coupling of violence and sex realizes considerable leeway in an **R** film.

This leeway leads to confusion in giving a film like *Basic Instinct* (1991) an **R** rating, and a less violent film like *Damage* (1992) an **NC-17** label. Why the difference? Hollywood columnist Martin Grove (1992, p. 8), searching for an answer, concludes that *Damage*, unlike *Basic Instinct*, proves more mental than physical in creating an attitude about erotic passion: "It recalls Hitchcock's classic shower stabbing scene in 'Psycho,' a case in which moviegoers thought they saw much more violence than there really was on the screen."

Advocates of the ratings system believe, of course, that the system, though not perfect, remains workable. Workable in the sense that the ratings keep unsupervised youngsters from seeing sexually explicit films. Still, given the kids' opportunities for slipping videotapes in the old VCR, and for watching cable movies when supervisors are busy elsewhere, what do you think? Does the system work?[1]

What Price Nudity?

Sex and censorship in movies, as in real life, relate to **nudity**. Physically, nudity concerns **decency**: the status of wearing the proper attire in the proper setting. If society deems you improper in attire or setting, watch out. (One legal case, for example, pertained to a woman's right to reveal her breasts; see Fahringer, 1992.)

Ask yourself this question: How many spots come to mind where you can go nude publicly or privately with no repercussions? Yes, not a large number. Now ask yourself a second question: How many spots come to mind where you would **want** to go nude? If you can't think of many, you have just given yourself another reason for going to the movies.

Psychologically, nudity refers to **sentiment**. Sentiment encompasses an individual's mental disposition, in this instance, a prudent adherence to society's norms for regulating sexual conduct. You can be fully clothed and therefore physically decent, but if you convulse suddenly into a flurry of pelvic thrusts, well, that's not proper conduct. You're still decent, although your immodesty makes it seem as if you are wearing no clothes (perhaps comparable to the play of sensuality that Michelle Pfeiffer exudes when she moves voluptuously atop that piano in *The Fabulous Baker Boys*, 1989).

The folklore, the politics, the morality of nudity begin with Adam and Eve, and, in particularly, with Eve's nakedness (Mullins, 1985, p. 57; Bal, 1986, p. 317). A naked female body has at various times been equated with sin, innocence, beauty, inequality, and, as always, commercialism (i.e., take a closer look at that butterfly in advertisements for *The Silence Of The Lambs*, 1991).

Nudity's delicate complexions play by **rules** of decency and sentiment that, like the shifting sands, depend on the nuances of a social situation and the mood of its participants. Cathy and David (Annette O'Toole and Martin Short) of *Cross My Heart* (1988) frolic in the joy of physical intimacy before orgasm, yet behave by different rules after orgasm. Cathy asks David to turn away from her as she slips on her undergarments. David, perplexed after her boldness in bed, obeys but does not understand.

Good nudity, of course, occurs in good movies, but also with good purpose. The female or male in the altogether need become neither exploitative nor perfunctory. Instead, the nudity can establish a needed link in character development or it can advance the plot. Thus, the nakedness of Isabella Rossellini in *Blue Velvet* (1986) creates a painfully humiliating presence to watch, so much so that any earlier thoughts of eroticism become lost through her victimization.[2] By contrast, the scampering antics of Annette Bening as she dashes *au naturel* into John Cusack's room provide the despairing tone of *The Grifters* (1991) with a sorely needed touch of gaiety.

Another variation finds Mariel Hemingway recovering from a lesbian love affair in *Personal Best* (1982). One scene shows Hemingway cavorting with her nude boyfriend (Denny Stiles). She even accompanies Stiles to the bathroom, standing behind him and holding his penis as he attempts to pee (he can't; guys are funny that way). This episode uses nudity without embarrassment to sustain a goofy bit of intimacy between new lovers. Earlier, the nudity displayed by Hemingway and her lesbian lover (Patrice Donnelly), and witnessed again with other females in a steam room, is incidental and unprepossessing; a natural state for female athletes accustomed to wearing little and to exhibiting their bodies.

Cinematic nudity, therefore, harbors a **nonerotic** property, although this feature receives less attention from filmmakers. A rambunctious "just-us-guys" outing at a pond during Victorian times shows frontal nudity with no hint of eroticism in *A Room With A View* (1985). The characters, including a clergyman, splash their way exuberantly through water games and chases around the pond, their personalities neutralized via nude bodies, and via concentration on indulging the boy in each of them. Boyish fun and games, that is, until some proper females chance upon them. Then, chaos ensues and the males' characters reassert themselves. One male gives a "Whoop!" as if the discovery caps off a fine romp in the pond. But other males express mortification as they scramble to hide their bare accessories.

These uses of nudity for entertainment indicate the fluid status of how filmmakers perceive sex and censorship. Conflicting attempts to define what is and is not pornography become less surprising when we realize the array of value judgments about nudity that enter into the equation.

Daniel Linz and Neil Malamuth (1993, p. 4), for instance, propose three normative positions on sex and censorship: (1) The **conservative/moralist** approach that finds censorship a lesser evil when compared to the offensiveness and conse-quences of graphic sexual displays, whatever their content; (2) the **pornographic/feminist** interpretation that also minimizes the dangers of censorship, but does so in the belief that squashing pornography will help release women from their recurring cinematic roles as sexual scapegoats; and (3) the **liberal/erotica** perspective which, as the odd position out, accords freedom from censorship a higher priority over the presumably harmless cosmetic fantasies that eroticism supplies to dramatize female and male sexual relations.

Thus, advocates of the first two positions willingly invoke censorship for what they perceive as the greater good: namely, keeping sexual promiscuity out of the public eye, and, for the pornographic/feminists specifically, preventing media presentations of females as sexual victims. Clearly the third position, the liberal/erotica viewpoint, charts a different course by endorsing a relaxed tolerance of sexual expression.

The key point for us concerns our moviegoing habits. We are more likely to see mainstream films than X-rated pornographic films, and more likely to see movies that show nudity and other erotica at least with some pretense of artistic integrity. How can we decide where to stand regarding sex and censorship, especially if none of the three normative positions meets our fancy? This question, naturally, is neither simple nor recent, and any answer requires a little cinematic history.

Sophistication

Compared to today's ratings game and viewers' casual acceptance of nude portrayals, sexual censorship during those earlier years of virginal attitudes and chaste encounters revealed a fang or two of "I mean business." Therefore, if we transport ourselves back to a period in movie history between 1934 and 1968, what shall we discover about the vigilance of these sexual guardians?

First, we will learn that the ratings analyst becomes a censor with a different verdict. The censor recommends (orders) a scene deleted, causing the actors to play out their passion on the cutting-room floor. Obviously the censor then is not the censor now. Culture moves on, as do attitudes about sexuality.

The mechanics of sex are rudimentary and hardly the stuff of a cosmopolitan outlook. But society's restrictions covering these mechanics introduce the opportunity for uncommon strategy. The **Production Code**, although in effect during the waning years of silent films, acquired its teeth in 1934 and continued in force until 1968. The Hays Office simply assumed a tougher stance in scrutinizing those films that dared to cross the line. Filmmakers, in response, met this opposition by finding ways to circumvent the Hays Code, via Practice #2.

The Code's influence produced a two-fold outcome. The Hays Office attempted to keep a powerful medium pure, a laudable goal that often received less regard than it deserved (Leff & Simmons, 1990, p. xiii; Gardner, 1987, p. 215). These persuasions were not a one-way street since studio and independent producers engaged in negotiation, skullduggery, and even harassment to keep certain scenes in, and the Hays Office out. Still, the Office held firm during the early years, and in doing so put its stamp on a second outcome: the promotion of distortions about sexual behavior. What remains remarkable, and a testimony to society's tardy revelations regarding sex, is that advocates of the Production Code maintained their attempts to regulate cinematic eroticism until 1968.

The Code covered crime, violence, religion, and other controversial issues. But to no one's surprise, the Code devoted three-quarters of its regulations to sex (Gardner, 1987, p. xx; also see Leff & Simmons, 1990, p. 283). No explicit treatments of adultery or illicit sex; no lustful, open-mouthed kissing; no graphic scenes of seduction or rape, not even as humorous portrayals; no positive treatments of abortion, nor any reference to sexual perversion; no themes concerned with sex hygiene or sexual disease; no dancing suggestive of immodest movements (remember Elvis and his gyrating loins in the 1950s?); no dirty words or unseemly references, such as fairy, goose, pansy, and S.O.B.; no immoderate uses of "damn" or "hell"; no nudity, not even in silhouette, unless the nudity pertained to native life in a foreign land (Gardner, 1987, p. 209).

No, No, No. The Hays Office permitted unwed lovers to kiss, but then added certain prohibitions, as in *Casablanca* (1942) when the censor decided that no bed could be shown when Rick and Ilsa embrace in Rick's apartment (Harmetz, 1992, p. 164). A bedroom scene depicting a husband and wife kissing required the kiss to last no longer than three seconds, and the man to have one foot on the floor. A man and woman, even if truly husband and wife, slept in twin beds, never together in one bed.

A pregnant woman remained slim and svelte, defying the anatomical changes that normally occur (Hong, 1994). A woman's breasts could protrude like cannons on a hillside, as scenes with blonde bombshells like Mamie Van Doren demonstrated, but cleavage must not receive exposure. The studios achieved this "cannon effect" by having its female players wear what the stars called a "bullet bra." Regardless of a female's ample or not-so-ample bust endowment, the bullet bra made all females appear superbly, nay, unbelievably endowed on the giant screen.

So, how does a filmmaker adroitly engage in Practice #2 and deliver sexual innuendo past the censors? One tactic, particularly useful for outwitting the Hays Office, involved **sexual sophistication**. Sophistication works in ways contrary to simplicity and openness. A sophisticate displays ingenuity in perceiving simple pleasures more complexly, but also delights in guile and misdirection.

Sophistication erects a front, a veil, a barrier that invites challenge. This barrier requires time to develop: An exchange of naiveté for worldliness occurs through maturity, and the exchange, to the disillusionment of some individuals, proves irreversible. Unlike the child/adult/child cycle which Charly Gordon traversed in *Charly* (1968), we cannot expect to return to the innocence of childhood. Sophistication, to whatever degree it manifests itself, captures us with a steely permanence.

Sophistication, well tended, can depict sex unconventionally. You do not think of a simpleton as erudite or urbane. Wit and wisdom belong, not to the humdrum mentality, but to the sly soul associated with sleight-of-hand cleverness. Wit and wisdom also constitute the mental paraphernalia to help establish a keen sense in presenting sexuality as entertainment. Sophistication does possess an ugly side--ugly in terms of snobbery and deceit. But this mannered conduct, virtuous or vile, demands careful cinematic treatment. Sophistication, portrayed thoughtfully, offers one avenue of escape from sex as a visceral affair.

Howard Hughes expressed his discontent at these restrictions by exercising a **direct challenge** to the Production Code. Unable to reach a satisfactory agreement with the Hays Office, he attempted to exhibit *The Outlaw* (1943), a lackluster western starring Jane Russell. Hughes apparently decided that the film's slim potential for artistic integrity must reside in Russell's breasts. He shot her bust using numerous camera angles, take after take, and even designed a special bra to accentuate her cleavage. (Unknown to him, Russell never wore his design but substituted her own creation; see Nash & Ross, 1986, p. 2305.) Hughes deliberately instigated a controversy by launching an enormous publicity saturation featuring Russell and her mammary glands. He finally realized a limited distribution of his movie, three years after its initial release in 1943.

A direct challenge also involved the principle of "overloading" a film with nudity and eroticism, knowing that the "worst of each" would be cut, but hoping that "some of each" might remain in the movie. *Tarzan And His Mate* (1934) includes an extended, nude underwater scene between Tarzan (Johnny Weissmuller, wearing briefs) and Jane (Maureen O'Sullivan, wearing nothing) that resembles an early Esther Williams' underwater aerobics routine. The swimming sequence, of course, was nixed. But the Hays Office permitted Jane to glide about in a skimpy jungle costume that revealed ample exposure of her hips and thighs. Tarzan and Jane, moreover, appeared to live an erotic existence in the trees, married only by nature, yet clearly enjoying their very physical relationship (Nash & Ross, 1987, p. 3282).

Other filmmakers opted for a finer sense of integrity by issuing an **indirect challenge** to the Code. This indirect challenge required greater artistry since the film must show nothing unseemly, yet infuse the characters and story with an undercurrent of sexuality that the censor would not detect, or, at best, misinterpret. Responding to the challenge, some moviemakers became adept at choreographing actors to engage in subtle gestures. Such gestures were proper in movement but wicked in intent, and depicted a slippery tactic for defying the Hays Office.[3]

Baby Doll (1956), a movie that disturbed numerous civic and religious groups, illustrates one example of the film-maker's indirect challenge. The actions in question pertain to the use of artful gestures and reactions, carefully laced with lust. This Tennessee Williams story concerns a Mississippi redneck, Archie (Karl Malden), who marries a young girl, Baby Doll (Carroll Baker), but agrees not to consummate the marriage until she reaches her nineteenth birthday. Archie, uneasy over the wiles of a scheming Silva Vacarro (Eli Wallach), sets fire to Vacarro's work equipment. Vacarro, suspecting Archie, gains revenge during a steamy scene that portrays him seducing Baby Doll as the two sit in a porch swing.

The film's provocative advertisement, showing Carroll Baker sucking her thumb, dressed innocently as she lay sensuously in an oversized crib, created a disturbing image for decency groups. But the porch scene becomes the episode of note, the incident of desire or consternation, depending on the viewers' sexual ethics and the liveliness of their Oz process.

Years later, Baker and Wallach commented that nothing extraordinary happened during the scene, although moviegoers fantasized Vacarro as a lecherous charmer who places his hands on suggestive curves of Baby Doll's anatomy. What Vacarro does, in fact, is intimidate Baby Doll by sitting close and caressing her face as he verbally draws her through a physical seduction. The film never explores what happens afterward, although presumably Vacarro's smooth delivery and Baby Doll's hesitant attentiveness combined to launch an erotic outcome in the audience's imagination. Vacarro's gestures in the porch swing are flirtatious yet suitable, despite the moviegoers' conviction that his hands strayed into forbidden territory.[4]

Orson Welles also found reason to chaff at the Hays Office. He wanted a scene from *Citizen Kane* (1941) to occur in a brothel, a desire that the Hays Office promptly squelched. Welles, undeterred, rehearsed the scene anyway, until a second warning forced him to abandon the idea. The Director surrendered the brothel scene, but not his animosity regarding the Code's constraints and alternative suggestions: He could, for instance, include the brothel if the plot called for it to be burned down.

Harlan Lebo (1990, p. 28), recounting the adventure and controversy of making *Citizen Kane*, notes that Welles unleashed his own "visual jab" at the Production Code in a later scene played by two of the story's characters, Leland and Bernstein (Joseph Cotton and Everett Sloane). Lebo explains, "When Leland and Bernstein are sorting through statues in Kane's office, the arm of one of the marble antiquities grabs Bernstein in the crotch. The Hays Office never noticed."

More telling, however, is the sophistication in sexual relationships that movies attained through **subtle dialogue**. Filmmakers who wished to indirectly challenge the Code and portray an illicit affair could use clever conversation to characterize the touchy subject of adultery.

The bantering between Fred MacMurray (Walter Neff) and Barbara Stanwyck (Phyllis Dietrichson) in *Double Indemnity* (1944) exemplifies this approach. He's a roving insurance salesman and she's a discontented wife. Their initial meeting results in dialogue that is playful and oblique in meaning, scripted by novelist Raymond Chandler and the film's director, Billy Wilder. Neff, after punctuating his sales pitch with teasing remarks, comments on the personalized anklet that Phyllis wears (Luhr, 1991, pp. 35-36):

WALTER: "Phyllis." I think I like that.
PHYLLIS: But you're not sure?
WALTER: I could drive it around the block a couple of times.
PHYLLIS: Mr. Neff, why don't you drop by tomorrow evening around 8:30. He'll be in then.
WALTER: Who?
PHYLLIS: My husband. You were anxious to talk to him, weren't you?
WALTER: Yeah, I was, but I'm sort of getting over the idea, if you know what I mean?
PHYLLIS: There's a speed limit in this state, Mr. Neff. 45 miles per hour.
WALTER: How fast was I going, officer?
PHYLLIS: I'd say around 90.
WALTER: Suppose you get down off your motorcycle and give me a ticket?

PHYLLIS: Suppose I let you off with a warning this time?
WALTER: Suppose it doesn't take?
PHYLLIS: Suppose I have to whack you over the knuckles?
WALTER: Suppose I bust out crying and put my head on your shoulder?
PHYLLIS: Suppose you try putting it on my husband's shoulder?
WALTER: That tears it! [*pause*] 8:30 tomorrow evening then?
PHYLLIS: That's what I suggested.
WALTER: Will you be here too?
PHYLLIS: I guess so. I usually am.
WALTER: Same chair, same perfume, same anklet?
PHYLLIS: I wonder if I know what you mean?
WALTER: I wonder if you wonder.

The ill-fated pair make it plain, without outwardly stating the fact, that they share a mutual attraction. Their transgression passes the censor's inspection because the lovers execute no sexual gymnastics, and because, ultimately, they pay the piper in the film's climactic scenes. The richness of their dialogue, however, implies a sexual invitation by Walter, and a "Maybe, Baby" response from Phyllis. It is this implied wit that tells perceptive moviegoers of the couple's true feelings, and of the couple's anticipatory arousal.

William Luhr, author of *Raymond Chandler & Film* (1991, p. 36), comments that "The dialogue is sufficiently crass, sufficiently subtle, sufficiently direct, sufficiently tentative, and sufficiently witty to establish the basis for the relationship, and for the film. Chandler once described good writing as resembling an iceberg: it has to carry a great deal more weight than what is visible."

The Oz process performs an imaginative leap here. Just as in *Psycho* where the viewers convince themselves that they see more of Marion (Janet Leigh) in the shower than actually occurs, so do moviegoers make the relationship between Walter and Phyllis more sexually seductive than what appears on screen. Sophisticated viewers, in particular, excel at the game of adding their own lustrous (and lustful?) closure to the prickly teasing between forbidden lovers like Phyllis and Walter.

Sexualities: The Pristine And The Exquisite

Filmmakers relied on **sexuality** to convey more sensuality in romantic relationships than some censors, or moviegoers, recognized in the literal conduct observed on screen (recall the erotic nibbling of Cary Grant and Ingrid Bergman in *Notorious*). Sexuality, compared to physical sex, encompasses an emotional and a physical attraction between female and male. Sexuality that "works" on screen reflects an appealing chemistry of femininity and masculinity, concocted to inspire all kinds of gratifying illusions.

Frankly, the censors appeared dominant as guardians of sexual restraint. But behind the scenes, these guardians found a clever filmmaker's portrayal of sexuality daunting. The Hays Office had no firm rules regarding the subjective dimension of male/female hedonism. The censors thought concretely--don't do this, don't do that--whereas sexuality propelled lovers into a domain of exquisite feelings and comprehensions. Sophistication, remember, engages life through a veil of unorthodox expressions. Sexuality certainly qualifies as an experience that some lovers revel in expressing personally and unconventionally.

Pristine sexuality depicts one such experience. "Pristine" is taken at face value to mean a virginal allure. A naive attraction between young lovers who, in their mutual ecstasy, discover the lessons of passion from scratch. The filmmaker's advantage in displaying these desires centers on the knowledge that viewers (and censors) **expect** a zestful eroticism where youth are concerned. The question becomes, How can this expectation be mined cinematically to achieve the desired sexuality?

Leonard Whiting as Romeo and Olivia Hussey as Juliet (*Romeo And Juliet*, 1968) personify this zest, this fresh-eyed enthusiasm of young love. A young love made more pure and delicious by the lovers' frenzied embraces, and their precarious existence amid the hostilities of two feuding families.

Director Franco Zeffirelli's interpretation of Shakespeare's drama unfolds in a four-day whirlwind of mischief, misunderstanding, impetuousness, and secrecy. Romeo and Juliet spark a calamity of woeful events with such vigor and recklessness that you wonder a little about their haste. Romeo characterizes the key to this breathless pace, magically forgetting all other adorations upon seeing the fair Juliet. He rashly embarks on a dangerous, passionate affair with his true love, as if the stars may grant them little time. And, indeed, Romeo and Juliet find their moments all too precious, all too brief.

The occasional prophetic utterings in Shakespeare's play leave an impression of unshakable tragedy, of a fledgling romance destined to a dire denouement. Before his meeting with Juliet, Romeo fleetingly imagines a forbidding future: "I fear, too early; for my mind misgives/Some consequence yet hanging in the stars/Shall bitterly begin his fearful date/With this night's revels and expire the term/Of a despised life, closed in my breast,/By some vile forfeit of untimely death" (Shakespeare, 1963, p. 64, Act I, Scene IV, Lines 106-111). Juliet, too, entertains misgivings as she seeks Romeo's identity after their sprightly exchange of affection: "Go ask his name.--If he is married,/My grave is like to be my wedding bed" (Shakespeare, p. 70, Act I, Scene V, Lines 136-137).

Previous dramatic productions of *Romeo And Juliet* included a film in 1936 with Leslie Howard and Norma Shearer, and in 1954 with Laurence Harvey and Susan Shentall (Nash & Ross, 1986, pp. 2664-2665). Both dramas paid cinematic homage to Shakespeare's tale, yet both dramas failed to rival Zeffirelli's 1968 work because of two developments. First, Zeffirelli orchestrated a glimpse of Romeo's nudity and Juliet's partial nudity, giving viewers (and their Oz process) a physical intimacy to share with the lovers that moviegoers did not realize in the earlier films. Remember that the Production Code, by 1968, had gums but no teeth. Nudity became a dimension for filmmakers to explore. Some directors, like Zeffirelli, used this emerging freedom prudently, whereas other filmmakers chose less circumspectly to embrace the belief that "more is better."

Second, and of greater importance, Zeffirelli's actors were true teenagers, the proper age of Romeo and Juliet, unlike those performers who portrayed the lovers in 1936 and 1954. The pristine sexuality of youth permitted a tenor to the lovers' relationship that heightened their tragedy: Star-crossed lovers whose promising affections die in yearning, possessing youthful passions unfulfilled. Death is death, but in the primal flush of life, death proves an elegiac loss of blossoming sexuality. Zeffirelli's rendering of this young love invokes a special lament that the earlier film versions using more mature players could not capture.

Pristine sexuality gains its appeal through a cherub nature of first-time lovers. Innocence is vanishing, as is time for some lovers, so the beauty of this sexuality lies in its delicacy and short life. Immature lovers do not claim much foresight in dwelling on the intensity of their delights and where these delights shall lead. The love is sufficient and no doubt capable of surmounting the requisite obstacles ahead, or so young lovers believe (see Driscoll, Davis, & Lipetz, 1972, on the Romeo & Juliet effect).

Wilma Loomas and Bud Stamper (Natalie Wood and Warren Beatty) of *Splendor In The Grass* (1961) believe so. Parental guidance--or some critics will claim misguidance--convinces the young lovers to repress their sexual urges. Pristine behavior, they are told, becomes preferable to the sordidness of fleshly desires. This chaste preference proves frustrating and ultimately disastrous. The lovers never fulfill the promise of their innocent attraction.

Five years and several heartbreaks later, Wilma visits Bud and finds him married to an Italian waitress--a very pregnant Italian waitress. The lovers' innocence behind them, Wilma observes that she has matured but Bud has not. He seems not to have prospered from his experiences with women, with sex, or with life. Wilma understands that the splendor of what they might have shared cannot be relived. Their innocence, so filled with exuberance then, vanishes into a wellspring of trying experiences.

Thus, although pristine sexuality need not bestow its charms exclusively on young lovers--new love can rejuvenate mature lovers, too--the innocence in question does call for a childlike wonder that normally only youth possess. What the rest of us aspire to, if we aspire at all, concerns exquisite sexuality.

Exquisite sexuality portrays allusions to physical sex as an enchanting venture. Exquisite lovers pass beyond the virginal stage and search for a sexual relationship more mature in commitment, in *savoir-faire* and *savoir-vivre*. They wish a love more fulfilling and ascendant than past loves. They certainly look for a love more gainful than the awkward joys and pains once remembered of a pristine sexuality. Exquisite sexuality marks the kind of ambitious relationship that Wilma ultimately sought, but that Bud appeared unable to comprehend.

Sometimes ambition dances with love to illuminate a stirring union of joy and commitment. Sometimes, however, the ambition outreaches the love, and bitterness results. Consider the classic murder mystery, *Laura* (1944), in which Laura (Gene Tierney), bright and lovely, establishes a career for herself under the tutelage of Waldo Lydecker (Clifton Webb). Lydecker struts and preens as a haughty columnist, luxuriating in his caustic wit. But one evening in her apartment, Laura apparently becomes the victim of a killer's shotgun blast. Mark (Dana Andrews), the detective assigned to the case, ponders her death and her portrait. (The portrait was actually a photograph of Tierney smeared with paint to better resemble her likeness; see Nash & Ross, 1986, p. 1628).

The portrait fascinates Mark and he fantasizes about why so desirous a creature had to die, finding himself unaccountably enamored of a woman he has never met. Even Waldo Lydecker, always the astute observer, comments on Mark's odd attraction: "Ever strike you--that you're acting strangely? ...You'll end up in a psychiatric ward. I don't think they've ever had a patient who fell in love with a corpse" (Nash & Ross, 1986, p. 1628).

Mark's fanciful thoughts on a rainy evening lull the detective to sleep in Laura's apartment. A noise awakens him and he turns to see his fantasy come to life. Laura, unharmed, enters the room. Her cool, sensuous presence evokes a mesmerizing vision that overwhelms the detective. Events bear out that another woman, similar in appearance to Laura, died that fateful night.

Laura's mystique poses a tantalizing puzzle: She becomes the indefinable beauty who charms a cynical sophisticate like Waldo Lydecker; and Waldo, in turn, perceives Laura as the object of his immeasurable frustration when she proves unattainable. For Waldo, Laura's appeal involves her exquisiteness as a woman. Clearly what Waldo seeks is something more than a mentor-protegee relationship, and yet something apart from fleshly gratification. We do not think of their bond as one that culminates in physical sex. But this possibility becomes quite prominent in Laura's attraction to Mark, together with Mark's prescience of his feelings about Laura that he experiences initially through her portrait.

Two obsessed men who harbor different sexual fantasies about the same woman: Waldo, to captivate Laura and monopolize her allure for his own ego-fulfillment; and Mark, to reach out and have Laura's portrait of loveliness become flesh, his to hold and to cherish. Finally and inevitably, it is Waldo who relinquishes his illusion and, destructively, confronts the reality of losing Laura.

Exquisite sexuality represented the filmmakers' saving grace during those years of heavy censorship. Consequently, if the Hays Office chose to surround normal overtures to physical sex with barbed wire, the intrepid filmmaker might at least find dramatic reality in the foreplay of a sophisticated sexuality. The more exquisite the expression, the more likely the censor would deduce little harm in the filmmaker's clever disguise of a sexual invitation: Two screen lovers who are so in tune sexually as to convey the essence of a sensuous relationship--and who manage to do so without revealing one inch of taboo anatomy.

A Slouching Censorship

The power to censor poses at least two dangers that prove intimidating to the advocates of free speech. One danger concerns a **definition of boundaries**. The Production Code suggested standards for decency and modesty in films, but how much authority did a censor possess to interpret what is decent and indecent? Modest and immodest?

Decency, described earlier, refers to appropriate attire, and modesty to acceptable conduct or sentiment. Censors conscientiously wished to counter indecency by prohibiting tell-tale cleavage and other glimpses of suggestive nudity. Censors also desired to monitor the actors' provocative gestures and postures in maintaining a decorum on body language. But how many revisions could a censor demand before encountering arguments that these alterations would ruin a film? Such proscriptions forced the Office to field accusations regarding its stranglehold over what could and could not reach the screen. These accusations had little effect in the early years because the censor's hand usually prevailed.

The Hays Office, moreover, was not alone in proclaiming its position on decency and modesty. Gossip columnists, such as Louella Parsons, Hedda Hopper, and Walter Winchell, commanded the power to "make" or "break" film stars during the 1930s and 1940s. Parsons enjoyed media power because of her column in a newspaper that belonged to William Randolph Hearst. It seems that Orson Welles used Hearst as one of the models to help characterize Charles Foster Kane, the story's central figure (Lebo, 1990, p. 133).

The film did not portray Kane favorably, an interpretation to which Parsons took offense. After demanding a special screening, she concluded that the movie reflected poorly on Hearst, sexually and otherwise. Right or wrong, Parsons believed she saw Hearst in the character of Kane--another instance of how the Oz process may enrich the viewer's imagination to "see more" than the screen legitimately shows.

The gossip columnist, who apparently perceived no boundaries to her influence over Hollywood, mustered opposition in an attempt to destroy the film's negative and prints. Fortunately, Parsons's self-appointed campaign failed, partly because the furor over suppressing *Citizen Kane* generated more public attention to the Kane/Hearst connection than the film would have created alone (Lebo, 1990, p. 166; also see Nash & Ross, 1985, p. 431).[5]

The point is not Kane's real or imagined ties to Hearst, but that one person should anoint herself the "madame of morality" and think nothing of killing a film that cost almost a million dollars. Going beyond the bounds of propriety is a temptation for those individuals who enjoy a measure of influence. The Hays Office at least consulted the Production Code to justify decisions on censorship, however picayune. But what authority did figures like Louella Parsons use as justification to condemn a film? Power, sheer power, some would say. The kind of power that defines its own boundaries of proper and improper conduct.

A second danger of censorship concerns its **inflexibility**. Sexual attitudes became more public and less constrained after the 1940s for a number of reasons, revised by the wave of social and economic changes that accompanied World War II. Scientifically, Alfred Kinsey and his associates analyzed thousands of sexual case histories into trends and figures that popularized two books, *Sexual Behavior In The Human Male* in 1948, and *Sexual Behavior In The Human Female* in 1953. Americans may not have read these books cover to cover, but Kinsey's message reached public awareness: namely, that people engage in more recreational sex privately than they admit publicly. Kinsey did not launch a sexual revolution, although his professionalism in researching sexual behavior countered the critics of change sufficiently to encourage further investigation (Martone, 1984, p. 28).

The movies, never an industry to shy from change, also became bolder and started to punch gaping holes in the Production Code. The censor's slouch began to show its droopy drawers. A modest comedy, Otto Preminger's *The Moon Is Blue* (1953), marked one such salvo against the Code's static position. This lightweight romance entails the attempted seduction of a young virgin by an older man. More to the point, the words "virgin," "mistress," and "seduction," thought too risqué by the Hays Office, were treated by Preminger as amusing and harmless. The movie gained theatrical release in spite of the Production Code and proved a box-office success. The timing was right and the mood was right: The power of the Hays Office had peaked and the Code's censorship now faced an uphill battle.

Another Preminger film, *Anatomy Of A Murder* (1959), scored a legal victory concerning more racy words. The film details the trial of Lt. Frederick Manion (Ben Gazzara), charged with killing a bar owner under the belief that the man had raped his wife, Laura Manion (Lee Remick). A portion of the trial involves Paul Biegler (James Stewart) seeking to prove that Laura did indeed suffer a rape. In that regard, actors voiced intimate words like "contraceptive," "sexual climax," and "spermatogenesis" in discussing the necessary evidence for a rape. Moviegoers had never heard these words in a movie theatre until *Anatomy Of A Murder* in 1959. A Catholic censorship board in Chicago sought to have the expressions eliminated before the movie's release, but Preminger refused and won a court decision to keep the film intact (Harris, 1987, p. 101).

Nothing so complex as a change in sexual thinking happens all at once. We do not have a night-and-day rebellion that centers on *The Moon Is Blue* or *Anatomy Of A Murder*. Instead, filmmakers throughout the regime of the Hays Office continually tested the Production Code and nipped away at its prohibitions. Finally, in *The Pawnbroker* (1965) the Code permitted a frontal view of a woman's bare breasts (Toll, 1982, p. 205). This notable compromise derived from the cumulative effects of a number of lesser-noticed compromises by the Hays Office over the years.

Preminger's open defiance occurred during a favorable time for sexual openness. He enjoyed the progress made by a legacy of filmmakers whose creative efforts, particularly in portraying the amorous subtleties of human sexuality, helped make Preminger's challenge successful. Performers could now throw off a few shackles and deliver a wicked moment or two. Naughty words and racy situations started to assume a measure of dramatic realism as well as comic potential. By contrast, the Hays Office began to see its power erode through changes in sexual attitudes that simply outdistanced the Production Code.

Sexual Permissiveness

The Code surrendered to a new ratings system in 1968, which the Motion Picture Association of America later revised in 1990 to monitor the current pulse of sex and violence in films. The philosophy behind the **G, PG, PG-13, NC-17,** and **X** letter system, as described earlier, tells moviegoers something about the extent of sex and violence present in a film.

Note the difference of intent between the early, influential years of the Production Code and the present Ratings System. The Code said to Filmmakers, you can't do this and you can't do that (which some filmmakers tried to do, anyway). The new System, however, does not prohibit a movie's release. It merely abbreviates the nature of sex and violence that a viewer will encounter in a given movie, and sets forth instructions on attendance. If filmmakers find the label unsatisfactory, they can snip footage here and there to gain a more desirable rating, or they can ignore the Board's judgment. Filmmakers can even release a censored version for theatrical distribution and a less-censored interpretation for the video market, as described in Endnote #1.

Such **sexual permissiveness**, nonetheless, carries obligations. The liberty to show lovers indulging their passions, warts and all, runs the risk of neglecting the finer virtues of sexuality. Censorship in previous years inspired filmmakers to search for creative ways around the Hays Office. But what about today's standards? A full-bodied display of flesh remains no substitute for a good script and a well-crafted movie. Hollywood, free of the Production Code in 1968, faces a modern dilemma: The opportunity to concentrate artistically on sexual taboos, such as rape, prostitution, and homosexuality; and the danger that some filmmakers will succumb to the almighty dollar and exploit these issues.

Succumb they have. The movies exhibited a bit of sexual gluttony during the 1970s, using sexual freedom to present provocative issues as entertainment. *Myra Breckinridge* (1970) examined transsexualism, the surgical and psychological transition of one gender becoming the opposite gender. *Carnal Knowledge* (1971) assumed a cynical air and pursued the sexual obsessions of two men as they moved from youth to middle age. And *Lipstick* (1976) dramatized the inequities of a rape trial, specifically the victim's slim chances for justice, unless she happens to be a good shot with a hunting rifle. *Carnal Knowledge* creeps out of the pack as the one example that brings some substance to the idea of sexuality, but clearly none of these films could have claimed a hearing in the heyday of the Hays Office.

Thus, where lies the salvation for sexuality in the movies? During the pioneering years, American films doled out physical sex in mincing, Puritanical tidbits. European films, by comparison, projected a more natural, earthy eroticism. An American scene showing a woman decently clothed and modestly behaved in bed underwent revision in the European version: The same scene depicted a woman with one breast innocently peeking over her slip, or a derriere teasingly exposed.

Today, these comparisons no longer apply. American filmmakers who value commercialism over artistic integrity now view sex as a hard sell. They're allowed to show it, so **show** it! The male and female on screen need not flirt or find ingenious ways to express their sexuality. The two lovers can just let it all hang out.[6]

Characters who compel a **destructive sexuality** cast a fascinating charm, regardless of the punishment that may or may not come their way. The healthy sexuality possible in reality hardly proves recognizable against the lure of the selfish sexuality highlighted in films like *Body Heat* (1981) and *Basic Instinct* (1992). Sexual permissiveness, particularly in combination with murder, metamorphoses into a manipulation of base thoughts and heaving thighs, neither of which lifts the "lovers" airborne.

The insidiousness of this metamorphosis concerns the fact that young viewers may have little means to appreciate the gentility of a very complex, very positive sexuality, as conveyed without the baseness or the thighs by Rick and Ilsa in *Casablanca* (1942), and by Laura and Mark in *Laura* (1944). To the contrary, young moviegoers see a sexuality so anchored with the flesh that the flesh suffices as a "loving" relationship.

Can filmmakers continue to peddle loosey-goosey sex and have their films retain a measure of creativity? Frankly, it depends on the movie's basic intent and its capacity to present viewers with a lurking intelligence. If the film centers on sexual relationships as a legitimate theme, then creativity becomes a matter of how artistically the filmmaker develops this theme.

The English film *Scandal* (1989) chronicles the Profumo affair, a series of sexual liaisons that involved call girls and eminent British figures. The questions of artistic integrity for this film boil down to a pair of inquiries: (1) Is the theme worthy entertainment? and (2) does the entertainment capture the spirit of the actual scandal? (See the book, *An Affair Of State*, a 1987 exposé of the Profumo case by Phillip Knightley and Caroline Kennedy, as an independent source to compare to the movie.)

Generally, the film received favorable reviews. One insightful comment by critic Roger Ebert (1993, p. 583) focused on John Hurt's portrayal of the scandal's undeserving victim, Stephen Ward: "In an early scene, Hurt's eyes light up as he sees a pretty girl walking down the street, and somehow Hurt is able to make us understand that he feels, not lust, but simply a deep and genuine appreciation for how wonderful a pretty girl can look on a fine spring day."

Remaining nonchalant about cinematic sex no longer indicates a carefree treat. Today, the matter becomes practical **and** academic. In this era of AIDS and the importance of protection against sexually transmitted disease, it is imperative that filmmakers present physical sex responsibly to the public (Abramson & Mechanic, 1983).

The exploitative filmmakers won't care, so we can rule them out. For those writers, actors, producers, and directors who do care, physical sex appears best relegated to a supporting role. Bodies writhing in sexual ecstasy are fine for a few moments, but these few moments need to count for something besides a gratuitous exhibition of whales in heat. What counts is how physical sex complements the lovers' sexuality, and how aptly the filmmaker--now with a permissiveness to show flesh and more flesh--uses this sexuality to develop the characters and advance the plot.

Fans of *An Officer And A Gentleman* (1982) will remember the sensuous love scene between Zack Mayo (Richard Gere) and Paula Pokrifki (Debra Winger).[7] The scene shows partial nudity, sufficient to satisfy most viewers who, vicariously, crave such interludes. More important, the lovemaking lends a reality to Zack and Paula's relationship. Zack shies from commitment because the people he attempts to love--his drunken father and a mother who kills herself--fail to return that love. Thus, Zack induces a conflict: An affectionate woman cares for him, although he remains aloof and insulates himself from further intimacy and disillusionment. Other subplots work through the film, yet it is the physical, and ultimately the emotional attraction that bring the lovers together in the film's visionary ending. Zack, in navy whites and a motorcycle as his steed, arrives to claim Paula and the love he almost denies.

A romp in the sack can become integral to characters and story, or it can become nothing more than a digression to bare some flesh. In *The Big Easy* (1987), Dennis Quaid (Remy) as a detective and Ellen Barkin (Ann) as an assistant district attorney make love on their second date. The fact that she's willing indicates her attraction to him; and the fact that he's beguiled suggests his interest in her goes beyond mere bed time. Consequently, this physical beginning enriches rather than exhausts the sexuality of their relationship. Remy and Ann dominate the movie, as indeed they must if the film is to work.

Complicating the lovers' mystique, then, constitutes one way to keep their relationship on edge. Because of the lovers' attachment, Remy and Ann convey the motivation to justify an ongoing conflict. The friction, which concerns graft, becomes a counterpoint to their affectionate entanglement: Remy's willingness to accept small gratuities as a police officer, a practice that Ann tells him is wrong and cannot be rationalized.

Remy's uneasiness in dodging this bit of ethics is interesting because the dodging has never bothered him until he meets Ann. Therefore, when a pair of crooked cops almost kill Remy's brother, mistaking him for Remy, the detective finds himself accepting Ann's viewpoint. The turnaround proves believable since the plot gradually moves Remy to think more and more about his honesty. And he thinks more about his honesty because of Ann. Their earlier lovemaking sets the stage for these later developments.

Sex and censorship conjure up a strange partnership. Each domain tugs at the other, resulting in outcomes that speak on occasion of an uneasy compromise. Sometimes, however, this compromise delivers guidance essential to a healthy sexuality. Without a tribute to constructive sexuality, physical sex shown as the sum total of a relationship leaves nothing for illusion. And sexuality robbed of its mystery, of its indefinable allure, leaves only a flat, pedestrian partnership for viewers to witness. That's not memorable entertainment, and that's not artistic integrity.

Lovers become more inviting if they retain the fantasy of their elusive attraction; if they engage in an exquisite sexuality that caters to the lovers' ability for sophisticated playfulness. A sophistication that uses physical sex as an entrée, as a mere beginning to whet the viewers' appetite for a relationship of intrigue.

Fortunately, since the old silents, movie history has brought us filmmakers--clever filmmakers--who realized the value of a thoughtful sexuality. Consider the creative passion in films like *Notorious, Laura, Casablanca,* and *An Officer And A Gentleman,* that gives us a better chance to savor sexuality's mystery--and a better chance to use our imagination.

Notes

1. MPAA ratings denote a voluntary compliance, so guess what happens when controversial films reach the video stage? Videos are released unrated, a commercial windfall that permits **NC-17** films to lose their designation. The no-label status also permits a flood of B-movie sexbusters to enter the market. These videos, sporting lower production values, are made specifically for home viewing (Landis, 1992). Indeed, video versions may prove more risqué and

titillating than film versions because the video format can include scenes cut from the film's original release.

2. Bob Greene (1983, p. 141), a journalist, recounts the day in which one woman discarded her robe and an undergarment (panties or a bikini bottom, no one is quite sure) to walk through downtown Chicago wearing a smile and nothing else. Weary big-city pedestrians had witnessed muggings and street fights, but a naked woman walking sedately on North Michigan Avenue represented a first.

Onlookers recognized, however, that she had not placed herself on exhibition as a stunt. Her demeanor, modest in behavior though indecent in appearance by society's standards, indicated a troubled woman. Until the police intervened to escort this lady to a mental health center, no one touched her or otherwise expressed sexual titillation at what they observed. Rather, they seemed to sense a woman on the edge, a fragile existence. Some of the onlookers even reported their relief when the police arrived to help.

3. The *Dracula* movies depicted one of the more sexually oriented monsters to grace the big screen. Dracula's thirst for young, nubile victims came with the symbolism of exchanging one form of sexual intercourse for another: a sensual approach (foreplay) to the taking of blood in the most intimate manner (intercourse). One of Dracula's offspring, *Dracula's Daughter* (1936), even includes a rapturous moment in which the daughter (played by Gloria Holden) rakes her eyes over the lily-white skin of a young girl, whose life blood is in jeopardy. The rapture implies a lesbian attraction, but the attraction--if there--occurs through a look too brief to pose a problem, apparently, for the Hays Office.

4. The ability of Baker and Wallach to convey an arousing seduction does them credit since they performed the porch scene on a cold day in November. Out of camera view, Baker and Wallach wore long johns and sucked on ice cubes before each take so that their breath would not show on screen. The scene and the actors' evaluation of its intent appear in a 1987 video, *Hollywood Uncensored*.

5. William Randolph Hearst, despite Parsons's pretentious actions, held himself aloof from the fray. The mogul's ambivalent posture inspired additional speculations as to whether he ever saw the film (Lebo, 1990, p. 167). The common ground that Kane and Hearst share remains argumentative, as does Welles's actual contribution to the screenplay (Carringer, 1985). But the name "Rosebud" prompts one interesting comparison. The characters in *Citizen Kane* never solve the puzzle of Rosebud, Kane's last utterance before he dies, although the audience learns that the name refers to a sled Kane possessed

during his childhood. Hearst did not have a sled, but he had a mistress, actress Marion Davies. And, according to one source, he had a pet name for her genitalia: Yes, yes, you guessed it (Gardner, 1987, p. xvii).

6. Well, almost. Performers of American films, for varied reasons, still display greater reluctance in showing casual nudity than do the actors of European films. How often in an American film, and certainly a television drama, have you viewed the nude female arise from bed and wrap herself discreetly in a sheet? And how often, pray tell, does this practice truly occur in the intimacy of one's bedroom (Clements, 1989)?

7. The business of shooting a love scene depends on how the actors feel about nudity, and how convincingly the director can arouse the performers to do what they're supposed to do (Rochlin, 1989). The love scene becomes an odd combination of dispassionate camera placements by a skeleton crew, and feigned (or not so feigned) passion by the actors. Reality, however, may not work well through the camera's lens. A lustful kiss, for example, appears more effective on screen if executed lightly in practice--as occurs between Harrison Ford and Sean Young in *Blade Runner* (1982).

Lesson 9

Sexual Traps

Time presses on. Attitudes concerning sexual taboos relax so that the perversions and deviations of yesteryear become the variations of today. Perversion sounds dirty and deviation implies an unusual, possibly shady happening. **Variation**, however, seems more democratic in setting our sexual compass.

Variation suggests flexibility without the stigma of aberration. This flexibility, for better or worse, indicates that the main stream is now a broader stream. Practices like masturbation and premarital sex suffer less scorn, whereas sexual harassment, sexual assault, and incest continue to prove unacceptable, and, indeed, currently spark greater visibility and more public controversy.

How have movies presented these disreputable sexual practices over the years? Why do filmmakers, for instance, favor dramatizations of sexual assault over stories of sexual harassment? Moreover, what differences in sexual permissiveness emerge when two films, created years apart, use the same characters and story to depict sexuality as a destructive force?

Cape Fear: **1962 & 1991**

The quiet ugliness of Max Cady (Robert Mitchum) in *Cape Fear* (1962) paints a chilling figure. Physically imposing, sporting a bullish build and bestial disposition, the man wears his evil through a fine layer of smirking civility. Cady's back from prison where he's nursed a hatred against Sam Bowden (Gregory Peck) whose testimony put Max away on a rape charge six years ago.

The lazy southern community complements Cady's leisurely plan to menace his target. He ogles Bowden's wife (Polly Bergen), but actually covets the family's 12-year-old daughter (Lori Martin). Sam is a respectable lawyer, has friends, and tries to rid himself of Cady, but Max knows the law and hires an attorney to protect his rights. Desperate, Sam and the family travel to a secluded creek in the cypress jungles of North Carolina and lay a trap for Cady.

The trap fails, of course. The brutish cleverness and physical prowess of Sam's adversary almost allow him his sadistic revenge. Almost. One scary outcome involves the fact that Sam Bowden wins only by a stroke of luck. Given the physical odds--such as Bowden's lanky frame against Cady's powerhouse physique--Sam Bowden should have died. You expect this kind of improbability in movies, but ponder the terror of a real Max Cady. The vision is frightening, as Sam Bowden learns, because most of us do not know how to defend against a psychopath, especially a resourceful psychopath (Hare, 1993, p. 6).

That, in brief, describes the story and characters of Director J. Lee Thompson's 1962 *Cape Fear*. The movie slips in comfortably as a black-and-white film, a testament to the model family: Husband loves wife, wife loves husband, both love their daughter, their daughter loves back. He's admired, she's a good homemaker, the daughter's dutiful. You can't ask more from such a solid (some may say stolid), domestic family. And it is this family that Max Cady lusts to shatter.

Now, here's *Cape Fear* again, and Peck and Mitchum are still in the film, but whoa. What gives? The movie's in color, and the Bowdens, well, the Bowdens appear nothing like the contented family we saw in 1962. A lot can happen in almost 30 years, and what's happened to the Bowdens falls just short of a domestic calamity.

Sam (Nick Nolte) is not so squeaky clean in 1991. He's still a lawyer, although he's held back incriminating evidence concerning a victim's sexual promiscuity that probably would have exonerated Max Cady (Robert De Niro) of a rape charge. The 1991 *Cape Fear* makes Sam more culpable for sending Cady to prison, this time to serve a 14-year term.

Give Sam a partial reprieve, nonetheless. He risks his illegal action in the moral belief that Cady truly did rape the woman, and raped her viciously. Bowden decides that Max needs incarceration, for everyone's safety. But, on another front, Sam receives a bad mark in domestic comportment because he indulged in an affair (now history) and his wife, Leigh (Jessica Lange), continues to feel pretty brittle about it.

Their daily lives make you nervous since the veneer holding this marriage intact plays rather thin. Eruptions of anger and betrayal challenge the family's fragile efforts to keep from sinking. The 1991 Bowden domicile hardly resembles the nuclear family we felt so secure with in 1962 (Kelly, 1991, pp. 281-282). Cinematically, it becomes more acceptable to throw Nolte's Sam a sexual curve in 1991 than to impose the same impropriety on Peck's Sam in 1962.

De Niro's Max, an illiterate when he enters prison, comes out with an awareness of letters--normally a step up for most people, though not for Cady. He knows a little about a lot, including superficial knowledge of prose and poetry. But, far worse for Sam, Max also comprehends the law and realizes that Sam did him dirt.

De Niro, lacking the impressive physique and swaggering grace of Mitchum's Cady, conjures up his own Cady as a clever, tattooed gospelmonger who speaks in tongues. This animal, wearing a contradictory cloak of geniality and coarseness, further believes that he possesses the right to beguile anyone whom he brands as his moral inferior. This irrational conviction fosters an arrogant attitude that encompasses everyone in Cady's Bible-spouting cross hairs. More important, Max recognizes from his surveillance that the

Bowdens are a family under stress, and he plans to parlay that stress to his lethal advantage.

A comparable scene in both movies shows Cady luring an unsuspecting female to his lair. Mitchum's Cady stalks back and forth in front of the bed, smashing his fist in his hand, reliving, you imagine, the many many nights he spent pacing his small cell. But he's out, he's unleashed, and he has a victim (Barrie Chase) who understands, sickeningly, that she's been duped and singled out for punishment. She's right, although we never see the beating. We observe the aftereffects, viewing a woman too terrified of the beast in Cady to testify against him. The scene plays with heart-skipping fear, and you need not witness the violence to understand the man's depravity.[1]

De Niro's Max Cady, however, delivers his wickedness on screen, or at least he erupts in a preview of coming attractions. Director Martin Scorsese gives us an early glimpse at the man's sadism. Cady, having trussed up a naive victim named Lori (Illeana Douglas), begins his ferocious assault by leaning over her face and biting a chunk of flesh from her cheek. The abused and sexually humiliated woman, as in the first *Cape Fear*, cannot muster the fortitude to testify against Cady. He's still free and moving closer to the Bowdens.

His next target is Danielle (Juliette Lewis), the Bowdens' sexually budding daughter. Cady's initial strategy arises as a shimmering seduction rather than a callous rape. **Foreplay**, the most creative process of lovemaking, fashions an attractive trap in the villain's sexual scheme. He lures Danielle to the basement of her high school on the pretext of conducting a drama class.

Wesley Strick (Kelly, 1991, pp. 289-290), who wrote the screenplay, recalls that the scene originally called for a conventional search-and-escape sequence between Danielle and Max--the kind of teasing pursuit engineered by Mitchum's Cady in 1962. But what transpires in the 1991 version, Strick notes, represents a departure from the script: A deceptive encounter of predator and prey materializes that carries both figures to the apex of a moment charged with sexual tension.

No, not sexual intercourse, but a conquest, nonetheless. Through script changes and improvisation from the two actors, the relationship of Danielle and Max begins with his soothing rendition of her virtues as a woman; a woman who desires sexual openness. He even refers to Henry Miller's works on sexuality, quoting a Miller line about the glories of penile erection as a "piece of lead with wings on it" (Kelly, 1991, p. 290). When you can disguise a sexual overture by dramatizing penile mechanics, and when the young innocent reacts not in horror but with captivating awe, you're home free.

This rationale is the evangelist's plan of invasion, his true intent. Danielle, wittingly or no, overlooks Cady's intellectual miscues. He's too mesmerizing for her sprouting urges to withstand. Max "talks" his thumb into her mouth, mollifying her anxieties, crooning to her needs, affording her the forbidden pleasures of orally massaging his miniature organ as an approbation to the real thing.

The passionate, full-bodied kiss that follows depicts a natural culmination of Cady's campaign to take Danielle. He knows her hidden wishes, her timid thoughts, and he uses this knowledge to control her. She cannot foresee his ultimate course. He brings her precipitously closer to the sexual gratification of her fantasies, but she possesses neither the wherewithal nor the experience to comprehend his satanic denouement.

Movies being movies, viewers rely on Oz to hope and expect that a propitious miracle will dispatch the Bible-abusing Max Cady to his deserving Hell. But what Max does in the seduction scene, he could not have done in the *Cape Fear* of 1962. Censorship via the Production Code, though waning, and the sexual climate, though changing, still prevented filmmakers from risking such physical intimacy between a lustful conniver like Max Cady and a nubile girl like Danielle Bowden.

Most telling, however, is the fact that Mitchum's Max Cady remains too coarse of breath to enact an engrossing seduction of a young girl. De Niro's Cady makes evil less direct, less detectable--unless it wishes to be detected--and more rapturous as an instrument of entrapment. Evil and goodness collaborate in De Niro's character as an unholy alliance. The perfect trap choreographed by an evangelical demon who believes, fervently, that he belongs on the side of the angels.

Cinematic Traps

Cinematic reality does not pose a straightforward relationship with true reality. There is no reason why it should. Cinematic reality represents entertainment: A saga of the absurd, made more or less believable.

Thus, when you are entranced by events of which you command little information, or of which you already hold a sympathetic prejudice, the movie becomes a persuasive experience. Oz nudges you to accept the movie's message--its theme--more readily because little reason exists for you to question the enchantment of a winning story, attractive actors, and good production values.

Unfortunately, if a topic proves provocative--and sexual topics usually are--the moviegoer risks assimilating misinformation. Misinformation becomes likely when the issue is poorly understood, and, particularly, when the presentation harmonizes with a sexual bias, already in place. Instead of the viewer maintaining a critical balance, the movie's emotional pitch strengthens the bias in question. After all, don't most rapists and murderers usually receive their comeuppance? And don't most individuals who survive a terrifying ordeal appear to emerge all the stronger for it?

These misguided thoughts, with all their glamour and allure, lead unsuspecting viewers to a **cinematic trap**: The risk that a moviegoer's fanciful preconceptions will ultimately lead to erroneous judgments. We could assume, of course, that since filmmakers concoct the message, filmmakers should hold themselves accountable for setting the cinematic snare. We could, but we won't. We won't because the filmmaker's first priorities are to entertain and make money. Whether the director intends the theme to persuade or merely to provoke, the final outcome--as interpreted through Oz--becomes an arguable matter. Viewers enjoy the prerogative, via Oz, to accept or reject the movie's message, however admirable or gawdawful.

Think of the process as a 1-2-3 strikeout: **Strike 1**: Filmmakers produce their share of obnoxious sexual portrayals. But along with this exploitation, some films comprise subtle scenes capable of cultivating insidious value judgments, inadvertent or not. These implicit prejudices--courtesy of the filmmaker--permeate the exhibition of sexually volatile issues, such as the industry's sacrificial treatment of female rape victims.

Strike 2: Filmmakers supply what the market will bear. We are the market. Without our patronage, fewer exploitation films will find the light of day, fewer misrepresentations of female victimization will arise, fewer scenarios on making women feel vulnerable will stream forth, and fewer distortions of sexual matters in general will surface.

We can stop at Strike 2. We can do so, especially if our awareness of the sexual content proves critical. We can do so, furthermore, if we have no intention of allowing a movie to sway us with its contrived facade. Because of our awareness, we view the questionable film as a mere treatment for escapism; a fleeting diversion that means nothing to us and fails to endanger our informed beliefs about sexual assault.

Strike 3, however, indicates a different proposition. The final strike says that we accept prejudicially what the film appears to endorse sexually. We thrill to the fear, for example, that women display on screen as they anticipate a sexual attack. We strengthen our biases, already intact, "knowing" that the rape victim "asks for it." Strike 3 designates an act of conversion from entertainment to personal reality. We enter the sexual trap and it's truly a deceitful web, far more despairing than our Oz process has the cognizance to imagine.

The deceit becomes challenging if the movie impresses us with fine acting and heart-stopping quivers of genuine anticipation. *Cape Fear*, more quietly in 1962 and more zealously in 1991, presents viewers with its stark characterizations of sexuality's darker paths. The potential for sexual destructiveness appears so real, yet so entertaining. This fascinating combination encourages uninformed moviegoers to subscribe to sexual myths about the dynamics of sexual assault. The combination of apparent reality and entertainment also helps viewers to ignore the aftereffects of a traumatizing episode, such as the reprieve given Sam and his family at the close of both versions of *Cape Fear*.

Aftereffects do not always consist of relief, forgiveness, and reconstruction. Sometimes, psychologically, the consequences of a sexual trauma result in slow death. No happy endings, no just desserts, no comfort to heal the wounded spirit--just the aftermath of victims who engage in fragile attempts to survive by living a very different, very difficult life.

The sexual trap of accepting women as appropriate victims of rape customarily skirts such an aftermath. Rather, dramatic and even comedic portrayals of sexual assault find legitimization in the minds of impressionable males, but also in the longstanding film practice of sexually humiliating women for fun and profit.

Rape As Entertainment

What kind of fun and how much profit? Well, Hollywood realizes a comfortable, if not huge, financial reward from the horror genre of films. Envision the following scene of a 1983 movie, *Curtains*:

> The masked "rapist" positions himself outside an apartment window, eyeing his beautiful "victim" as she does all the lazily erotic things that a victim goes through before retiring. Finally, with the movie audience appropriately taut in anticipation, our stealthy predator pounces upon his glamorous prey--and both erupt into laughter. Foreplay between lovers, it appears, has become more and more bizarre (Wilson, 1991, p. 138).

Viewers should know that a spoof of anything requires people to recognize the "thing" in question. Finding humor in a customarily tragic happening, like sexual assault, depends on adding a clever twist to the familiar cinematic formula of sexual suspense. This formula does not rely so much on "Will she get it" (yes, she will) or "Why," but on "When and How." Horror fans watching horror flicks express less concern about Why, although Why becomes the crucial question.

What about Why? Stripped of entertainment value and viewed harshly as an act of sex and violence, **rape** functions to demean womanhood and manhood. The statutes on rape as an offense have shown greater complexity in recent years, so that the unwelcome penis-in-the-vagina entry no longer denotes the sole, governing definition.

Therefore, for our purposes, let's personalize the legal status of sexual assault and examine at least four ways in which a female fails to give consent for sexual intercourse: (1) She says "No!" and means "No!"; (2) she's pressured to say "Yes" when she really means "No!" (as in a date rape); (3) she can't say "No" or "Yes" because she's unconscious or otherwise unable to reply; or (4) she's under the age of consent, and it matters little whether she consents or not (as in incest or child molestation).

These four conditions spell rape, although the first and last statements permit the most likely opportunity for due process. Still, even the first statement--when "No!" truly means "No!"-- may not suffice in bringing an attacker to justice if the assault is not a "prosecutable rape." Susan Estrich (1987, p. 4) describes this liability as the difference between an aggravated rape and a simple rape.

Aggravated rape concerns the legal ideal of proving sexual assault by a stranger or strangers that includes severe violence and threat with a weapon. Put another way, the victim must undergo an appreciable beating and then agree to display these injuries in order to have her day in court. **Simple rape** denotes the more muted experience of sexual assault by a known party that does not customarily involve severe physical abuse or a weapon threat. Estrich's point is that any hint of mitigating circumstances, as in a victim's familiarity with the rapist, or any incriminating behavior on her part, such as using alcohol or being in the rapist's quarters, and she can kiss her legal retribution goodbye.[2]

Regardless, why does rape hold such cinematic appeal?

The witchery of rape seems durable, yet selective. **Sexual harassment** as a form of emotional rape does not warrant the same attention in movies. Why? Filmmakers may have salivated at the thought of capturing the national audience that watched the Clarence Thomas/Anita Hill hearings. Did he make those lewd remarks to her, or didn't he? Did she tell the truth about their early relationship, or didn't she?

Certainly the hearings provided the kind of drama that has propelled many a movie plot. But sexual harassment plays as an insidious, seemingly covert offense in comparison to physical rape. Such tactics represent an ongoing persecution that, over time, reduces the conflict to HER word against HIS word (Kaplan, Cohn, McDaniel, & Annin, 1991; Smolowe, Gorey, Johnson, & Traver, 1991). The drama's entertainment may be there, but not the "explosive culmination" that has made physical rape a staple industry of sex and violence over the decades.[3]

The captivation of rape as entertainment concerns the process and the victim. The process involves a rapist's **preparation** and **execution** of the act. Exploitation films, for example, translate preparation and execution into cinematic strategies called the stalk and the attack. The victim, by sad tradition, is female. Oh, you may recall *Deliverance* (1972) and thus remember the terror of a male sodomized by backwoods yokels. But probably you don't recall *The Rape Of Richard Beck* (1985) in which a macho police officer is sexually assaulted--an experience that he finds sufficiently humiliating to soften his perception of women as rape victims.

The movie list of males relative to females ravaged by rape is a short list. Also in short supply is a third stage of the process bearing on preparation and execution. This third stage concerns the **aftermath** of a sexual assault, a period that can include many years of suffering for the victim. Filmmakers evidence less interest in rape's aftermath because they favor the dramatic suspense and shock vested in the rapist's preparation and execution of sexual violence.

Movie Rape: Integrity And Exploitation

Filmmakers, therefore, become more or less creative in their attempts to embellish the preparation and execution of an aggravated rape. The consequences of this creativity allow cinematic rape to service an illusion, although, understandably, such an illusion misses the mark of reality. Still, how damaging is this miss to the integrity of a real rape? What kinds of sexual traps arise when art imposes its glamorous sheen over the blemishes of an actual rape?

Integrity refers to the aptness and honesty of judging a person or event, when that person or event proves worthy of evaluation (McFall, 1987). To speak of integrity calls for speaking of matters that boast substance and importance. Movies are subject to integrity when aptness depicts a dramatic response, event, or character that seems more appropriate than any other interpretation. And honesty in movies denotes an expression that sounds true, looks true, feels true. Because a movie constitutes an illusion and need not be true to reality, a well-performed, plausible film can make its characters and story appear quite reasonable to the Oz process.

A movie rape possesses **artistic integrity** when it conveys a natural and logical action, perfectly suitable and credible to the scheme of a cinematic narrative. The course of a movie's rape, from the rapist's motivation to the victim's aftermath of suffering, should receive believable treatment. Poorer treatment, then, concerns the gratuitous intervention of a rape that exercises little impact on a movie's story or characters. Regrettably, many movies that use rape as entertainment do not respond well to the higher standard of artistic integrity.

The point remains that whether moviegoers view a rape presented with artistic integrity or without it, sexual traps exist. A movie's depiction of rape must realize its judgment not only from the film's context, but beyond that context. So, even if sexual assault finds legitimate cinematic expression and can lay claim to a measure of artistic integrity, it may still illustrate a moderate, even humorous act compared to the harshness of an actual rape.

The comedy in *Young Frankenstein* (1974), for instance,

shows the monster abducting his creator's fiancée and forcing himself upon her sexually. The "victim" resists until she catches sight of the monster's "instrument of pleasure." What follows amounts to the "victim" singing about life's sweet mystery, which is the film's farcical way of portraying sexual gratification. These hijinks permit viewers to cushion the fact that the monster begins this sequence as a rapist. Indeed, sexual traps are easier to overlook or dismiss when the sexual content plays as an unabashed farce than when the content plays as exploitation (see Lesson 6).

Speaking of unabashed treatments, the worst of the worst involve **exploitation films**. These overstated dramas range from sleazy, low-budget movies (*I Spit On Your Grave*, 1980) to slick productions (*Lipstick*, 1976) that use rape deceptively for wanton effect. *I Spit On Your Grave* and *Lipstick*, for example, portray a raped heroine who wreaks personal revenge by killing. *I Spit On Your Grave* represents the cruder movie, but *Lipstick* the more dangerous. Why? Because *Lipstick* boasts higher production values and better performances, making the use of sexual assault more credible.

No doubt many rape victims desire retribution, but the sexual trap of triumphant gratification in vanquishing a rapist proves improbable. The consequences of such retaliation are too risky and too likely to end in noncinematic fashion. The true rape victim may find her retaliatory attempts ineffective, or she may discover that her attempts at revenge inspire a "backlash effect," causing her even more grief. These prospects hardly match the cinematic gratification experienced by the heroines of *I Spit On Your Grave* and *Lipstick*.

Ugly films that exploit female rape also tell us something enduring about the movie rating system: namely, that it serves as a lame guideline for parents (see Lesson 8). Pornography, for instance, claims an association with the **X** rating. What does that rating encompass? Before answering, consider once more the notorious film, *I Spit On Your Grave*. The girl in this movie suffers graphic depictions of rape and sodomy when caught by a gang of youths in the woods, and suffers again when they assault her repeatedly and leave her for dead.

The film, described by Roger Ebert (1989, p. 359) as a "vile bag of garbage," gives the girl her turn at violence. She survives to exact vengeance resourcefully by killing her attackers, each in an artistically expressive way, of course. Full frontal nudity for the girl, explicit sex scenes, and vivid violence--these features seem to indicate a pornographic movie. But the film received an **R** rating, apparently because it does not show the penis of any of her assailants (although, "discreetly," she does "relieve" her first rapist of his tally-wacker). The letter system leaves one to wonder what remains for an **X** rating to cover (see Donnerstein, Linz, & Penrod, 1987, p. 180).

Movie Rape: Docudramas And Melodramas

Fortunately, not all movies fall under the spell of exploitation. A second classification, **docudramas/melodramas**, focuses on sexual assault as a theme, giving the subject of rape at least an appearance of legitimacy.

Docudramas and melodramas highlight rape issues, such as the rape victim's plight after her attack (*A Case Of Rape*, 1974); the rapist's attempts at rehabilitation (*Rage*, 1980); confusion over whether the alleged victim gives her consent under stress (*When She Says No*, 1984); the vagaries of taking an accused date rapist to trial (*She Said No*, 1990); the legal ambiguity surrounding marital rape (*Rape And Marriage: The Rideout Case*, 1980); and the anguish suffered when a man finds himself accused falsely of rape (*Blind Justice*, 1986).

These productions depict television movies that pursue an instructive function, occasionally based on true happenings, but also founded on fictional characters and stories that seek to squeeze entertainment from a rape issue. Viewers, however, may not recognize the mingling of facts and falsehoods unless they have access to factual sources elsewhere. True cases are easier to judge than pretend cases, but viewers still need independent information to substantiate either version.

Docudramas and melodramas as entertainment call for a standard of artistic integrity to prevail within the movie's

purview. A docudrama or melodrama's plot and characters
should display aptness and honesty according to the story's
logic of pushing the plot and characters forward. But, too,
docudramas and melodramas as commentaries on the
complexities of sexual assault require an additional criterion
to meet these concerns. This criterion transcends the movie
and relates to the known information about the issue in
question.

The Boston Strangler (1968) becomes a case in point. The
movie offers a mix of fact and fiction in characterizing the
serial murderer and sexual slayer, Albert DeSalvo (played by
Tony Curtis). The film suggests that DeSalvo went insane, in
part through the catalyst of police questioning--a questioning
designed to force him to recognize the "evil side" of his
personality. The film closes with DeSalvo viewed as a
catatonic inmate (a person in a state of assumed immobility),
too overwhelmed by the recognition of his evil self to
function, and presumably remanded to spend his remaining
years inside a mental institution.

The story's integrity, though introduced with reasonable
logic during the film's first half, falls into disrepute as the
film's second half winds to a faulty conclusion. Mental health
officials, frankly, are not likely to permit law enforcement
representatives to "hammer" a patient into an emotional
never/never land. What happened, in fact, is that DeSalvo
wished to stay in a mental ward, but the murderer's emotional
problems failed to prevent his transfer to a state prison. Other
than perhaps DeSalvo's acting ability, no catatonic state
emerges to indicate mental incompetence. If you do not know
of Gerold Frank's (1966) biography on the murderer's career
however, or of other sources concerning DeSalvo's actual
behavior, you would leave *The Boston Strangler* with the
belief that DeSalvo simply withdrew as a mental case.

A filmmaker can, of course, do whatever it takes to make
a production entertaining. But to alter real events for purposes
of dramatic license carries with it an obligation to set the
record straight, or at least to acknowledge the filmmaker's
preference in charting a different course. The reason for this
obligation concerns the power of entertainment to influence an

audience. If viewers, especially young, impressionable viewers, hold little perspective on reality except what a film or television movie delivers to them, they may accept the movie's content as gospel. Viewers need to know more, and filmmakers need to act so that the audience **does** know more.

Television dramas more so than theatrical films possess the power to awaken viewer consciousness, tie up phone lines, and make the matter of rape a prolific buzz word. Television, even without a script, can accomplish this feat: Look no farther than the 1991 William Kennedy Smith trial that presented date rape for national consumption. Lest anyone forget, a **date rape** demands persuasive evidence to merit a trial; evidence that the prosecution did not have in the Smith case. A jury acquitted William Smith of the charges against him, although with television's capacity to touch so many people so rapidly, the stigma of Smith's participation will continue to surface. The accused, though "free" from the charges directed at him, will find that his freedom denotes a relative state.

The sheer publicity of William Kennedy Smith's family name shall link him to the issue of date rape for years to come--just as Ted Kennedy's past continues to prompt reminders of that fateful night at Chappaquidick. The massive concentration of viewers for television docudramas and melodramas, compared to the more scattered audience for theatrical films, permits consequences that may alert the public quickly to examine formerly low-profile controversies like sexual harassment, date rape, and incest.

Incest refers to a child or adolescent at the mercy of a closely-related individual who engages in the sexual intimacies of coercive fondling, oral contact, vaginal and anal penetration, or the watching of such activities (Darnton, Springen, Wright, & Keene-Osborn, 1991; Gorman, Dolan, & Horowitz, 1991; Maltz, 1990). Incest, like sexual harassment, relies on longstanding, repetitive practices of sexual intrusion. The love and lust of this repetitive practice are sometimes misperceived and accepted temporarily by the child victim, although legally, incest depicts a forced intimacy.

The television movie, *Something About Amelia* (1984), uses

incest as its theme to show a father/daughter tragedy, and to conclude--perhaps too happily--that the father can change. The movie's father (Ted Danson) shows remorse even as he commits the abusive intimacy, and the family, though scarred, manages to stay together.

A contrasting picture, achieved by realizing information independent of the movie, suggests that incestuous fathers are less remorseful and more premeditated when they plan their sexual abuse than the father portrayed in *Amelia* (Crewdson, 1988, pp. 83-88; Browning & Boatman, 1977). Television's immediacy, nonetheless, overrides these minor objections by showing that a program like *Something About Amelia* can shock the American public into confronting the taboo of child sexual abuse:

> Deftly acted and dramatically understated, *Amelia* contained a message that child-protection workers had been trying to convey for years--that the sexual abuse of children in America is not uncommon, and not bound by class or culture. Nearly half of those who watched television that night were watching *Amelia*, and when it was over, child-abuse telephone hotlines across the country began to ring. The callers numbered not in the hundreds or the thousands, but in the tens of thousands. They included children who said they were being sexually abused, children who thought their friends were being abused, mothers who thought their daughters and sons were being abused, grown women and not a few men who said they had been abused as children--even a handful of child abusers wanted to help (Crewdson, 1988, p. ix).

Movie Rape: The Classics

Theatrical films dealt with incest much earlier than the docudramas and melodramas of television, yet no comparable outcry about sexual abuse ensued. Indeed, ten years before *Amelia*, one such film used incest as the heart of its private-eye tale set in Los Angeles in the 1930s.

We don't learn about the incest until late in the story, but the revelation means something because the victim, Evelyn Cross Mulwray (Faye Dunaway), becomes familiar to us as a beautiful yet fragile character. She intrigues a cynical private detective, J. J. Gittes (Jack Nicholson), who finds himself attracted to her as a person, but even more so as the key to a mystery. Gittes follows Evelyn to a private residence where she attends to a teenage girl. He confronts Evelyn in a dramatic scene, slapping her as she blurts out her terrible secret: She's my daughter, my sister, my daughter, she's my daughter **and** my sister!

The villain of the piece, Noah Cross (John Huston), conveys an artful blend of graciousness and malevolence. He is a murderer (of Evelyn's husband), but a wealthy murderer and a man of vision. Among other untoward developments, he wants the offspring of his incestuous relationship, and, in an unconventional ending, he reclaims the girl.

Evelyn attempts to escape with her daughter/sister, but in what can pass only as bad judgment by Evelyn and the police, she dies in a burst of gunfire. J. J. Gittes is left with another tragedy to bear: Evelyn Mulwray is dead, and Noah Cross has Evelyn's daughter, plus the money to combat a murder charge. The classic film *Chinatown* (1974), as the title suggests, offers us an inscrutable, nihilistic experience where nothing turns out well for reasons that have more to do with fate than logic.

The classics, consequently, differ from the docudrama/melodrama classification. Classic movies showcase artistically significant productions to make a singular statement about life. These films attain their extraordinary status by sustaining integrity in characterization and story, an exceptional accomplishment for the movies.

Notably, the classics offer a deft treatment of sexual assault, choosing to subordinate the issue and to emphasize the drama's basic intent.[4] *Chinatown*, for example, relegates incest as a taboo to serve the greater story of political corruption. Incest in the narrative of *Chinatown* does not become a "theme of the week." Instead, the movie's lurking intelligence merely intertwines the pathos of this offense with other dark happenings to softly reveal incest as an understated tragedy.

Classic films are more likely to show how the aftereffects of sexual assault cause anguish for the victim and the victim's social relationships--a perspective on rape that exploitation films neglect. Thus, classic movies depict more admirably the

complications of rape's aftermath. The bitter repercussions of
this haunted lingering are finely illustrated in *A Passage To
India* (1984), *Johnny Belinda* (1947), *A Streetcar Named Desire*
(1951), and *To Kill A Mockingbird* (1962).

A Passage To India uses an attempted rape that may or
may not have occurred as a fulcrum to examine the contrast of
character and culture involving a British lady (Judy Davis) and
an Indian doctor (Victor Banerjee).   Both characters are
victims, but very different victims as their lives change
through the echoes of the alleged rape attempt.   One
identifying feature of a classic film concerns its originality in
not providing the easy, formulaic answer. You certainly learn
about the mysteries of India and the prickly heat of Victorian
sensuality, but you won't have your curiosities laid to rest by
pat resolutions.

Nor is life a simple matter for Jane Wyman, who plays a
deaf mute in *Johnny Belinda*. She experiences, among other
indignities, a rape by the town bully. But from this rape
comes a child, and Belinda's child characterizes a turning point
that gives momentum to the story. In *A Streetcar Named
Desire,* rape creates a fitting though violent climax to the
increasingly tense relationship between Blanche Debois
(Vivian Leigh) and her brother-in-law, Stanley Kowalski
(Marlon Brando). Blanche, emotionally delicate, has her wispy
illusions of love and chivalry shattered by Stanley's brutal
assault.

A false charge of rape in *To Kill A Mockingbird* brings
forth a due process that can only lead to one verdict. A white
woman makes the charge against a black man in a small,
Southern community during the Depression years.   This
tragedy becomes more than the man's suffering as an innocent
victim of prejudice: His attitude of hopelessness after the
conviction and his fatalistic efforts to escape result in a moral
lesson for the community's children and adults.

Classic films unveil the darkness of sexuality, yet these
artistic works foster a grander message than that realized in
exploitation films and docudramas. The stories and characters
do not prevail to signify rape as an overshadowing presence.
Rather, the dynamics of sexual assault arise in the classics as

part of a more intricate fabric of social issues; and, as with *To Kill A Mockingbird*, a social fabric capable of coarsely denying sexual innocence during an age enmeshed in racial destiny.

Sexual Traps And Sexual Myths

So, where has our journey taken us? We know that slick, exploitation films portray the character and lifestyle of rapists and rape victims in an exceedingly "pleasing" fashion. Predatory males taking advantage of vulnerable females hardly passes as a revelation. But, less obviously, we find that classic films--films that creatively defy the rapist/victim stereotype--also suffer the presence of sexual traps. This problem implies that just because a movie rates as a classic does not mean that the elite film plays "trap free."

Remember, a sexual trap involves the filmmaker's sexual bias in a movie that **you** choose to interpret according to your convictions. Remember, too, that sexual traps lurk in any film, good or bad. And remember, finally, that what a film **doesn't say** about a sexual issue can denote another form of sexual bias through its silence. When a filmmaker decides not to include a certain perspective, this selective omission may go unnoticed by less-informed viewers. What the filmmaker omits can proved detrimental, especially for those moviegoers who erroneously accept dramatizations of sexual assault at face value.

Viewers who trigger sexual traps give service to a logjam of sexual myths. The **sexual myth** defines a recurring theme that relates to gender, to sexual fantasies, to physical sex, to anything argumentative about sexuality. But the sexual myth also presents a theme wholly or partially enveloped in falsehood (if partially enveloped, we speak of a half-truth).

Therefore, we have a dangerous tandem: The sexual trap consists of questionable evaluations that you draw from cinematic presentations of sexual content. The sexual myth concerns mistaken beliefs you already harbor, independent of the movie you are to see--or mistaken beliefs that you formulate anew, in part because of what the film's sexual content suggests to your Oz process. Either way, the sexual myth becomes bait for a film's sexual trap.

Viewers who know of circumstances that counter the sexual myth in question, will find themselves less susceptible to the kinds of sexual traps that movies inspire. But viewers who embrace sexual misbeliefs--even positive misbeliefs, such as the assumption that most rape victims can shrug off the experience--will find themselves more vulnerable to the enticements of a sexual trap. Sexual myths encourage moviegoers to seek out films that strengthen their inclinations--usually negative inclinations--about controversies surrounding victims like gays, prostitutes, transsexuals, and...women who suffer rape.

Sexual myths regarding rape represent the misguided notion that women who suffer rape also, somehow, suffer the responsibility of bringing this action upon themselves (Brinson, 1992). The act of rape, viewed objectively, appears to characterize a straightforward plan of sexual coercion: He wants it; she doesn't want him to have it; he tries to get it, anyway. What could be simpler? Two people in disagreement as to the advisability of sexual penetration, whether oral, anal, or vaginal. She fails to give consent, he acts to disregard her lack of consent, and that's that.

Well, no, not quite. A fuzzy cloud of misdirection may hover over "alleged" rape encounters. Sometimes a woman charges "rape" for reasons that call into question the actual happening. A **false accusation** of rape carries grave repercussions for the accused, but how frequently do women use the charge as a weapon? Considering that only a small percentage of rapes are actually reported, false estimates, too, remain low. Typically this estimate approximates 2 percent, comparable to the false claims made in other crimes (Salholz, Mason, Barrett, Talbot, King, & Yoffe, 1991; Katz & Mazur, 1979, p. 212).

Films using rape as a source of drama, however, overstate these false reports. One survey indicates that 7 of 26 films invoking rape as entertainment rely on false testimony about sexual assault, presumably to enliven the accused's torment and to create suspense in the search for justice and the real culprit (Wilson, 1988). We cannot afford to forget that entertainment comes first, instruction second.[5]

The same 26 films also depict the **futility** of a victim attempting to resist the rapist. One lonely film from this cluster, *Blackmail* (1929), directed by Alfred Hitchcock, shows the victim successfully defending herself against sexual assault. Sad to say, a rape attempt that proves a failure also risks becoming anathema as entertainment. A failed rape does not fulfill the entertainment wishes of expectant males who regard a sexual conquest by force as the supreme male fantasy. We noted earlier that women can become more ferocious and victorious than they know in preventing rape (Bart & O'Brien, 1985). Too many films, regrettably, suggest otherwise.

Revenge, either personal or legal, also plays deceptively in the world of Oz. Films depicting the sexually wronged heroine as a gladiator, someone who assumes the empowerment to judge and execute her attacker, serve the essence of exploitation. Simply put, it's fun to see the bastards blown away in vehicles like *Lipstick* (1976), *I Spit On Your Grave* (1980), and *Sudden Impact* (1983), the last film a Dirty Harry episode. Conversely, reality dictates a different script, one that makes personal justice not only unlikely to occur but also dangerous to the victim. She may really, REALLY desire retribution, but her better judgment is to walk away.

Legal revenge offers less drama for the exploitation crowd, although more fascination for those moviegoers who prefer the lawfulness of using due process to wage an "honorable" retaliation. "Innocent until proven guilty" sounds a hollow ring when you gaze at the defendant (the alleged rapist) in a court of law. He's there, he's been charged, so **something** must have happened to make him a suspicious soul. Movies can play the scene this way, as we observed earlier in films dealing with false charges of rape. But movies about rape also can extend the victim's agony as she seeks to vindicate her word against his word in a legal arena.

The Accused (1988) offers a textbook case of how the unsavory complications of a gang rape lead achingly to a second "rape" for the victim as she pursues the legal options due her (Madigan & Gamble, 1991, p. 73). Sarah Tobias

(Jodie Foster) hardly presents herself as the ideal poster girl. She drinks too much, dresses provocatively, dances the same way, and does all three in the wrong place at the wrong time. Her "night out" deteriorates to a gang bang atop a pinball machine.

She emerges from her ordeal seeking revenge, already down by three points: (1) Sarah faces a criminal justice system whose advocates do not share her earnestness. (2) She seeks redress against a community whose inhabitants prefer to blame her. And (3) she sports a salty past that presents her as less than an eloquent victim. Facing these obstacles, Sarah Tobias knows that only one witness will come forward to set the record straight about this brutal saga--herself.

Sarah overcomes these hurdles by virtue of her ferocity, her tenacity, and her sheer determination to make a jury believe her. Jodie Foster won an Oscar for her spirited performance as the victim who worked to right a wrong. But does her victory constitute a wave of inspiration for real rape victims?

Perhaps yes, perhaps no. Sarah's success may not dispel the belief that legal retribution proves just another litany of horrors. Sarah's gauntlet will seem overwhelming to some women, particularly those shy individuals who cherish their anonymity. Knowing the need to bring charges, yet understanding the reality of their own scars and woes, how many females harbor Sarah Tobias's resilience? Regardless of the oft-heard plea to go public and search for legal amends, the emotional solution for certain rape victims involves charting a different course.[6]

Two other recurring themes of movie rape concern the victim's **aftermath of suffering**, and oddly, the **victim's pleasure**. We noted previously that movies neglect rape's aftermath: A cacophony of anguish, guilt, rage, and loathing that imbues some victims to live a radically altered lifestyle. The sin, again, is a sin of omission.

The cinematic omission denotes what you don't see, and therefore what you are less likely to consider in comprehending the full scope of a sexual assault. For those women who suffer dearly beyond their rape, the road to recovery can be hell, if "recovery" stays in the picture at all. A few productions, classics like *Johnny Belinda* (1947) and melodramas like *A Case Of Rape* (1974), dwell on rape as a lingering malady, although most movies do not.

Finally, after all the negative commentary on sexual assault, can a woman possibly gain "pleasure" from a rape attack? If you wish to believe in rape as entertainment, she can. She does, actually, in *Gone With The Wind* (1939) and in *Straw Dogs* (1971). Scarlett (Vivian Leigh) resists Rhett (Clark Gable) as he hauls her up the stairs to have his way, but the next morning she greets us with a big smile. A sweet night of passion apparently redeems even the forcible actions of an overly determined lover. And Amy (Susan George) of *Straw Dogs* tries to say no as an ex-boyfriend drags her by her hair to the couch. Passion again overcomes all and she relinquishes her body, at first reluctantly, then with abandon.

The myth that when a woman says "No" she means she needs persuading--gently, seductively, or otherwise--becomes the most flagrant misconception about rape. The "otherwise" constitutes an aberration of rape's true humiliation. More than an aberration, the cinematic myth that "She really wants it" sends encouragement to prospective rapists. Don't stop, even if she says stop. Keep trying, twist her arm a little (or a lot), and she'll thank you later, flushed with pleasure at your sexual prowess.

Indeed, that belief and a dime will get the male a bag of confetti and a party hat. He can keep the fantasy alive by giving himself a little parade. I doubt, however, that she will be joining him.

Give movies credit where credit is due. Most films, including the exploitative vehicles, present rape as a terror of invasion and shame. The movie's reasons may not rival the best reasons for portraying rape in this fashion, but at least the experience does not fabricate a loving interlude for the female. By contrast, the well-made films that suggest rape as pleasurable for the victim are truly dangerous illusions for Oz to assimilate.

Sexual traps abound in movies, with the better films

exercising more complex schemes. The content is there because the filmmaker provides it (Strike 1), and because the filmmaker believes that a profitable market exists for this entertainment (Strike 2). But the trap does not become a trap until the viewer accepts the entertainment as a reasonable pronouncement on reality (Strike 3).

So, in closing, play a little game with me. Compare what you know about sexual assault from the movies against what you know from other, more legitimate sources. Specifically, imagine the entertainment value of a rape in terms of recalling movies concerned with false accusations, with the victim's futility of resisting, with the victim's chances of revenge, with the time devoted to the victim's suffering, and with the victim actually realizing pleasure from the assault. Now, think about each of these issues and their likelihood of occurrence in real life.

How do your comparisons fare? They shouldn't be close, you know. They really shouldn't.

Notes

1. The finale of the 1962 *Cape Fear* includes a deliberately paced rape attempt by Max Cady of Sam's wife, Peggy Bowden (Polly Bergen). Reprising the incident in an Arts & Entertainment tribute, *Robert Mitchum, The Reluctant Star* (1992, October 14), Polly Bergen recalls that she and Mitchum got "into the scene" to the point that Mitchum had to be physically pulled away from her, before either of them realized that the director had said "cut." After the separation, Mitchum recovered and held Bergen in his arms, rocking her softly back and forth, saying "I'm sorry, I'm sorry..."

Performing the scene, Mitchum smashed his fist through the wrong cabinet--one that was not set up to collapse--and bloodied his fist. He kept going, pushing Bergen into a door that was supposed to give way quickly, but did not, leaving Bergen as a battering ram used by Mitchum to crash through the door. Movies are supposed to constitute illusion, except, now and then, a sprinkling of reality causes the performers to glisten a bit more truthfully.

2. Ladies, the grand solution, of course, is not to get raped. Certain precautions will help such as installing deadbolt locks on bedroom doors, placing only the initial of your first name in the phone book, arranging for escort service if you must walk somewhere at night, or having a trusty German

Shepherd at your side. But no precaution is foolproof. A well-fortified bedroom door will not keep a determined assailant out, although the delay can give you time to prepare a welcome with your Louisville slugger; or, better still, plan accordingly to pursue an alternative escape route.

Sadly, no formula exists to guarantee success for the potential victim when you meets the rapist face to face, be he familiar or unfamiliar. If you are a talker, talk. If you are a doer, talk first, and if that ploy looks hopeless, physically resist your attacker. If you are neither, you must not allow him to take advantage of your timidity and tie you up. Never, ever, agree to that demand.

If a formula lurks in the wings, it probably concerns the feat of **letting go**. Letting go involves an acceptance to care less about demeanor and comportment, and care more about your willingness to explode verbally and physically as a person who fiercely defends herself. Programs with varying names play to this key, calling on a cheering chorus of women who urge the "victim" to let go and give the "rapist" hell.

This technique exposes females to the simulated attacks of a man encased in 40 to 50 pounds of protective gear. The gear is necessary because the women are exhorted to kick, punch, bite, or do whatever it takes to discourage their attacker. Occasionally, they succeed more ably than the "rapist" expects, such as knocking him unconscious. The heart of this program, though, involves the group support that encourages a woman to overcome a lifetime of polite behavior and to lash out--as she must in a real assault. Figures, claimed by one workshop, the **Model Mugging Program**, indicate that 30 of 32 members subsequently dissuaded their attackers in a real confrontation (Freeman & Wilhelm, 1989). Therefore, since filmmakers are less likely to give rape prevention much screen time, females should avail themselves to know the score, including the need to be vigilant out there.

3. The dynamics of sexual harassment resolve mostly into a male creation. Generally speaking, **quid pro quo** refers to an exchange of considerations: You scratch my back and I'll scratch yours. Sexually speaking, you want this promotion? Okay, it's yours, providing... The other general condition, that of a **hostile environment**, involves lewd comments and, frankly, any ridicule or intimidation that make the victim--usually female, but sometimes male--sexually uncomfortable, day after day.

Proving either condition is difficult, especially since the company's interpretation and resolution of sexual harassment charges likely represent policy derived from a male perspective (Carlson, Gorey, & Traver, 1991); Ehrenreich, 1991; Riger, 1991). Men, as the all-male senate committee in the Hill/Thomas hearings demonstrated, realize one way of evaluating sexual harassment, whereas women adopt a different perspective. Under these circumstances, you shouldn't need to guess which party assumes a relaxed, liberal position on the nature and seriousness of sexual overtures, and which party prefers a stricter, conservative appraisal. But compared to rape as cinematic fare, sexual harassment appears less focussed and too lukewarm for frequent dramatic treatment.

4. Sexual assault has been a cinematic institution since filmmakers began churning out the Silents. Alfred Hitchcock included a rape scene in both an English silent and sound version of his early film, *Blackmail* (1929). The heroine joins a stranger in his apartment and then kills him when he attacks her sexually. The struggle occurs inside a curtained bed and remains unseen by the audience, but the circumstances incriminate the woman and prevent her from reporting the assailant's death. Hitchcock, naturally, sees to it that the heroine pays dearly for her indiscretion throughout the film.

Johnny Belinda in 1947 apparently became the first major American film to use a successful sexual assault--committed off screen--as a telling event that changes the story's characters and direction. Interestingly, Ida Lupino, a well-known actress in her own right, may have been the first female director to examine sexual assault in a modern American movie. Lupino's first directorial production, *Outrage* (1950), tells of rape's aftereffects and of a young woman, played by Mala Powers, who struggles to overcome her trauma and return to a more constructive life. Lupino's film suggests but does not show the sexual assault, preferring to emphasize the anguish that follows.

5. The cluster of 26 films concerns a **convenience sample**. This sample is just what it says, a search for videotapes that proved accessible to study. The convenience sample in this instance captures neither a condition of **representativeness**, nor a condition founded on **random assignment**. Representativeness implies that the sample gives us a valid estimate in assessing the population of videotapes dealing with rape, i.e., what happens in the sample also happens much the same way in the population. The safest assumption here, however, is that representativeness remains in question.

Many films over the decades have used rape as entertainment, but without more information we cannot assume that the present sample of 26 movies represents a microcosm of those movies comprising the population of dramas portraying rape. "Those movies" include stories concerned with false reports of rape, with victims unable to defend against rape, with the revenge factor, and other plot developments.

Random assignment refers to the chance selection of videos for study from a larger pool of videos available. This kind of chance assignment did not occur. We simply searched for any and all videotapes at hand from the stores in our vicinity. Consequently, the sample of 26 movies occupies a tentative status of reference, but a reference nonetheless.

6. Two stories behind *The Accused* are worth mentioning. Kelly McGillis received first choice of the film's two major roles, Sarah, and Sarah's attorney, Katheryn. She chose Katheryn, the less colorful, less sympathetic character. Why? McGillis notes that Sarah's tragedy echoes her own real-life pain, a remembrance that McGillis decided not to relive, even as entertainment. The actress, before she became known professionally, suffered a rape by two men. Both assailants were convicted, but the indignity they inflicted remains a dark memory. Hence, McGillis holds a special interest in *The Accused* and its message for rape victims (Sabulis, 1988).

The other story concerns the real Sarah, Cheryl Araujo, who inspired the film version of her ordeal. Cheryl's crucible began in 1983 at Big Dan's Tavern in New Bedford, Massachusetts, and became more tortuous than that of Sarah, her fictional counterpart. The real victim had to testify not once, but twice at two separate trials, morning and afternoon. Defense attorneys grilled Cheryl about her contradictions in reporting the incident, her sexual history, her drinking, and other improprieties in an effort to discredit the victim and her claims. But Cheryl Araujo persevered and, unlike the film story, four Portuguese defendants found themselves convicted of aggravated rape (Beck & Zabarsky, 1984).

Sadly, Cheryl could not master her personal life with the same perseverance, nor did she feel secure in New Bedford. Fearful of retribution from the family members and friends of the defendants, she moved to Florida. The fear didn't cease with her change of scenery, and neither did the drinking. A story appeared in January, 1987, of a car crash on a rain-slicked road during the day of December 14, 1986. Two children survived the accident, but the mother died instantly when a utility pole collapsed and struck her on the head. A later report indicated that the mother had three times the legal limit of alcohol in her blood. Cheryl Araujo was 25 (Agus, 1987).

Lesson 10

Endings

Maybe Rhett shouldn't have said what he said to Scarlett. Maybe he should have given a damn. Imagine the delight of a happy ending after so much misery. Rhett Butler and Scarlett O'Hara, united at last. Working together to bring Tara back to life. Standing firm, arm in arm, to help revitalize a new South. A finale to capture all the golden qualities of true romance. So, why didn't it happen?

It didn't happen because too much had already happened. Too many promises unfulfilled, too many sacrifices made, too many deaths between them. Rhett and Scarlett held a relationship too weary for renewal. And Rhett, well, Rhett just didn't give a damn anymore. Scarlett would have to think about tomorrow without him.[1]

The bell tolls, the bough breaks, shadows fall, and the movie ends. Some movies end too soon, others continue for a millennium. But all films seek a resolution to the misunderstanding, anguish, chaos, or disharmony of its characters. The story must wind down, and the audience must find closure. If we seldom see "THE END" emblazoned across the movie's final scene (and I miss it), we know that when the credits roll the movie has run its course.

Consequently, whatever you feel about *Gone With The Wind* (1939), whether it's the Classic of classics or the Melodramas of melodramas, the parting of Rhett and Scarlett holds true. A credible ending is not always welcome, of course. Movies are supposed to entertain, and we enjoy the entertainment more if it gratifies our expectations via Oz.

Film and television dramas achieve this aim so well that viewers seem unlikely to notice phony sentiment or a contrived ending. And when viewers do notice, they may not care. After all, "It's only a movie," said Alfred Hitchcock. But the slighting of creativity in entertainment represents a common occurrence. This slighting diminishes the drama's lurking intelligence. Some moviegoers, unable to imagine the truer character or better ending, never know that they have taken a cheap shot from the filmmaker.

A cheap shot, incidentally, suggests a bargain-basement treatment of sexuality. We may not wish our hero and heroine to part company as in *The Way We Were* (1973), but a baloney ending that repairs an unreparable romance does not represent filmmaking with integrity.

The Filmmaker's Achilles' Heel

Typically, the movie begins with a **complication**. Something goes wrong. A problem emerges, characters are stressed, disaster threatens. These complications progress into the **body** of the film. We encounter elaborations through the development of subplots: An articulation of storylines that move forward in time, although occasionally a subplot retreats using flashbacks. In any event, we move in some direction. The story gains momentum and complications intensify. The **ending**, therefore, requires a gathering of subplots and a culmination of character conflicts--to wrap up mysteries that linger and confrontations that dangle.

Filmmakers frequently enjoy greatest success in dramatizing the complication (Makoul, 1989). An unexplained

sequence of events mesmerizes viewers at the movie's
beginning. First impressions of the hero and heroine, and
seeing how villainous the villain can be, realize an advantage
in novelty.

The movie at this early juncture still holds promise. But
eventually the filmmaker must give substance to a movie's
sensational opening salvo. The practice of endowing players
with characterizations that sustain viewer interest distinguishes
greater directors from lesser directors. Possessing the potential
to unfold fascinating personalities spells the difference
between a good script and a lukewarm effort; between a
portrayal of exquisite sexuality and of a sexuality labored,
trite, and empty.

A movie needs to legitimize its happenings. The
convenient coincidence comprises one cinematic gimmick that
helps to befuddle movie reality and diminish creativity. When
the coincidence occurs, a cheap shot is in progress. Note, for
example, the happy use of coincidence in this hypothetical
thriller: "Surprised to see me, my daring? Thought you had
taken care of me, eh, my love? Well, sweetness, here I am.
The guy who climbed in my car only looked like me. We
wanted you to think that, so when the car blew up..." Integrity
is out to lunch in such a concoction. Coincidences happen, but
when they happen too often, or in bizarre fashion, these
improbable events weaken a drama.

You may argue that holding entertainment to such a lofty
standard seems unfair. You want to be entertained, not
receive a heavy dose of reality. And you don't mind
glamorizing revenge or suffering a few coincidences. Listen,
it's only a movie. Or a television drama. Or a docudrama. Or
a documentary. Or a newscast. Where does entertainment end
and responsible communication begin? A mediocre movie still
requires a measure of credible craftsmanship to document its
artistry.

This artistry meets its acid test with the film's ending. A
movie's denouement often shoulders the burden of clarifying
earlier events, and of giving the story whatever coherency it
will command. The ending also constitutes a moviegoer's
"high" for savoring justice, realizing character fulfillment,

languishing in love's sweet refrain, and celebrating victory over incredible odds. To give viewers these scintillating experiences, and to do so honestly, marks a real achievement in filmmaking.

Pictures and memories vary, of course, but endings probably convey a disproportionate influence on how viewers evaluate a film. Who can forget the final "freeze frame" in *An Officer And A Gentleman* (1982)? Zack (Richard Gere), a shining knight in his navy whites, rescues Paula (Debra Winger) from her drab factory job and carries her into the bright sunlight of a new beginning.

Dismiss the heartaches and heartbreaks that occurred previously. The turmoil that Zack and Paula suffered, unlike the anguish of Scarlett and Rhett, makes the fairy-tale climax precious. The nature of their characters hardly suggests a future relationship of idyllic magnitude, but who cares about future reality at this point? The ending does not indicate reality, or that viewers should worry about reality as they must in *Gone With The Wind*. Zack and Paula's reunion offers the lasting impression of a magic moment when love conquers all.

Multiple Endings

A film, in truth, customarily engages the audience through more than one ending. These **multiple endings** become essential to conclude each of the subplots that a director threads into a story. Before the glowing finale of *An Officer And A Gentleman*, Zack Mayo closes out a storyline involving his friction with Sergeant Foley (Louis Gossett, Jr.). The two antagonists stage a macho, martial-arts "kickout" and Zack loses. His defeat, nonetheless, solves a problem for him and leads to his reconciliation with Paula.

Picnic (1955) features two love stories, major and minor, with happy endings for each to double the moviegoers' pleasure. The minor plot features Rosalind Russell as Rosemary Sydney, a teacher desperate to marry and dreading the beginning of another school year as a spinster. Her target is Howard Bevins (Arthur O'Connell), a lifelong bachelor who takes a hard look at his homey surrounds, his resident pinup picture, and tells himself "No!". He drives over to tell Rosemary "No!" as painlessly as he can, but never gets the chance. Rosemary assumes what she needs to assume--that Howard arrives to take her away. He finds himself over-whelmed by the gusto of Rosemary's exuberance, and the next thing Howard knows, they're driving off for the marriage license with everyone's good wishes.

The major love affair concerns an aging jock, Hal Carter (William Holden), and a small-town Kansas beauty, Madge Owens (Kim Novak). Like Rosemary, Hal hears his clock ticking, and realizes that if he's to make anything of his aimless life, Madge must be a part of it. The closing scenes show Hal literally pulling Madge from her possessive mother, telling Madge "You love me! You know it! You love me!" Hal shouts these words as he races for a freight train to leave town ahead of the police. Madge hears his call and makes her big decision: She will join him and take a chance on the kind of man he is to try for a happy marriage. The final scene depicts an aerial view of a train heading out in synchrony with a bus carrying Madge, moving across the lush Kansas countryside toward, you hope, a better future.

Likewise, our focus in *The Big Easy* (1987) remains on Remy (Dennis Quaid) and Anne (Ellen Barkin), although a minor plot about gangland killings influences the lovers' relationship. Remy and Anne barely survive intact as they resolve the minor plot (ending #1). After the violence and dust settle, a closing scene reveals the lovers frolicking as newlyweds (ending #2). This postscript requires no dialogue to tell viewers that Remy and Anne have laid their disagree-ments to rest. Ending #2 outranks ending #1 in importance to the story, although both resolutions function in tandem because the major and minor storylines are intertwined.

Ending #2 in *The Big Easy* works as a **cinematic postscript.** This afterthought denotes the aftermath of a crisis, confrontation, or revelation. The purpose of a postscript is to clean house, thus the movie's afterthought exudes little or no suspense. Tension passes and an accounting of all characters and plots is at hand.

Psycho (1960) introduces three postscripts following the unmasking of Norman (Anthony Perkins) as Mother Bates. First, a psychiatrist arrives to explain Norman's sexual identification with his mother and why "she" murdered Marion (Janet Leigh). Second, we see Norman staring at the camera, giving us his little, crooked smile, and relating the thought that he wouldn't harm a fly. Finally, the closing scene shows Marion's car (with Marion in the trunk) being towed from the pond where Norman had submerged it.

Each of the three postscripts carries a different intent: one to explain Norman, one to show what happens to Norman, and one to reveal that Marion will receive a decent burial. If you're counting, *Psycho* winds down with four endings, only the first of which packs any horror (capturing Norman). Or, if you wish to include Marion's death in the shower as an "early ending," then nudge the score to five.

Postscripts sometimes assume the essence of a curtain call, an encore, or a peek at the future. After dispatching the villain to satisfy the dramatic climax in *Charade* (1963), Cary Grant and Audrey Hepburn, in a post-climatic scene, reassure the audience that they intend to continue their romantic relationship. Following this assurance, viewers see a humorous encore of earlier scenes in the movie.

Likewise, in *Stripes* (1981) the escape from East Germany by the film's oddball characters comprises a violent, yet humorous ending. The film's afterthought includes a triumphant homecoming for the unlikely victors, after which viewers see a "curtain call" of the patriots and a frivolous aside about their future prospects. On a more somber note, the episodic antics of high schoolers in *American Graffiti* (1973) also are placed in future perspective at the movie's end. This curtain call reveals what happens to each youngster, although the outcomes vary dramatically from light-hearted to darker-hearted prospects.

Curse The Lame Ending

As moviegoers, we can be a picky lot. Movies with **lame endings** bring out the beast in us.[2] We've paid our money and we don't wish an ending that's tantamount to waffling through warm spit. Something interesting must happen, something **very** interesting to send us out the door, satisfied: Not an ending tired and conventional, not an ending unbelievable, and not an ending overly sentimental and saccharine.

A solid ending generates its own power, yet derives logically from the film's preceding events. The ending, after all, delivers the moment of truth. And the truth had better be worth the wait. A lame ending denies the moviegoer's Oz that special pleasure.

An **enigmatic ending** offers more, although moviegoers will split on their reactions to an ambiguous resolution. Frank Galvin (Paul Newman) in *The Verdict* (1982) wins his case and gains a reprieve on his self-esteem as an alcoholic lawyer. But an earlier betrayal by Laura Fischer (Charlotte Rampling) mars the victory. Laura posed as his lover, though secretly in legion with the opposing legal camp. The last scene finds Galvin at his desk and the phone ringing. Laura, having confessed her duplicity to him, presumably is calling to reestablish their relationship. The phone rings and Galvin sits there. The scene ends and the movie ends, with no indication of Galvin's decision.

The optimist believes that Galvin will answer the phone and get his love life back on track. The pessimist concludes that the phone will keep ringing, and wonders about Galvin's fortitude to stay away from the bottle. The character of Frank Galvin allows ample latitude to accommodate either ending and still retain the character's integrity. Using a little imagination to create one outcome or the other isn't a hardship, although some viewers want their endings etched in stone: "I deserve to know what happens so don't leave me hanging!"

Patrons curse the lame ending, but may accept an enigmatic conclusion if that conclusion sparks their interest in arguing for or against the ambiguous resolution. Filmmakers, however, count their blessings when they inspire fanfare over a **twist ending**. If the twist receives enough publicity, it can draw filmgoers just to savor the ending. The trick of the twist, nonetheless, is to play fair. Surprise the audience, but surprise them credibly.

The Jagged Edge (1985) surfaced from nowhere to become a well-received puzzle of "Who's the murderer?" The movie stars Jeff Bridges as Jack Forester, a newspaper publisher charged with murdering his wife, and Glenn Close as Teddy Barnes, his defense attorney. *The Jagged Edge* undermines its reality by having Barnes fall in bed and in love with her client, although their romance helps to further the story's suspense.

This exchange in the cinema is known as trading honesty for expediency. Regardless, the important point involves the ending. Our concern hinges on whether Forester is guilty of killing his wife. Roger Ebert (1993, p. 337), in his review of the film, speculates that since the movie works so diligently to be deceptive, the audience should not learn the killer's identity. Leave viewers, in other words, to contest the ambiguity of an enigmatic ending rather than the revelation of a twist ending. Let them imagine the final solution.

Moviegoers want closure, however, especially when the closure involves a murder mystery. *The Jagged Edge* chooses to unmask the killer as he makes a failed attempt to terminate Teddy. The murderer is Forester. A quick shot of the killer's face at an odd angle left numerous viewers confused (see Ebert, 1993, pp. 337-338). They could not ascertain that the face belonged to Bridges. Possibly, desirous of a happy ending, these moviegoers wished the face **not** to belong to Bridges.

This revelation may not satisfy some individuals, but Forester's guilt gives *The Jagged Edge* a more believable ending, and a more plausible story. Teddy finds a typewriter in Jack's closet, one used to write incriminating tips about the murder. Another killer could have planted the typewriter, of course. But if not, this clue leads logically to Forester as the killer. More important, Forester's guilt permits moviegoers to reflect on Bridge's eerie portrayal of a seemingly earnest

young man who wants to clear his name and return to his first
love--publishing a newspaper, a job he does well. Because the
jury finds Forester not guilty, he cannot stand trial again for
his wife's murder. Teddy, nonetheless, can besmirch Jack's
reputation. He must eliminate her. The film's characterizations of Jack and Teddy achieve an honesty that would have
suffered had the filmmaker opted to compromise these
characters and impose a happy ending. *The Jagged Edge*
cannot manage a happy ending and retain its spirit of sinister
duplicity. One experience has to go.

Happy Trails

We do like **happy endings**, though.[3]   Most movies end by
giving us an uplifting moment. Life has more than its share
of grim reminders, so it's nice to find sanctuary in make-
believe. We can live forever (*Cocoon*, 1985); or if not forever,
we can freeze a glorious instant and bypass death's ugly sting
(*Butch Cassidy And The Sundance Kid*, 1969). But if we must
die, let's die outrageously and blow ourselves to kingdom come
like James Cagney ("Made it, Ma. Top of the world!" from
White Heat, 1949); or we may opt to bow out leisurely like
Warren Beatty and Faye Dunaway (death in slow motion from
Bonnie And Clyde, 1967). Mostly, however, we just want to
escape reality's doldrums.

Consider the notion, then, that as doldrums worsen, happy
endings become more important. During the Depression years,
happy endings proved almost a godsend to escape grim reality:
the working class out of work; the working class sifting
through garbage to survive; the working class finding shelter
in shanties, asking only for the chance to earn a livelihood.

My Man Godfrey (1936) chronicles the disenchanted
working stiff in a screwball comedy starring William Powell as
Godfrey and Carole Lombard as Irene. Godfrey, born into a
wealthy family, resides at the city dump for reasons involving
a failed marriage and, more disillusioning, the conviction of
a failed life. He lives with other disenfranchised souls as one
of the "forgotten men" who sees monied families indulging

themselves, conveniently ignoring the less fortunate members
of society. Irene, although from such a family, projects an
unaffected warmth as the impulsive daughter who has yet to
learn the distinction between wealth and poverty. Indeed, it
is Irene who functions as the catalyst by imposing her
dithering ways on Godfrey's quiet, ordered existence.

Irene wrangles Godfrey a job as butler for her eccentric
family, an interesting lesson of humility and patience for
Godfrey--and an opportunity for Irene to nurture her growing
attraction to the new manservant. When a woman chases a
man as breathlessly and devotedly as Irene, we find ourselves
watching either a comedy like *My Man Godfrey*, or a sinister
upheaval of gender roles as in *Play Misty For Me* (1971). Not
much middle ground exists to accommodate those females who
put males on the defensive.

Godfrey, in his urbane fashion, helps Irene's family out of
financial difficulty, and then leaves to accomplish his ultimate
aim. He creates a plush nightspot, appropriately called "The
Dump," at the very site where Godfrey and the other forgotten
men eked out an existence. His plans include renovating the
dump site for affordable housing, and giving the forgotten
men the jobs they so richly deserve. As for himself, Godfrey
reassuringly supplies his failed life with new meaning. He has
smoothly touched all bases, save one. A friend asks him why
he left the family and Godfrey replies, "I...felt that foolish
feeling coming on again." He refers to Irene, and the foolish
feeling that leads him too close to matrimonial waters.

Irene, naturally, thinks otherwise. In the club she comes,
breezing through the place and marching straight to her true
love, up in his face, remarking, "You know, there's no use
struggling against a thing when it's got you. It's got you and
that's all there is to it. It's got you." Godfrey, off-balance,
outmatched, and bewildered, remains speechless. Irene serves
up a marriage ceremony on the spot, pulling a dumbfounded
Godfrey into position, and cooing to him, "Stand still,
Godfrey. It'll all be over in a minute."

A fetching giggle follows this line, like a soft exclamation
point to Irene's dedicated pursuit. Godfrey's twitterpated. He
knows it, the audience knows it, and Irene has never doubted

it. Moviegoers of the solemn 1930s had much to cheer
concerning *My Man Godfrey*. The forgotten men are shown
to be as stalwart as the rich are idle. The shantytown of old
gives way to a nightclub that rises from the ashes to showcase
the revival of good times. But most enjoyable, the viewers
appreciated a romance that defies wealth and poverty to bring
two decent people together. Thus, not one, but several happy
endings helped moviegoers, at least temporarily, to keep the
gloom of the Depression era at bay.

Filmmakers, therefore, know the risks of relinquishing a
happy ending for a sad one. These risks prove more than
artistic, they become commercial. A film like *Blow Out* (1981)
received favorable critical reviews, but did poorly at the box
office. Why? John Travolta (Jack) and Nancy Allen (Sally)
star in this well-crafted movie that possesses its share of
heroism, villainy, and suspense--except that *Blow Out* ends
bleakly. Jack, rushing to rescue Sally from death, arrives too
late.

Here, unlike *The Jagged Edge* where we anticipate Bridges
as the possible murderer, Travolta's failure to fulfill the hero's
function appeared to sharply deflate moviegoers and their Oz
of expectations. The viewers' sentiments did not agree with
the film's cynicism (Sally participates in blackmail, and Jack
works as soundman for a seedy film outfit). Still, the ending
claims artistic integrity because it addresses that cynicism.
More concretely, the viewers' discontent probably focused on
the downbeat ending: Jack fails to save Sally. Why the
failure? He saves her from drowning earlier in the story, so
why not at the end?

Happy endings exercise such a stranglehold on how a
movie concludes that it takes a determined filmmaker to try
for something nobler--if the movie calls for something nobler.
A star's persona, for instance, may dictate against the nobler
finish. Charles Bronson as Paul Kersey in *Death Wish* (1974)
learns that hoodlums have killed his wife and sexually
assaulted his daughter, who goes into a coma. Working
through his grief, Kersey decides to play vigilante and handle
street crime with a smoking .32-caliber revolver.

He survives, but so does the disturbing theme that a person can solve his personal problems best through killing. A better ending would have sacrificed Kersey to underscore the more honest theme that relying on violence can lead to greater tragedy. But you do not sacrifice Charles Bronson unless Hell freezes over. His macho image thrives on conquering the odds, and in not jeopardizing the movie's box-office potential due to a fit of vulnerability. Bronson's survival also kept him intact to appear in a string of profitable, although less-than-admirable sequels.

Permit filmmakers their just desserts, therefore, when they challenge the status quo. Remember *The War Of The Roses* (1989) from Lesson 6? Oliver Rose (Michael Douglas) and Barbara Rose (Kathleen Turner) begin with a flash romance that, over the years, changes course. Oliver becomes too busy to think much about Barbara, and Barbara gradually loses her affection for Oliver. The friction escalates as each character assumes a defined role: Barbara wants him out with no reprieve; Oliver wants to stay and, on his terms, bring Barbara back to the fold.

The flagrant antics of husband and wife reach a point wherein the "ideal house" they both covet metamorphoses to a war zone. Dirty tricks become commonplace. How can such a marriage realize reconciliation? The answer is, it can't. Barbara and Oliver, through their selfish twists of character, perish at the end. But just before they succumb, recall that Oliver weakly places his hand on Barbara--and Barbara, weakly, yet contemptuously, pushes his hand away. Their final chance for salvaging the relationship falls short, even at the brink of death.

An ending proves the victim of all that's gone before. For Barbara and Oliver, like Scarlett and Rhett, too much has happened. What serves to lighten the Roses's demise is Danny DeVito's narration. He relates the Roses's rise and fall, not as a tragedy, but as a cautionary tale, told with a measure of resigned wit. DeVito takes the edge off the bleakness of two people who once loved so much, only to die so foolishly. Despite this added touch, allowing your main stars to die represents a gamble at the box office. The gamble, this time, succeeded.

Rejection, The Black-Eyed Monster

Before discussing our final film, *Fatal Attraction* (1987), let's consider the ideas of jealousy and rejection, the dual dynamics that drive the film's story and characters. **Romantic jealousy** popularly refers to the green-eyed monster, a state of mind that influences the unhappy lover to view himself or herself as involved in an unbalanced relationship.

The jealous lover's expectation of faithfulness and affection does not possess the equity it needs to keep both partners joyous and content (White, 1981a, 1981b; Walster, Walster, & Berscheid, 1978, p. 143). Real or imagined, one party suffers negative feelings--and they are always negative--about the other party diddling with a third party (for a classic, comic treatment of pathological jealousy, see the 1948 film, *Unfaithfully Yours*).

The mere hint of a romantic triangle can galvanize the injured partner into action. Susan Hayward plays Mary Thompson, a rural pastor's wife in *I'd Climb The Highest Mountain* (1951). Mary, a city woman, marries William Thompson (William Lundigan), a circuit rider, whose pastoral assignment leads the newlyweds to the red clay hills of Georgia where surreys are still in fashion.

Mary, finding the life of a minister's wife more than a little trying, snaps to when her handsome William begins to receive visits from Mrs. Billywith (Lynn Bari). Billywith, poised and stylish, wishes to have the pastor "clarify" some troubling passages in the Second Book of Samuel. The trouble, Mary decides, is not with the Second Book of Samuel but with the wily Mrs. Billywith.

Their confrontation kindles one of the most delightful episodes of verbal jousting that the movies have to offer: Two women spar over a man, William, an innocent in this triangle. He remains blissfully ignorant of the happening, and quite dense to the females' way of settling accounts. Mary invites the seductress to the front porch, and to a sermon that sends Billywith scurrying home to her husband, who happens to be named Sam: "I've been thinking," says Mary, "that what you need is to stay at home more and try to interpret your own Samuel...He seems to me a very neglected prophet, too." Goodbye, Mrs. Billywith, and fare-thee-well.

Now, step back and gaze at a broader fabric. The jealous partner obviously fears losing his or her beloved, but note this fear also includes the possibility of a deeper anguish, namely, that of personal rejection. **Rejection** offers no happier state than jealousy, except that it harbors a greater potential to invoke dire consequences (Rubin, Peplau, & Hill, 1981; Hill, Rubin, & Peplau, 1976).

Why? First, a jealous state holds the promise, likely or not, of winning back the beloved. Something good may come of the negotiations to stay together...perhaps. A rejected state, however, suggests finality. Once the scorned lover accepts this finality, a different course of action looms forth. Nothing to lose now, so no more begging or cajoling or prostrating one's heart and soul at the lover's feet.

Rejection rouses its ugly head as the black-eyed monster that seeks vindication. Rejected lovers--male and female-- have gone beyond the pale to underscore their despair: a car belonging to the ex-lover, stolen or trashed; wilted flowers delivered as a parting shot; a live grenade handed to one ex-girlfriend, who, thoughtfully, gave it and her ex-boyfriend to the police; a plane piloted by one rejectee crashed into the house of the rejecter (the pilot survived, though with skull fractures); and, at the alter of the Ebenezer Baptist Church, a groom about to say "I do," received, instead, a bullet from a .38-caliber revolver, courtesy of his ex-girlfriend.

Rejected lovers can walk away, of course. Most of them do, albeit with visions other than sugarplums of what they would wish on their depraved ex-partners. We all suffer rejection of some nature in life. It pains us, it's not easy to forget, but, usually, we will not cross the line with vengeance. The point, however, is that rejection carries the propensity to make certain individuals commit extraordinarily destructive acts. A ton of bitter feelings weighs on the rejected lover and she, or he, must retaliate. Filmmakers adore this kind of propensity; indeed, they have adored it since the first cameras began cranking our celluloid stories of human conflict.

Adultery represents a favorite theme of such stories because adultery spells danger. It spells taking a risk. It hints at the lurking possibility of discovery. And if the discovery happens, it glories in the trouble that ensues. Trouble with a capital T that complicates three lives (at least), and, that at some juncture, gets worse before it gets better. Real life offers its share of triangles, but movies do it so much better. Adultery conjures up the stuff that makes filmmakers gloat with anticipation.

What transpires, however, when two people go to a film on adultery and leave with differing opinions regarding the film's entertainment value?   Specifically, how do moviegoers' feelings about adultery influence their feelings concerning its portrayal as entertainment?   We can define **adultery** as voluntary sexual relations between a spouse and someone other than that spouse's marital partner, with an emphasis on the word *voluntary*.[4]

One moviegoer finds artistic credibility in the adultery theme, the other doesn't. The movie conveys sufficient ambiguity about character and story so that two people disagree on how they interpret the film. How can anyone say anything meaningful about artistic accomplishments, or about adultery, under these circumstances? We can, although our arguments must allow for a measure of uncertainty.

Creativity in movies depends on structure but also harbors a telltale whiff of subjectivity. **Subjectivity** permits film critics and filmgoers to dispute the worth of a movie, whereas **structure** supplies enough evidence of the movie's cinematic construction to foster a legitimate argument. The disagreement, in other words, remains anchored to something substantial, something arguable, and not something that constitutes a quagmire of wild speculations. Thus, we can acknowledge subjectivity--the number of reasonable interpretations possible--and still concentrate on integrity's calling card: the substance, aptness, and consistency of a film's characters and story.

Cinematic creativity therefore manages a deft adaptation of subjectivity and structure. The content of this adaptation-- adultery--carries with it a history vested in reality and in the cinema. Adultery's cinematic history involves recalling such tragedies as *The Postman Always Rings Twice* (1946/1981), *Double Indemnity* (1944), *Topaz* (1969), *Body Heat* (1981), *Blood Simple* (1984), *Dangerous Liaisons* (1988), and *Valmont* (1989). But adultery also relies on the humorous potential of infidelity to entertain, expressed in movies like *Adam's Rib* (1949), *The Apartment* (1960), *Bob & Carol & Ted & Alice* (1969), *Hannah And Her Sisters* (1986), *A Fish Called Wanda* (1988), and *Husbands And Wives* (1992).

The question arises as to how your personal conception of adultery rivals Hollywood's attempts to make an essentially illicit act interesting as entertainment. If you regard an illicit affair lightly, you may bring an openness to the business of how a filmmaker treats adultery. But if you hold serious misgivings about the violation of marital sanctity, you will find it difficult to appreciate any filmmaker's efforts to dramatize adultery, humorously or not. These attitudes characterize extreme value judgments however, and do not account for mood and circumstance.

Fatal Attraction Promises Artistic Integrity

To wrestle with the problem of what you carry to the subject of adultery, and what the filmmaker brings in the way of creativity, suppose we examine a film that unsettled millions of moviegoers. *Fatal Attraction* (1987) denotes an excursion into the uses and abuses of artistic integrity. Originally, the film offered a promise of integrity concerning its first ending. But the desire for a more commercial film dictated a new conclusion. Integrity, in this change, suffered artistic abuse: A semblance of integrity remained, though less elegant and more the ugly duckling.

The movie concerns an intense woman and a casual man committing adultery. Such a liaison presents moments of erotic frenzy at the risk of substantial loss. This risk serves as

part of the affair's wrongful appeal. The relationship of Alex
Forrest (Glenn Close) and Dan Gallagher (Michael Douglas)
goes from uninhibited sexual exploration to a disturbing series
of intrusions by Alex into Dan's otherwise genial, domestic
life. He wants their brief fling over and forgotten; she
doesn't.[5]

Dan, a lawyer, prompts an introduction to Alex, more out
of curiosity than with an affair in mind. When circumstances
bring them together, Dan pursues the next step by inviting
Alex for a drink. The invitation is innocent but still made,
and Alex's provocative sexual overtures during their
conversation evoke little resistance from him. The number of
males who have eased their way into episodes of sexual hooky
are many, but the thought lingers that Dan rings the doorbell.
However unwittingly, he presents himself as a passive though
willing participant (Dennis, 1992, p. 233).

Because Dan has a lovely wife and daughter, he views his
affair with Alex as the male's sexual windfall: fleeting but
pleasant, a weekend's respite from the lawyer's routine. The
fact that Dan is happy before he meets Alex, and evidences
guilt after the episode, leads to the puzzling question of Why
the affair? Alex, in a flash of insight, asks a telling question
when Dan declares his happiness: "So what are you doing
here?" Dan has no answer, although he finds Alex intriguing
and sexually potent (Gilmour, 1988, p. 71). Their illicit pact
is made and trouble follows. Dan finds Alex a disturbed
personality whose behavior is never adequately explained, but
whose possessiveness of Dan extends to her dying breath.
Alex also is pregnant, apparently by Dan, and wants to have
the child--his child.

The film's original ending had Alex commit suicide using
a knife that held Dan's fingerprints: Alex's perverse way of
framing him for her "murder." References to *Madame
Butterfly* occur in earlier, peaceful scenes between Dan and
Alex. Dan plays music from the opera that closes with a
young girl committing suicide. The operatic suicide poses an
eloquent analogy to Alex's suicide in the movie's first ending.
But if you have seen the film, you know that Alex does not

take her life. The original finale went on the shelf. How
come?

Fatal Attraction Compromises Artistic Integrity

Plainly put, preview audiences did not care for the original
ending.[6] They wanted to see Alex "get it"--and get it she does
in a brutal bathroom climax that ends with Dan attempting to
drown her. Alex appears to succumb. But no, as in so many
films where the villain only looks dead, Alex retains a spark
of life. Predictably, when Dan turns his back, she rises from
her watery shroud to inflict further mayhem. Fortunately for
Dan, his wife, Beth (Anne Archer), has retrieved a gun and
plugs Alex through the chest. This time she doesn't get up,
although a sequel to *Fatal Attraction* would no doubt do
wonders for her resurrection.

Let's give the second ending its due. Viewers wanted a
good murder, that is, they wanted to see Alex--who, other
than the rabbit, manages to kill no one--punished for the
misery she wrought. A good murder occurs when the hero or
heroine kills a villain, frequently in self-defense, and under
circumstances that convince an audience the villain must die
(Wilson, 1991, p. 2). Apparently in Alex's case nothing short
of a life-and-death struggle would do.

Logically, Dan cannot kill Alex since he remains the
flawed catalyst who set her off. Earlier in the film we witness
Beth's pain when Dan tells her of his unfaithfulness. The
sparkle leaves her eyes and the warmth leaves her marriage.
Dan suffers from Alex's threats, but he hasn't suffered enough
to deserve killing her. No, only Beth has that "right." Beth is
the most (remember that word, *most*) innocent party of the
three, and she becomes the fitting member to terminate what
her husband has initiated: a thoughtless sexual indiscretion
that unleashes an abnormal personality. Feminists may
suggest, moreover, that Beth deserves a second shot at you-
know-who.

The revised finale clearly provides a more commercial ending. The bathroom's small space, white and brightly lit, offers an interesting technical challenge. The director, Adrian Lyne, has to choreograph the complicated, close-up movements of three people in a lethal dance. Lyne does not use shadows or distant shots to diversify this scene. The struggle appears on screen as intimate, forceful, and continuous.

Viewers, especially male viewers, it seems, feel themselves part of the contest. They desperately want Alex to die (Faludi, 1991, p. 112). And thus, the movie captures an intense relationship that says something to moviegoers: On rare occasions rejected lovers become dangerous to themselves and to others. They can be quite vindictive. It hurts to find that someone doesn't want you. Perhaps a number of viewers lived that experience. If so, *Fatal Attraction* captures a breath of real tragedy--and a modicum of integrity in the process.

What the new ending achieves commercially, however, it loses artistically. The visceral treatment of Alex's killing diminishes her character and the complexities she once conveyed. Her violent attack and death cloud the meaning of the operatic suicide mentioned earlier in *Madame Butterfly*, and it denies us the opportunity to see Dan **really** suffer for Beth's disillusionment.

Dan, framed for murder in the original ending, must find a way out. How he does it--or more appropriate, how Beth manages to save his tail--would have contributed an unusual dimension to the suspense. (Belatedly, viewers finally realized their chance to see both endings in a video reissue of *Fatal Attraction*.)

Another criticism surfaces concerning the commercial ending. Beth fires the fatal shot, presumably to keep Alex from stabbing Dan in the back. But stabbing, if you're not a professional at it, generally requires numerous strikes to inflict serious injury. The thought arises therefore that perhaps Beth need not shoot Alex to stop the horror. Can't Beth and Dan, together, subdue Alex? Dan, after all, almost drowns her by himself.

Recall the earlier comment that Beth was the "most" innocent of the three figures. Most innocent, though not wholly innocent. Beth, too, nurtures a point of fury: Alex played havoc with Beth's marriage, and, more unforgivable, kidnapped Beth's daughter, an act that drove the mother frantic and ultimately put her in the hospital. No, Beth pulls the trigger, possibly for reasons in addition to the bathroom crisis. What Beth accomplishes is to kill Alex **and** Alex's unborn child. A double killing, although the law exonerates Beth's lethal behavior as self-defense. Still, ask yourself the unpleasant question: Is Beth blameless?

Fatal Attraction's subjectivity allows for argument over the two outcomes, but the suicide ending appears less contrived and more suited to Alex's character. An earlier episode in the film shows Alex with her wrists slashed when Dan tries to leave. She punishes herself to make him stay. Alex's suicide in the original ending follows the same principle: She sacrifices herself, the ultimate punishment, to frame Dan for murder. This principle is self-defeating because Alex fails to overcome her futile behavior. She works throughout the film for a cause she can't win. Alex becomes a truly tragic figure by hurting herself more than she hurts Dan; and Dan, in the first ending, becomes less sympathetic for triggering her suicide.

The second ending, by comparison, sacrifices these subtleties to make Alex the horror stereotype and Dan the traditional man of action who rushes to save his wife. Both Alex and Dan suffer a simplification of character in the way that Alex dies. The movie gains commercially, but compromises its creativity by demeaning the characters' original integrity.

Fatal Attraction overcame these contrasting appraisals, of course. The film accumulated more than 150 million dollars in a successful box-office run. The film's backers, in fact, can laugh at the controversy because the preview audiences dictated a change in endings, a change occurred, and the movie prospered financially. The end result is a risk not taken. The chance of a different ending, very possibly a more creative ending, slips by in favor of Hollywood's first priority--producing a commercial product. Worry less about the old bromide that violence solves the complications of adultery and other ills of society, and worry more about the tough, competitive world of promoting a real winner. Artistic integrity be damned.[7]

The Tenth Viewer

The **personal taste** approach offers the assumption that individual preferences dominate. Whatever the moviegoer decides is paramount. If the viewer experiences entertainment, no matter how trashy the vehicle or sordid the sex, it's the entertainment that counts. If the viewer wants to see Alex get blasted to eternity in *Fatal Attraction*, so what? The bottom line is to enjoy the movie; nothing else matters.

Personal taste deserves consideration, if only to assert that any responsible person should be free to see any movie. Entertainment, after all, relies on mood and expectation in giving Oz its measure of anticipation. If you're in the mood for the Three Stooges or a romp in the boudoir with Madonna, fine. Slapstick has its cinematic legacy in the great silent comics, and the packaging of erotica holds endless fascination, whether it's Madonna, Marilyn Monroe, or Mae West.

The personal taste orientation self-destructs, however, with the impression that movies are too subjective to merit analysis. This impression carries the idea of subjectiveness to an absurdity. Movies **are** subjective, but few social scientists or film critics find them so helter skelter as to defy systematic evaluation. Personal taste alone denotes a dead end, scientifically.

Concerning sexuality, the assumption is that you and I and others follow a **cinematic sexual script** for being entertained. The script allows for divergences from our usual viewing pleasures, as these pleasures pertain to sexuality. But usually the script identifies you and I and others as characteristically preferring certain kinds of films. People, like movies, can be subjective yet show that their sexual preferences, too, possess structure.

Creativity in movies requires confirmation. Filmmakers can build high expectations as to a movie's success, only to find that the audience remains stone silent at the "funny" sex scenes, and laughs uproariously during the film's dramatically tender moments. Moviegoers don't make a good movie bad, but they can persuade filmmakers to reassess a film's artistry. Nor does the moviegoers' persuasion have to point downward toward a less substantive ending, as occurred in *Fatal Attraction*.

Place yourself in the role of preparing to see a movie. Normally, you harbor expectations about the kind of entertainment that awaits. You enter the theatre or rent a video with preconceptions about how you hope to be entertained. Oz, in other words, goes through a priming process.

Let's assume that you're among 10 people viewing *Fatal Attraction*. After the film, five people indicate enjoyment, noting that the characters and events are what the moviegoers expected. These five viewers have no reason to grouse over the movie's ending, or, indeed, to think about the film other than to note the riskiness of extramarital affairs.

Three people like the movie even better than they anticipated--Oz receives a bonus boost--and proceed to point out why the film exceeded their expectations. A ninth individual, and you, the tenth, dislike the film, but for different reasons. The ninth person expresses frustration over the lack of gore. He grumbles that the bathroom ending should have played a lot bloodier. You disagree, and state your displeasure over the film's hackneyed conclusion because it appears gratuitous and does not derive logically from earlier events in the story.

The first five viewers agree with the **cinematic payoff** that *Fatal Attraction* delivers. They sit through the film watching Alex unleash one indignity after another, first on Dan, then on Beth and her child. The entire business of Alex, for them, becomes unconscionable. Something must happen to this woman, something bad. Something worse, apparently, than committing suicide. If we can't always give villains their just due in reality, we should certainly sock it to them in the movies. Don't worry about the artistic right or wrong of it, just kill the bitch. These feelings satisfy the first five viewers so that *Fatal Attraction*, to them, denotes little more than another evening's entertainment.

The final five viewers (yourself included) constitute a different matter. Expectations of entertainment are surpassed for three moviegoers, prompting them to explain **why** they enjoyed the film so much: "I thought it was just another love triangle, I didn't realize it would be, well, so intense!" "I can't believe what Alex did to that rabbit!" Or, "For sure, I'm going to lock the door next time I bathe." If their comments aren't all that revealing, they do make one point: Viewers feel the need to understand why the movie played beyond their expectations.

The same principle holds true for Viewer Nine, except that *Fatal Attraction* doesn't "rise" to the "standard" he anticipated. The ninth person claims a standard, although not one in danger of provoking enlightenment. He has an opportunity to creatively assess a movie that fails to meet his entertainment needs, and yet his comments suggest a shallow philosophy. Shallow viewers study a film's characters and story to produce (what else?) shallow critiques: "Disappointing, not enough blood." "Well, it wasn't realistic. No one takes a girl prisoner without doing something to her sexually." "I don't understand why they went on the roller coaster. I figured someone would fall or get pushed off, and they didn't even do that."

Finally, there's you. *Fatal Attraction* doesn't fill your bill either because the movie fails to produce a trustworthy ending. The other nine viewers may not understand your complaint, and you will not change their evaluations, but that's the nature of moviegoers. If they don't agree, okay, that's their business. Still, the ten of you together do not exhibit a simple declaration of personal taste.

The ten people who watched *Fatal Attraction* illustrate a relative frame of reference. Five people saw it, liked it, and contributed little that they did not find already self-contained in the film. But the remaining five viewers attempted in different ways to justify their viewing experience. They did so because their experience--the cinematic payoff--departed from what they had imagined the movie to be.

These variations do not suggest chaos via the personal taste approach. They indicate simply that individuals differ among themselves, and sometimes within themselves, in how they respond to a film.[8] Perhaps you feel in the mood to see a sexually teasing yet tasteful movie like *Pillow Talk* or *A Fish Called Wanda,* even though normally you shy from attending such films. You digress, for whatever reason, but you digress in a quirky departure from your viewing habits. You digress for escapism, or for a friend who persuades you to go, and not because your values have changed regarding the use of sex for comedy.

The viewer has a voice, however small, to proclaim a film's creative strength--or weakness--in presenting sexuality as an art of substance. The most resounding voice is, If you don't care for a film because of its shoddy treatment of sexuality-- spread the word. Believe me, if a number of moviegoers choose not to go, their missing patronage at the box office and the video store will send a chill through any filmmaker's heart.

Do filmmakers really have a heart? Well, it's a crass testimony to Hollywood's conscience, but the testimony still seems appropriate today. Fred Allen, a comedian during our country's "radio years," offered this telling summary of tinseltown: "You can put all the sincerity in Hollywood in a flea's navel and still have room for four caraway seeds and the heart of an agent" (Christy, 1986).

If Allen's proclamation echoes a bit harshly, just remember that someone must hold filmmakers accountable for how they portray sexuality as entertainment. Exquisite sexuality is a cinematic beauty to behold. Sexuality with a dash of mystery, a wave of imagination, a breath of sophistication. This kind of Oz is an Oz worth savoring, an Oz worth teaching to the younger generation.

We need teachers and we need guardians to man the gun mounts. Most of all...we need that tenth viewer.

Notes

1. Margaret Mitchell wrote the ending to *Gone With The Wind* first, then wrote various narratives that eventually led to the final chapter. As essayist Richard Harwell (1987, p. xxi) declared: "She had no intention of publishing any new book until she was satisfied that it was as well done as *Gone With The Wind*. Neither had she any intention of writing a sequel to GWTW. For her the story ended when Rhett left Scarlett. For what happened after that she, like Rhett, did not give a damn."

By contrast to Mitchell's solo performance as author, the screenplay for *Gone With The Wind* underwent revision at the hands of 17 writers (among them, F. Scott Fitzgerald; see Harwell, p. xx). Margaret Mitchell also held her own counsel as to who should play Rhett Butler--and it wasn't Clark Gable. Serious or not, her candidates included Maurice Chevalier, Vincent Price, and...Groucho Marx (Christy, 1991; Grant, 1982).

2. In Steven Spielberg's television movie, *Duel* (1971), a vicious truck driver wheels his ugly vehicle across country, seeking to make mincemeat of an innocent car driver (Dennis Weaver). The ABC Network powers demanded that the truck explode at the end. Spielberg, however, entertained a more innovative climax. He wanted the "villainous" truck, which hurtles over a cliff, to "die" slowly. Dying slowly included a low, agonizing wail--not unlike a lover's passionate moaning during the throes of intercourse--as the truck plunged downward. A close, camera scan of the truck's remains chronicles the following: A fan in the cab that still runs, a wheel that slowly spins down, and the final death murmurs of a dying monster. Spielberg almost didn't receive his chance, but the movie's producer, George Eckstein, convinced ABC executives to go with the slow-death ending (Crist, 1984, p. 360).

3. Studios also pant over happy endings--for monetary reasons. The Alfred Hitchcock film, *Suspicion* (1941), relies on the suspense of a husband who may or may not be attempting to kill his wife. Hitchcock wanted an ending that reveals the husband as the murderer, but the studio desired a happy finish. Hitchcock lost this round. Likewise, studio heads called for the film, *Days Of Wine And Roses* (1962), to end happily. Jack Lemmon and Lee Remick play a husband and wife caught up in demon rum, telling the harsh story of how alcohol ravages each life. Lemmon, in an interview, relates how they led the studio to believe a positive ending was planned, but actually filmed a sadder, more realistic conclusion. Lemmon then flew to Europe and prevented the studio from calling him to re-shoot the film's finale. The plan worked and *Days Of Wine And Roses* ends on a stronger note of cinematic reality, with Lemmon fighting to stay sober, and Remick refusing to make the effort.

4. Adultery denotes a legal term and invoked severe repercussions under Roman law. The husband, absolved of any requirements to remain faithful, could, if he desired, "terminate" the adulterer of his unfaithful wife. The wife's father, however, reserved the option to kill or not kill his daughter. Medieval canonists reworked the meaning of adultery, making the idea and the punishment more equitable between husband and wife. The canonists decided, for example, that adultery might involve any kind of sexual lust, including a husband demonstrating excessive desire to have sexual intercourse with his wife (Brundage, 1982, pp. 131-132).

Adultery, known more benignly as "extramarital relations," has never reflected a simple history, and is not simple today. If both husband and wife agree to outside entanglements, then we speak of "co-marital relations." Thus, the one-million dollar offer by Robert Redford to spend an evening with Demi Moore in *Indecent Proposal* (1993) indicates co-marital relations. It does so because Redford's offer carries the reluctant approval of Woody Harrelson, Demi's husband in the film. The problem for Demi Moore concerns less the fact that she loans her body for a price, and more the feelings that she believes she should have, but does not experience after the episode. Perceptively, Redford tells her, "You don't hate me. You *wish* you hated me."

Adultery demands that one spouse disapprove of the other spouse engaging in either an emotional or a sexual relationship outside of marriage. Beyond this requirement, infidelity proves quite murky. The marriage, for instance, need not be particularly troubled for either husband or wife to stray, as is the case for the husband (Michael Douglas) in *Fatal Attraction*. But the termination of an adulterous relationship, or of a marriage because of adultery, can lead to acts of revenge.

Journalist Wendy Dennis (1992, pp. 258-259) describes this story of a newlywed husband who knew a bitter secret: "...One woman reported that she attended a wedding reception where the guests were just digging into the fruit cocktail when the groom stood up to make his speech. After a few gracious welcoming words, he announced in a jocular way that he was 'going to leave now.' Expecting a punch line, the guests chuckled. Then they got it: 'I just want to let everyone know,' he went on, 'that for the last five months my wife has been screwing my best man.' After delivering his coup, he turned on his heel and walked out." No, not a character in a movie. Just someone with an exquisite sense of timing.

5. James Dearden, the writer of *Fatal Attraction*, initially conceived the idea and presented it in 1979 as a 42-minute British drama called *Diversion*. This earlier drama conveys a more muted portrayal of the characters, placing the husband at center stage as the transgressor. The story ends enigmatically with the woman making a phone call. The wife prepares to answer the phone...and that's all you see.

But the script and casting for *Fatal Attraction* pursued a bolder, melodramatic approach, creating more sympathy for Dan and less for Alex. The shift of sympathy from Dearden's original story occurs by transforming Alex into a ferociously obsessed mental case, just a bite away from the Wicked Witch of Oz (see Faludi, 1991, pp. 117-123; Thompson, 1992). A cottage industry of sorts has emerged because of the film. Feminists, in particular, dislike the "shrill" treatment given to Alex's personality. A characterization that, in effect, lets Dan off easier than he deserves, and presents Dan's wife, Beth, as the dutiful, traditional housewife (see Babener, 1992, for an introduction to eight articles on the film; and Smith, 1989, p. 32, for logical flaws imposed on Alex's character).

6. Interestingly, an item in *The Hollywood Reporter* (Hachem, 1987) notes that Japanese preview audiences preferred the suicide ending. The regular Japanese showing of *Fatal Attraction*, nonetheless, kept the bathroom scenario intact. But this particular scene provoked a complaint from another quarter. British director Michael Anderson contended that the violent "bathroom" sequence matched too closely a similar scene in an earlier suspense film, *The Naked Edge* (1961), starring Gary Cooper and Deborah Kerr. The director of *Fatal Attraction*, Adrian Lyne, denied the charge but admitted that one moment in the bathroom episode--the clearing of a fogged mirror to suddenly reveal Alex's presence--was inspired by a scene from *Closely Watched Trains*, a 1966 Czechoslovakia film (Grant, 1988). Ah, Hollywood.

7. True to form, Hollywood also pursues its favorite parlor game of churning out sequels. Imitations of a box-office success become a foregone practice because imitations represent good business sense. Capture at least a reasonable proportion of the audience that viewed the original product and you have more marketability for your film than do most filmmakers. One variation on *Fatal Attraction* involves *Body Chemistry* (1990), a film about a happily married couple--happy that is until the husband precipitates a raucous love affair with an unstable psychologist. Sound familiar? The acting, dialogue, and story of *Body Chemistry* are not dreadful, but neither does this movie express the artistry of *Fatal Attraction*'s better scenes.

8. Sometimes the response includes movie sex that "goes home" with the viewer. One survey of Human Sexuality students indicated that certain films facilitated sexual arousal and helped to initiate one or more sexual practices. Practices, the students attested, that probably would not have happened except for the movie. These sexual acts, listed according to their decreasing frequency of occurrence, included sexual intercourse, oral/genital contact, and, that old standby, masturbation (Wilson & Liedtke, 1984). Sharpest gender differences emerged when males favored the male fantasy *"10"* (1979), and females liked

the romanticism of *Endless Love* (1981). One student even became excited over Walt Disney's *Lady And The Tramp* (1955). So, you never know.

Appendix

Sir Alfred Hitchcock

Alfred Hitchcock directed his first movie in 1925 (*The Pleasure Garden*), and his final film in 1976 (*Family Plot*). These alpha and omega features encompass a span of 51 directorial years and 53 theatrical films, not to mention occasional directing stints on his television series, *Alfred Hitchcock Presents*.

He symbolizes the consummate professional, busy at creating a life's work that defined the genre of suspense, and spanned the spectrum from witty romance to dark comedy. Some films, of course, do not attain the entertainment level expected of Hitchcock. But the exhaustive, risky business of masterminding 53 films in 51 years represents a remarkable achievement in artistic longevity.

And "masterminding" seems an apt expression. If you ask "Who directs the director?", you really ask what "wherewithal" directors use to guide their decisions. What muse do directors tap to guide a movie through treacherous waters? Posing this question invites a controversy about the director's power to shape a film. This power concerns **auteur theory**, or the assumption that directors command a singular status by dominating the creative process (Thomson, 1977, p. 230).

Indeed, Hitchcock personifies auteur theory since he desired to control every facet as the pre-eminent author of a "Hitchcock" movie. For him, the challenge involved solving technical problems scene by scene before shooting a foot of film. Camera angles, camera movements, the positioning of actors--he orchestrated these tasks with loving care. The actual filming, by contrast, presented less a challenge, and, for Hitchcock, sometimes marked a boring aftermath to the creative effort.

He seldom offered much direction to his performers. Hitchcock accepted suggestions, as long as they fell within his purview of the movie. He agreed, for example, with Anthony Perkins in *Psycho* (1960) to have quirky Norman Bates eat candy as Norman watched Janet Leigh's car (and Leigh) sink out of sight in a pond (Rebello, 1990, p. 88). But Hitchcock, who (perhaps facetiously) referred to actors as "cattle," left performers mostly to their own motivation.[1]

Opponents of the auteur attitude, however, contend that a movie remains a collaborative project (Spoto, 1983, p. 108). The director, even one like Hitchcock, can reach only so far in revising a script, inspiring actors to act, and coordinating the artistry of so many parties.

Alfred Hitchcock, nonetheless, enjoyed sufficient creative control over his body of films to develop cinematic ideas about a number of fundamental issues, including sexuality. Because of his work ethic, it becomes possible to examine the artist's changing thoughts regarding gender, love, sex, and other matters that comprise sexuality's entourage.

More important, these changing thoughts derive primarily from a single orientation, namely, the suspense film. Hitchcock argued that his challenge was to make viewers nervous and tense, not for a quick surprise, but for the duration of the movie (Kapsis, 1992, pp. 23-24). Despite this seemingly elementary ambition, the gift to carry an audience through such extended tension requires a rare talent--and rarer still to do so film after film.

The Master's career would have mustered a mere footnote had he churned out only minor variations of his suspense motif. Instead, Hitchcock mined the suspense lode for a diversity of messages and moods (Kapsis, 1992, p. 74). Such diversity, in particular, does not permit a simple take on his treatment of cinematic sexuality and its attendant issues.

The thesis of this appendix concerns Hitchcock's use of secrecy to influence sexuality, and the presence of sexuality to induce secrecy. **Secrecy** and **sexuality** denote a two-way relationship, and, in Hitchcock's hands, the dual phenomena combine dynamically to foster an array of apparently contradictory interpretations.

These interpretations attain clarity, however, when they are examined according to Hitchcock's **mood** in telling a story. Secrecy, for instance, plays a minimal role in his stories of lighthearted romance, such as *The Thirty-nine Steps* (1935). Deception and duplicity contribute to the action, to move everyone from "A" to "B," but these secrets exert little effect on the eventual disposition of the lovers and their romantic entanglements.

Secrecy applied to more serious endeavors, nevertheless, plays an increasingly complicated role in the characters' outcome. Graver considerations of sexuality are afoot, and what a character does or doesn't know can prove crucial in determining that individual's resourcefulness to repair a troubled relationship.

Secrecy and sexuality, therefore, depend on Hitchcock's conception of the story's mood, and what the story requires in cinematic logic. Hitchcock exercises his own peculiar designs on these conditions of secrecy and sexuality--designs that call for a special classification of his films.

What we learn of Hitchcockian sexuality on screen, still, does not mean that we know Hitchcock's thoughts about the subject off screen (see Leitch, 1991, Chapter One). Certainly the person and the professional are not wholly independent personalities. But Hitchcock understood the value of showmanship, not to mention the contrivances of exaggeration and implausibility that fuel entertainment. He understood how to create suspense, and how to heighten this suspense through the lure of appealing sexualities.

Suppose, then, we pursue Hitchcock's views on secrecy and

sexuality as entertainment by creating not one, but three Hitchcocks. Each persona will offer a perspective on sexuality that reflects the Master's state of mind concerning a particular cluster of films.

Hitchcock, The Romanticist

"The Thirty-nine Steps." Sounds ominous, and it is. "The Thirty-nine Steps" represents an organization of spies who want to steal this air force secret, and, um, you know, it's about espionage.

What it's really about, though, is romance. *The Thirty-nine Steps* (1935) concerns the feisty relationship between two independent lovers. They go through considerable discomfort to realize their mutual attraction: the kind of discomfort that only a keen and mischievous mind could concoct. The mind belongs to Hitchcock and the challenge consists of interpreting his allusions as sexual allusions. *The Thirty-nine Steps* plays as a blithe romance, punctuated by episodes of sexual tension, and, of lesser importance, encounters concerning life or death.

We know little of Richard Hannay (Robert Donat), our Hitchcockian hero, except that he's Canadian and in London on business. Hannay enters a rowdy music hall for an evening of relaxation. His relaxation ends abruptly when the stage attraction, a mnemonist called Mr. Memory (Wylie Watson), fails to control a rambunctious audience and a melee ensues. Two shots are fired and people stampede for the exits, among them Hannay, who shepherds a woman to safety. Free of the crowd, the woman looks up and asks, point blank, if she can go home with him. Momentarily put off, but only momentarily, Hannay replies, "Well, it's your funeral."

His reply suggests that he's a bachelor, and that he does not shock easily. We do not know, however, whether Hannay expects a one-night stand and views the woman's request as a sexual windfall--or whether he's simply a very accommodating man. We fail to discover much about this suave gentleman, other than to learn that he can behave very resourcefully (Rothman, 1982, p. 118). Resourcefulness, truly, becomes a paramount trait in Hitchcock's world of romantic adventure.

The woman, known only as Annabella Smith (Lucie Mannheim), does not last long.[2] While both are asleep in separate rooms (which means that Hannay chose to be accommodating), Annabella is knifed in the back. She staggers to Hannay and collapses, giving him a vivid view of the knife. Thus, his expression, "Well, it's your funeral," constitutes a foreshadowing, unfortunately a literal one for Annabella. Why the perpetrators did not also dispatch Hannay as he slept denotes one of those little implausibilities that Hitchcock permits. Cinematic logic does not require common sense to be rigorously observed. Suffice to say, having received some clues from the late Annabella, Hannay needs to resolve the mystery of the thirty-nine steps.

First, he must find a way to avoid the two assassins awaiting him outside. Hannay meets a milkman and asks for the man's white coat as a disguise. Interestingly, the milkman refuses to believe Hannay when told the truth, so Hannay segues into a fabrication about a married lady that he's "just visited" and now seeks to avoid her husband. **This** story the milkman understands, and Hannay is on his way.

Circumstances find him on a train for Scotland, desperately seeking sanctuary as the police close in. By happy, cinematic coincidence, Hannay selects the compartment of an attractive blonde, Pamela (Madeleine Carroll). Madeleine Carroll inaugurates the "cool blonde," a favorite Hitchcockian image that recurs in his later films. Hitchcock wanted an elegant, classy lady who **understated** her sex appeal, because the understatement, for him, made her sexuality more compelling (Spoto, 1983, p. 147). He held little relish for women like Marilyn Monroe who exaggerated their womanly wiles (can you imagine, then, what Hitchcock would have thought of Madonna?).

Hannay rushes in, mumbles "darling," and gives Pamela an impassioned kiss as the police pass by. Now Pamela, upon recovering from the initial shock of this amorous intrusion, can do a number of things. She can pull back and scream, but doesn't. She can bite his lip in anger, but doesn't. She can force him away and slap his silly face, but doesn't. Instead, as the camera lovingly records, she opens her eyes wide, then closes her eyes, and finally, in a state of vulnerability, drops her reading classes. Pamela allows Hannay to give her a long, wet kiss. Only after the kiss does she alert the police to this handsome stranger, perhaps as much out of irritation with herself over the ecstasy experienced, as to her sense of duty. But, not to worry. Cinematic logic dictates that she and the handsome stranger shall meet again.

Hannay has become an old hand at eluding the police, and does so once more. Searching for a professor living in Scotland, he stops at a crofter's house to spend the night. Hitchcock, always preferring the visual to tell a tale, shows by reference to the eyes that (1) Hannay sees a story on Annabella's murder in the crofter's paper; (2) the crofter's wife, Margaret (Peggy Ashcroft), sees what he sees and benevolently understands; and (3) the crofter sees both of them, misinterpreting their eye contact as signals for a tryst behind his selfish, greedy back.

The Thirty-nine Steps enters its darkest period with this strange triangle. The police, patrolling the Scottish moors for Hannay, are pressing in again. Hannay, forced to reveal his story to the crofter, pays the man to keep his presence a secret. But Margaret does not trust her husband, and for good reason. She quickly gives Hannay her husband's overcoat and urges him to leave.

Hannay, concerned for her safety, is told by Margaret that she will only be "prayed at," a convenient lie. Her husband will do worse to her. Margaret's story becomes the movie's true tragedy: A sad, sensitive woman who has left a town that she loves to spend her life in a desolate countryside, with a man who thinks of her as a possession. A marriage, one assumes, that surely did not arise through any voluntary choice by Margaret. She gives Hannay a slim chance to continue his freedom, a chance denied her (Spoto, 1992, p. 45).

Hannay, barely a few breaths ahead of his pursuers, locates the house of a Professor Jordon (Godfrey Tearle). The Professor amicably arranges to deceive the police, but he does so with amusement because Jordon is the villain, not the friend that Hannay believes. Jordon's magic moment comes,

Hitchcockian style, when Hannay makes reference to a mastermind who has his little finger missing (having received this clue from Annabella):

We see, and see that Hannay does not see, the Professor give a momentary start on the words, "I believe she was coming to see you about some Air Ministry secrets. She was killed by a foreign agent who's interested too." Hannay sips his drink as the Professor turns to face him. "Did she tell you what the foreign agent looked like?" "Wasn't time. Oh, there was one thing. Part of his little finger was missing." "Which one?" "This one, I think," Hannay says, holding up his hand. "Sure it wasn't...this one?" (Rothman, 1982, p. 144).

And the Professor, gleefully we suspect, shows his missing finger to Hannay. Film experts have likened the missing finger to a pair of devilish horns, to cloven hooves, and even to a symbol of castration (Rohmer & Chabrol, 1988, p. 42; Wood, 1989, p. 275). The point, for us, is that Hannay faces a man who outclasses him, a man who almost makes our adventurer pay the ultimate price. After toying with Hannay by offering him a chance to commit suicide, the Professor fires his weapon and hits Hannay in the chest. End of Hannay? No, not quite. But, yes, end of Part One.

Part Two opens with Hannay surviving his apparent demise through the physical help of a hymnal, the bullet having struck the hymnal in his overcoat. The crofter's overcoat, actually, which means the crofter indirectly saves a life that his tormented soul probably cannot rejoice over.

Hannay, as his custom, eludes the police and finds himself in a meeting hall. He's mistakenly taken to the podium as a political candidate who, naturally, must speak his political mind...on what? Hannay does not know. Surrounded by the Professor's henchman, he nonetheless gives an impassioned speech to a cheering audience, declaring the need to stop neighbors from waging war on neighbors, a message close to the Canadian's heart. Hannay's captured, however, with Pamela there to identify him and both are whisked away, ostensibly to the police station, but in reality to the Professor's lair.

Handcuffed, Pamela and Hannay escape from the

Professor's escorts and make their way to an inn for the night. Pamela, still disbelieving and quite reluctant, allows Hannay to pose them as newlyweds who have eloped.[3] The scene in their room, with Pamela grudgingly yet provocatively removing her wet stockings--as Hannay's handcuffed hand follows her movements--establishes a physical intimacy that illuminates the male's sexual fantasy. Hannay, in charge as he has been since their escape, realizes a sense of lecherous pleasure at Pamela's feminine plight. He accommodates her, as he did Annabella, yet keeps Pamela on edge with insinuations of himself as a murderer.

The male game sounds dominating, but Pamela reaches some inward conclusion about Hannay, one of which concerns the likelihood that he's not a murderer. She finds herself dependent on him since he knows more about the adventure, yet Pamela holds her own in the verbal exchanges. William Rothman (1982, p. 133), who offers the most detailed analysis of *The Thirty-nine Steps*, suggests that Hannay's skills at improvisation appear checked when he meets a woman important to his freedom. Pamela, for instance, doesn't wholly succumb to his charms in their earlier encounter. And, later, Hannay requires the generous help of Margaret, the crofter's wife, to flee the police. Pamela, therefore, characterizes more of a match for Hannay than their circumstances indicate.

Nothing happens physically, of course. They share a bed, and subsequently, as Hannay sleeps, Pamela slips out of the handcuffs. Her attraction to him has strengthened more than she admits. Still, Pamela moves to alert the two men who have come searching for them, only to realize just in time that Hannay speaks the truth. She returns to the room, covers Hannay with a blanket, then curls up on the settee to sleep. Chilled, she has second thoughts about how comfortable Hannay deserves to be, and cheerfully pulls the blanket from him to cover herself.

Hannay awakens, gratified at Pamela's trust in him. Their affection, nurtured ambivalently and stifled during the ordeal, now appears unleashed. The unleashing leads to their first "post-handcuff" argument, when Hannay learns that the men have come and gone. He fusses at her about the loss of valuable time, thereby asserting his dominance and her dependence once more, this time without the handcuffs.

They return to London, knowing from what Pamela overheard as she eavesdropped on the two henchman that the Professor will be at the London Palladium. The Palladium represents another Hitchcockian fondness for the swell finish, using an elaborate setting to create suspense and achieve a grand finale. At the Palladium, in a return to the music hall atmosphere that began the adventure, Richard Hannay learns of the thirty-nine steps. He discovers that Mr. Memory, on stage again, embodies the crucial link: It is Mr. Memory who commits the secret to his admirable gray cells, and it is Jordon who plans to take Memory out of the country and extract the secret from those gray cells.

Needless to say, Hannay wins, and Jordon, true to his castration curse, loses his freedom, together with the mastery that he wielded so effectively. Mr. Memory, in due payment for his complicity, is fatally wounded by Jordon, but sets his earthly record straight by revealing the secret to erase his debts, and, expeditiously, to clear Hannay of suspicion.

The camera pulls back from Mr. Memory and focuses behind Richard and Pamela. Two hands slowly intertwine-- with a pair of handcuffs dangling from one--a relic of previous bondage that proves essential no longer. Pamela and Richard effect a voluntary meeting of intentions: They inspire a bonding through their earlier forced intimacy that, under duress, led to a quickening of the lovers' attraction for each other (Brill, 1988, p. 64).

The implausibility of their meeting via Hannay's improvised kiss in the train compartment, their reunion in the meeting hall, their volatile feelings of attachment on a chain (the handcuffs), their "wedding night" that became only partly a pretense at the inn, and their final grasp of resolved bliss at the Palladium--these cinematic instances of sexual tension and ultimate relief comprise the ingredients that define Hitchcock, the Romanticist.

Indeed, what Richard and Pamela can do as an encore to rival their arousing adventure forecasts a mystery that goes beyond fair play in Hitchcock's world. But considering the friction that marriage creates in Hitchcock's world--as illustrated by Margaret and her crofter husband--Pamela and Richard may yet confront their greatest challenge.[4]

The Thirty-nine Steps introduces a mosaic of Hitchcockian devices to dramatize the Director's Romanticist views. First, a romantic and suspenseful vehicle must motivate its players with a very secret secret, referred to by Hitchcock as a **MacGuffin** (Spoto, 1992, p. xi). A MacGuffin functions to drive the characters forward and keep the plot moving, although a MacGuffin, as such, exercises little relevance to the movie's theme.

What **is** relevant are not the secrets, which serve as accessories to keep everyone jumping, but the lovers' embroilments designed to test their **trust** and **mutual attraction.** Mr. Memory controls the MacGuffin in *The Thirty-nine Steps*, yet the nature of the secret matters little-- only that the information be of reasonable importance to justify all the shenanigans regarding its revelation. The main thrust concerns the lovers' attempt to sustain an uneasy trust, and to deduce which role they must play that will get them past the next crisis (Leitch, 1992, pp. 88-89).

A second Hitchcockian device involves the hero's **resourcefulness.** Hannay's an innocent regarding espionage, but he clearly can handle himself, even under the extraordi- nary circumstances of repeatedly escaping his pursuers. Naturally a little luck helps, such as having that hymnal in the right spot to stop the Professor's bullet. Mostly, though, Hannay makes more of his slim chances to succeed than one has any right to expect in reality. Still, it's not reality, is it? It's cinematic reality at our disposal, and, cinematically, Richard Hannay epitomizes the admirable romantic hero: resilient, quick-thinking, daring...not to mention that he sports the charisma of a ladies' man who has been around the block a few times.

The third device from Hitchcock's revision of the Romance tradition dwells on Hannay's masculine appeal and the feminine wonderments of his opposite-sex nemesis, Pamela. The lovers conjure up a **prickly relationship** because, to the

Romantic Hitchcock, that relationship holds the greatest promise for humor and interest. Two people, thrown together in an attraction/repulsion partnership, who use intimacy and bickering to surmount their status as strangers and nurture a windblown affection.

The idea of slipping some pepper into the broth becomes a cinematic recipe that Hitchcock uses repeatedly in his characterizations of romantics at peril. He presents romantics in danger from outside forces, as they work to bond themselves through an intimacy of sheer survival. But the Master also explores romantics who wrestle with inside forces. Hitchcockian lovers find these inner conflicts over attraction and repulsion less comprehensible and more disturbing than outward perils, yet quite beguiling. That's Romanticism, Hitchcock style.

Finally, given these elements of suspense, where's the violence? Customarily, Hitchcock presents **violence** as a tool rather than an obsession. A tool used discreetly in his Romanticist philosophy to provide (1) a sense of terror, as does the knife in Annabella; (2) a sense of irony, as by Hannay's good fortune with the crofter's hymnal; or (3) a sense of vindication, as with Mr. Memory's disclosure of the thirty-nine steps before his demise.

Romantically, violence can't be too intrusive and risk darkening the mood of two lovers on a sprint for their lives.[5] The bleakest moments of *The Thirty-nine Steps* concerns the crofter and his wife, Margaret. Hitchcock indicates Margaret's claustrophobic hell through her unhappy marriage, and her confinement to a runty cottage set in the expansive middle of nowhere. But Hitchcock does not dwell on Margaret's plight. She's a brief and transient sadness in the film's grander purpose to enthrall viewers romantically. Indeed, remembering Margaret and her travails makes the adventurous attachment of Richard and Pamela appear all the more precious.

Now consider this theme: The hero is innocent of a murder, he must clear himself of suspicion, and he needs the help of a reluctant but admirable heroine to bring the real murderer to justice. Sound familiar? No, not a remake of *The Thirty-nine Steps*, but an updated revision of a tried and true Hitchcock formula, called *North By Northwest* (1959).

Roger Thornhill (Cary Grant) appears the successful advertising executive, complete with all the material trappings of a man on the move. We first see him walking down a hall dictating to his secretary, who nervously attempts to match his pace. Thornhill seems so pressed for time, he must have his secretary travel with him to his first destination.

What we also learn, however, is that all does not fare well in Rogerland. Thornhill likes his booze a little too much, has two failed marriages, and finds himself somewhat intimidated, if affectionately so, by his mother. Even his full name, Roger O. Thornhill, reflects the man's modus operandi. The "O" stands for "nothing" and his initials spell out R. O. T., characterizing the busy male who traipses through a round of drinks and appropriate chit-chat, then makes appointments for more of the same.

He relies on a civilized savvy and the drive of a hard-nosed businessman to find satisfaction in his life. But it's a life leading nowhere, not in any sense liberating him to search for the kind of rewarding relationship that he needs. (The business of "going nowhere" will appear in other Hitchcock films, often expressed through a circular or a **spiraling effect**.) Roger Thornhill, to put it nicely, is heading down the tubes. Thornhill's "women," moreover, have become affairs that he reduces to "reminders," asking his secretary to send them candy and a trite thank-you message.

Consequently, what happens to unsettle the old Roger Thornhill, ten minutes into the movie's plot, concerns the real heart of *North By Northwest*. He finds himself mistaken for a government spy, George Kaplan; he finds himself hustled away by two men to an unknown destination; he finds himself stripped of his luxuries, conveniences, and routines (Wood, 1989, p. 134). Roger Thornhill, in short, finds himself removed from his state of inertia, forced to clear his reputation (such as it is), and compelled to practice the fine art of staying alive.

Unlike Richard Hannay, Roger Thornhill comes to us a

flawed character. Not tragically flawed, since *North By Northwest* plays as a comedy adventure, but Roger's hardly the staunch stuff of heroes. He is, nonetheless, Cary Grant, and Grant's image cannot help but provide reassurance that Roger Thornhill will persevere. Grant may represent the perfect Hitchcockian hero because he conceals a silent nature that keeps you, the viewer, from fully comprehending his intentions (Rothman, 1982, p. 122; Spoto, 1983, p. 408).

This silent nature shows its darker side in the auction scene. Roger meets Eve Kendall (Eva Marie Saint) on a train as he flees from the police, and, as happens in Hitchcock's stories, male and female spark an instant attraction. Later, Roger returns from a near-death experience, courtesy of a crop-dusting plane. The flatland episode with the plane monopolizes our attention, portraying Thornhill as no more out of his civilized element than in this wide-open countryside (Wood, 1989, p. 137).

The flatland episode, however, becomes more important for what it subsequently causes Roger to experience: The first shadow of distrust concerning Eve because she sent him to this trap. Eve betrayed him, a stigma of treachery that females named Eve appear stuck with through eternity (Leitch, 1991, p. 88). Therefore in the auction setting, risking a confrontation with the master villain, Vandamm (James Mason) and his gay assistant, Leonard (Martin Landau), Roger launches a scathing verbal assault on Eve.[6]

He speaks bitterly, vehemently, with little regard for his safety. What Thornhill does not suspect is that Eve cares for him. What he also does not know is that she's a government agent for a man called the Professor (Leo G. Carroll). Eve has her own checkered past. Impulsively, she fell in love with Vandamm, an impulse that led her to still another disillusion. Now, seeking to accomplish something with her life, she agrees to spy on him. (What do you think? Does Eve qualify as a "prostitute," the value judgment made against Annabella Smith in *The Thirty-nine Steps*?)

Humor keeps *North By Northwest* from sagging into melodrama.[7] And humor, used as a weapon, can rival a physical attack in its spirit of viciousness. Roger, denouncing

Eve at the auction, notes that everyone's been in her hotel room (a line drawing an "oooh" from college students when they viewed the film in a movie course).

Roger, however, feels the sting when he, his mother (Clara, played by Jessie Royce Landis), two of Vandamm's killers, and other passengers are in an elevator. Roger signals to his mother that the two men are the same individuals who tried to dispatch him the previous evening in a drunk-driving "accident." Clara, still skeptical, looks at the two men and asks them pointedly, "You gentlemen aren't **really** trying to kill my son, are you?" To cover their complicity, the two men begin to laugh, Clara begins to laugh, and the other passengers join in. Everybody's laughing except one person. The elevator incident is telling because it shows Roger Thornhill in his most ineffectual position. Even Clara believes her son's reputation as a rummy before she will accept the truth about his mistaken identity.

Most of the humor remains sprightly, a jousting of wits. Roger's "frame" in the United Nations building of apparently killing a delegate arises as one example. The mistake plays so ludicrously--including a photograph of him holding the knife--that it seems quite in keeping with his run of bad luck (Brill, 1989, p. 18).

The jousting continues with sexual teasing between Roger and Eve on the train. Their amorous dialogue permits cinematic logic to create an abbreviated courtship, and, *vite*, a discreet reunion in Eve's compartment. There, the lovers inject fanciful references to murder as a Hitchcockian prelude for kissing and caressing. Humor greases the wheels to keep the implausibilities flashing by, and to remind us that the real search does not concern government secrets--our MacGuffin--but the resolution of two lovers who truly need each other.

Ultimately the wheels lead to Mount Rushmore, and the lovers' final test. Leonard learns of Eve's deception, leaving her expendable in Vandamm's eyes. The rehabilitated Roger, far removed from the old Roger, intervenes to rescue Eve and they dash for safety in and around the four stone faces. Viewers may interpret the steadfastness of Mount Rushmore as a hallmark of Roger Thornhill's progress to stability (Wood,

1988, p. 138). Compared to the shallow personality who ran in circles at the story's beginning, Roger constitutes a more forceful, concentrated personality at the monument.[8]

Roger and Eve triumph and Vandamm fails, of course. No news there since a comedy adventure builds to an expectant Oz regarding these finishing touches. What intrigues, however, is the kind of love that succeeds in a Hitchcock caper, and the kind of love that destroys itself. Vandamm's love of Eve proves destructive, generated by an egotistical and possessive man who cannot change, as Roger has changed (the auction scene depicts Vandamm's hand curling about Eve's neck, displaying a gesture of danger and ownership).[9]

Vandamm's affection for Eve proves neither wholesome nor lasting. His love, instead, hobbles along under the constraints of logic. Vandamm expresses pain when he learns of Eve's betrayal, but he hurts, not at losing her, but in having his ego bruised through her deception. Vandamm prepares himself quickly to arrange her death, without thought of doing the illogical and attempting to salvage the relationship.

And Roger's love? A quite different passion from Vandamm's selfish affections, lacking logic and born of implausibility (Brill, 1988, p. 20). Roger, who indeed found himself betrayed by Eve, forgives this transgression and risks all to save her--knowing that by saving her, he saves himself. The key note is forgiveness, a sentiment that Vandamm cannot produce. Eve sent Roger into the teeth of considerable harm. Once he learns of her secret as a government agent, Roger rallies to her cause. Eve's hidden agenda surfaces as the only secret in *North By Northwest* that carries a decisive influence on the lovers' fate. Other secrets, such as the fictional spy, George Kaplan, affect Thornhill's movements but do not change his character.

Roger's hands deliver Eve from sure death on Mount Rushmore, and in a clever segue to the next scene, pull her up to a train berth for a new life (Hitchcock often uses hands to reflect intimacy). The one symbol Hitchcock admits to, a closing shot of the train going into a tunnel, appears an unnecessary reminder that the lovers have "earned" their happiness, and all the sex that comes with it. We already

understand that Roger and Eve are more sexually fulfilled
together than either could hope to realize apart.

So, the romantic Hitchcock begins to materialize. His
cinematic faith resides in a quick love, a saving love. He
promptly establishes a sterling connection between female and
male, an emotional awakening, which, when absent, leaves
each lover wanting. Roger, for instance, has embarked on his
share of affairs. But Eve's mystique, the secrecy of her
sexuality in effect, draws him to her. Remember that
sexuality can induce secrecy, and thus can inspire the curiosity
of a searcher like Roger Thornhill to desire to know more.
Secrets abound in Hitchcock's romantic world, but these
subterfuges usually bear on external events rather than
influence character development.

The Thirty-nine Steps and *North By Northwest* denote only
two films, but I invite you to examine other romantic efforts
by Hitchcock and determine for yourself if his Romanticism
does not rule the day over any and all obstacles. Consider, for
example, *Young And Innocent* (1937), *The Lady Vanishes*
(1938), *Foreign Correspondent* (1940), *Saboteur* (1942), *To
Catch A Thief* (1955), and *The Trouble With Harry* (1956).
These films include innocent and often inexperienced parties
drawn into risky, well-planned schemes. They survive
because their love becomes too precious to forego, allowing
them to beat odds that, realistically, do not hold much hope
for victory.

The Hitchcockian devices previously described come into
play, leaving no doubt that the lovers will prevail. In one
story, for instance, the heroine's father surfaces as the villain.
Logically, such a rude surprise should damage or at least strain
a lovers' relationship. But for Hitchcock the Romanticist, no
secret can prove so ugly, so tragic, or so personal as to
jeopardize the lovers' mission.

Hitchcock, The Bittersweet Philosopher

Secrecy claims only a passing fancy for the Romantic Hitchcock, but assumes a prominent role, a darker role, in other Hitchcock films. Romance stutters, stumbles, and turns a shade gray. The lovers struggle more distressingly with distrust and misunderstanding. Hitchcock's tremulous high-wire act, this time without a net, offers viewers less security as to how hero and heroine will fare. Emphasis shifts from chases and other bits of derring-do to a more intense character study. Something's still rotten in Denmark, but it takes longer to detect the Rotter's villainous intentions.

Secrecy concerns the disposition of information and feelings that, in Hitchcock's bittersweet mood, influence characters and story. Concealment assumes practical value because you dare not reveal everything you feel about someone else. Secrecy permits sanctuary in this regard. But secrets, especially for entertainment, find common exploitation through our fascination with negative happenings.

This fascination draws us into a domain that bars intrusion. Part of the enchantment concerns trying to discover what we shouldn't know. Or, conversely, trying to reduce the uncertainty of what we wish to know. Either way, secrecy fascinates and keeps us searching. The secret holder, by contrast, experiences a sense of power, or the **illusion of power,** to control others (Appelbaum, 1978). Now, make this secret dangerous to the concealer if revealed, and dangerous to others if not revealed, and you have the makings of drama.

The drama becomes more Hitchcockian when the secrecy depends on sexuality. Imagine a beautiful woman who knows a Nazi spy, a spy who finds himself lured to her sensual presence. She pursues a promiscuous and aimless existence, indeed a rebellious lifestyle to express anger at her father for turning against his country. Add a government agent who finds her appealing, yet fights to squelch these feelings because of his contempt for her conduct. Put both the woman and the man in a position to learn the covert doings of the spy, and you have a volatile triangle in which secrecy rides uneasy on the head of each party. You have a time bomb ticking

away, made more precarious by sexual tensions. And, amid
the glamour of Rio de Janeiro, you have a dandy film of
suspense called *Notorious* (1946).

Alicia Huberman (Ingrid Bergman) seeks to drink and
party herself ad nauseam to forget her traitorous father. She
acts "sexy," although we suspect that the act is really an act.
Later, when she reverts to her more stable personality, Alicia
conveys a different sexuality. The distinction between "sexy"
and "sexual" is the difference between enforced frolicking and
the spontaneous, natural behavior that reflects Alicia's true
femininity (Wood, 1989, p. 322).

Devlin (Cary Grant), a government agent, recognizes her
true appeal, but wrestles with his own torment. This conflict,
never fully explained, keeps him from revealing his genuine
affection for her (a telling secret). Alicia, more sensitive to
their relationship than Devlin, comments at one point, "Why
don't you believe in me, Dev--just a little?" She feels a sense
of communion with him, and searches for an opening to
undermine his detachment.

Devlin, perhaps to fend off his fear of becoming
vulnerable, retreats to the unsympathetic mission of exercising
control. When Alicia, smashed to the four winds, decides to
go for a drive, Devlin places a scarf around her bare midriff
to "keep her warm." The scarf and later a rented necklace
appear to symbolize this control (Wood, 1989, p. 323;
Modleski, 1988, p. 68). She's a hired hand and claims no
power except that granted to her by the government. Males
pull her strings because males hold the power. Their
monopoly, although not necessarily their sense of the human
condition, puts them in charge of the war and everything else
of consequence. Notably, when either the U.S. Agency or the
Nazis hold their high-level meetings, women have no place at
the table (Wood, 1989, p. 324).

This patriarchal picture is not so simple, however. Alicia,
the centerpiece of *Notorious*, holds the key--literally and
figuratively--to what males desire of her. The "literal" key
leads to Alexander Sebastian's (Claude Rains) wine cellar and
the bottling of uranium ore, Hitchcock's MacGuffin. The
"figurative" key concentrates on Alicia's pained ability to play

her role well, including a reluctant agreement to marry the spy, Alexander, whom she does not love. This "agreement" carries a whiff of sexual enslavement, not unlike the expedient bondage that surrounded Annabella Smith in *The Thirty-nine Steps* and Eve Kendall in *North By Northwest* (Spoto, 1992, pp. 147-148). Alicia's sexuality helps her to maintain the government's secret intentions from Sebastian (remember that secrecy and sexuality can enact a mutual relationship).

Secrecy creates misunderstanding between Alicia and Devlin; it generates suspicion between Alicia and Sebastian; and provokes sexual jealousy for Devlin and Sebastian. The business of harboring these secrets, in short, does not make for a happy triangle of secret bearers. Devlin's more responsible for the misunderstanding than Alicia. She's trying to tell him she's unhappy, but he seems more interested in convincing himself that Alicia is, verily, a fallen woman. If Devlin can persuade himself of this low-brow image, perhaps he can pull away and forget her.

Sebastian, one of the more sympathetic villains on the scene, truly wants his marriage with Alicia to succeed. Indeed, it had better succeed because he has defied a formidable figure called m-o-t-h-e-r (Mme. Sebastian, played by Leopoldine Konstantin) to bring a rival into the home. Mme. Sebastian practices the high art of "sinister niceness" toward Alicia, leaving neither woman with any illusions about a lasting friendship.

Devlin and Sebastian observe each other guardedly. Both men wonder who bests whom in the male game of sexual competition. Alicia's willingness to marry Sebastian persuades Devlin, for a time, that his sardonic view of Alicia's womanhood is correct. Sebastian, however, continues to seek reassurance from Alicia that she really has no interest in his competitor. Sebastian, you see, relies on logic. Compared to Devlin, he's older, shorter, less handsome, and he's got mother hovering in the wings. Something's amiss here, but Sebastian finds himself too enamored of Alicia to face the prospects of overturning his male fantasy.

Sadly, Alexander's fantasy flies apart at a party when he happens upon Devlin and Alicia in a passionate embrace.

Their embrace, only partly pretense, occurs to divert Sebastian from the fact that Devlin and Alicia were in the wine cellar discovering the MacGuffin. The diversion does not hold. Sebastian snoops about and uncovers their discovery. His love, as with the "romantic affection" of other Hitchcock villains, vanishes quickly, leaving him a cold, ruthless adversary, desiring revenge.

Mme. Sebastian resumes her dominance. A pathetic scene plays out when Sebastian, realizing the danger of knowing Alicia's secret, calls softly to awaken his mother. He sits dejectedly in her bedroom, head bowed, again at her beck and call. She has won. She, not Alexander, engineers a plan to kill Alicia slowly by poison. A plan designed to hide Sebastian's mistake from his Nazi peers.

Alicia's dying, but doesn't know it. Instead of telling Devlin that she feels ill, his apparently callous attitude prompts her to lie and tell him of a hangover. A hangover, he understands. She returns the scarf, her way of telling him goodbye. The scarf serves a fragile connection, a razor-thin semblance of continuity between the anguished lovers. Her return of the scarf puzzles Devlin, who surely needs to decipher a few quick answers.

Weak and disoriented, Alicia realizes what the Sebastians are doing to her. She gazes dreamily at them as they turn from figures to shadows, and from two shadows to one: Sebastian and his mother merge as her common enemy. She knows their lethal secret, yet she also fathoms that her revelation comes too late. She's at their mercy, and going fast.

The lover who loves illogically, who takes chances because of love, this impassioned soul is the figure who wins in Hitchcock's world of romantic conflict. Roger Thornhill managed such a win in the Romantic Hitchcock, and Devlin does so in the Bittersweet Hitchcock. Concerned about Alicia and moving against the judgment of his superior, Devlin seeks Alicia at Sebastian's house. He risks his life to save her, an ordeal that he must face to pay for his insensitivity to her needs (Wood, 1989, p. 326). Devlin has suffered too, though a suffering not clear to us except that it seems to occur of his own bullheadedness (Modleski, 1988, p. 70).

The final sequence sees Devlin, his arm around Alicia, escorting her down the winding staircase of the Sebastian home.[10] Alexander and his mother try to intervene, but Devlin has one trump to play--another secret. Sebastian's suspicious lot of Nazi corroborators gaze at the four individuals descending the stairs. Devlin tells Sebastian that he will inform Sebastian's "friends" of the truth about Alicia. Mme. Sebastian, realizing more quickly the danger to their existence, prods her son to tell a lie, to say that Alicia is simply being taken to the hospital.

Sebastian feebly offers the lame excuse, so feebly that you wonder why he doesn't see the transparency of his behavior. Devlin and Alicia climb in the car, but Devlin reaches over and locks the door, shutting Sebastian out. Sebastian's lie depends on his going to the hospital. But Devlin denies him that excuse, and both mother and son find their fate determined.

Devlin and Alicia drive away. The Nazi leader waits at the top step, looking down at a beaten man. Impotent as a husband, as a son, and, now, as a Nazi. Ominously, the leader asks Sebastian to come inside. You see and hear the massive door close. (Sigh.) End of Sebastian. End of the final secret. End of movie.

Secrecy fascinates. It fascinates because of the power that we assume concealment gives us. When the secret's usefulness depends on sexuality, the game of deception becomes doubly complicated. Alicia commands a sliver of domination over Alexander, playing on his attraction to her. She commands sufficient leverage to mask her true purpose, although, as Alicia learns, not sufficient to retain Sebastian's trust when he observes her in Devlin's embrace. Here, Secret #1, Alicia's awareness of Sebastian's desperate desire to believe in her, permits Secret #2, Alicia's use of this desire to spy on him.

Secrecy's witchery arrives with a price, however. Disclosure may be wrenching. Sometimes we discover information that we prefer not to discover. Surely Alexander can relate to such a painful disclosure with his tale of woe regarding the truth of why Alicia married him. As can Alicia, when she comprehends that her "illness" lies in the scheming hands of the Sebastians.

Sexuality provokes a backlash here. Alicia not only rejects Alexander but seeks to deceive him. Everything about her that Alexander cherished so dearly, now reminds him of his vulnerability. Sexuality so luscious in the morning light, now becomes reprehensible in reality's rush of darkness. Alicia must pay for her loveliness. And, as the Bittersweet Hitchcock completes his handiwork, she almost does.

Hitchcock's most direct assault on secrecy occurs in *Rear Window* (1954). The issue of responsibility assumes a new guise through the prying eyes of an injured photographer, L. B. Jefferies (James Stewart). Jefferies likes to get close to his subjects, but this philosophy leaves him with a busted left leg when a race car careens out of control. The normally roving photographer finds himself forced to recuperate in a small Greenwich Village apartment--his world now reduced to a rear-window view of life. This life concerns an apparently mundane tempo of summer activities in the courtyard and apartments that fall within Jefferies' horizon.

The photographer's temporary incarceration feeds an idle curiosity. Jefferies knows his neighbors: a newlywed couple, a songwriter, a busybody, a spinster, a dancer, and others--but he knows them only as a spectator. He stereotypes their lifestyles, noting that Miss Lonely-Hearts (the spinster) lives alone and seeks male companionship, whereas in an upstairs dwelling, Miss Torso (the dancer) also lives alone but appears to have no lack of male suitors. Jefferies favors a detached, one-way intimacy and realizes little empathy with these figures, or with the woman who loves him, Lisa Fremont (Grace Kelly) (Leitch, 1991, p. 171).[11]

Lisa and Jefferies share a genuine affection, yet they appear at odds. She's into fashion and the gilded gaiety along Park Avenue. He's into high excitement and the attraction of any far destination except where he is. The lovers' contrasting interests become subverted, however, by what Tania Modleski (1988, p. 77) calls a "gender reversal." Jefferies portrays the Hitchcock hero, though a passive hero by circumstance; Lisa adorns the heroine role, yet a role that will prove enterprising and daring. The customary man of action is chairbound, and the customary woman of inaction is out and about.

Across the courtyard we have Lars Thorwald (Raymond Burr) and his wife. Contrary to Jefferies, Thorwald is active, indeed, possibly too active for his wife's well-being. Contrary to Lisa, Mrs. Thorwald parallels Jefferies as an inactive, confined tenant. She becomes, soon enough, (1) quite inactive, and (2) the missing link to a puzzle.

A murder occurs, or does it? Jefferies suspects Mr. Thorwald of chopping up the nagging Mrs. Thorwald. He sees Thorwald, a salesman, leave with his sample case several times in the wee morning hours. And he doesn't see Mrs. Thorwald again. The uncertainty that comes with not knowing begins to haunt the photographer. Logical explanations fail to convince him. Jefferies, like Hitchcock, finds the illogical happening more fascinating.

He also finds himself impressed with Lisa, who, after some skepticism, joins as an ally to wonder about Thorwald. This union, however tentative, offers sweet relief to the comments and attitudes that Hitchcock imposes on the merry state of marriage. Jefferies invests himself with an orientation that envisions matrimony as a loss of freedom. Thorwald's situation, moreover, heightens this loss of freedom. His wife, who has him at her command, appears capable of doing more than remaining bedridden. Instead, she taunts Thorwald, giving him ample motive to imagine life without her.

Hitchcock, in a parallel venture, presents us with a dual maelstrom that mocks wedded bliss: The marriage desired by Lisa evokes a discordant note from Jefferies, and the Thorwalds' present marriage inspires one spouse apparently to murder the other. The idea of marriage suffers further irony when you realize that if Thorwald does kill his wife, he risks doing so for reasons other than money. One reason that whets Jefferies' appetite concerns the possibility of an illicit affair involving Thorwald--one that, conceivably, may lead the salesman into yet another "marital trap." Love, in Hitchcock's *Rear Window* world, experiences rough treatment on several fronts before earning its true colors (Leitch, 1991, p. 170).

Privacy harbors its own paradox. The secretive business of living life behind closed doors, of not trespassing on posted property, of being denied access to privileged parties--these exclusive happenings seem proper, legal, and necessary. The common cry arises that such instances of deserved privacy suffer violation too frequently. By contrast, invasion via government files, electronic bugs, and fax machines, and from trespassers, hackers, reporters, and snoopy neighbors with binoculars (like L. B. Jefferies), keep privacy in a state of flux.

The paradox occurs when we consider the implications of too much privacy. The paradox arises especially when we contemplate the people and practices that privacy endangers (Keisling, 1984): AIDS contacted by a medical doctor who refuses to inform the patients he treats until his symptoms become obvious; spouse abuse that the abuser and often the abused seek to hide from outsiders; child molestation inflicted on a young victim for years, who remains fearful that others may discover this shameful secret. And...the possibility of a domestic murder, suspected only through the husband's unusual behavior and the wife's abrupt absence.

Lisa and Jefferies piece together observations on changes in the Thorwalds' usual routine. Still, even if these conclusions are correct, their invasiveness requires justification. The right to privacy constitutes, allegedly, an inalienable right: Leave me alone, stay off my turf, don't darken my door! Do voyeurs therefore, despite a supposedly admirable cause, claim the right to monitor the personal behavior of a stranger like Lars Thorwald?

Jefferies, Lisa, and Stella (Thelma Ritter, Jefferies' physical therapist) tussle with the morality of their Peeping Tomism, although they express little anguish in searching for an answer. Frankly, the characters expend minimal effort on the matter of privacy, and greater concern on the promise that something nasty happened across the way. The Peeping Toms want a murder. They know that they shouldn't, but can't help themselves--they need a killing to make their snooping acceptable (Leitch, 1991, p. 171; Rohmer & Chabrol, 1988, p. 125). Our spectators also realize gratification in privately peeping the other tenants, all of whom, Hitchcock ensures, will have something unsettling to say about love and marriage.

When Thorwald leaves his apartment, Lisa sneaks inside to search for Mrs. Thorwald's telltale wedding ring. She finds the ring, but Thorwald returns. A struggle begins, one that Jefferies and Stella watch in horror from Jefferies' apartment, helpless to intervene.[12]

Voyeurism has its drawbacks, not the least of which is the embarrassment of discovery. The police arrive to salvage Lisa, but she's located the ring and wears it on her finger, wiggling this finger so that Jefferies will know of her triumph. (A triumph with more than one meaning since a wedding ring on the appropriate finger spells the "loss" of Jefferies' male freedom.) Unfortunately for Jefferies, Lisa wiggling her finger also attracts the attention of Thorwald. He looks across the courtyard, directing his unnerving gaze into the sanctuary of his spy (and at us, the audience, Jefferies' co-conspirators) (Spoto, 1992, p. 221). The voyeur's cover is blown. He has been "de-peeped."

Hitchcockian circumstances prevail to bring Thorwald and Jefferies to a confrontation in Jefferies' apartment. Thorwald then asks the question that sums up the enigma of privacy's fascination: "What do you want of me?" Jefferies has no answer since his early observations of Thorwald began through idle curiosity, not the soundest motive for launching a surveillance (Rohmer & Chabrol, 1988, p. 128; Truffaut, 1985, pp. 218-219).

Thorwald is perplexed. He has no money. He appears to exude little charm, a talent usually endowed generously to Hitchcock's villains. He's a nobody, a lost face in the crowd. And he can't understand, nor does Jefferies fully comprehend, why anyone should take an interest in him.

The implausible reigns again: "What do you want of me?" Thorwald becomes of interest because of what our observers do not know about him. Their enchantment concerns his potential for murdering a nagging wife, a potential they use to vindicate their continued prying. But a potential that, with precious little evidence at first, hardly merits an invasion of privacy.[13]

Jefferies and Thorwald fight, but the die is cast. Thorwald

is doomed. He loses, he confesses, he once more slips into anonymity. A bad marriage, a bad decision--an unlucky decision given his neighbors--and he retreats to nowhere. Jefferies looks even better than he should, since, aside from Thorwald, his perception of Miss Lonely-Hearts--or more accurately, Stella's intuitive awareness of her distress--saves the woman from a suicide attempt.

Hitchcock gives us a final reading on each tenant's story. Miss Lonely-Hearts finds comfort with the songwriter upstairs. Miss Torso, for all her handsome suitors, squeals with delight when her true soldier love, a shrimpish-looking gent, returns home and immediately goes to the fridge. And the newlyweds, who practiced their marital acrobatics behind a pulled window shade during the entire movie, now emerge, and, counter to the other stories, end on an abrasive note by engaging in their first argument.

No one views these scenes from Jefferies' apartment, however. Jefferies sleeps with his back to the courtyard, as if he no longer cares to show a peeping interest in his neighbors' affairs. Or, perhaps he no longer dares to show such curiosity for fear that he will not be so fortunate again in seeing his voyeurism rewarded.

Lisa, though, emerges the real winner. She sits comfortably, knowing that she has passed Jefferies' test of hardship and adventure. Comfortable, too, knowing that she has her own designs to finesse (Leitch, 1991, pp. 173-174). Lisa reads a magazine on the Himalayas until she's certain that Jefferies lies asleep. Quietly, confidently, she puts down the Himalayas and picks up a fashion journal, *Harper's Bazaar*. Discreetly, she raises her true colors, and, given the lady's resourcefulness, who's to say that these colors will not rule?

Other films like *Rebecca* (1940) and *Dial M For Murder* (1954) speak of Hitchcock's treatment of love triangles and their uneasy resolution. Still other Hitchcock efforts-- *Suspicion* (1941), *Spellbound* (1945), and *Marnie* (1964) in particular--show how the female and male must struggle to achieve any kind of relationship that has a chance to survive. And in these efforts, the female searches for the strength and resiliency to continue, having to earn her Hitchcockian medals before she can deserve a happy ending.

Hitchcock's bittersweet forays into secrecy and sexuality portray his prickly position on affection and intimacy. An intimacy desired by males, but threatening to them. Love at the loss of masculine wayfaring for a Devlin or a Jefferies, yet a love, no matter how clouded, that's basically needed. Love that shows the female as more attractive in character and more open in her quest. A love to take chances for, to even behave illogically and implausibly for, but an affection that demands the price of commitment. The torturous path to realize this commitment becomes the substance of the Bittersweet Hitchcock in the ambivalent relationships of *Notorious* and *Rear Window*.

Hitchcock, The Somber Judge

Cynics, tax collectors, and aging rock stars have the kiss of death about them. Pretend, pretend, and pretend, but they still come across as cynics, tax collectors, and aging rock stars. Time has no obligation to reform, nor love to rejuvenate. Sometimes justice does not endure. Sometimes a hero or heroine takes the fall, and stays down.

Hitchcock hints at the somber dynamics of sexuality even in his Romanticist films. Remember Margaret, the crofter's wife in *The Thirty-nine Steps*? And the auction scene in *North By Northwest*? Roger Thornhill bitterly denounces Eve Kendall in front of Vandamm, impugning her sexual character because she deceived him. But Roger's bitterness also stems from his vulnerability to her, and she betrays that vulnerability by sending him, C.O.D., to a brush with death. The Romantic Hitchcock, however, permits Roger to right his mistakes, forgive Eve her transgressions, and gallantly save her life.

Gallantry and forgiveness wear out their welcome under a Somber Hitchcock. No miraculous escapes or regenerations of spirit soar forth to elevate the lovers. No Devlin comes along to rescue Alicia from the fading moments of her existence.

No hand appears with a firm Rogerian grip to save Eve Kendall from her perilous fall. And no troops swoop across the courtyard to salvage what's not broken in L. B. Jefferies.

Rather, Hitchcock offers us a dark fable about a woman who makes the grievous decision to steal 40,000 dollars (the MacGuffin). She never makes her decision explicitly, but simply drifts to the idea; an idea that she foolishly believes will solve a problem. Sadly, her theft reaps a savage punishment. Sadder still, the theft need not have happened. Her "problem" would have been solvable if only the man in question had said, "Yes."

Psycho (1960), for better or worse, becomes the one film most identified with Alfred Hitchcock. To commemorate 30 years of *Psycho* longevity, Stephen Rebello's *Alfred Hitchcock And The Making Of Psycho* (1990) tells you the conception, inception, and deception of this seemingly slight, black-and-white movie. The film's inspiration traces back to one Ed Gein ("rhymes with mean"), a Wisconsin odd-jobber and recluse, who follows his own agenda for companionship and recreation. This agenda includes:

> ...two shin bones. Two pairs of human lips on a string. A cupful of human noses that sat on the kitchen table. A human skin purse and bracelets. Four flesh-upholstered chairs. A tidy row of ten grimacing human skulls. A tom-tom rigged from a quart can with skin stretched across the top and bottom. A soup bowl fashioned from an inverted human half-skull. The eviscerated skins of four women's faces, rouged, made-up, and thumbtacked to the wall at eye level. Five "replacement" faces secured in plastic bags. Ten female heads, hacked off at the eyebrow. A rolled-up pair of leggings and skin "vest," including the mammaries, severed from another unfortunate (Rebello, 1990, p. 3).

And so, Norman Bates (Anthony Perkins) is born. Oh, not all at once. From the 1957 discovery in Gein's farmhouse, to Robert Bloch's novel in 1959, to Hitchcock's film treatment in 1960, a few changes occur. Gein's farmhouse gives way to the Bates Motel, and the Bates' friendly mansion out back. The 51-year-old Gein magically regains his youth as the adolescent Norman. And, whereas the authorities transport Ed Gein to an asylum (he died there on July 26, 1984), no one yet suspects

Norman of anything other than some hard luck regarding his mother.

The camera's eye hesitates, then peeks into a shabby hotel room where Marion Crane (Janet Leigh) and Sam Loomis (John Gavin) have spent themselves on sexual intercourse. Now, partially clothed, they return to the business at hand: Marion wants to marry, pronto, and Sam wants to wait, interminably it seems. He has inherited his father's debts and prefers to wait until expenses are more manageable. Besides, there's that monthly alimony to his ex-wife, and, well, Sam Loomis does not move fast. Truth be told, he hardly moves at all.

Sam represents *Psycho*'s premise--the reason for everything that follows. Indirectly, he shoulders responsibility for two deaths and considerable anguish. Sam conveys the kind of character who finally decides to say "Yes," but his "Yes" comes too late for Marion. "Too-late" Sam, the story of a male reluctant to commit, and when he does commit, the tale of a man who's missed the boat again. But this time, his tardiness sets in motion dire consequences.

Sam and Marion have no reason not to marry. Marion senses that her biological clock is saying, "It's time." And Sam's debts at the family hardware store in another town comprise a lame excuse for denying himself companionship. Perhaps he balks at marrying Marion because of the Hitchcockian fear that debts and marriage constitute, not a helpmate, but a prison. The kind of prison Sam suffered with his ex-wife. Whatever his elusive motive, Sam's reluctance encourages Marion to pursue an illogical course of action. She embarks on the type of radical journey that makes for suspense in Hitchcock's somber world.

Given 40,000 dollars to deposit by her boss, Marion absconds with the money, but does so carelessly and with a dash of bad luck. (Symbolically, Marion wears white undergarments before the theft and black undergarments afterward.) By Hitchcockian chance, her boss passes the car and notices Marion as she waits for a light to change. Later, after Marion pulls off the highway to take a nap, she's awakened by a police officer and, rattled, gives him

questionable answers. Finally, after trading her car for
another to delay police identification, she observes the officer
watching her from across the street. Marion even gives the car
salesman cause to wonder when she accepts his first offer too
easily. Contrary to her attempts at anonymity, Marion only
calls attention to herself as a "wrong one."

These incidents are crucial since they allow us to recognize
Marion's basic decency. We sympathize with her because,
first, we know that the money belongs to her boss's client, a
lecherous braggart whose manhood depends on the money he
can spend (Rothman, 1982, pp. 259 & 264). Second, Marion's
intimidation by the policeman reminds us how vulnerable and
frightened the theft makes her. And third, Marion's decency
wins out when she decides that somehow she and Sam will
enjoy life without the 40,000 dollars.

Ironically, Marion's turnabout arises from her conversation
with Norman Bates. Marion, already imagining a joyful
existence with Sam and the money, speaks to Norman of
escaping to her private island, free from immediate cares.
Norman, perceptive like the beady-eyed bird he is, reflects
that all of us have private traps we hope to leave. But he
resigns himself to his little world, he says, because Mother
needs attention.

Unwittingly, Norman provides Marion with the inspiration
to return to Phoenix and work out a solution to her private
trap. Prophetically he says, "We all go a little mad sometimes."
More prophetically, Marion replies, "Sometimes just one time
can be enough" (Brill, 1988, p. 236). She refers to her sin of
thievery, but we know that this line sums up her fate at the
hands of Mad Momma Bates.

The decision made, Marion retires to her room and her
shower. Norman, too intrigued with Marion for Mother's
welfare, lifts a painting to uncover his trusty peephole so that
he may spy on Marion's nudity (viewed in one interpretation
as an "implicit rape"; see Leitch, 1991, p. 217).[14] He returns to
the house, hesitates and looks upstairs, then wanders into his
kitchen. Hindsight suggests that Norman engages in a
momentary conflict as to Marion's fate. The conflict does not
arise between Norman and Mother, since Norman is mostly

Mother. The indecision may result from Mother trying to determine her next step. And Mother, regrettably for Marion, chooses to scurry forth in her garb as Norman's protector (Leitch, 1991, p. 219).

The **shower scene** graces the screen as a classic bit of cinema. Technically, Stephen Rebello (1990, pp. 100-118) examines the scene and tells all that you will wish to know about lights, camera angles, and the fuss over who really directed this brief montage of horror. Psychologically, William Rothman (1982, pp. 292-310) analyzes the sequence into three stages, speculating rather liberally about Marion, the shower head, her murder, and what it means when blood and water spiral down the drain. The blood and water sweep into a dark hole, only to dissolve into another dark recess as we, the audience, spiral out of Marion's dead eye. I prefer to modify Rothman's organization by thinking of the shower episode less elaborately, choosing instead to structure Marion's crucifixion as a matter of foreplay, violation, and aftermath.

Foreplay assumes many guises, not all of them requiring sexual intercourse to follow as the main event. Sometimes, foreplay serves its own designs. Lovers caress, kiss, and mumble affectionate tidbits to each other, without obliging themselves sexually to pursue orgasm. When Marion steps into the shower and the water flows forth, she clearly finds physical pleasure in the cleansing (Sterritt, 1993, p. 108). Whether the cleansing washes away her sin of thievery and makes her feel virginal again, whether the cleansing arouses her sexually, or whether the joy of cleansing merely confirms her new look at life, she appears ecstatic under the shower. You receive the impression that, barring interruption, Marion may have continued her cleansing foreplay for some time.

The **violation**, when it comes, retains a suddenness, a brutal change of tempo that shocks even upon repeated viewing. Ripping aside the shower curtain constitutes the deepest invasion of privacy and security, and the commencement of Marion's rape. This rape does not involve the literal meaning of physical sex against the woman's will, but a broader interpretation of taking Marion by force. One possibility concerns portraying the shower curtain as a womb torn asunder, comparable to defiling Marion's fantasy of her private island (Rothman, 1982, p. 364). Another possibility points to Norman (as Mother) depriving Marion of her new-found freedom, the kind of freedom that Norman will never attain (Wood, 1989, p. 148).

The generic explanation, however, considers Marion's (unknowing?) sexual arousal of Norman, and Mother's inordinate retaliation to annihilate Marion in a rage of sexual jealousy. Whatever interpretation fits your fancy, Marion's song dies with her. A fantasy dying, the stream of water blurring Marion's defenseless body, the shadows masking her intruder.

Technically, the slashing knife does not touch her body (arguably with one exception). Artistically, it doesn't matter whether she's touched or not since we grasp the conclusions that Hitchcock desires. Marion draws for us a picturesque solo of dying, shrouded in mist and accompanied by a discordant shrieking of musical strings to heighten the barbarity (Sterritt, 1993, p. 108). Marion's fabled death is not that of grit and grime, but a death launched in secrecy and sheathed in delusion.

The intruder gone, Marion beseeches us, reaches a hand to us, but we cannot help (Brill, 1988, p. 231). A Somber Hitchcock won't allow it, and we must relinquish her. You may construe the **aftermath** of water and blood swirling down the drain and the camera's recording of this swirling from her eye as a journey of death, indeed, as the birth of Marion's death (Wood, 1989, p. 149; Rothman, 1982, p. 309). Whatever you construe, you will see a still face, glazed against the white-tiled floor, with a tear below her unseeing eye. We have lost Marion, and we have lost the eroticism she conveyed during the shower's foreplay and during the agonies of her violation.

Marion, not Norman, embodies the centerpiece of *Psycho*. Her murder proves a wrenching loss, one from which we do not recover. Hitchcock permits us time to feel for Marion, to live with her vulnerability, to make her fears our fears. We miss her too much to blithely dismiss her presence. Reminders of Marion through her sister, Lila (Vera Miles), her slow-footed lover, Sam, the jittery, pathological Norman, and the Bates Motel as her final stay, keep Marion very much with us.[15]

Psycho, truly, unfolds itself as one continuous fountain of duplicity, deception, and denial.[16] As Marion leaves us, the movie resolves its characters into a matter of secrets dying, secrets created anew, and secrets forced into discovery: Marion's secret to return the money dies with her, and Lila and Sam fabricate a story of husband and wife to stay at the motel and search for clues. Ultimately, however, the dreaded secrecy of the Bates Motel and the mansion on the hill find revelation. Norman surrenders himself to Mother, and it is Mother who relates the killing of Marion and of Arbogast (Martin Balsam), a private detective. Note, nevertheless, that the confession derives from her viewpoint. The psychiatrist, in a scene designated solely for exposition, authoritatively tells us of Mother's statement. Yet we know more than the psychiatrist because we have seen more. We know that not all mothers deserve our trust, and certainly not one particular Mother.

Psycho ends with Marion's car (and Marion) being removed from the swamp. What vindication we receive in Mother going to an asylum, and in Marion's recovery for a decent burial, hardly redeems her unjust murder. The unjust act is not easy to crystallize since Norman, as Norman, affords us glimpses of a winsome personality.

But he also deftly exposes Mother on occasion. Norman does so in a dialogue with Marion when he mentions the horrors of a mental institution. And he does so with Arbogast. When the private detective can pump no further information from Norman, he departs, intending to return. As he leaves, he leaves not Norman but Mother. We see a self-indulgent smirk on Mother's face, the kind of knowing smile that telegraphs her feelings of superiority to this clod, Arbogast. The dangers of a fantasy world are clearly evident here. Mother, imagining herself so clever in deflecting intruders and in seeing through the secrets of others, becomes in truth a pathetic creation of false security.

Marion's death remains unsettling because had she not

stopped at that damn Bates Motel, she would be alive. If we have trouble venting our hostility at the flickering, mentally ill persona of Mother/Norman--who is not responsible by law for the pathological behavior of murder--we also experience trouble in coming to terms with a murder that occurs by the bad luck of the draw. Hitchcock's implausible connections haunt us once more. If the rainstorm had not been so severe to cause Marion to take the wrong road; if, knowing she was close to her destination, she had decided not to spend the night; if the forsaken motel had been any other inn than the Bates Motel. If, if, if.

A Somber Hitchcock does not allow much tolerance for mercy or hope. The Bates' mansion and motel characterize a secrecy too overwhelming to permit escape. As Donald Spoto (1993, p. 314) comments, "For this film is really a meditation on the tyranny of past over present. It's an indictment of the viewer's capacity for voyeurism and his own potential for depravity" (Spoto, 1993, p. 314).

In *Psycho*, secrecy and sexuality work momentously against the troubled soul. A smothering secrecy that enmeshes the conflicted player deeper into a web of destruction. A secrecy perpetrated by shadowy, turbulent forces that unleash catastrophic entanglements, beginning with Marion's theft of 40,000 dollars. And Marion's sexuality, given Sam's failure to appreciate her urgency to marry, that guides Marion unwittingly to an erotic rivalry with the one adversary only a Solemn Judge like Hitchcock could engender--Mother.

The loss of Marion lingers, as does the sense that some calamities in life hold no promise of redemption. These happenings are not just, cinematically. Movies usually correct such inequities--a triumph of good over evil, the satisfying resolutions we come to expect from the Romantic and even the Bittersweet Hitchcock. But the Somber Hitchcock besets us with confusion, not gratification. The clock misses a tick, the evil creeps forth without its comeuppance, and the main characters, our alleged stalwarts, fail to find release from their self-made cells.

Hitchcock, on a dispiriting roll, anticipates *Psycho* in 1960 with a 1958 blood relative called *Vertigo*. Despite differences in how the two films look--their color and location--*Psycho* and *Vertigo* share a few bleak connections: Both films lose a central character as the story develops; both films include the "too-late" theme, Hitchcock's way of serving notice on the pain of what "might have been"; and both films use the spiraling effect to indicate a character's descent into despair and loss of identity (Brill, 1988, pp. 221 & 227).

Vertigo begins with Scottie Ferguson (James Stewart), a police detective, who rushes after an officer as the two of them chase a crook across the rooftops of San Francisco. The first indication of viewer trouble is that the crook escapes. The second indication is that Scottie stumbles and finds himself dangling high above the street. The third indication is that the officer, trying to reach for Scottie's hand, slips and falls to his death.

The fourth indication is that we never see Scottie rescued, despite his precarious hold on a rain gutter. Indeed, the next scene shows him visiting an old friend, Midge (Barbara Bel Geddes), as he recovers from his ordeal. What do these slips in logic and justice mean so early in the story? They suggest that instead of offering us a comfortable formula film, Hitchcock chooses to conjure up a labyrinth of lies and illusions as he sends our hero plunging into perdition.

Scottie now suffers vertigo: a dizzying sensation of swaying amid stable surroundings. For Scottie, vertigo stems from a fear of heights, the dread of falling coupled with the illogical desire to let go, to surrender and be pulled down (Wood, 1989, p. 110; Brill, 1988, p. 205). The detective's benign appearance and manner mask an unstable personality. His near death brings him closer to mental collapse, but Scottie's lack of purpose in life also hints at a long-term inadequacy: He escapes commitment by "wandering" (Sterritt, 1993, pp. 87 & 90; Spoto, 1992, p. 281). And in Hitchcock's vocabulary, "wandering" becomes another condition for spiraling, for going nowhere.[17]

Our first clue involves his relationship with Midge. She's a commercial artist of bras and other lingerie, a task beneath her abilities as an artist. Years before, Midge engaged, then

disengaged herself of a romantic relationship with Scottie.
Why did she break away? He asks her this question rhetorically and she refuses him a straight answer, nor does he expect
one. She saw a Scottie not fully committed to her, or to any
woman. Midge, always practical, chose to back off. Now
their companionship reflects a brother/sister, or perhaps a
mother/son arrangement, complicated by romantic undertones
that Midge continues to harbor.

Scottie represents the vulnerable male about to exchange
his aimlessness for a deepening mystery...and the first real love
of his life. An old school acquaintance, Gavin Elster (Tom
Helmore), unexpectedly enlists Scottie's help as a retired
detective to follow Madeleine (Kim Novak), Elster's wife.
Scottie refuses initially, wishing to remain the wanderer. But
Elster's suspicions intrigue the ex-detective since they include
Madeleine's belief that she will die at a young age as did an
earlier figure in her family, Carlotta Valdes. Madeleine
identifies with this tragic personality, sitting and gazing at
Carlotta's portrait, wearing her hair in the same fashion, and
buying a cluster of flowers similar to the flowers in the
portrait. Madeleine, Elster worries, may commit suicide at age
30, as occurred with Carlotta.

Scottie becomes mesmerized when he first sees Madeleine.
The attraction, as Hitchcock often engineers, happens
instantly. Scottie's hooked, and he stays hooked as Madeleine
leads him on a puzzling trail of visits to Carlotta's grave,
Carlotta's portrait in a museum, and other haunts. These visits
entail long stretches of silent exposition. During Scottie's
surveillance, Madeleine appears and disappears like a dream.
She impresses us as an ephemeral creature of Old San
Francisco. Contact between the two finally transpires when
Madeleine throws herself into the bay, and Scottie leaps in to
save her.   He transports Madeleine, unconscious, to his
apartment, undresses her, and waits for his dream to awaken.

Once they meet, their relationship changes complexion.
The reticent Madeleine and the obsessed Scottie move closer
together: Madeleine, desperately trying to understand the
mystery of Carlotta's hold over her, and Scottie, feverishly
seeking to unravel the puzzle and free Madeleine for himself.

Scottie's descent into illusion carries him farther than he knows. What begins as a favor to track a friend's wife, now accelerates to a Scottie who feels *responsible* for Madeleine (Sterritt, 1993, p. 94). He must know--MUST KNOW--the reason for Carlotta's possession of her.

Midge, mystified and curious, strives to recapture the old Scottie by painting a humorous portrait of herself as Carlotta. But she misjudges Scottie's immersion in the mystery, and in Madeleine. The sexualities of Midge and Madeleine clash because one portrays the familiar, maternal love of a friend, and the other exudes the unfamiliar, tempting allure of a mysterious woman (Wood, 1989, pp. 113-114). Midge can't compete, and her ill-conceived portrait alienates Scottie. She's lost him, not just to another woman but to another fate, the kind of obsessive descent that Midge cannot touch or change.

An apparent solution to Carlotta's mystique lead Scottie and Madeleine to a Mexican mission, San Juan Bautista, a short distance from San Francisco. There, Scottie explains away the landmarks that Madeleine describes in her dreams. She was imagining reality after all, he insists, merely a past reality rather than some mysterious spell.

Scottie embraces her in the livery stable, a setting that contains artifacts of Carlotta's time. He assumes the mystery solved and that Madeleine, though still married, somehow belongs to him. But Madeleine cannot shake Carlotta's spirit and breaks free of Scottie to enter and climb the bell tower of an old church. Scottie, perplexed, chases her only to find that he cannot reach the bell tower because of his vertigo. Collapsed on the steps, he looks in horror through a small window and sees Madeleine flash by in a fall to her death.

Others rush to Madeleine's body, but Scottie, disoriented and in shock, staggers from the scene. At the inquest, the coroner exonerates Scottie of any legal responsibility for Madeleine's death, yet cruelly assaults his character as a man who also was implicated in another death (the officer falling). Scottie, reliving the horror, loses himself in a nightmare sequence. Dark fantasies spiral forth to indicate that Scottie, grappling not only with Madeleine, also finds himself in puzzling scenes with Carlotta and Elster.

His obsession, however, permits him no solution to
Madeleine's strange suicide. Too, you may interpret Scottie's
nightmare as a suspicion that maybe, just maybe, he's been
duped (Spoto, 1992, p. 288). His experience as a police
detective could lead him to that unconscious idea.

Whatever you conclude, Scottie's illusion of Madeleine
leaves him desolate, uncommunicative (as in melancholy), and
in an asylum. Midge, ever faithful, visits and plays a selection
from Mozart, hoping the music will draw Scottie back to an
awareness of reality. But Scottie remains too distant for
Midge, or for anyone but Madeleine to reach. Madeleine's
gone, yet her presence overwhelms him, and Midge realizes
the futility of her own position (Brill, 1988, p. 208).

Madeleine, though no longer a physical rival, continues to
defeat Midge as a sexual rival. Midge stops by the psychiatrist's office and comments sadly, "I don't think Mozart's going
to help at all" (Wood, 1989, p. 119). We last see her walking
down a long, bleak corridor, where she pauses at the far end
as the scene fades black (Sterritt, 1993, p. 94). Exit Midge; a
dismal end to her participation in Scottie's life, and a sober
finis to Story #1.

Story #2 commences with Scottie sufficiently recovered to
become the wanderer once more. His wandering, however,
evokes a quasi-purpose since he morosely touches base with
past happenings and locales that cause him to recall Madeleine.
One day he spots an attractive woman, different in dress and
cosmetic appearance from Madeleine, but still eerily
reminiscent of his lost love. Scottie, in the boyish yet bold
manner that actor James Stewart has conveyed throughout his
career, approaches the woman, Judy (also played by Kim
Novak), and asks for a date.[18]

Judy, naturally hesitant, acquiesces. And Scottie, growing
more determined, regains his illusion. Not the original dream
he craves--not yet--but a stellar substitute. They walk, they
eat, they dance, they engage in all these activities at a sedate
pace, although they go nowhere; they spiral. *Vertigo*'s opening
credits illustrate a female's eye, and a spiraling effect from her
eye, a proximal variation on the drain-and-eye sequence used
in *Psycho*. But since spiraling denotes a bad omen in

Hitchcock's vernacular, we sense trouble ahead.

Trouble begins when Judy realizes Scottie's true intention: He wishes to transform her, body and soul, to Madeleine. Judy, less the dream image of Madeleine and more the hard-nosed working girl, refuses. But Scottie's pleading, most frantically the pleading of his eyes, slowly wears her down. Scottie, not content with Judy, must have Madeleine, or as close to her as his reconstruction will allow. When Judy asks Scottie why he is putting her through these changes and why he won't accept her as she is, Scottie has no sensible reply. He lamely says, "I just want to take care of you." A spiraling answer, an answer of "responsibility," only this time Scottie's possession of Judy proves comparable to Carlotta's claim over Madeleine.

He comes nearer than even he anticipates. Judy, wearing Madeleine's clothes, Madeleine's hairdo, Madeleine's make-up, emerges from her bathroom in a green, mystic glow created by Hitchcock, and traditionally used in stage plays to mark the presence of ghosts (see Spoto, 1992, p. 282). The green glow simulates earlier lush surroundings associated with Madeleine. She is reborn, and we know so because we see Scottie's naked-eyed confirmation: Madeleine is back. His illusion reasserts itself. Scottie and Madeleine/Judy embrace on a carousel of time, their surroundings a blend of the livery stable's past and the apartment's present. Thus, if Judy wishes to keep Scottie, she must vanquish herself into his illusion. She must sacrifice her natural self to a sexual rival of the past.

Pause now and realize the fragility of this relationship. Scottie's obsession churns away but it can't last...and doesn't last. Judy makes a mistake, and in the lore of a Solemn Hitchcock, it only takes one mistake. Preparing to go out she decides to wear a necklace, and worse, asks Scottie to help her with the clasp. He does so, then glances into the mirror and sees the necklace--the same necklace that Carlotta wore in her portrait, and that Madeleine wore when she was "alive."

Suddenly the puzzle yields a devastating solution. A bizarre scheme, too illogical to play in Peoria, but just so for Hitchcock's somber perception of a twisting, spiraling San Francisco. Scottie's rebirth of Madeleine proves too successful: Judy *is* Madeleine.   The overriding secret that has stretched its tentacles throughout, abruptly finds revelation for Scottie. Madeleine never existed, only Judy pretending.

Madeleine characterizes a true illusion, a woman fictional in all respects, save one: Judy's genuine love for Scottie, both as Madeleine and as herself. For a Romantic or a Bittersweet Hitchcock, that love would be enough. It would offset all the other insults imposed on Scottie.   But for the Solemn Hitchcock, the love arrives "too late," bearing too much emotional treachery. Judy's affection fails to derail Scottie's fundamental inadequacy: his fanaticism to possess a dream. Midge wouldn't do, nor could any woman satisfy his illusion-- until Madeleine.

He drives Judy back to San Juan Bautista, back to the church, back to the bell tower. He forces her and himself to relive the dark scenario. Scottie does so to coerce Judy through the anguish that he suffered. But, further, to vent his rage that Judy, as Madeleine, was first concocted by another man--by Elster--as a nemesis to Scottie's dream (Modleski, 1988, p. 98).

Up the winding steps they go, up to the bell tower, up where Scottie could not ascend before because of his vertigo. During Story #1, Gavin Elster has his wife here, already dead. When "Madeleine" arrives, the real wife "falls" from the tower. The two then secret themselves away, leaving Scottie to struggle through his dark journey. For sheer logic, surely an easier plan exists to dispatch one's spouse. But illogically, we experience the depths of passion and obsession that can deliver a wanderer who innocently places himself at a scoundrel's mercy, and unwaveringly commits himself to an illusion.

A return to the church's belfry provokes Judy to confess. Yes, Elster hired her to become Madeleine. Yes, he knew that Scottie's vertigo would stop him from reaching the bell tower. Yes, she wanted to come to Scottie later, but felt that she could not. And yes, she loved Scottie as Madeleine, and she loves him now. Scottie, still dazed from his discovery, says it's "too late."   Too late, he realizes at last, for recapturing Madeleine, a woman who never was. And seemingly too late for Judy, since she irrevocably falsifies all that Madeleine means to him.

Judy's pleading draws the two star-crossed lovers to an embrace amid a crazed kaleidoscope of past and present entanglements. Scottie whispers, "I loved you so, Maddie," a peculiar expression stated not only in the past tense, but an admission that Leslie Brill (1988, p. 219) cites "...is neither 'Madeleine' nor 'Judy' but an amalgam, a new being, both and neither."

A darkness looms for Judy, a ghostly presence that spirits to her a message of retribution. A time to pay. Judy lunges back in fear of this apparition that dooms her, falling from the bell tower as a real victim. The shadowy figure moves to light and becomes a nun who heard them in the tower. A benign figure who transforms to a specter of self-deception for Judy, just as Judy transformed herself to Madeleine in deceiving Scottie.

Vertigo ends with Scottie perched on the bell tower staring down at Judy...at Madeleine...at a paradise lost again. His past dwells below, not to be reprised with another Madeleine. Hitchcock does not ask whether Judy deserves such punishment. Nor does he ask if Scottie will survive his new loss. Instead, Hitchcock leaves Scottie frozen in place: A tragically flawed man who suffers a twice-told tale. Scottie hurts because a secret so diabolical in its allure invaded his customary detachment to ruin his life and other lives, past and present.

Scottie hurts because he desired a sexuality too divine for his illusion to persevere. A wasted life seeking an ideal that could not in any sense of reality, exist (Spoto, 1992, p. 298). A dream that never was, and never will be.

Hitchcock's somber mood carries moviegoers into other quarters of helplessness and confusion. He proffers no surge of resourcefulness to make his beleaguered characters any happier. Indeed, the endings of *Shadow Of A Doubt* (1943), *The Wrong Man* (1956), *The Birds* (1963), and *Frenzy* (1972) leave his survivors tattered and torn in psyche, wondering how to recoup.

Uncle Charlie and his malignant charm do not escape

retribution in *Shadow Of A Doubt*, but his lingering darkness
ensnares a small-town American family that must live with the
uncle's murderous deeds. *The Wrong Man* and its gritty reality
ends more positively (and against Hitchcock's wishes) than did
the experiences of the family that inspired this film. The
birds of *The Birds* could have won the Bodega Bay skirmish
against their feeble human opponents, and are perched as if
they **will** triumph omnipotently in Hitchcock's ominous
ending. And *Frenzy* vindicates Hitchcock's hard-luck hero
from accusations of serial murder, but in the process he loses
his job and his girl, causing his prospects of a better life to
look no brighter at the story's end than at the story's
beginning.

Morbidity represents a hard sell as entertainment, but
morbidity with a Hitchcockian twist sends forth a message
worth considering. Secrecy and sexuality are inlaid intimates.
Exquisite sexuality beguiles, and such beguilement invites
secrecy of the darkest order. In sexuality's guise of a
spellbinding presence, crucial secrets are less detectable by
obsessive, vulnerable players like Scottie Ferguson. These
wanderers learn, too late, that they have lost control of their
lives.

Hitchcock, recognizing the honesty necessary in a somber
world of pathological cravings and fragile innocence, gives his
figures no extraordinary powers of resurrection. Sometimes
they die, sometimes they cause others to die, and, always, they
mourn.

Hitchcock's Three Personas

The three personas do not presume an exhaustive classification
of Hitchcock's work, nor do they encompass the nuances that
arise in other perspectives on his films. (If you wish to
explore additional interpretations of Hitchcock's films, note
those authors cited in the text.) My treatment of Hitchcock's
moods regarding secrecy and sexuality reflect a less ambitious
interpretation. Hitchcock's three personas provide glimpses of
what the man had to say about love and the sexes, and about

the perturbation of intimate relationships.

The Romantic Hitchcock used secret formulas and deception to move his players together, render them apart, and bring them in proximity again. The sexual attraction bursts outward with a quicksilver quality--fast, feisty, and Forward Ho! with no obstacles too great or emotions too wrenching to subdue. But the secrets assume more a technical flourish to create action, and less a telling influence on the intimate parties in question. The attraction evidenced by Hannay and Pamela and by Roger and Eve seems to kickstart itself and thrive spontaneously, despite the whirling, buzzing confusion of danger that surrounds them. The events drive the characters, but the lovers forge their own interludes of charm and passion at opportune moments--and during those moments they care little about the push and pull of secret messages.

The Bittersweet Hitchcock asks more of love. Lovers must earn their affection rather than expect its prickly bliss to sweep them clear of harm. The male more often frets and fritters away chances to commit, as the wiser female searches for an opening that will jolt her denser partner to his senses. Thus, Alicia wonders how to crack Devlin's ice shield, and Lisa contests Jefferies' evasive movements as he seeks to preserve his idea of intimacy. The secrecy, this time, ingratiates itself into the lovers' personal lives. Deception and denial, especially in *Notorious*, almost work their black magic via Devlin's inner conflicts to keep him away from Alicia. Almost, but in Hitchcock's world of weathered redemption, not quite.

The Somber Hitchcock abandons all hope of sweet refrains and second chances. Secrecy and sexuality muster a simply monstrous duality that no mere mortal can easily phantom, much less defy. Both Norman and Scottie find themselves products of a woven fabric long in the loom. Their flaws are not born of momentous happenings, but of lives gone awry years before. Norman had already killed out of sexual perversion, and had he not murdered Marion, he would still be doomed. Scottie trenchantly shirked reality by wandering, seeking a vision of love that by all reasonable measures was irrational, yet in his warped fantasies this vision represented the only love he could imagine. These characters become primed--however implausible the events appear--to pursue sexuality's most forbidding paths.

"It has been observed of Hitchcock's films, both disparagingly and sympathetically," David Sterritt (1993, p. 87) notes, "that things happen *to* his characters--that they are more acted on than acting." Suffice to say, the Master calls the shots. Technically, he positions his players with loving care, not to honor the players, but to address his spatial conception of what it takes to tell a story. Psychologically, he encourages his players to run the emotional gamut, ushering forth the Hitchcockian sentiments--sexual and covert--that the story and mood demand.

If prickly and carefree, Romance blossoms a fragrant rose. If the fragrance is denied yet sustains itself under turbulent waters, a Bittersweet kiss brushes the lips. If gloomy and unrepentant, A Somber love loses its flowering, too late to recover.

Whichever persona you prefer, the six films spotlighted for discourse--so different in particulars yet so similar in their motif of suspense--derive from a single fount of restless creativity: Vintage Hitchcock.

Notes

1.   Hitchcock, in one interview, cryptically clarified his remark about actors. The Director contended he never made the statement that actors are like cattle. Instead, Hitchcock argued that actors should be treated like cattle.

2.   Robin Wood (1989, p. 278), in his evaluation of *The Thirty-nine Steps*, speculates that Annabella functions as a prostitute.   A loose woman who deceives Hannay temporarily by soliciting him for refuge, and also a spy who lends her talents to the highest bidder. Annabella's prostitution is not sexual, at least not in this instance, but concerns a willingness to sell herself over to the service of espionage.

3.   Filmed out of chronological sequence, as typically occurs in a shooting schedule, Robert Donat and Madeleine Carroll had just met prior to being handcuffed together.   Hitchcock led the pair through rehearsals, and

then...conveniently lost the key to the handcuffs. Donat and Carroll stayed inextricably paired until late afternoon, none too happy over the experience (Spoto, 1983, p. 148). Hitchcock, ever the prankster and a believer in the terror of bondage, may have gained a sliver of sadistic delight from their discomfort. He also may have decided that their turbulent relationship on screen could be better served with a little turbulence off screen.

4. Hitchcock had shot an extended ending to *The Thirty-nine Steps*, showing Richard and Pamela in a cab. Hannay, seeking to play another ace on Pamela, informs her that under Scottish law they are already married. A marriage by declaration, which occurred when the lovers arrived at the inn, posing as husband and wife before witnesses (Taylor, 1978, p. 130). Pamela's reply to this tomfoolery is not known. Hitchcock liked the idea but decided against the added footage. He concluded that the two hands, clasped in love, gave the audience all the continuity they needed to savor a happy ending.

5. An exception to this rule occurs in *Torn Curtain* (1966), a thriller concerned with espionage, but a thriller that lacks the tart romance and sly humor associated with Hitchcock's other Romanticist films. The Director choreographed a scene of extended violence to show the difficulty of bare-handedly killing someone, especially when that someone is prepared to defend himself (see Kapsis, 1992, p. 97). Paul Newman and a peasant woman endure a considerable struggle to accomplish this feat, almost exhausting themselves as they stab, beat, and finally gas to death a KGB agent. The film, however, seems neither fish nor fowl. The resiliency and craftiness of Newman's character are never in doubt, but *Torn Curtain* does not attain the free spirit to romp through troubled waters as do the participants in *The Thirty-nine Steps* and *North By Northwest* (1959).

6. Leonard hovers near Vandamm, conveying his gay nature quietly, as was necessary in 1959. His reptilian manners suggest an ice-cold personality, although he manages a humorous swipe on occasion ("Call it my woman's intuition") (Brill, 1988, p. 9). He also marshals a frosty rage of sexual jealousy when Eve becomes the target of Vandamm's affections (Wood, 1989, p. 140). Leonard's character does not do much for the gay image, but at least he succeeds in rendering an intelligent, restrained presence.

7. Hitchcockian humor extends to cosmetic effects and film titles, as well as dialogue. The Director enjoyed "warping reality" by introducing little touches of incongruity. Before Thornhill's abduction, he sits at a hotel table with other businessmen preparing for a martini "lunch." But the martini glasses appear as oversized vessels, in line with the hero's voluminous taste for booze. Add to this touch Hitchcock's choice of background music as Thornhill enters

the hotel for his "liquid lunch" and you have a mischievous foreshadowing of trouble to come. The music? "It's A Most Unusual Day" (Spoto, 1992, p. 307).

Film titles, too, sometimes carry a history. Originally entitled *The Man On Lincoln's Nose* and later *In A North-westerly Direction*, the head of the MGM script department suggested *North By Northwest* as more appropriate (Taylor, 1978, pp. 247-248). Fortuitously, this title bears on remarks made in *Hamlet*, Act 2, Scene 2, when Hamlet speaks to Rosenkrantz and Guildenstern: "I am but mad north-north-west; when the wind is southerly I know a hawk from a handsaw" (see Spoto, 1992, p. 307; and Nash & Ross, 1986, p. 2192). To speculate, Roger Thornhill behaves at times as if possessed by madness (the auction scene, for example). To speculate further, his madness derives as much, if not more, from a conflict of positive and negative feelings toward Eve, as from confusion over his own misadventures.

8.   Using blanks, Eve had previously "shot" Roger as a ruse to strengthen her position with Vandamm (watch the background closely before Grant is shot and you will see a boy put his fingers to his ears in anticipation of the noise). The Department of Interior denied Hitchcock an opportunity to film on the real Mount Rushmore, and even denied allowing the actors to position themselves on the four presidents' features in a huge replica of the monument built on the studio lot.

Hitchcock originally wanted to place Grant in Lincoln's nose, and have Grant go into a sneezing fit. The Director also wanted an episode at a car assembly plant in which Roger walks with a worker as a car is put together from scratch, piece by piece, in the background. Then, at the end of its production, someone opens the door of the newly assembled vehicle...and a corpse falls out (Truffaut, 1985, pp. 256-257). Hitchcock never found a way to use these ideas, which tells us how much a film may differ depending on what stays in, and what doesn't.

9.   Strangling carries an erotic connotation, and Hitchcock, notably in *Strangers On A Train* (1951) and in *Frenzy* (1972), uses this form of execution to dramatic effect. Its most artistic presentation occurs in *Strangers On A Train* when Guy Haines (Farley Granger) and Bruno Antony (Robert Walker) become acquainted on a train, and Bruno suggests that they "trade" murders to avoid suspicion. Bruno will murder Guy's estranged wife so that Guy can pursue his new sweetheart and a political career, and Guy will dispatch Bruno's father who, for Bruno, keeps too tight a check on him. Guy thinks Bruno is talking hypothetically, but Bruno, a psychopath, is not.

He proceeds to keep his end of the "agreement" by following Miriam (Laura Elliott), Guy's wife, and her two male companions to a fairground. Bruno hangs back and makes eye contact with Miriam. Miriam is curious. She sizes up this stranger with knowing glances that pass as sexual foreplay, but

Miriam has too much ego wrapped up in her bespectacled attractiveness to imagine the lethal game that Bruno intends. He waits until she goes through a tunnel of love and arrives at the park's "Magic Isle." Once she separates from her boyfriends, Bruno approaches Miriam and, having her acknowledge that, yes, she is Miriam, he quietly strangles her (Brill, 1988, p. 81). Strangling as a sexually intimate form of execution occurs here via a distortion viewed through the lens of Miriam's eyeglasses that have fallen to the ground. Bruno's large hands appear larger still in the lens. Unwittingly, Guy is now committed to Bruno's secret, and to the psychopath's pestering presence.

10. Thomas Leitch (1991, p. 126), in his evaluation of Alicia and Devlin, note that both are "homeless" with respect to the idea that a home represents a sanctuary: "Hitchcock emphasizes Alicia's homelessness in *Notorious* by providing her with too many homes, none of which is truly hers. She is repeatedly put under stress in public places: the courtroom where she first hears her father sentenced to prison, the airplane where she gets the news of his death, the racetrack where she meets her lover Devlin (Cary Grant) as Sebastian watches them through field glasses, the park bench where she and Devlin meet secretly. But the private places, the potential homes which ought to offer a refuge from the publicity that follows her, turn out to be equally public."

11. Hitchcock again uses music to advance a movie's theme, this time to characterize the lead character's philosophy on love. For *Rear Window*, Bing Crosby sings a song, "To See You Is To Love You," endorsing a kind of cosmetic love that Jefferies embraces, thereby keeping genuine love--and Lisa-- at a comfortable distance (Spoto, 1992, pp. 220-221).

Jefferies' somnolent position on love receives a harsh counterpunch when Thorwald catches Lisa in his apartment. Suddenly the comfort of a lazy, safe, one-way affection vanishes, replaced by an excitement about Lisa that Jefferies did not know he possessed. As Robert Kapsis (1992, p. 149) comments, "...Jeffreys [Jefferies] becomes most aroused by his girlfriend when her life is in jeopardy."

12. Well, no, not really helpless. Jefferies and Stella could scream across the courtyard for Thorwald to stop, thereby alerting the other tenants. Who knows how Thorwald would react to this incursion? He just might stop. Jefferies, in fact, does yell across the same courtyard to the police when he has **his** struggle with Thorwald. Chalk up this inconsistency to Hitchcock's penchant for not worrying much about such lapses in logic.

13. Given Jefferies' precarious reasons for spying, consider this scenario: Before Thorwald assaults Jefferies, the basis for arresting him on a charge of murder rests with the speculations of a Peeping Tom (Jefferies), Peeping

Tomette (Lisa), and with the circumstantial evidence of a wedding ring that Mrs. Thorwald presumably would not leave behind. But the police have no body. Thorwald can contend that his wife went on a visit, then disappeared. Perhaps the police may still find substantial cause to detain him, except that a case with no corpus delicti is a problematic case.

Hitchcock, of course, lets Jefferies off the hook when Thorwald moves to attack him. Possibly the Director decided that Jefferies' going out a window and breaking his other leg should prove more exciting, and more convenient to sidestep the question of Thorwald's right to privacy. Too, Jefferies' busting his other leg may represent Hitchcock's punishment for being a voyeur, even one with good intentions.

14. The painting that Norman removes, which normally viewers will disregard, depicts one of Hitchcock's fine details. The picture describes a rape of Susanna, a Biblical woman taking her bath. Voyeurs spy on her but become aroused and seek to have "their way." The whole enterprise, if you're interested, finds its source in the Book of Daniel, Chapter 13 (Spoto, 1983, p. 424).

Voyeurism in *Psycho* assumes a more enveloping and sinister tone than in *Rear Window*. Marion feels the anxiety and the self-alienation of being watched by others, a feeling that intensifies when she takes the money and commences her escape (Leitch, 1991, p. 215). The "Susanna" portrait also illustrates a foreshadowing of Marion's tragedy, and suggests to me that Hitchcock scholars, to spot little clues like the painting, must have examined his films with a scouring pad.

15. The ironies of identifying with a character arise just after Marion's death. Whereas you originally kept tune with Marion and condoned her stealing the 40,000 dollars, now you must concentrate on Norman. The lad, apparently blameless in the murder, assumes the chore of cleaning up after Mother and disposing of Marion and her car. Marion goes in the trunk, as does the newspaper containing the money. (How would Norman have reacted if he had known that Marion left the money inside a rolled-up newspaper? Think about Norman and what might have transpired.)

The car sinks partly into the swamp...and stops. Hitchcock has turned his mischievousness on villains before, and he does so with Norman. The youth eats his Kandy Korn, looks nervously about, and places his hands over his mouth. The car begins to sink again, and Norman gives a sigh of relief. But so do you (Spoto, 1993, p. 320). Why? You liked Marion and she's in the trunk. Why empathize with Norman? A little pop psychology may be in order here. Let's say you identify with Norman's positive features--he has a few--and you wish his mop-up operation to be a success. You wish closure for him. This rationale makes sense in the swamp scene, although less sense when you consider the overall story of Marion's murder and Norman's madness.

16. *Psycho* also resolves itself into an arsenal of foreshadowings and symbols. So much so that the viewer needs an atlas to monitor Hitchcock's drum roll of artistic and droll touches that he dispatches throughout the film--or, in some instances, that Hitchcock scholars **say** he dispatches. **Mirrors** pop up everywhere and apparently become important for their symbolism of introspection and split-personalities (see Spoto, 1992, p. 317). **Eyes** also prove intriguing, ranging from the camera's eye as it first peeks in on Marion and Sam, to Marion's lifeless eye that reveals nothing--a loss of human identity (see Leitch, 1991, p. 218). References to **birds** include Norman's hobby of taxidermy, his bird-like eyes, Marion's last name of "Crane," and Bernard Herrmann's musical score of violins that sound like shrieking birds (Spoto, 1993, p. 325).

For the Freudians, David Sterritt (1993, Chapter 6) chooses to grace the dynamics of *Psycho* with an **anal-compulsive** theme. (Hitchcock became the first director to offer the audience a closeup of that hygienic taboo, a toilet flushing.) Sterritt prefers to think of the 40,000 dollars as excrement, the swamp as another toilet that almost doesn't flush when Norman tries to sink the car into its swarmy depths, and the license plate on Marion's first car--ANL-709--as too convenient to be a Hitchcockian coincidence.

Just as fascinating, however, is Hitchcock's use of architecture and camera angles to manipulate the viewers' emotions in *Psycho*. The vertical spaciousness of Norman's Victorian house and the motel's horizontal closeness invite different possibilities for portraying violence (Spoto, 1993, p. 318). In the murder of Arbogast as he climbs the stairway, for instance, Hitchcock attempts an unusual camera shot. Fearful that the audience will become suspicious of Norman if the camera reveals only Mother's back as she comes out to kill the detective, Hitchcock placed the camera above "her" instead. He filmed down on "Mama" Bates's head to distract viewers and have them think of the shot rather than of Norman. The director then follows up this disorienting angle by an unusual closeup of Arbogast as he propels backward, down the stairs (Truffaut, 1985, p. 273; Rothman, 1982, p. 246).

17. Like *Psycho*, *Vertigo* contains its share of symbols and little Hitchcockian touches. David Spoto (1993, pp. 275-277) observes that "The image of the spiral is more than an innovative and arresting design suggesting the dizziness of vertigo; it is the basic image on which the entire structure and design of the picture are based." Thus, Hitchcock shows a winding staircase, a spiral in the hair styling of Carlotta Valdes (copied by Madeleine), a cemetery walk that curls around, and a camera that appears to circle about Scottie and Madeleine (the actors were actually on a turntable). Hitchcock even arranges

for Madeleine to wear a pin, a gold mockingbird on her suit. Spoto (p. 287) explains that "the German word [for the pin] is *Elster*. Not only is this apt for Hitchcock's lifelong theme of the birds of chaos, but of course this Madeleine is a 'mocking bird,' one woman imitating another."

18. James Stewart's credibility as an actor includes his talent for portraying the "disciplined fanatic." Playing Glen Miller in *The Glen Miller Story* (1954), he single-mindedly searches for the "right sound" to his music. Bringing alive Charles Lindbergh in *The Spirit Of Saint Louis* (1957), Stewart refuses to relinquish his dream of the first transatlantic solo flight. Becoming Monty Stratton of *The Stratton Story* (1949), the actor makes you feel the dedication of a ball player who strives to overcome the loss of his leg in a hunting accident. Stewart's fanaticism doesn't unleash drool and dribble. Instead, he drives himself on a narrow track, using his intensity to achieve a seemingly impossible goal. The achievement, however, comes at the price of ignoring alternatives and compromises that most reasonable individuals would accept. Scottie in *Vertigo* pays a dear price for his fanaticism.

Bibliography

Abbey, A. (1982). Sex differences in attributions for friendly behavior: Do males misperceive females' friendliness? *Journal of Personality and Social Psychology, 42*(5), 830-838.

Abramson, J. (1991, January). Burying the X. *Premiere*, pp. 28-30, 34.

Abramson, P., & Mechanic, M. (1983). Sex and the media: Three decades of best-selling books and major motion pictures. *Archives of Sexual Behavior, 12*(3), 185-206.

Adair, G. (1981). Drama. In D. Pirie (Ed.), *Anatomy of the Movies* (pp. 294-303). New York: Macmillan.

Adams, G. (1977). Physical attractiveness research. *Human Development, 20*, 217-239.

Agus, C. (1987, January 4). Fears follow assault victim to her death. *Dallas Times Herald*, p. A-12.

Alderman, E., & Kennedy, C. (1992). *In our defense*. New York: William Morrow.

Alley, T., & Cunningham, M. (1991). Averaged faces are attractive, but very attractive faces are not average. *Psychological Science, 2*(2), 123-125.

Altman, D. (1982). *The homosexualization of America*. Boston, MA: Beacon Press.

Aman, R. (1979). On the etymology of *gay*. *Maledicta, 3*(2), 257-258.

Appelbaum, J. (1974, February). Secrets: simple, sinister, and sublime. *Harper's Magazine*, p. 3.

Babener, L. (1992). Introduction: *Fatal Attraction*, feminist readings. *Journal of Popular Culture*, *26*(3), 1-3.

Bakan, D. (1967). *David Bakan on method*. San Francisco, CA: Jossey-Bass.

Baker, M., & Churchill, Jr., G. (1977). The impact of physically attractive models on advertising evaluations. *Journal of Marketing Research*, *14*, 538-555.

Bakos, S. (1990). *Dear superlady of sex*. New York: St. Martin's Press.

Bal, M. (1986). Sexuality, sin, and sorrow: The emergence of female character (a reading of Genesis 1-3). In S. Suleiman (Ed.), *The Female Body in Western Culture* (pp. 317-338). Cambridge, MA: Harvard University Press.

Bardis, P. (1980). A glossary of homosexuality. *Maledicta*, *4*(1), 59-63.

Barocas, R., & Karoly, P. (1972). Effects of physical appearance on social responsiveness. *Psychological Reports*, *31*, 495-500.

Bart, P., & O'Brien, P. (1985). *Stopping rape*. New York: Pergamon Press.

Barthel, D. (1988). *Putting on appearances*. Philadelphia, PA: Temple University Press.

Basow, S. (1980). *Sex-role stereotypes: Traditions and alternatives*. Monterey, CA: Brooks/Cole.

Bateson, M., & Goldsby, R. (1988). *Thinking AIDS*. New York: Addison-Wesley.

Bauer, H. (1992). *Scientific literacy and the myth of the scientific method*. Chicago, IL: University of Illinois Press.

Beck, M., & Zabarsky, M. (1984, April 2). Rape trial: 'Justice crucified'? *Newsweek*, p. 39.

Bell-Metereau, R. (1985). *Hollywood androgyny*. New York: Columbia University Press.

Benderly, B. (1987). *The myth of two minds*. New York: Doubleday.

Benedict, R. (1938). Continuities and discontinuities in cultural conditioning. *Psychiatry, 1,* 161-167.

Berscheid, E., & Walster, E. (1974). Physical attractiveness. *Advances in Experimental Social Psychology, 7,* 157-215.

Biema, D. (1993, June 14). But will it end the abortion debate? *Time,* pp. 52-54.

Blow, S. (1992a, July 26). Abortion foes' acts: Triumph or terrorism? *Dallas Morning News,* p. A-33.

Blow, S. (1992b, August 5). One doctor down, more to follow? *Dallas Morning News,* p. A-19.

Bok, S. (1982). *Secrets.* New York: Pantheon Books.

Boorstin, D. (1987). *The image* (25th Anniversary Edition). New York: Atheneum.

Boorstin, J. (1990). *The Hollywood eye.* New York: Harper Collins.

Boswell, J. (1980). *Christianity, social tolerance, and homosexuality.* Chicago, IL: University of Chicago Press.

Breines, W. (1992). *Young, white, and miserable.* Boston, MA: Beacon Press.

Brill, L. (1988). *The Hitchcock romance.* Princeton, NJ: Princeton University Press.

Brinson, S. (1992). The use and opposition of rape myths in prime-time television dramas. *Sex Roles, 27*(7/8), 359-375.

Brooks-Gunn, J., & Furstenberg, Jr., F. (1989). Adolescent sexual behavior. *American Psychologist, 44*(2), 249-257.

Brown, R. (1988). *Starting from scratch.* New York: Bantam.

Browning, D., & Boatman, B. (1977). Incest: children at risk. *American Journal of Psychiatry, 134*(1), 69-72.

Brownlow, K. (1990). *Behind the mask of innocence.* New York: Alfred A. Knopf.

Brundage, J. (1982). Adultery and fornication: A study in legal theology. In V. Bullough & J. Brundage (Eds.), *Sexual Practices & The Medieval Church* (pp. 129-134). Buffalo, NY: Prometheus Books.

Caine, M. (1990). *Acting in film*. New York: Applause Theatre Book Publishers.

Callahan, J. (1990, May). Profanity poll. *Premiere*, p. 21.

Cardwell, D., Coto, J., Matzer, M., Pearlman, C., & Thompson, A. (1991, September 6). The summer's most important movie. *Entertainment Weekly*, pp. 36-39.

Carlson, M. (1991, June 24). Is this what feminism is all about? *Time*, p. 57.

Carlson, M., Gorey, H., & Traver, N. (1991, October 21). The ultimate men's club. *Time*, pp. 50-51.

Carringer, R. (1985, September). Who really wrote *Citizen Kane*? *American Film*, pp. 43-49, 70.

Cavell, S. (1981). *Pursuits of happiness*. Cambridge, MA: Harvard University Press.

Cetola, H. (1988). Toward a cognitive-appraisal model of humor appreciation. *Humor*, *1*-3, 245-258.

Champlin, C. (1981). *The movies grow up*. Chicago, IL: Swallow Press.

Chesser, B. (1980). Analysis of wedding rituals: An attempt to make weddings more meaningful. *Family Relations*, *29*(2), 204-209.

Chism, O. (1992, November 29). Oohs and Oz: Was money the message? *Dallas Morning News*, p. J-8.

Christy, G. (1986, March 5). The great life. *The Hollywood Reporter*, p. 34.

Christy, G. (1991, October 4). The great life. *The Hollywood Reporter*, p. 51.

Clements, M. (1989, September). Nudity in American movies. *Premiere*, pp. 72-74.

Coles, R., & Stokes, G. (1985). *Sex and the American teenager*. New York: Harper Colophon.

Coontz, S. (1992). *The way we never were*. New York: Basic Books.

Corliss, R. (1991, March/April). By the book. *Film Comment*, pp. 37-46.

Corliss, R. (1994, February 7). The gay gauntlet. *Time*, pp. 62-64.

Courtney, A., & Whipple, T. (1983). *Sex stereotyping in Advertising*. Lexington, MA: Lexington Books.

Crewdson, J. (1988). *By silence betrayed*. Boston, MA: Little, Brown.

Crist, J. (1984). *Take 22*. New York: Viking.

Crivello, K. (1988). *Fallen angels*. Secaucus, NJ: Citadel Press.

Cross, J., & Cross, J. (1971). Age, sex, race, and the perception of facial beauty. *Developmental Psychology*, *5*(3), 433-439.

Crowe, C. (1981). *Fast times at Ridgemont high*. New York: Simon and Shuster.

Crowley, J. (1992, July 5). The road to hell is paved with yellow bricks. *The New York Times Book Review*, p. 7.

Darnton, N., Springen, K., Wright, L., & Keene-Osborn, S. (1991, October, 7). The pain of the last taboo. *Newsweek*, pp. 70-72.

Davies, C. (1982). Sexual taboos and social boundaries. *American Journal of Sociology*, *87*(5), 1032-1063.

DeAngelis, T. (1991, July). Weapons can lessen witnesses' accuracy. *APA Monitor*, pp. 40-41.

Deaux, K. (1993). Commentary: Sorry, wrong number--a reply to Gentile's call. *Psychological Science*, *4*(2), 125-126.

Dennis, W. (1992). *Hot and bothered*. New York: Viking.

Diamond, J. (1991, September 6). The heart of the Hood. *Entertainment Weekly*, pp. 40-41.

Donnerstein, E., Linz, D., & Penrod, S. (1987). *The question of pornography*. New York: The Free Press.

Doyle, J., & Paludi, M. (1991). *Sex and gender* (2nd edition). Dubuque, IA: Wm. C. Brown.

Driscoll, R., Davis, K., & Lipetz, M. (1972). Parental interference and romantic love: The Romeo and Juliet effect. *Journal of Personality and Social Psychology*, *24*(1), 1-10.

Eagly, A., Ashmore, R., Makhijani, M., & Longo, L. (1991). What is beautiful is good, but...: A meta-analytic review of research on the physical attractiveness stereotype. *Psychological Bulletin*, *110*(1), 109-128.

Ebert, R. (1988). *Roger Ebert's movie home companion* (1989 edition). Kansas City, MO: Andrews and McMeel.

Ebert, R. (1989). *Roger Ebert's movie home companion* (1990 edition). Kansas City, MO: Andrews and McMeel.

Ebert, R. (1993). *Roger Ebert's movie home companion* (1994 edition). Kansas City, MO: Andrews and McMeel.

Ehrenreich, B. (1991, October 21). Women would have known. *Time*, p. 104.

Ekman, P., Friesen, W., O'Sullivan, M., & Scherer, K. (1980). Relative importance of face, body, and speech in judgments of personality and affect. *Journal of Personality and Social Psychology, 38*(2), 270-277.

Ephron, N. (1991). *When Harry met Sally...* New York: Alfred A. Knopf.

Estrich, S. (1987). *Real rape.* Cambridge, MA: Harvard University Press.

Fackelmann, K. (1990, December 15). Zona blasters. *Science News*, pp. 376-377, 379.

Fadiman, C. (1972). Humor as a weapon. *The Journal of Creative Behavior, 6*(2), 87-92.

Fahringer, H. (1993). Equal in all things: Drawing the line on nudity. *Criminal Law Bulletin, 29*(2), 137-146.

Fairfax, J., & Moat, J. (1981). *The way we write.* New York: St. Martin's Press.

Faludi, S. (1991). *Backlash.* New York: Crown.

Feingold, A. (1992). Good-looking people are not what we think. *Psychological Bulletin, 111*(2), 304-341.

Fischer, L. (1992). Birth traumas: Parturition and horror in *Rosemary's Baby. Cinema Journal, 31*(3), 3-18.

Foucault, M. (1978). *The history of sexuality* (Volume 1). New York: Pantheon.

Frank, G. (1966). *The Boston strangler.* New York: New American Library.

Fraser, J. (1974). *Violence in the arts.* New York: Cambridge University Press.

Freedman, E., & Hellerstein, E. (1981). Introduction. In E. Hellerstein, L. Hume, & K. Offen (Eds.), *Victorian Women* (pp. 118-133). Stanford, CA: Stanford University Press.

Freedman, R. (1986). *Beauty bound.* Lexington, MA: Lexington Books.

Freeman, P., & Wilhelm, M. (1988, July 18). Kicking and screaming, women master Matt Thomas' get-touch tactics for self-defense. *People*, pp. 62-65.

Fyfe, B. (1983). "Homophobia" or homosexual bias reconsidered. *Archives of Sexual Behavior*, *12*(6), 549-554.

Gagnon, J. (1971). Physical strength, once of significance. *Impact of Science on Society*, *21*(1), 31-42.

Garber, M. (1992). *Vested interests*. New York: Routledge.

Gardner, G. (1987). *The censorship papers*. New York: Dodd, Mead & Company.

Gass, W. (1976). *On being blue*. Boston, MA: David R. Godine.

Gentile, D. (1993). Just what are sex and gender, anyway? *Psychological Science*, *4*(2), 120-122.

Gerosa, M. (1992, July 17). Heeding the cat's call. *Entertainment Weekly*, p. 10.

Gerosa, M., & Thompson, A. (1990, October 12). How the X got axed. *Entertainment Weekly*, p. 23.

Gilliant, P. (1990). *To Wit*. New York: Charles Scribner's Sons.

Gilmour, H. (1988). *Fatal attraction*. New York: Signet.

Glass, L. (1984). Man's man/ladies' man: Motifs of hyper-masculinity. *Psychiatry*, *47*(3), 260-278.

Glassner, B. (1988). *Bodies*. New York: G. P. Putnam's Sons.

Gorman, C., Dolan, B., & Horowitz, J. (1991, October 7). Incest comes out of the dark. *Time*, pp. 46-47.

Gottman, J. (1994). *Why marriages succeed or fail*. New York: Simon & Schuster.

Gramick, J. (1983). Homophobia: A new challenge. *Social Work*, *28*(2), 137-141.

Grant, H. (1982, November 2). Rambling reporter. *The Hollywood Reporter*, p. 3.

Grant, H. (1988, March 4). Off the cuff. *The Hollywood Reporter*, p. 24.

Greenberg, H. (1975). *The movies on your mind*. New York: Saturday Review Press\E. P. Dutton.

Greene, B. (1983). *American beat*. New York: Atheneum.

Grove, M. (1992, December 7). 'Damage' didn't deserve NC-17. *The Hollywood Reporter*, p. 8.

Guilbault, R. (1989, September 18). More than a minor nuance lost on the translation of 'macho'. *Dallas Times Herald*, p. A-9.

Haas, K., & Haas, A. (1993). *Understanding sexuality*. St. Louis, MO: Mosby.

Hachem, S. (1987, November 30). 'Silence' will be next Lyne project. *The Hollywood Reporter*, pp. 1, 13.

Hailey, E. (1991, April). The essence of storytelling: Dramatize, dramatize. *The Writer*, pp. 9-11, 43.

Hall, E. (1989, September). When does life begin? *Psychology Today*, pp. 42-46.

Hall, H. (1988, July/August). Marriage: Practice makes imperfect? *Psychology Today*, p. 15.

Hare, R. (1993). *Without conscience*. New York: Pocket Books.

Harmetz, A. (1992). *Round up the usual suspects*. New York: Hyperion.

Harris, M. (1993, January 15). Abridged too far? *Entertainment Weekly*, pp. 26-29.

Harris, T. (1987). *Courtroom's finest hour in American cinema*. Metuchen, NJ: Scarecrow Press.

Harvey, S. (1989). *Directed by Vincente Minnelli*. New York: Harper & Row.

Harwell, R. (1987). Introduction. In R. Harwell (Ed.), *Gone With The Wind as Book and Film* (pp. xv-xxi). New York: Paragon House.

Haskell, M. (1987). *From reverence to rape* (2nd edition). Chicago, IL: The University of Chicago Press.

Haun, H. (1986). *The movie quote book*. New York: Bonanza Books.

Hawkins, R. (1980, January). The Uppsala connection: The development of principles basic to education for sexuality. *SIECUS Report*, 8(3), 1-2, 12-16.

Heilman, M., & Saruwatari, L. (1979). When beauty is beastly: The effects of appearance and sex on evaluations of job applicants for managerial and nonmanagerial jobs. *Organizational Behavior and Human Performance*, 23, 360-372.

Higashi, S. (1990). Silent cinema. In A. Kuhn & S. Radstone (Eds.), *Women In Film* (pp. 365-368). New York: Fawcett Columbine.

Hildebrandt, K. (1983). Effect of facial expression variations on ratings of infants' physical attractiveness. *Developmental Psychology, 19*(3), 414-417.

Hill, C., Rubin, Z., & Peplau, L. (1976). Breakups before marriage: The end of 103 affairs. *Journal of Social Issues, 32*(1), 147-168.

Hobson, B. (1987). *Uneasy virtue.* New York: Basic Books.

Hong, T. (1994, March 26). Cradles and cameras. *Dallas Morning News*, p. C-5.

Horn, J. (1991, January 21). NC-17 marks the spot. *Dallas Morning News*, p. C-5.

Hubbard, R., & Wald, E. (1993). *Exploding the gene myth.* Boston, MA: Beacon Press.

Hughes, G. (1991). *Swearing.* Cambridge, MA: Blackwell.

Huss, R., & Silverstein, N. (1971). Tone and point of view. In F. Marcus (Ed.), *Film and Literature: Contrasts in Media* (pp. 53-70). Scranton, PA: Chandler Publishing Company.

Indigestion turns into labor pains (1984, April 4). *The Daily Sentinel*, Nacogdoches, TX, AP item, p. B-10.

Jackson, L. (1983a). The influence of sex, physical attractiveness, sex role, and occupational sex-linkage on perceptions of occupational suitability. *Journal of Applied Social Psychology, 13*(1), 31-44.

Jackson, L. (1983b). Gender, physical attractiveness, and sex role in occupational treatment discrimination: The influence of trait and role assumptions. *Journal of Applied Social Psychology, 13*(5), 443-458.

Jaehne, K. (1987, June). Hooker. *Film Comment*, 25-32.

Jay, T. (1980). Sex roles and dirty word usage: A review of the literature and reply to Haas. *Psychological Bulletin, 88*(3), 614-621.

Jay, T. (1992). *Cursing in America.* Philadelphia, PA: John Benjamins.

Johnson, W. (1993, May/June). Heart of the matter. *Film Comment*, pp. 8-10, 16-18.

Kaplan, D., Cohn, B., McDaniel, A., & Annin, P. (1991, October 21). A moment of truth. *Newsweek*, pp. 24-32.

Kapsis, R. (1992). *Hitchcock: The making of a reputation.* Chicago, IL: The University of Chicago Press.

Katz, S., & Mazur, M. (1979). *Understanding the rape victim.* New York: Wiley.

Kawin, B. (1987). *How movies work.* New York: Macmillan.

Keisling, P. (1984, May). The case against privacy. *The Washington Monthly*, pp. 12-28.

Kelly, M. (1991). *Martin Scorsese.* New York: Thunder's Mouth Press.

Kendall, E. (1990). *The runaway bride.* New York: Alfred A. Knopf.

Keough, W. (1990). *Punchlines.* New York: Paragon House.

Kinsey, A., Pomeroy, W., & Martin, C. (1948). *Sexual behavior in the human male.* Philadelphia, PA: W. B. Saunders.

Kinsey, A., Pomeroy, W., Martin, C., & Gebhard, P. (1953). *Sexual behavior in the human female.* Philadelphia, PA: W. B. Saunders.

Knightley, P., & Kennedy, C. (1987). *An affair of state.* New York: Atheneum.

Kolodny, A. (1993, January 31). Among the Indians: The uses of captivity. *The New York Times Book Review*, pp. 1, 26-29.

Korabik, K., & Pitt, E. (1980). Self concept, objective appearance, and profile self perception. *Journal of Applied Social Psychology, 10*(6), 482-489.

Kuhn, A. (1988). *Cinema, censorship and sexuality, 1909-1925.* New York: Routledge.

Lakoff, R., & Scherr, R. (1984). *Face value.* Boston, MA: Routledge & Kegan Paul.

Landau, T. (1989). *About faces.* New York: Anchor Books.

Landis, D. (1992, October 7). Unrated videos escape the stigma. *USA Today*, p. D-7.

Langlois, J., & Roggman, L. (1990). Attractive faces are only average. *Psychological Science, 1*(2), 115-121.

Langlois, J., Roggman, L., Casey, R., Ritter, J., Rieser-Danner, L., & Jenkins, V. (1987). Infant preferences for attractive faces: Rudiments of a stereotype? *Developmental Psychology*, *23*, 363-369.

Langlois, J., Roggman, L., Musselman, L., & Acton, S. (1991). A picture is worth a thousand words: Reply to "on the difficulty of averaging faces". *Psychological Science*, *2*(5), 354-357.

Lebo, H. (1990). *Citizen Kane*. New York: Doubleday.

Leff, L., & Simmons, J. (1990). *The dame in the kimono*. New York: Grove Weidenfeld.

Leitch, T. (1991). *Find the director and other Hitchcock games*. Athens, GA: The University of Georgia Press.

Lesser, A. (1980). Love and lust. *Journal of Value Inquiry*, *14*(1), 51-54.

Liggett, J. (1974). *The human face*. New York: Stein and Day.

Linden, G. (1971). The storied world. In F. Marcus (Ed.), *Film and Literature: Contrasts in Media* (pp. 157-163). Scranton, PA: Chandler Publishing Company.

Linz, D., & Malamuth, N. (1993). *Pornography*. Newbury Park, CA: Sage.

Lipton, M., & Armstrong, L. (1992, June 22). Agony of choice. *People*, pp. 77-80.

Luhr, W. (1991). *Raymond Chandler and film*. Tallahassee, FL: The Florida State University Press.

Maccoby, E. (1990). Gender and relationships. *American Psychologist*, *45*(4), 513-520.

Machotka, P. (1979). *The nude*. New York: Halsted Press.

Madigan, L., & Gamble, N. (1989). *The second rape*. New York: Lexington Books.

Makoul, R. (1989, February). The living end. *The Writer*, pp. 7-8.

Maltz, W. (1990, December). Adult survivors of incest. *Medical Aspects of Human Sexuality*, pp. 42-47.

Martin, E. (1987). *The woman in the body*. Boston, MA: Beacon Press.

Martone, M. (1984). *Alive and dead in Indiana*. New York: Alfred A. Knopf.

May, R. (1972). *Power and innocence*. New York: W. W. Norton.

McCary, J. (1971). *Sexual myths and fallacies*. New York: Schocken.

McFall, L. (1987). Integrity. *Ethics, 98*(1), 5-20.

McKibben, B. (1992). *The age of missing information*. New York: Random House.

McWhirter, D., & Mattison, A. (1984). *The male couple*. Englewood Cliffs, NJ: Prentice-Hall.

Mellen, J. (1977). *Big bad wolves*. New York: Pantheon.

Miller, C. (1974). Emission control: It makes a vas deferens. *The Worm Runner's Digest, 16*(1), 59-62.

Miller, M. (1993, December 10). The selling of "Philadelphia." *Newsweek*, p. 99.

Miller, M. (1973). *Plain speaking*. New York: G. P. Putnam's Sons.

Modleski, T. (1988). *The women who knew too much*. New York: Methuen.

Montagu, A. (1967). *The anatomy of swearing*. New York: Collier Books.

Morowitz, H., & Trefil, J. (1992). *The facts of life*. New York: Oxford.

Mosher, D. (1991). Macho men, machismo, and sexuality. In J. Bancroft, C. Davis, & H. Ruppel, Jr. (Eds.), *Annual Review of Sex Research* (Volume 2) (pp. 199-247). Lake Mills, IA: The Society for the Scientific Study of Sex, Inc.

Mullins, E. (1985). *The painted witch*. New York: Carroll & Graf.

Nash, J., & Ross, S. (1985). *The motion picture guide* (Volume 2: C-D). Chicago, IL: Cinebooks.

Nash, J., & Ross, S. (1986). *The motion picture guide* (Volume 3: E-G). Chicago, IL: Cinebooks.

Nash, J., & Ross, S. (1986). *The motion picture guide* (Volume 5: L-M). Chicago, IL: Cinebooks.

Nash, J., & Ross, S. (1986). *The motion picture guide* (Volume 6: N-R). Chicago, IL: Cinebooks.

Nash, J., & Ross, S. (1987). *The motion picture guide* (Volume 7: S). Chicago, IL: Cinebooks.

Nash, J., & Ross, S. (1987). *The motion picture guide* (Volume 8: T-V). Chicago, IL: Cinebooks.

Nash, J., & Ross, S. (1987). *The motion picture guide* (1987 Annual). Chicago, IL: Cinebooks.

Nash, J., & Ross, S. (1988). *The motion picture guide* (1988 Annual). Evanston, IL: Cinebooks.

Newcomb, M. (1986). Cohabitation, marriage, and divorce among adolescents and young adults. *Journal of Social and Personal Relationships*, *3*, 473-494.

Nilsson, L. (1990). *A child is born*. New York: Delacorte Press/Seymour Lawrence.

Paglia, C. (1992). *Sex, art, and American culture*. New York: Vintage books.

Patzer, G. (1985). *The physical attractiveness phenomena*. New York: Plenum Press.

Perrine, L. (1956). *Sound and sense*. New York: Harcourt, Brace.

Phillips, G. (1975). The boys on the bandwagon: Homosexuality in the movies. In T. Atkins (Ed.), *Sexuality in the Movies* (pp. 157-171). Bloomington, IN: Indiana University Press.

Pilipp, F., & Shull, C. (1993). TV movies of the first decade of AIDS. *Journal of Popular Film & Television*, *21*(1), 19-26.

Pinkerton, S., & Abramson, P. (1992). Is risky sex rational? *The Journal Of Sex Research*, *29*(4), 561-568.

Pittenger, J. (1991). On the difficulty of averaging faces: Comments on Langlois and Roggman. *Psychological Science*, *2*(5), 351-353.

Pleck, J. (1982). *The myth of masculinity*. Cambridge, MA: The MIT Press.

Prince, V. (1985). Sex, gender, and semantics. *The Journal of Sex Research*, *21*(1), 92-96.

Rebello, S. (1990). *Alfred Hitchcock and the making of Psycho*. New York: Dembner Books.

Reno, J. (1989, September). Ridgemont redux. *Premiere*, p. 24.

Renshaw, D. (1990, June). Cohabitating before marriage. *Medical Aspects of Human Sexuality*, p. 58.

Riger, S. (1991). Gender dilemmas in sexual harassment policies and procedures. *American Psychologist*, *46*(5), 497-505.

Rochlin, M. (1989, September). How to shoot a love scene. *Premiere*, pp. 66-68.

Rohmer, E., & Chabrol, C. (1988). *Hitchcock: The first forty-four films.* New York: Continuum.

Rosenberg, D., Miller, M., & Leland, J. (1994, February 14). Homophobia. *Newsweek*, pp. 42-45.

Rosenblatt, R. (1992). *Life itself.* New York: Random House.

Rothman, W. (1982). *Hitchcock--The murderous gaze.* Cambridge, MA: Harvard University Press.

Rubin, Z., Peplau, L., & Hill, C. (1981). Loving and leaving: Sex differences in romantic attachments. *Sex Roles*, *7*(8), 821-835.

Russo, V. (1987, 1981). *The celluloid closet.* New York: Harper & Row.

Ryman, G. (1992). *Was.* New York: Alfred A. Knopf.

Sabulis, T. (1988, October 13). Foster, McGillis dispute perception of rape. *Dallas Times Herald*, p. E-1.

Salholz, E., Mason, M., Barrett, T., Talbot, M., King, P., & Yoffee, E. (1991, December 16). Sex crimes: Women on trial. *Newsweek*, pp. 22-23.

Sayre, N. (1982). *Running times: Films of the cold war.* New York: The Dial Press.

Schank, R., & Childers, P. (1988). *The creative attitude.* New York: Macmillan.

Schickel, R. (1991, June 24). Gender bender. *Time*, pp. 52-56.

Schwartz, K. (1985). *The male member.* New York: St. Martin's Press.

Schwarzbaum, L. (1994, March 11). The mommy track. *Entertainment Weekly*, pp. 12, 15.

Seger, L. (1992). *The art of adaptation: Turning fact and fiction into film.* New York: Henry Holt.

Selnow, G. (1985). Sex differences in uses and perceptions of profanity. *Sex Roles*, *12*(3/4), 303-312.

Sennett, T. (1989). *Hollywood's golden year, 1939.* New York: St. Martin's Press.

Shakespeare, W. (1963). *Romeo and Juliet.* New York: Signet Classics.

Shapiro, L., Murr, A., & Springen, K. (1991, June 17). Women who kill too much. *Time*, p. 63.

Shotland, R., & Craig, J. (1988). Can men and women differentiate between friendly and sexually interested behavior? *Social Psychology Quarterly*, 51(1), 66-73.

Simon, W., & Gagnon, J. (1984). Sexual scripts. *Social Science and Modern Society*, 22(1), 53-60.

Simpson, J. (1992, April 6). Out of the celluloid closet. *Time*, p. 65.

Slotkin, R. (1992). *Gunfighter nation.* New York: Atheneum.

Smith, J. (1989). *Misogynies.* New York: Fawcett Columbine.

Smith, R. (1991, March 31). Gays on the screen: A target of protest. *Dallas Morning News*, p. C-1.

Smolowe, J., Gorey, H., Johnson, J., & Traver, N. (1991, October 21). She said, he said. *Time*, pp. 36-40.

Solomon, S. (1976). *Beyond formula.* New York: Harcourt Brace Jovanovich.

Spoto, D. (1983). *The dark side of genius.* Boston, MA: Little, Brown.

Spoto, D. (1992). *The art of Alfred Hitchcock.* (2nd edition). New York: Anchor Books.

Sternberg, R., & Whitney, C. (1991). *Love the way you want it.* New York: Bantam Books.

Sterritt, D. (1993). *The films of Alfred Hitchcock.* New York: Cambridge University Press.

Suls, J. (1975). The role of familiarity in the appreciation of humor. *Journal of Personality*, 43(2), 335-345.

Sussman, S., Mueser, K., Grau, B., & Yarnold, P. (1983). Stability of females' facial attractiveness during childhood. *Journal of Personality and Social Psychology*, 44(6), 1231-1233.

Tannen, D. (1990). *You just don't understand.* New York: William Morrow.

Taylor, J. (1978). *Hitch.* New York: Pantheon.

The many faces of *Thelma & Louise*. (1991/1992). *Film Quarterly*, *45*(2), 20-31.

Thompson, J. (1992). From *Diversion* to *Fatal Attraction*: The transformation of a morality play into a Hollywood hit. *Journal of Popular Culture*, *26*(3), 5-15.

Thompson, S. (1990). Putting a big thing into a little hole: Teenage girls' accounts of sexual initiation. *The Journal of Sex Research*, *22*(3), 341-361.

Thompson, T. (1976). *Blood and money*. Garden City, NY: Doubleday.

Thomson, D. (1977). *America in the dark*. New York: William Morrow.

Thomson, D. (1982, March/April). Falling in love again. *Film Comment*, pp. 9-17.

Toll, R. (1982). *The entertainment machine*. New York: Oxford University Press.

Tribe, L. (1990). *Abortion: The clash of absolutes*. New York: W. W. Norton.

Truffaut, F. (1985). *Hitchcock*. (Revised edition). New York: Touchstone.

Tuchman, M. (1983, April). Dustin Hoffman. *American Film*, pp. 26-28, 69-72.

Unger, R., & Crawford, M. (1993). Commentary: Sex and gender--the troubled relationship between terms and concepts. *Psychological Science*, *4*(2), 122-124.

Updike, J. (1993). Even the Bible is soft on sex. *The New York Times Book Review*, pp. 3, 29.

Vornholt, J. (1992, August). Play fair with your readers. *The Writer*, pp. 9-10.

Walster, E., Walster, G., & Berscheid, E. (1978). *Equity: Theory and research*. Boston, MA: Allyn and Bacon.

Webster, M., & Driskell, J. (1983). Beauty as status. *American Journal of Sociology*, *89*(1), 140-165.

Weddington, S. (1992). *A question of choice*. New York: Grosset/Putnam.

White, G. (1981a). Some correlates of romantic jealousy. *Journal of Personality*, *49*(2), 129-147.

White, G. (1981b). A model of romantic jealousy. *Motivation and Emotion*, 54), 295-310.

Wilson, W. (1981). Five years and 121 dirty words later. *Maledicta*, 5(1+2), 243-255.

Wilson, W. (1988). Rape as entertainment. *Psychological Reports*, *63*, 607-610.

Wilson, W. (1991). *Good murders and bad murders*. Lanham, MD: University Press of America.

Wilson, W., & Liedtke, V. (1984). Movie-inspired sexual practices. *Psychological Reports*, *54*, 328.

Winokur, J. (1986). Writers on writing. Philadelphia, PA: Running Press.

Wolf, N. (1991). *The beauty myth*. New York: William Morrow.

Wood, R. (1989). *Hitchcock's films revisited*. New York: Columbia University Press.

Zillmann, D., & Bryant, J. (1986). Exploring the entertainment experience. In J. Bryant & D. Zillmann (Eds.), *Perspectives on Media Effects* (pp. 303-324). Hillsdale, NJ: Lawrence Erlbaum.

Zillmann, D., & Bryant, J. (1991). Responding to comedy: The sense and nonsense in humor. In J. Bryant & D. Zillman (Eds.), *Responding to the Screen* (pp. 261-279). Hillsdale, NJ: Lawrence Erlbaum.

Zorn, E. (1990, November 5). Please return the word gay. *Newsweek*, pp. 10-11.

Zurawik, D. (1989a, May 15). Drama brings court case to life. *Dallas Times Herald*, p. C-1.

Zurawik, D. (1989b, May 15). Groups split on whether film is fair. *Dallas Times Herald*, p. C-1.

Zurawik, D. (1989c, May 15). Principles agree show is accurate. *Dallas Times Herald*, p. C-1.

Film Index

Person Index

Subject Index

About The Author

Wayne J. Wilson is professor of psychology at Stephen F. Austin State University in Nacogdoches, Texas. He received B. A. and M. A. degrees from Southern Methodist University, and the Ph.D. degree from Texas Christian University. He has penned a previous work with the University Press of America, *Good Murders And Bad Murders*, published in 1991. The present title, *Sexuality In The Land Of Oz*, derives from the author's teaching and research interests in Human Sexuality, the Psychology of Aggression, and Psychology & Movies.